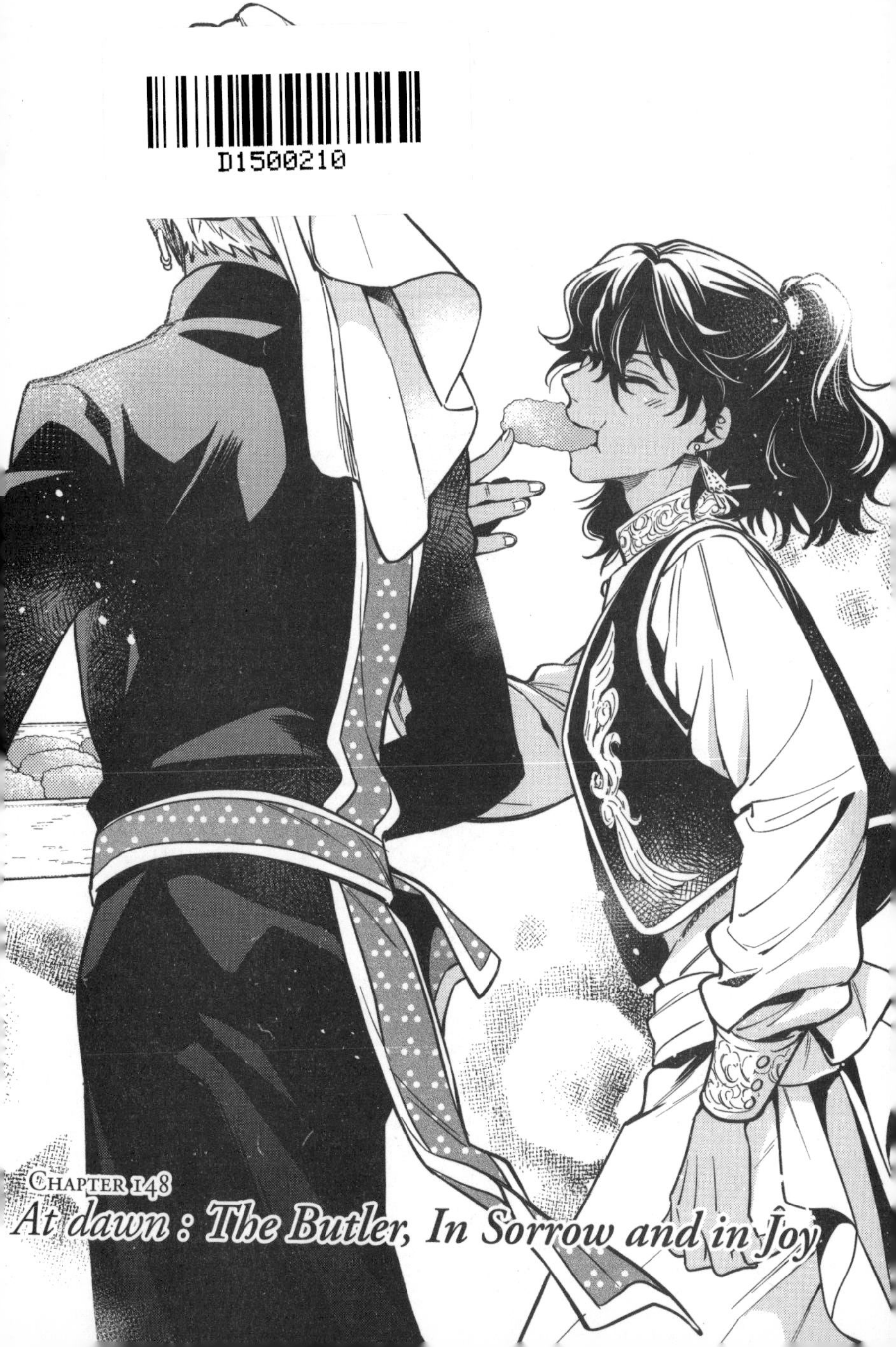
CHAPTER 148
At dawn : The Butler, In Sorrow and in Joy

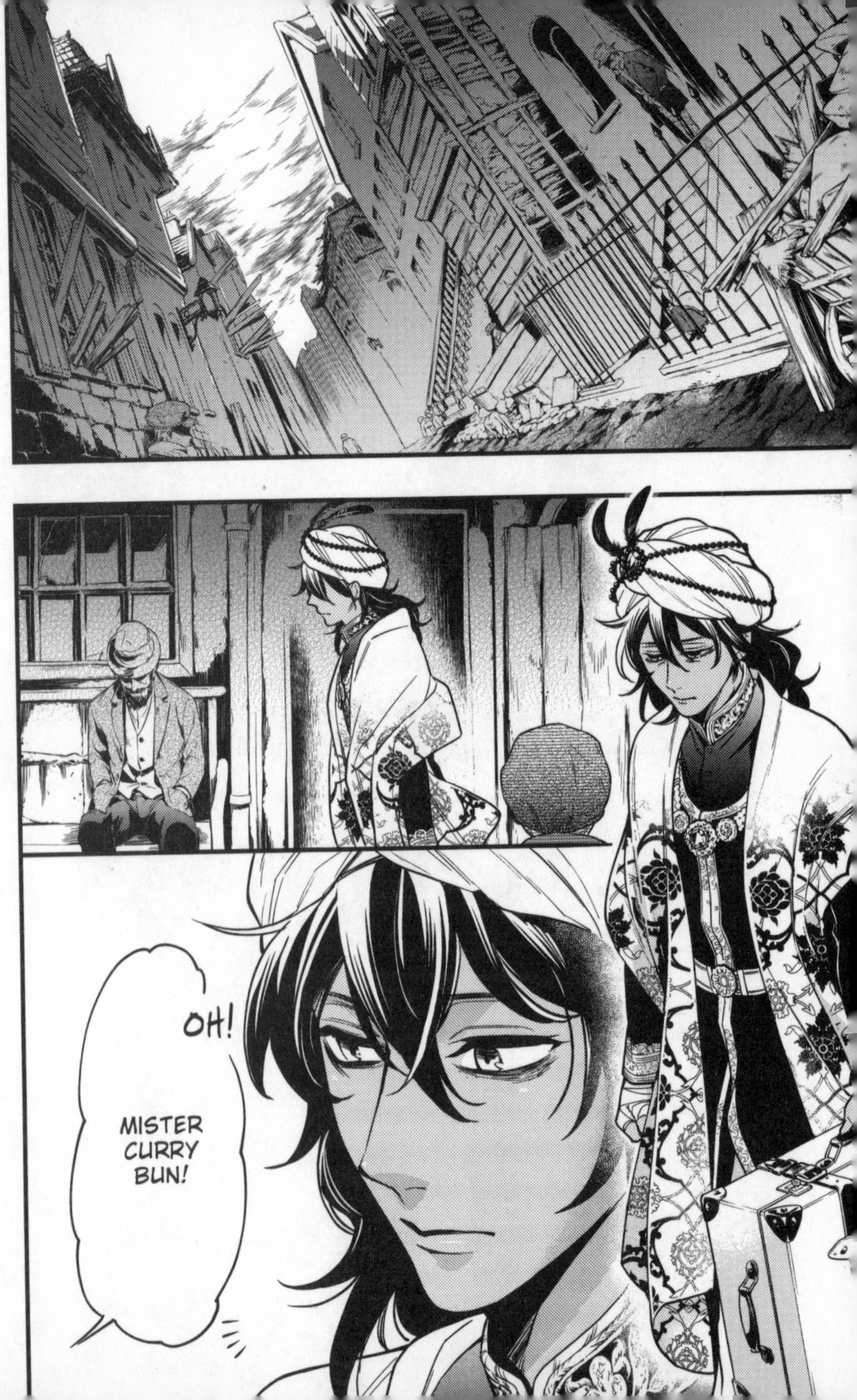
OH!
MISTER CURRY BUN!

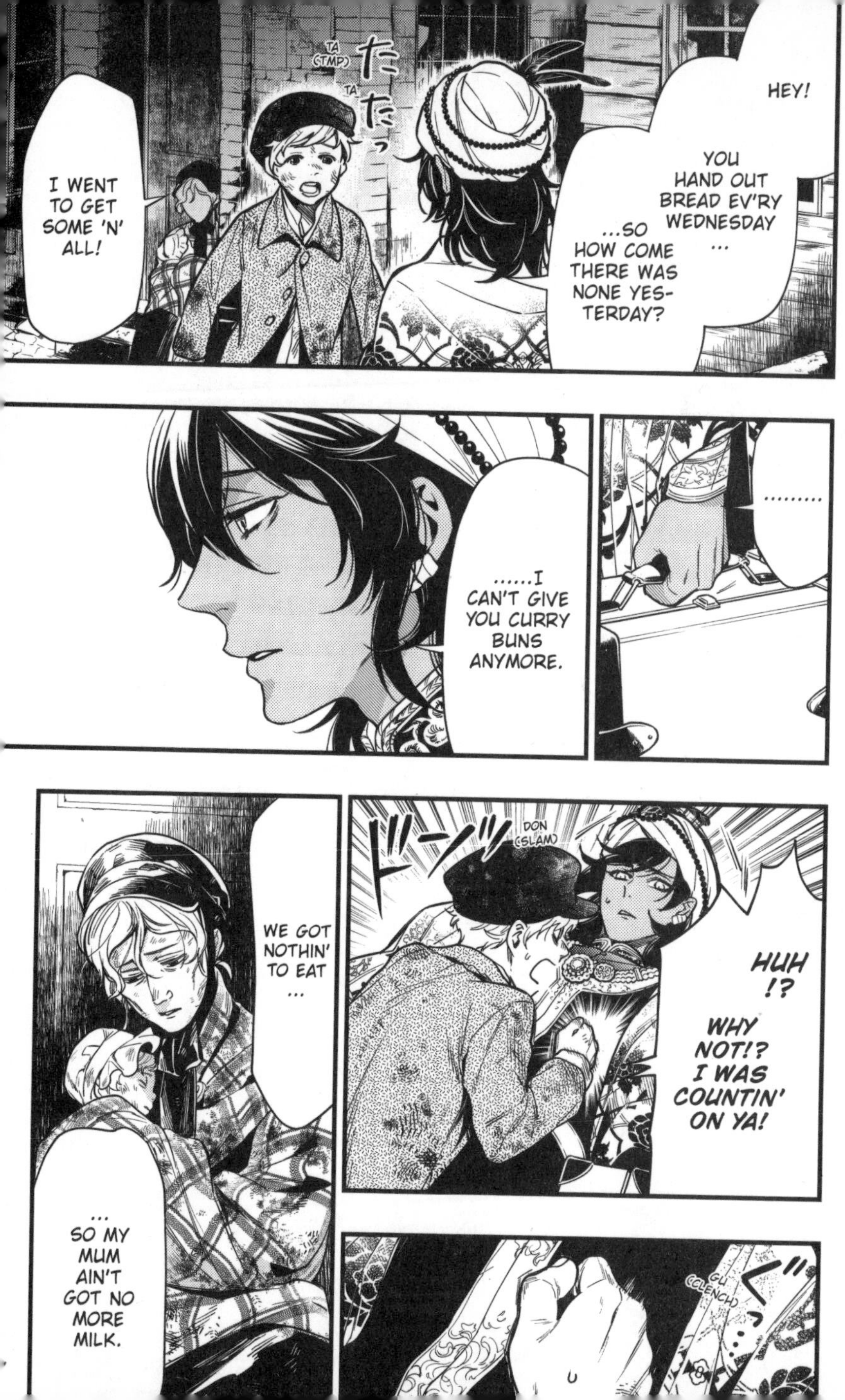
HEY!
YOU HAND OUT BREAD EV'RY WEDNESDAY ...
...SO HOW COME THERE WAS NONE YESTERDAY?
たたっ
TA (TMP) TA
I WENT TO GET SOME 'N' ALL!
....
......I CAN'T GIVE YOU CURRY BUNS ANYMORE.
ドーン
DON (SLAM)
HUH!?
WHY NOT!? I WAS COUNTIN' ON YA!
ぐっ
GU (CLENCH)
...
WE GOT NOTHIN' TO EAT ...
... SO MY MUM AIN'T GOT NO MORE MILK.

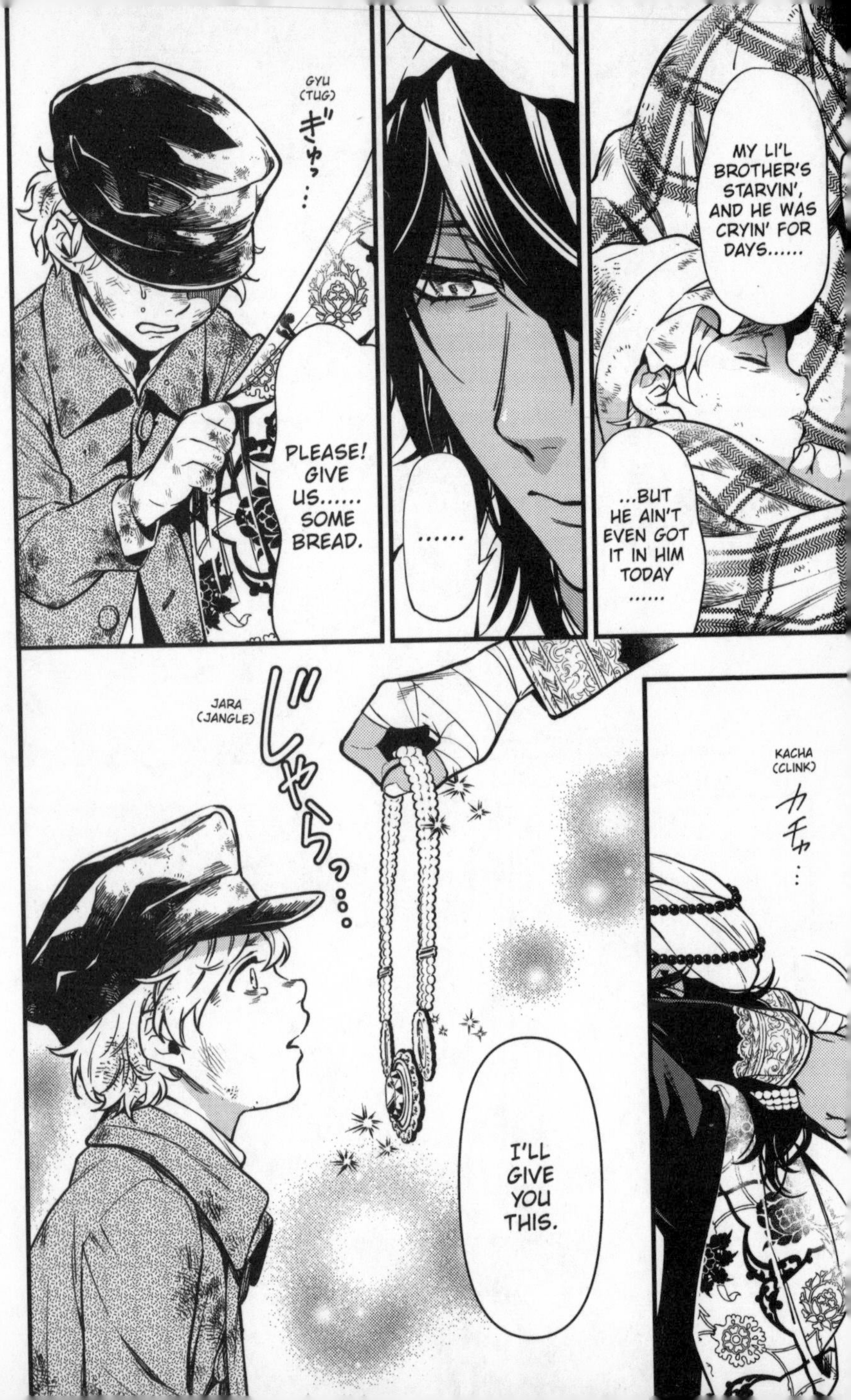
MY LI'L BROTHER'S STARVIN', AND HE WAS CRYIN' FOR DAYS......
...BUT HE AIN'T EVEN GOT IT IN HIM TODAY ......
......
GYU (TUG)
ぎゅっ…
PLEASE! GIVE US...... SOME BREAD.
KACHA (CLINK)
カチャ…
JARA (JANGLE)
じゃらっ…
I'LL GIVE YOU THIS.

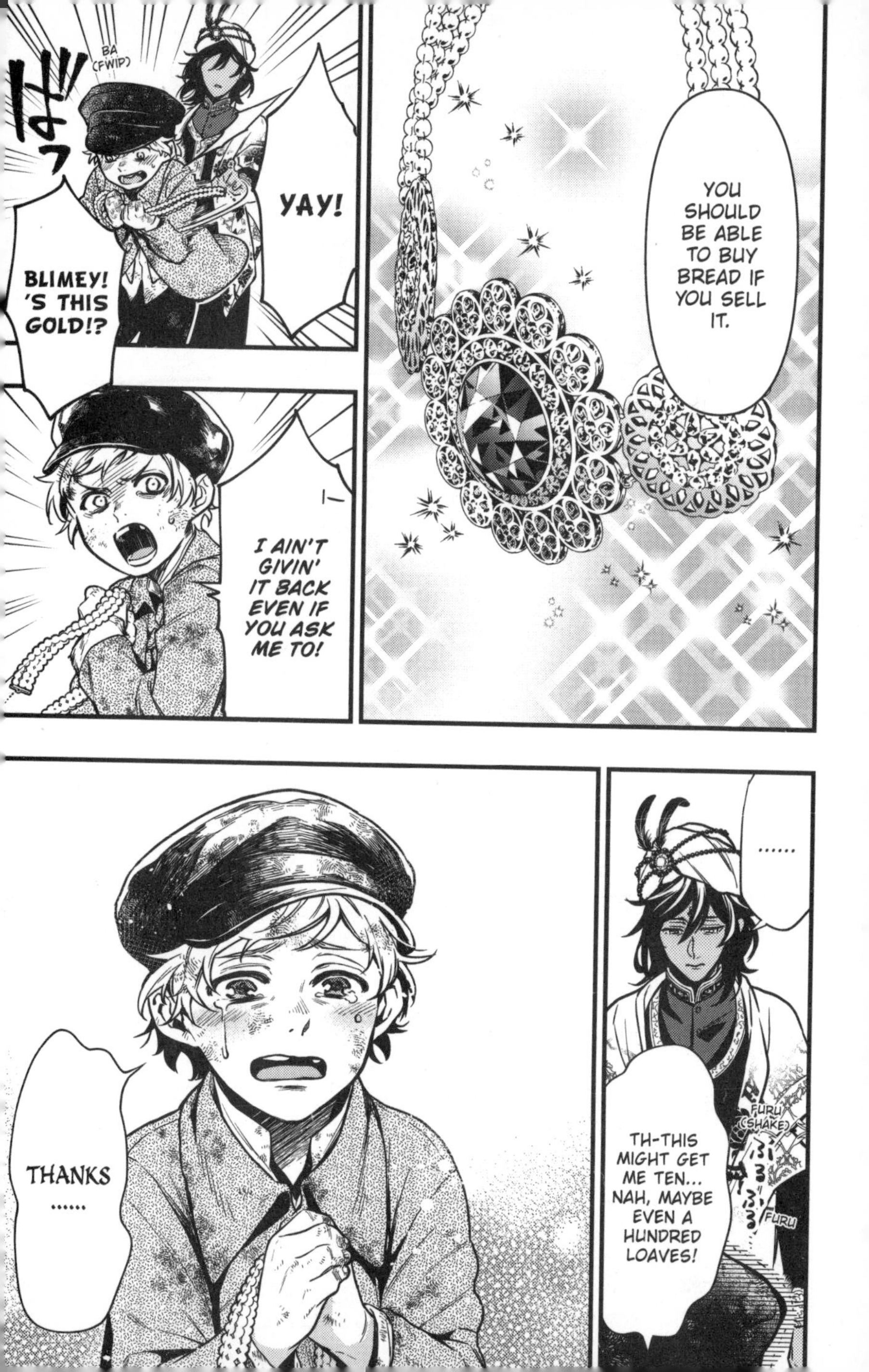
YOU SHOULD BE ABLE TO BUY BREAD IF YOU SELL IT.
YAY!
ばっ
BA (FWIP)
BLIMEY! 'S THIS GOLD!?
I AIN'T GIVIN' IT BACK EVEN IF YOU ASK ME TO!
......
ふるふる
FURU (SHAKE)
FURU
TH-THIS MIGHT GET ME TEN... NAH, MAYBE EVEN A HUNDRED LOAVES!
THANKS ......

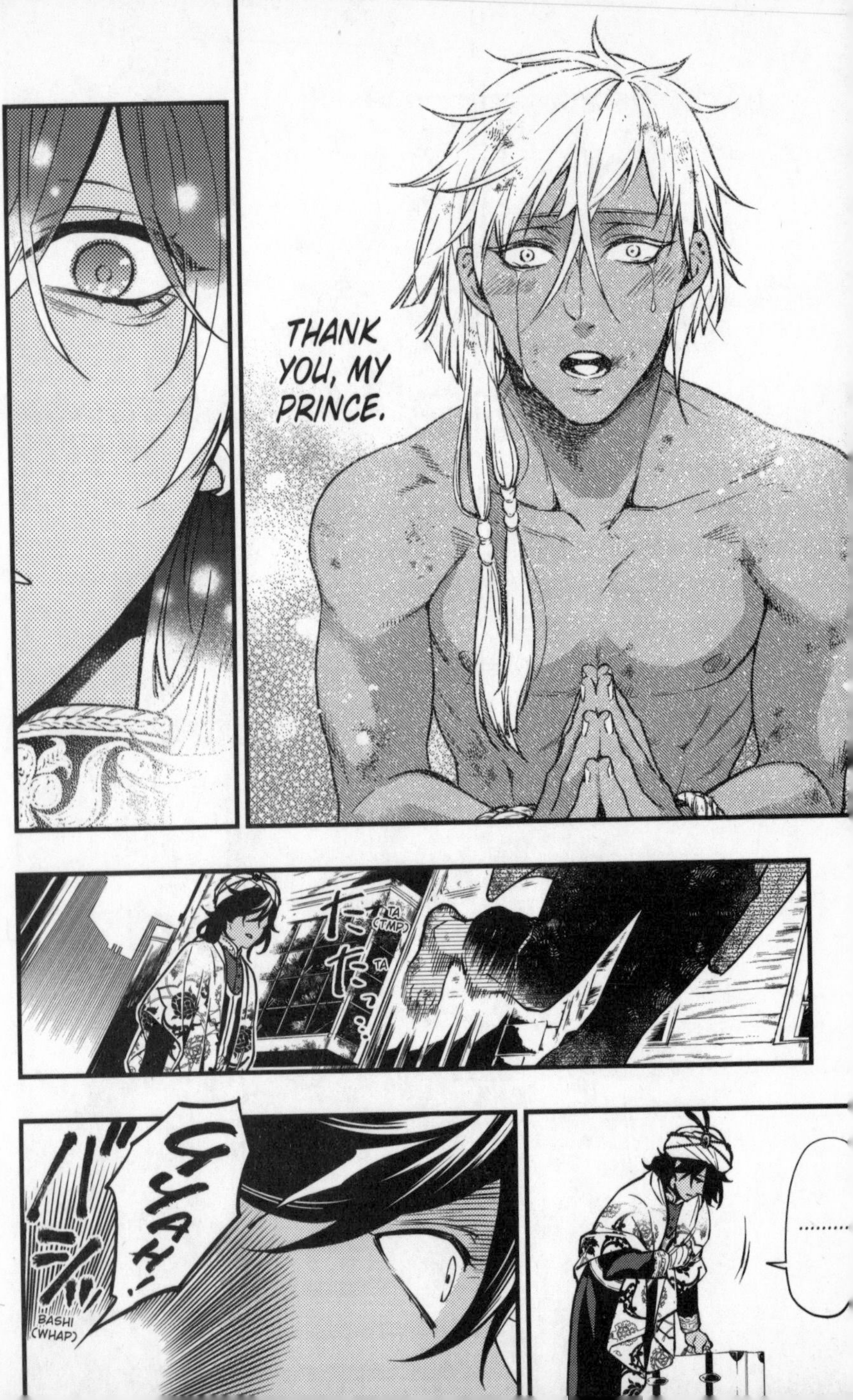
THANK YOU, MY PRINCE.
TA (TMP)
TA
......
GYAAH!
BASHI (WHAP)

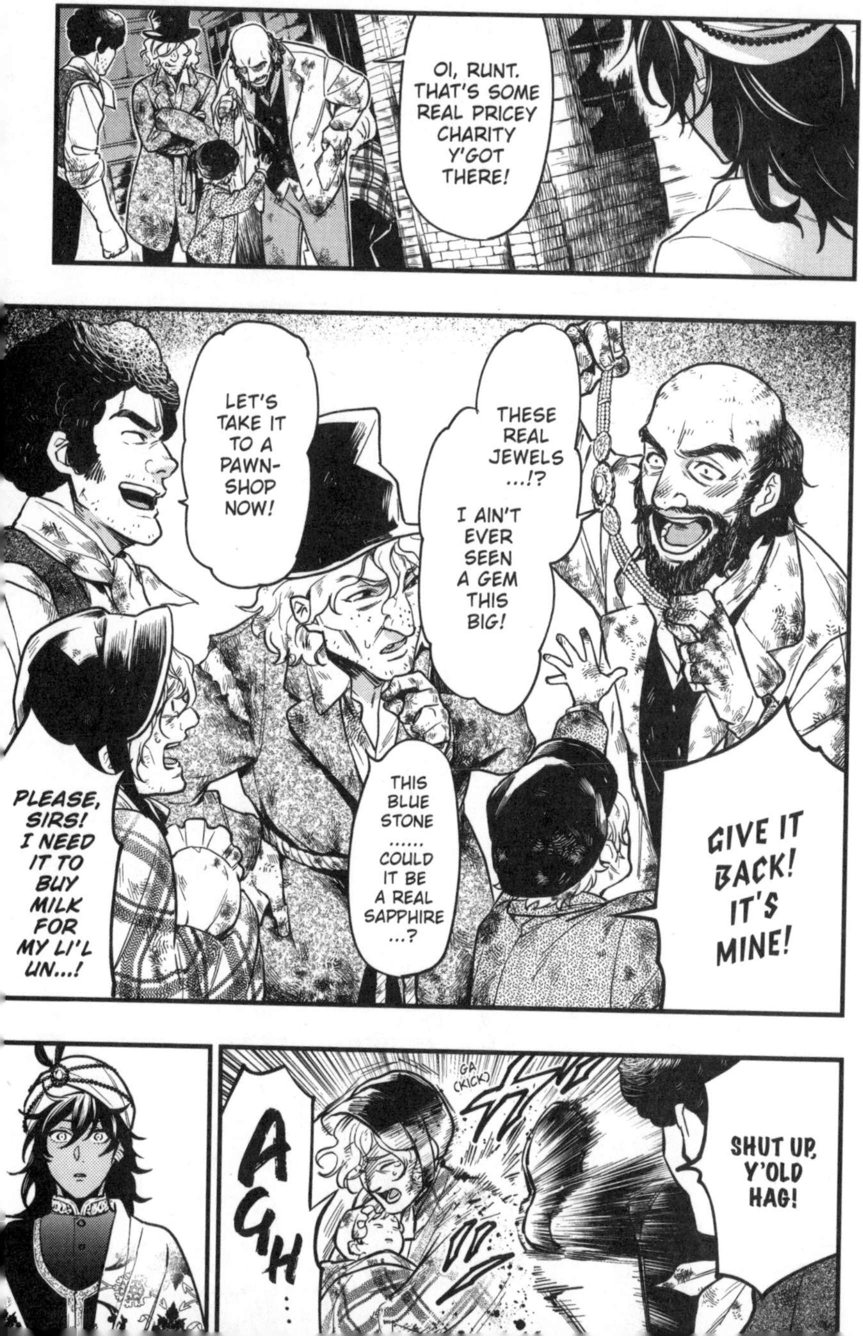
OI, RUNT. THAT'S SOME REAL PRICEY CHARITY Y'GOT THERE!
THESE REAL JEWELS ...!?
I AIN'T EVER SEEN A GEM THIS BIG!
LET'S TAKE IT TO A PAWN-SHOP NOW!
GIVE IT BACK! IT'S MINE!
THIS BLUE STONE ...... COULD IT BE A REAL SAPPHIRE ...?
PLEASE, SIRS! I NEED IT TO BUY MILK FOR MY LI'L UN...!
SHUT UP, Y'OLD HAG!
GA (KICK)
AGH...

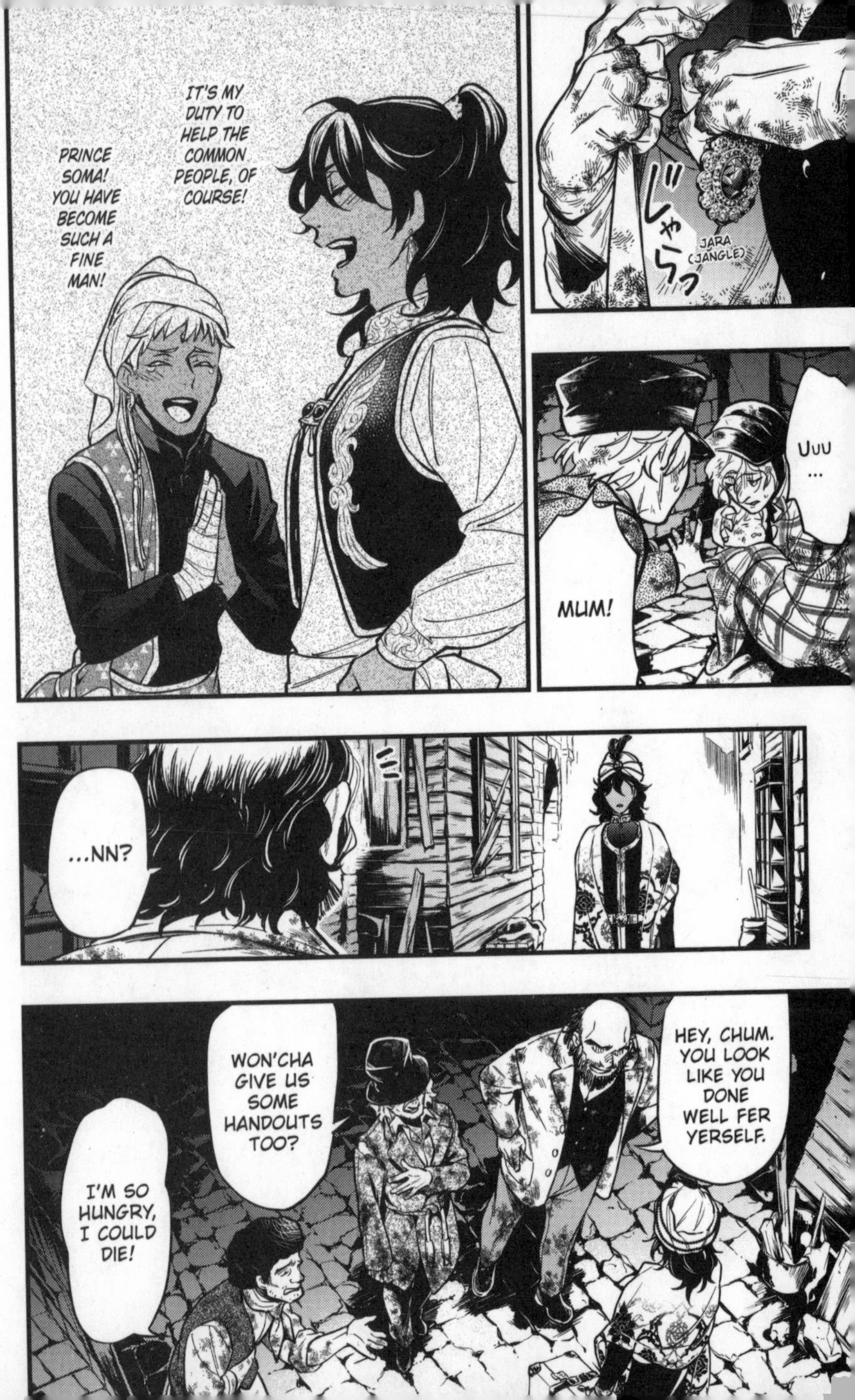
じゃらっ
JARA (JANGLE)
UUU ...
MUM!
IT'S MY DUTY TO HELP THE COMMON PEOPLE, OF COURSE!
PRINCE SOMA! YOU HAVE BECOME SUCH A FINE MAN!
...NN?
HEY, CHUM. YOU LOOK LIKE YOU DONE WELL FER YERSELF.
WON'CHA GIVE US SOME HANDOUTS TOO?
I'M SO HUNGRY, I COULD DIE!

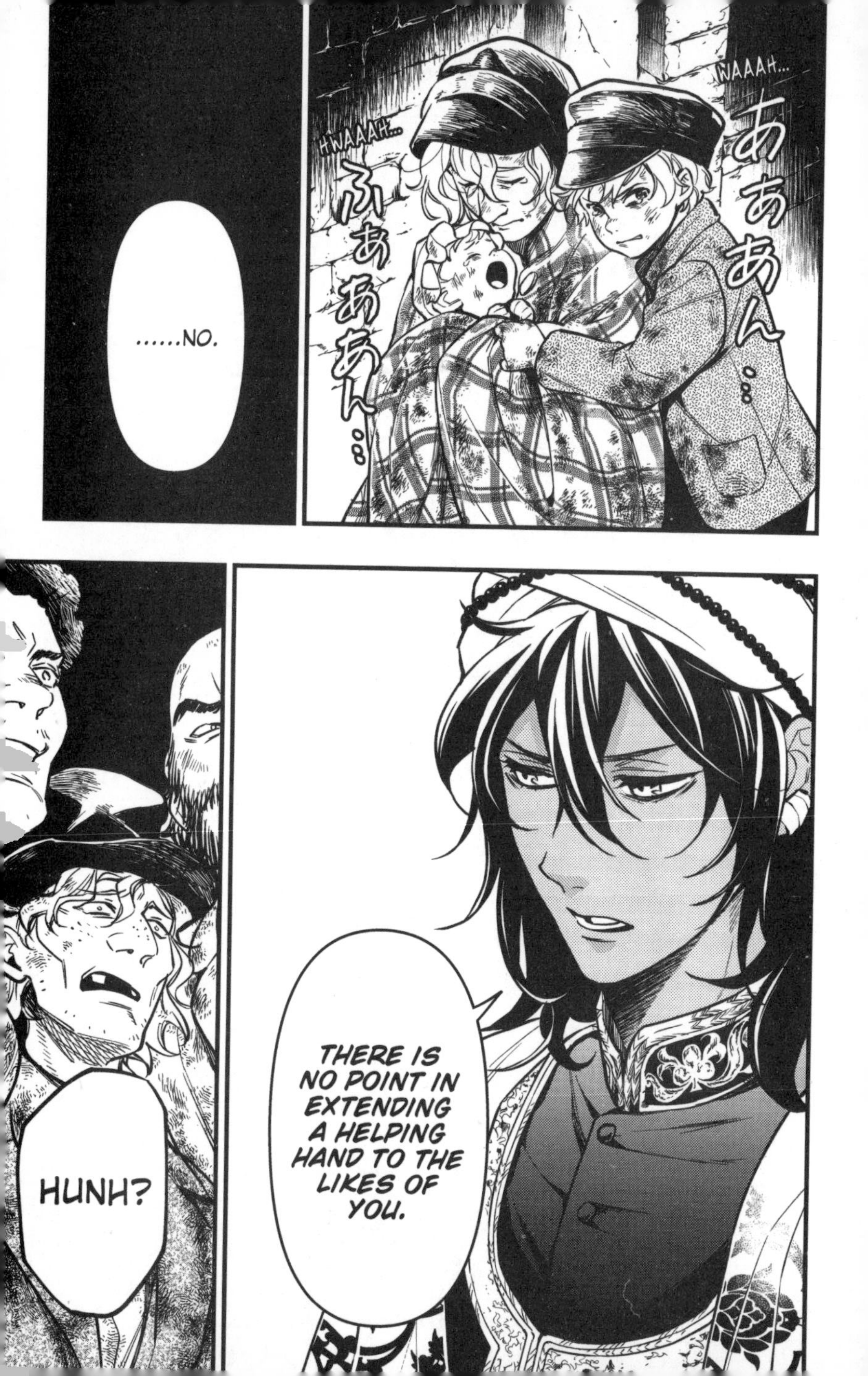
WAAAH...
あぁあん。。
HWAAAH...
ふぁああん。。
......NO.
THERE IS NO POINT IN EXTENDING A HELPING HAND TO THE LIKES OF YOU.
HUNH?

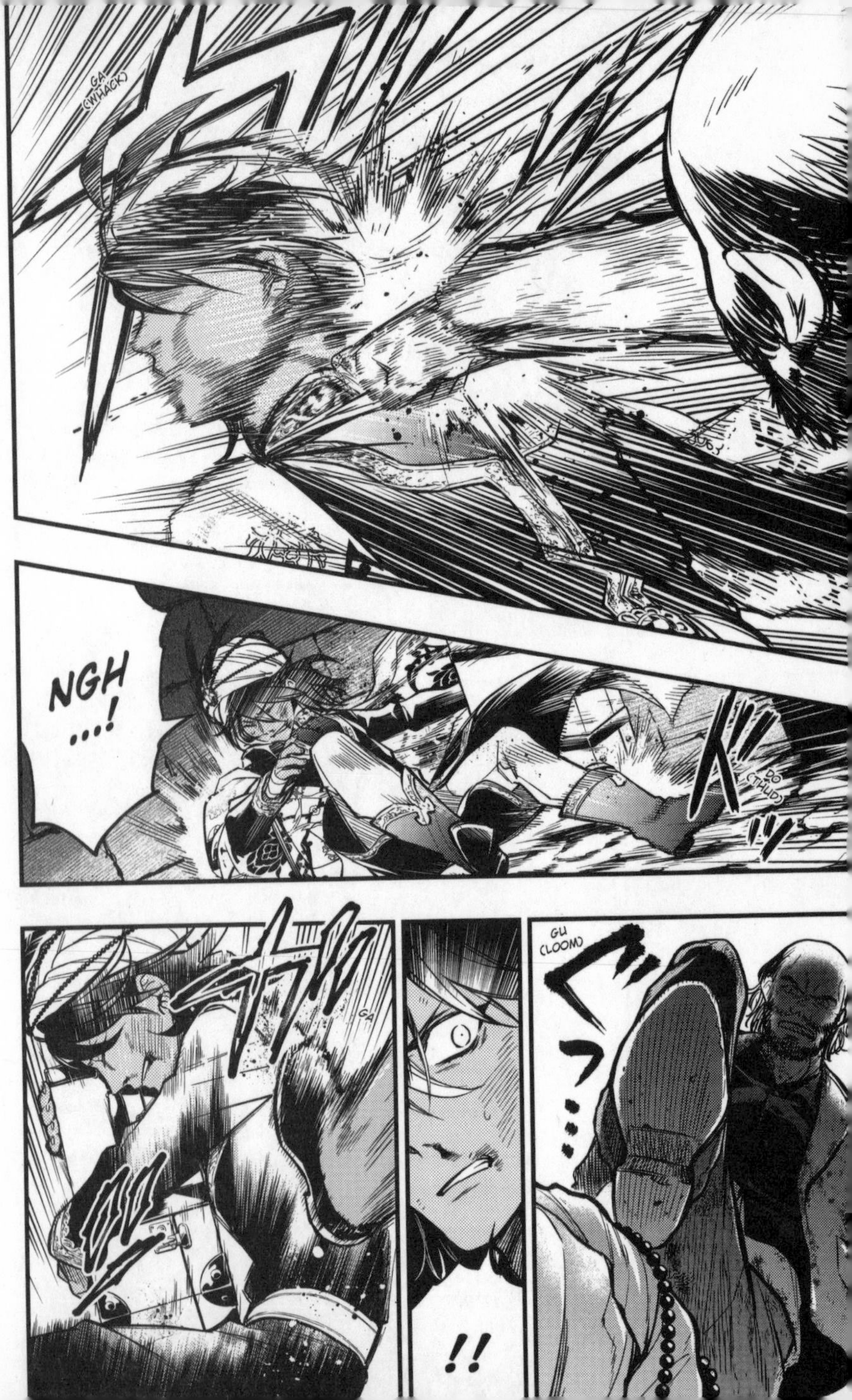
GA
(WHACK)
DO
(THUD)
NGH
...!
GU
(LOOM)
!!
GA

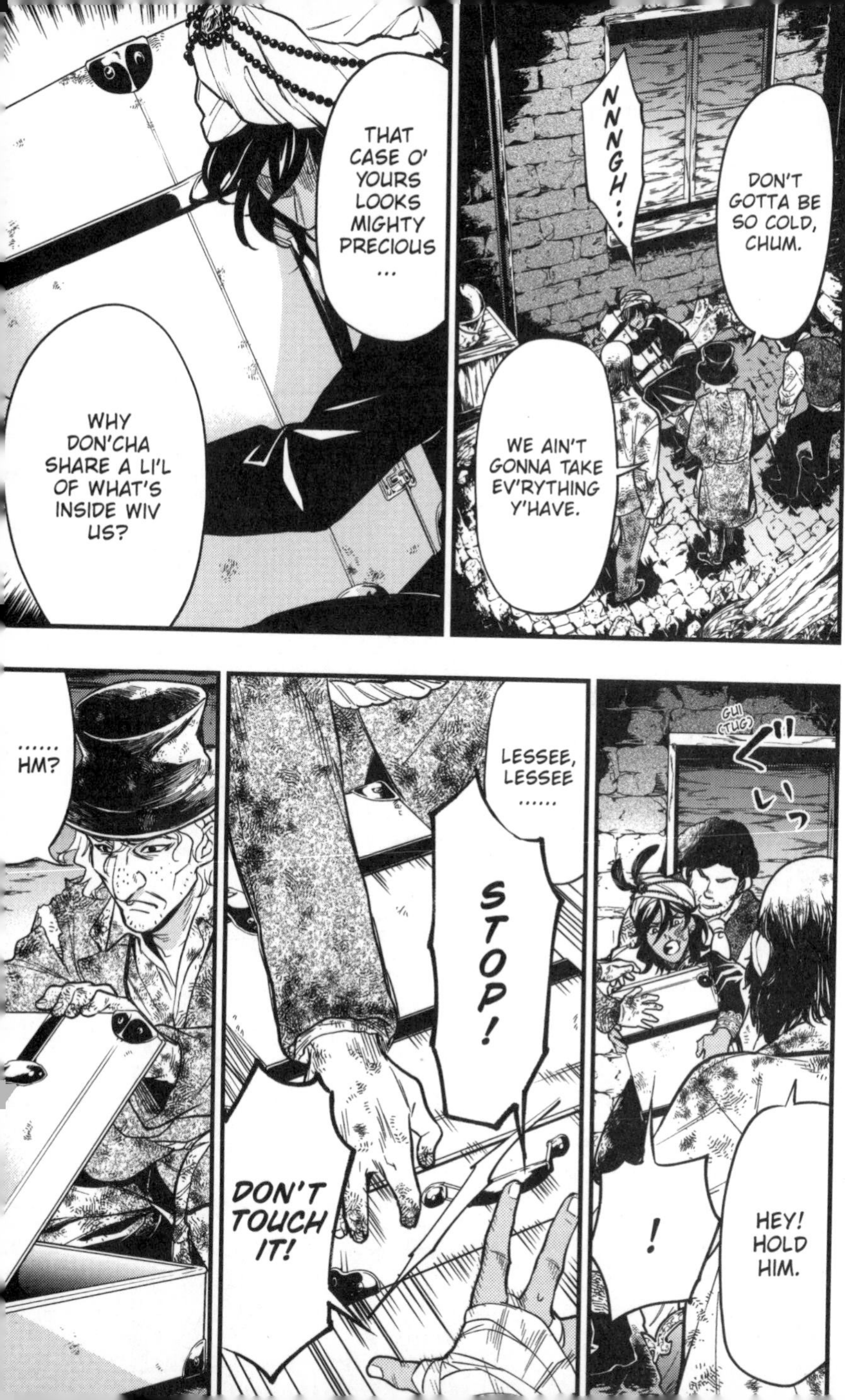

DON'T GOTTA BE SO COLD, CHUM.
NNNGH...
WE AIN'T GONNA TAKE EV'RYTHING Y'HAVE.
THAT CASE O' YOURS LOOKS MIGHTY PRECIOUS ...
WHY DON'CHA SHARE A LI'L OF WHAT'S INSIDE WIV US?
GUI (TUG)
HEY! HOLD HIM.
!
LESSEE, LESSEE ......
STOP!
DON'T TOUCH IT!
...... HM?

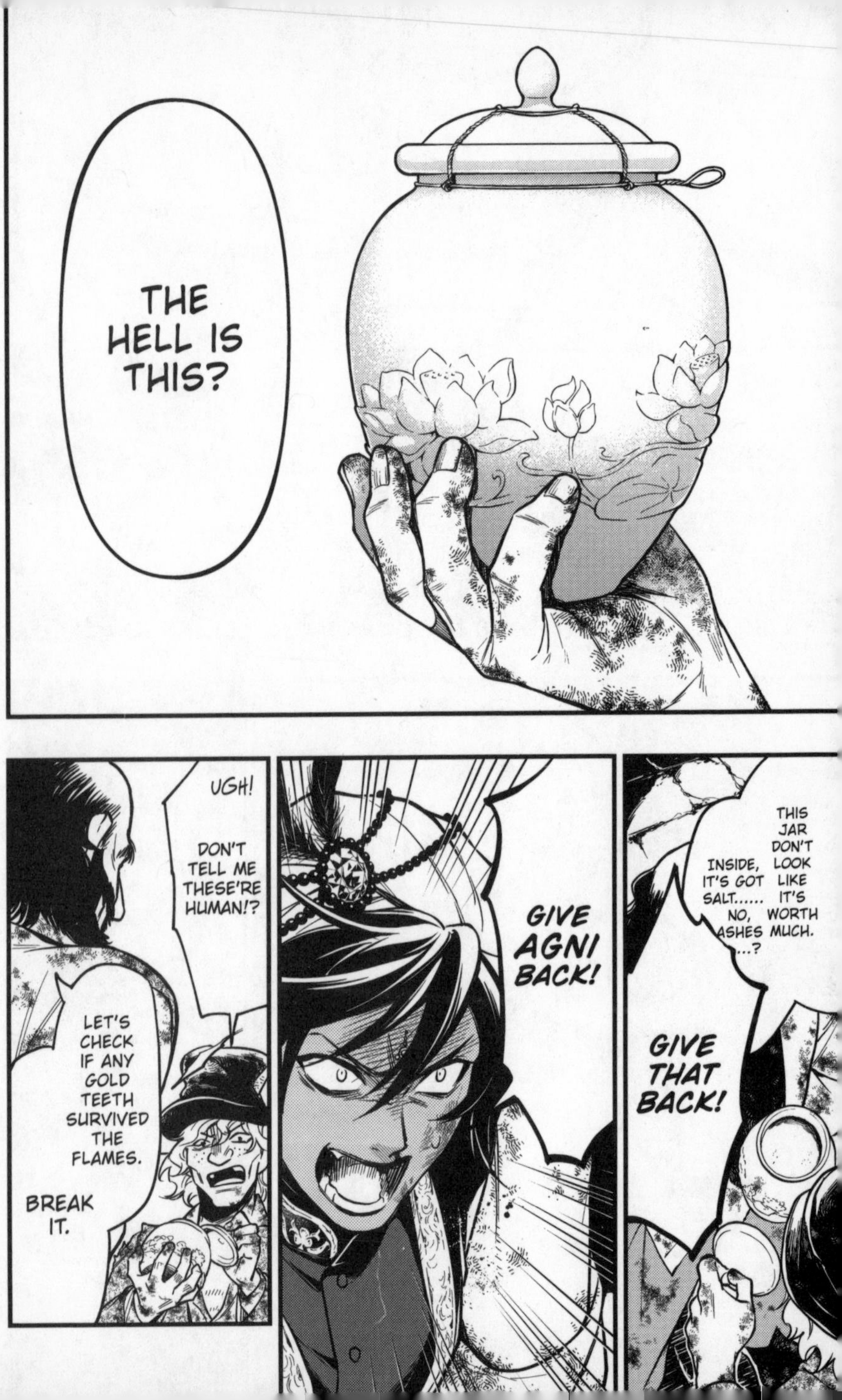
THE HELL IS THIS?
THIS JAR DON'T LOOK LIKE IT'S WORTH MUCH.
INSIDE, IT'S GOT SALT...... NO, ASHES ...?
GIVE THAT BACK!
GIVE AGNI BACK!
UGH!
DON'T TELL ME THESE'RE HUMAN!?
LET'S CHECK IF ANY GOLD TEETH SURVIVED THE FLAMES.
BREAK IT.

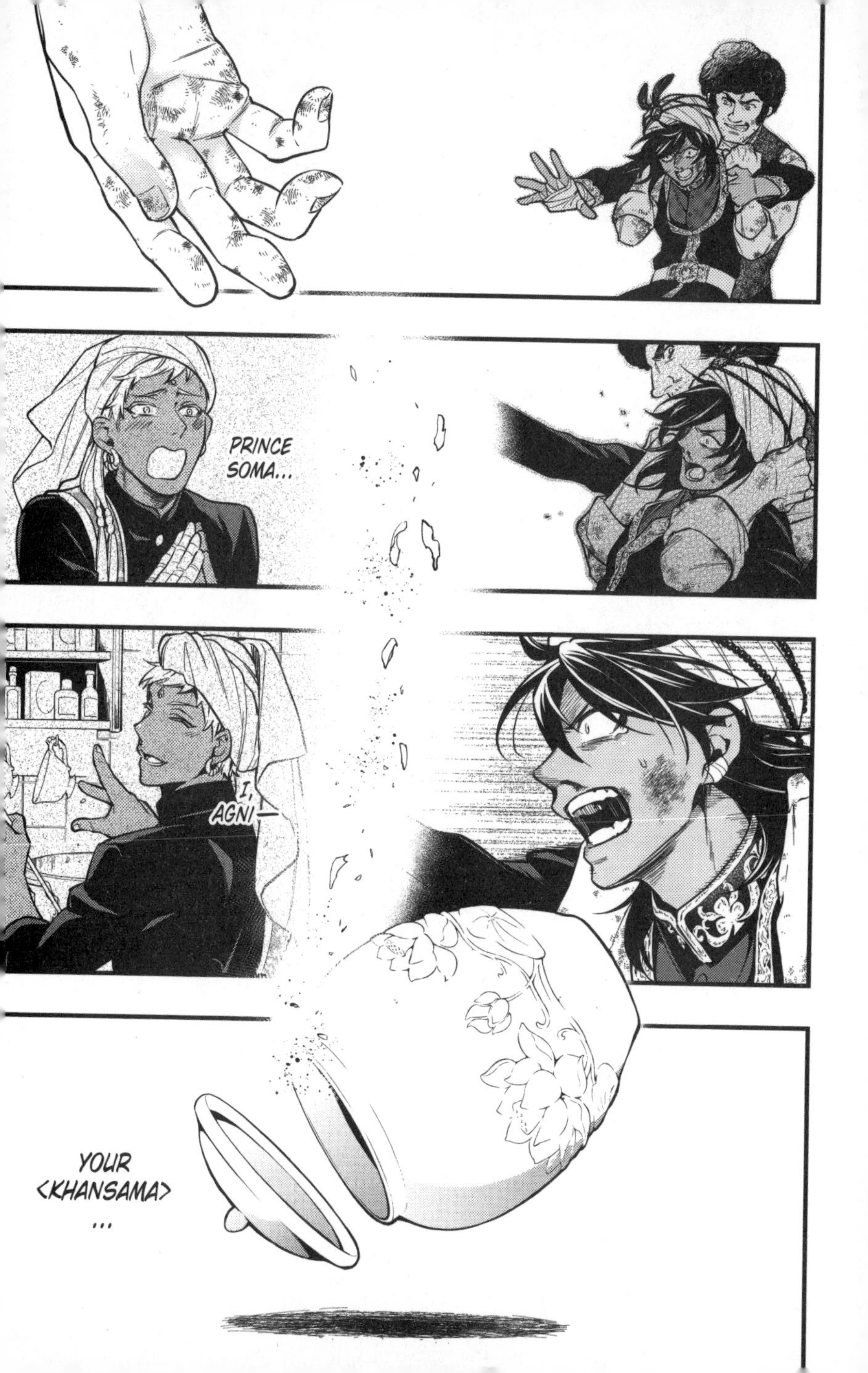
PRINCE SOMA...
I, AGNI—
YOUR <KHANSAMA> ...

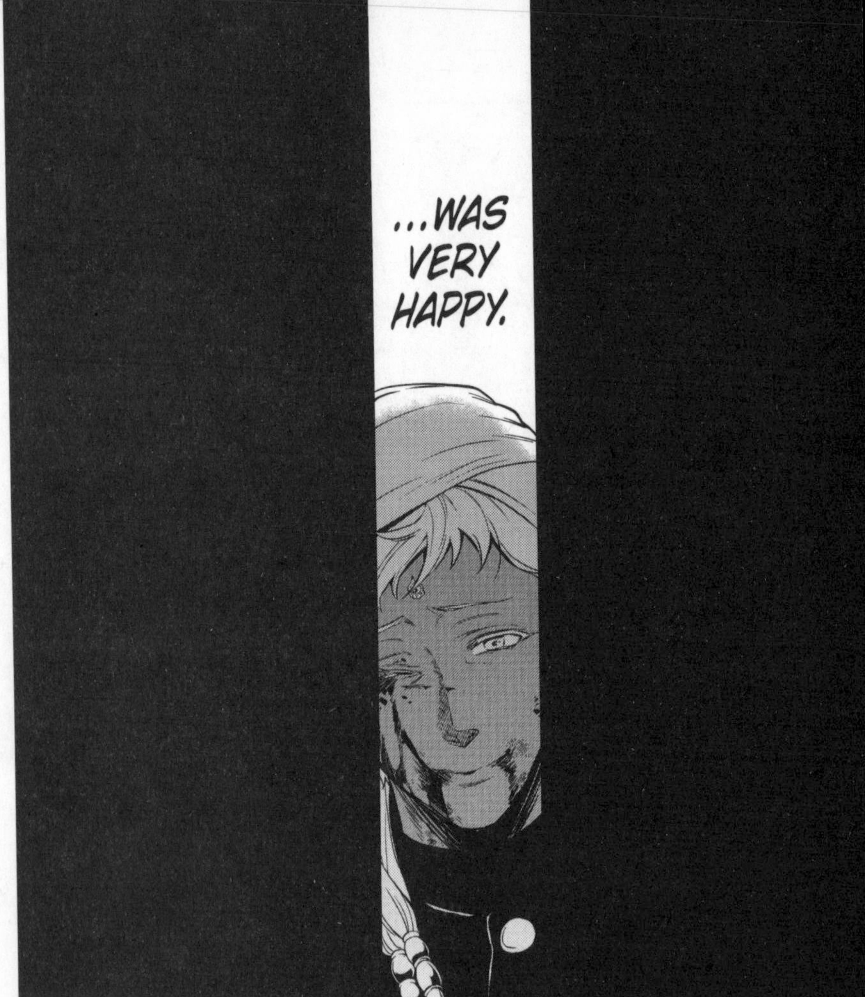
...WAS VERY HAPPY.
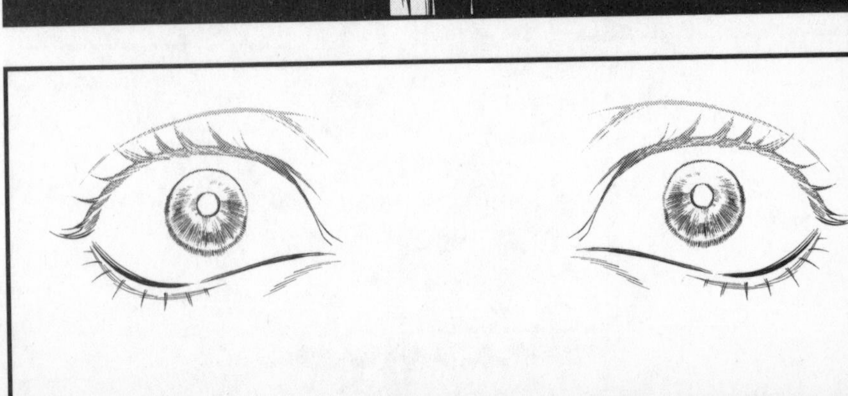

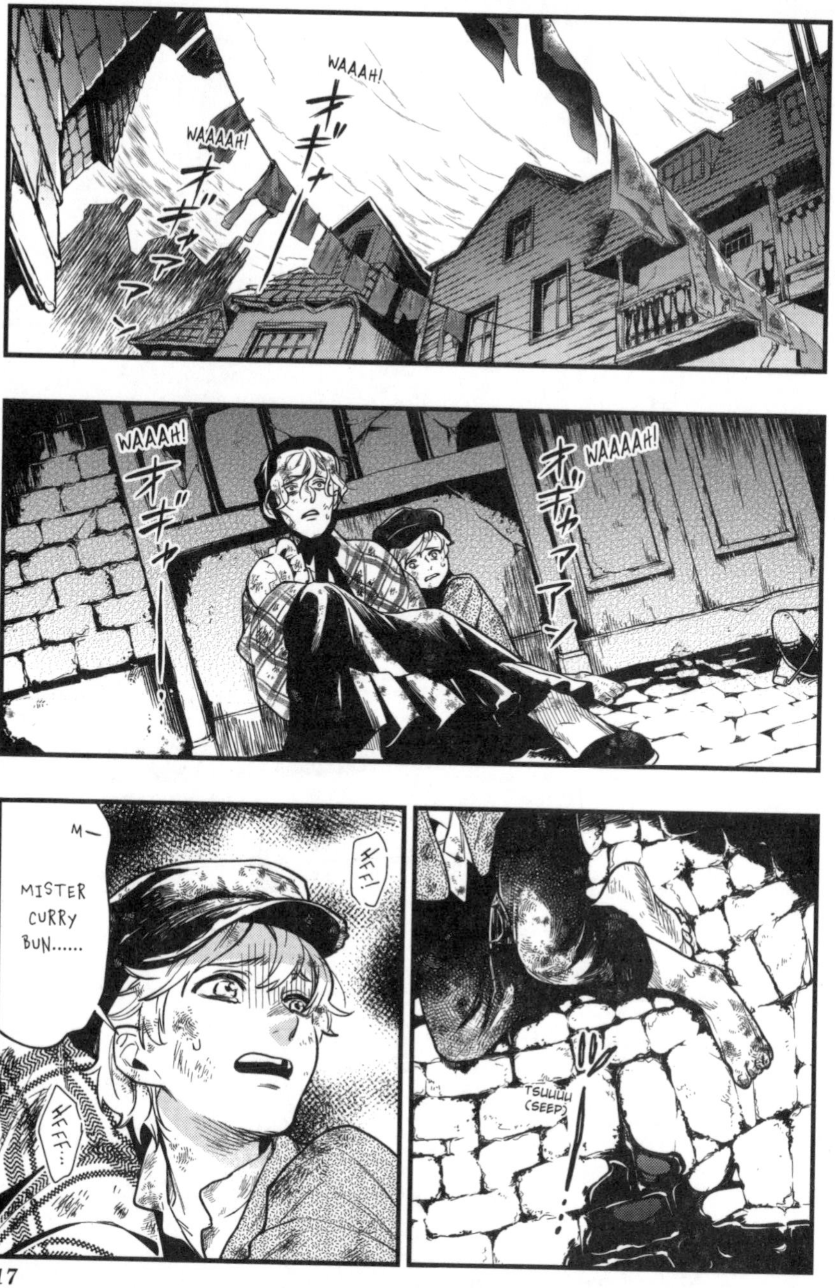

WAAAH!
オギャー
WAAAAH!
オギャァアン
WAAAAH!
オギャァアン
WAAAH!
オギャー
TSUUUH (SEEP)
HFF!
M— MISTER CURRY BUN......
HFFF...

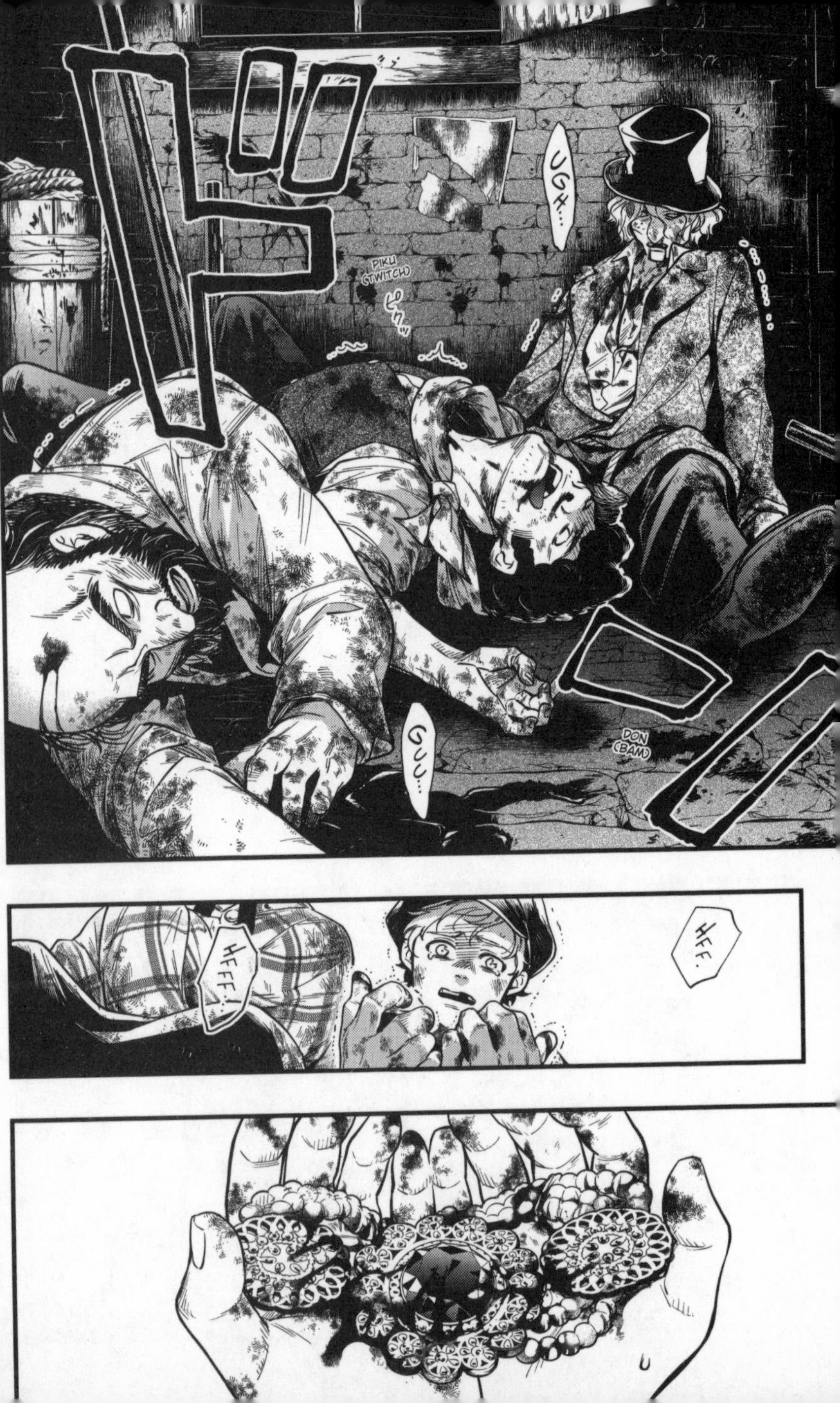
UGH...
PIKU (TWITCH)
DON (BAM)
GUU...
HFF.
HFFF...!

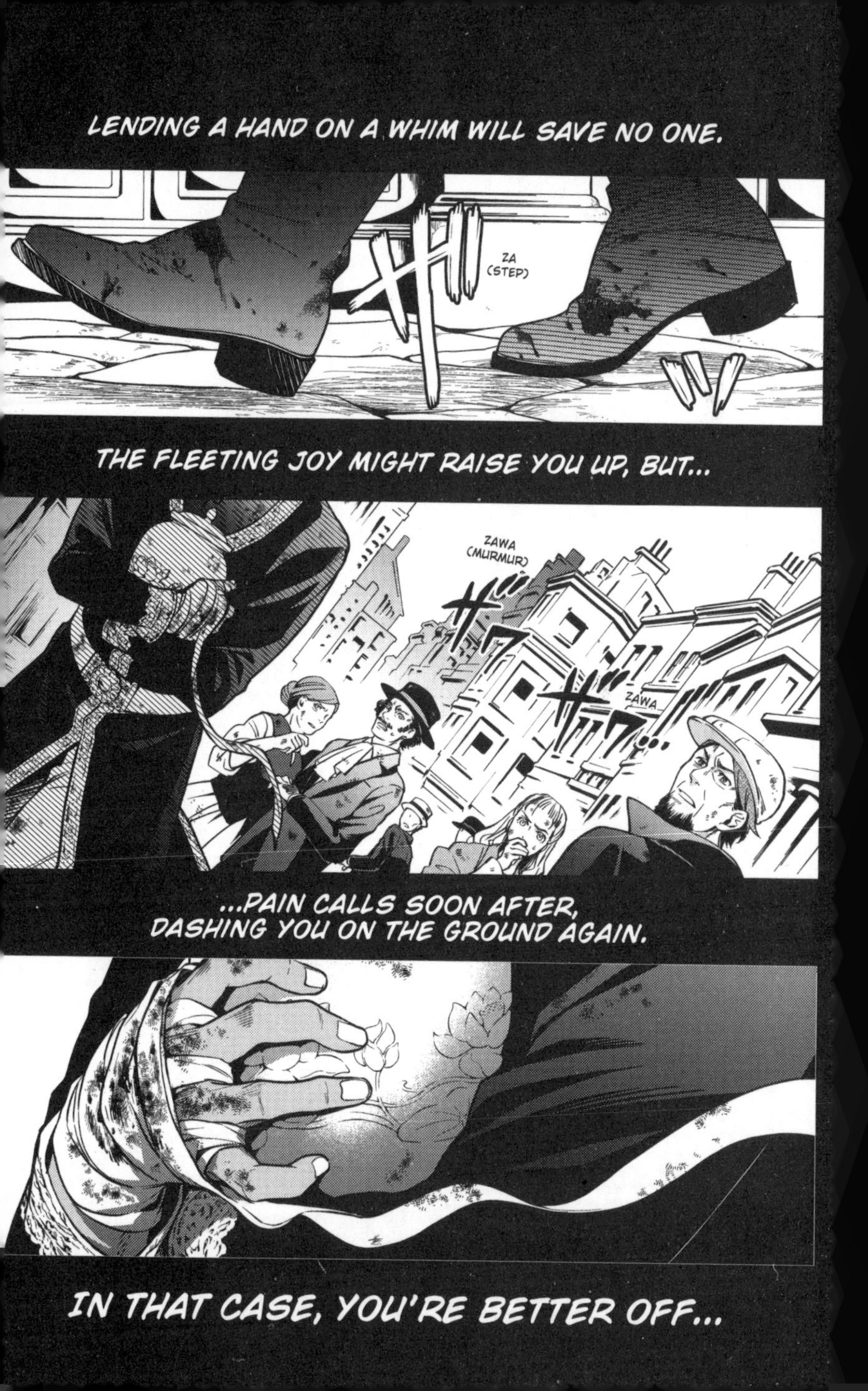
LENDING A HAND ON A WHIM WILL SAVE NO ONE.
ZA (STEP)
THE FLEETING JOY MIGHT RAISE YOU UP, BUT...
ZAWA (MURMUR)
ZAWA
...PAIN CALLS SOON AFTER, DASHING YOU ON THE GROUND AGAIN.
IN THAT CASE, YOU'RE BETTER OFF...

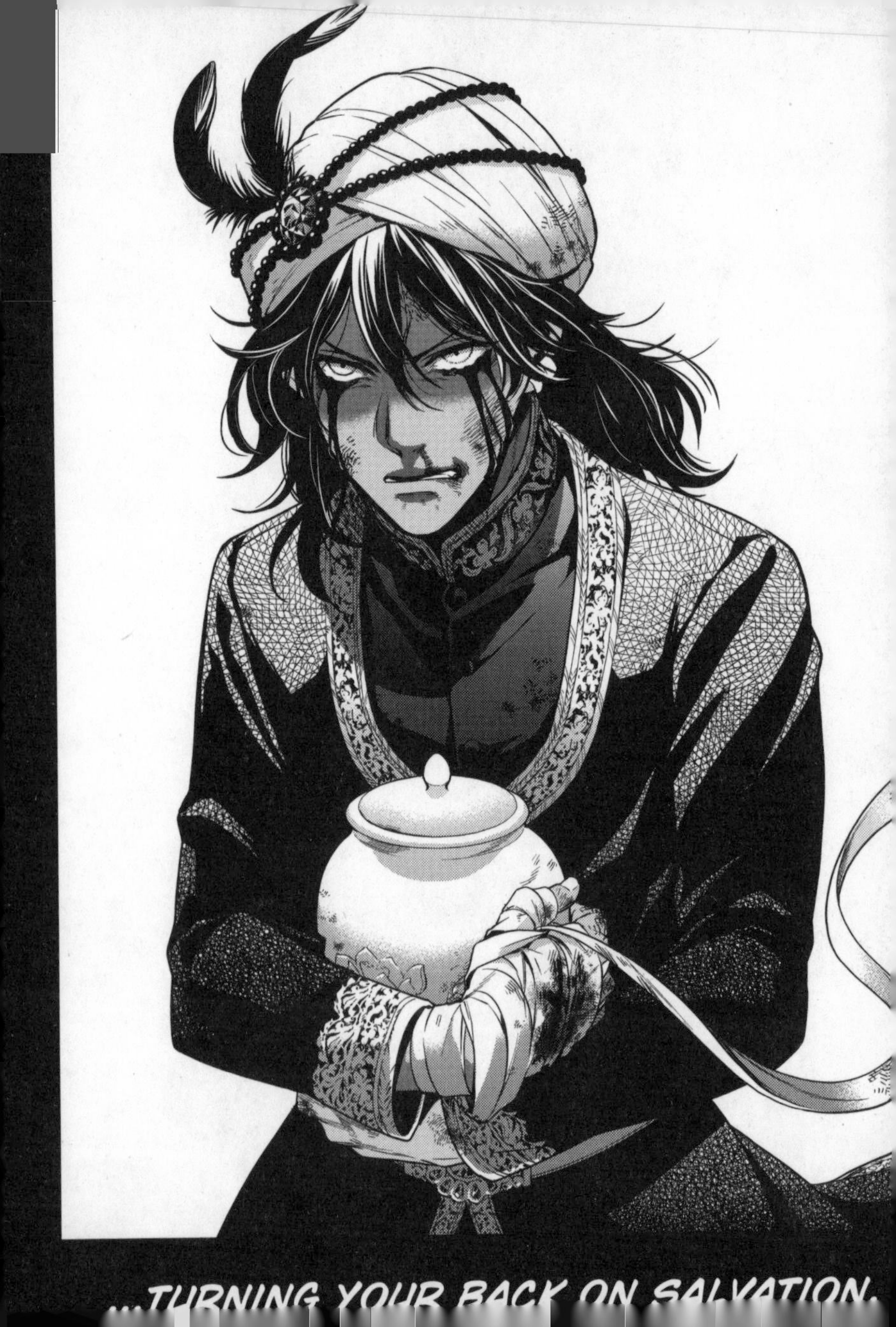
...TURNING YOUR BACK ON SALVATION.

Black Butler

Chapter 149

In the morning : The Butler, Rallying

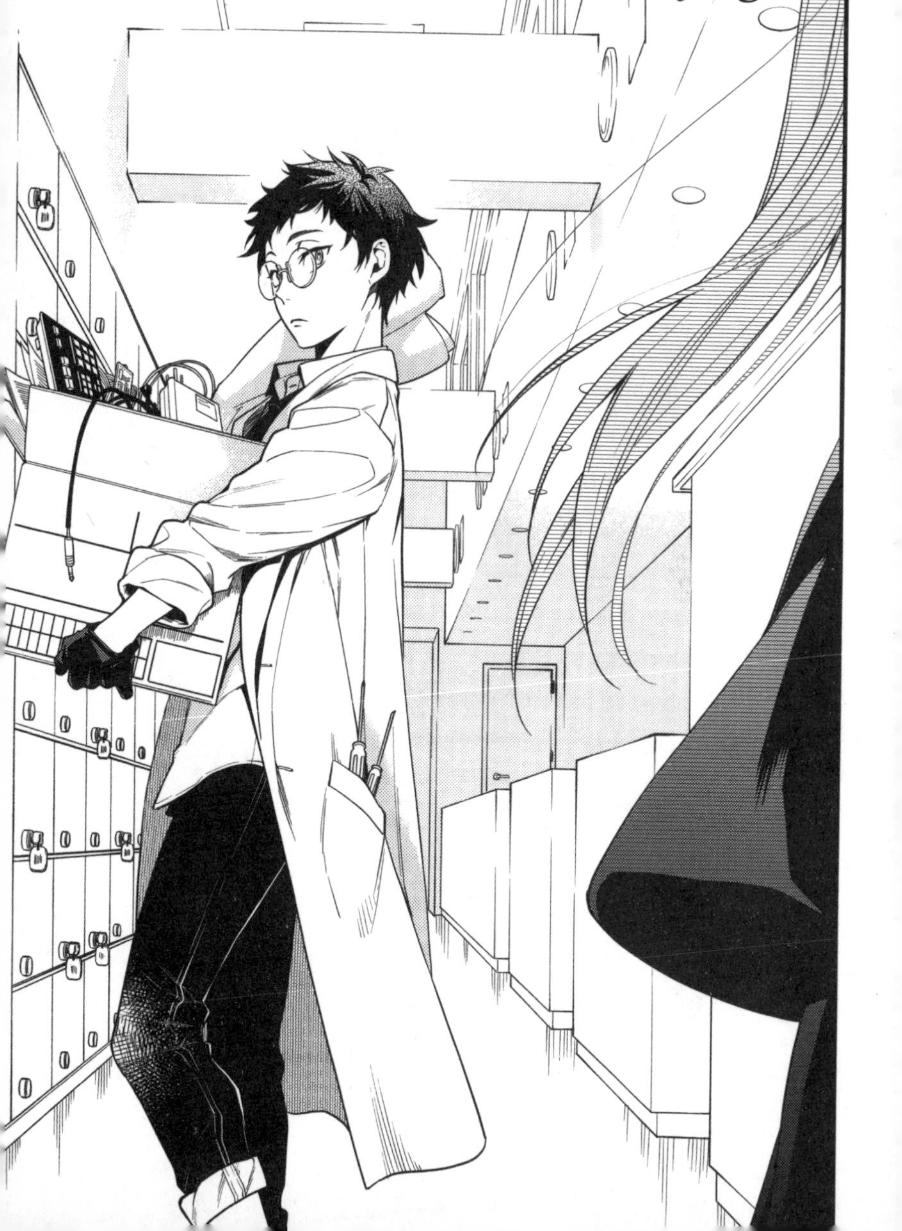

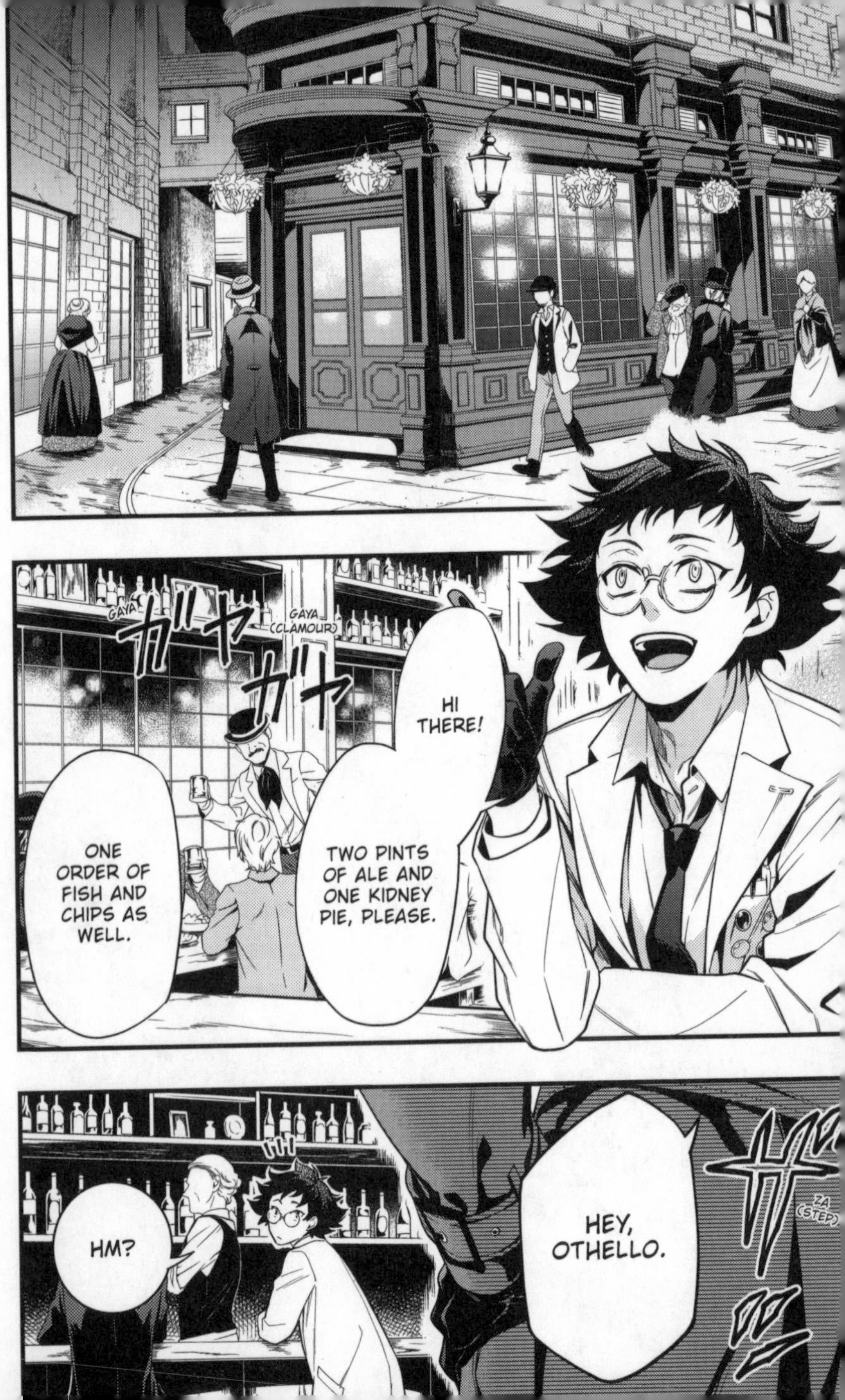
HI THERE!
GAYA
GAYA (CLAMOUR)
TWO PINTS OF ALE AND ONE KIDNEY PIE, PLEASE.
ONE ORDER OF FISH AND CHIPS AS WELL.
ZA (STEP)
HEY, OTHELLO.
HM?

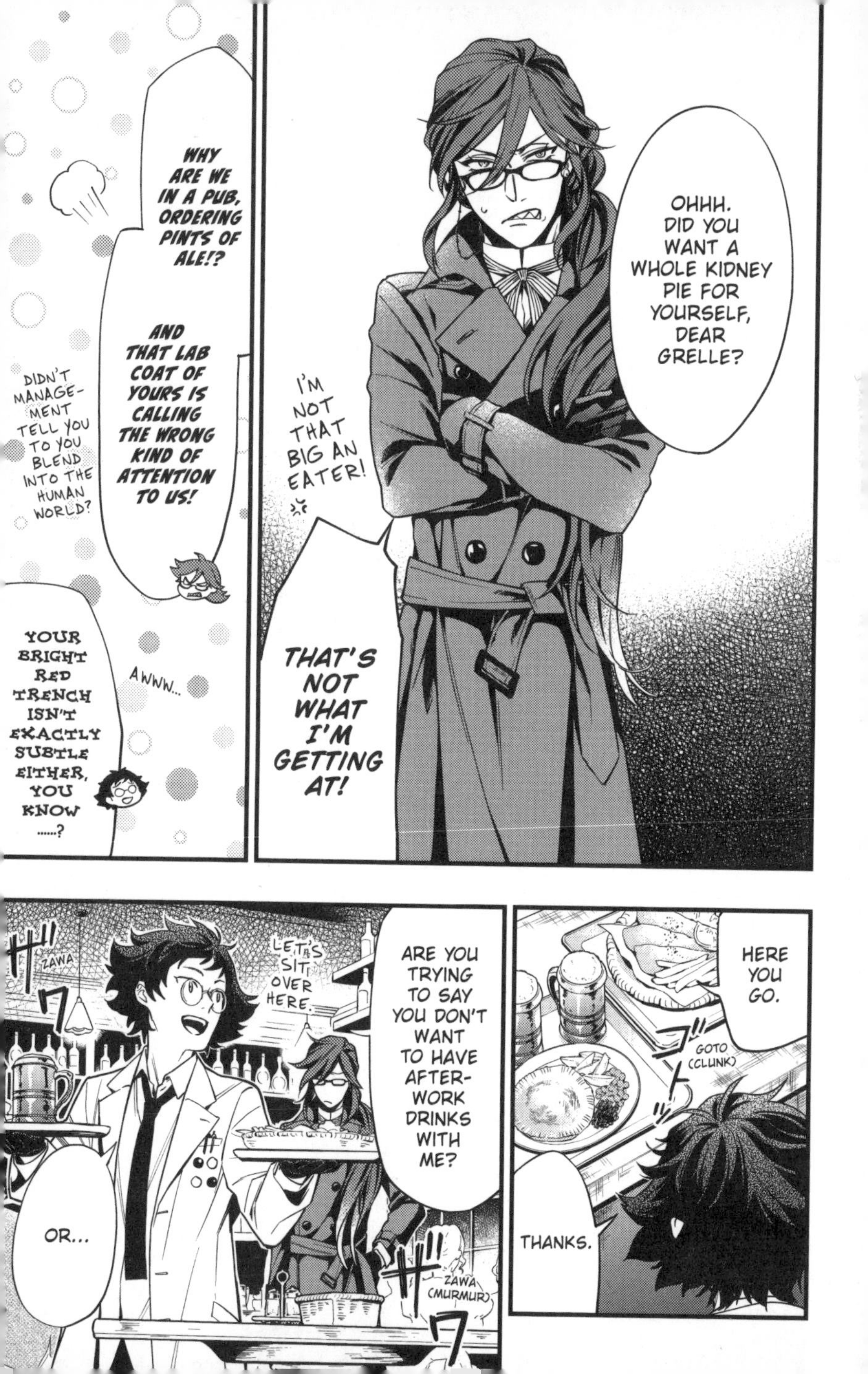
OHHH. DID YOU WANT A WHOLE KIDNEY PIE FOR YOURSELF, DEAR GRELLE?
I'M NOT THAT BIG AN EATER!
THAT'S NOT WHAT I'M GETTING AT!
WHY ARE WE IN A PUB, ORDERING PINTS OF ALE!?
AND THAT LAB COAT OF YOURS IS CALLING THE WRONG KIND OF ATTENTION TO US!
DIDN'T MANAGEMENT TELL YOU TO YOU BLEND INTO THE HUMAN WORLD?
YOUR BRIGHT RED TRENCH ISN'T EXACTLY SUBTLE EITHER, YOU KNOW......?
AWWW...
HERE YOU GO.
GOTO (CLUNK)
THANKS.
ARE YOU TRYING TO SAY YOU DON'T WANT TO HAVE AFTER-WORK DRINKS WITH ME?
LET'S SIT OVER HERE.
ZAWA
ZAWA (MURMUR)
OR...

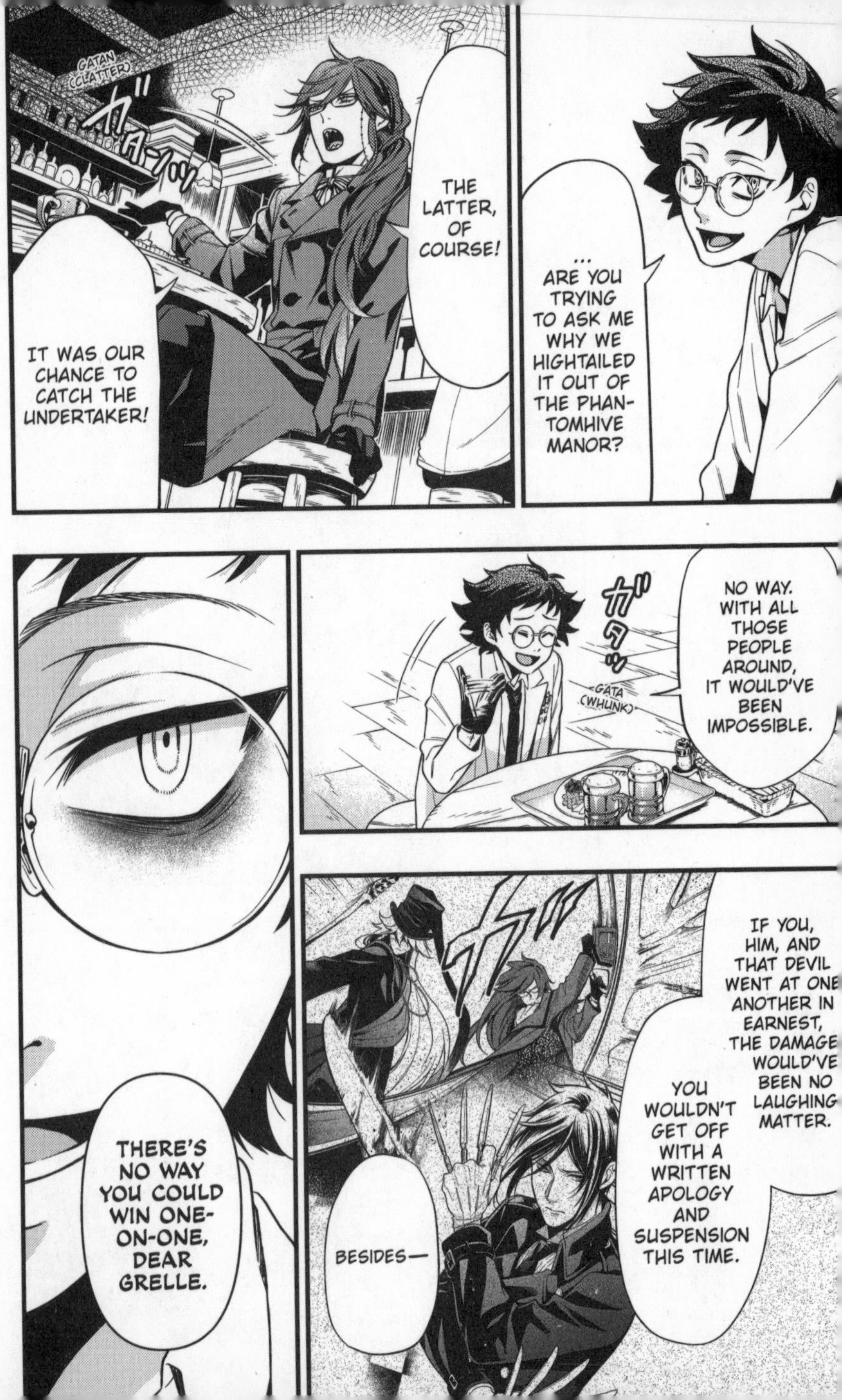
...
ARE YOU TRYING TO ASK ME WHY WE HIGHTAILED IT OUT OF THE PHANTOMHIVE MANOR?
THE LATTER, OF COURSE!
GATAN (CLATTER)
IT WAS OUR CHANCE TO CATCH THE UNDERTAKER!
NO WAY. WITH ALL THOSE PEOPLE AROUND, IT WOULD'VE BEEN IMPOSSIBLE.
GATA (WHUNK)
IF YOU, HIM, AND THAT DEVIL WENT AT ONE ANOTHER IN EARNEST, THE DAMAGE WOULD'VE BEEN NO LAUGHING MATTER.
YOU WOULDN'T GET OFF WITH A WRITTEN APOLOGY AND SUSPENSION THIS TIME.
BESIDES—
THERE'S NO WAY YOU COULD WIN ONE-ON-ONE, DEAR GRELLE.

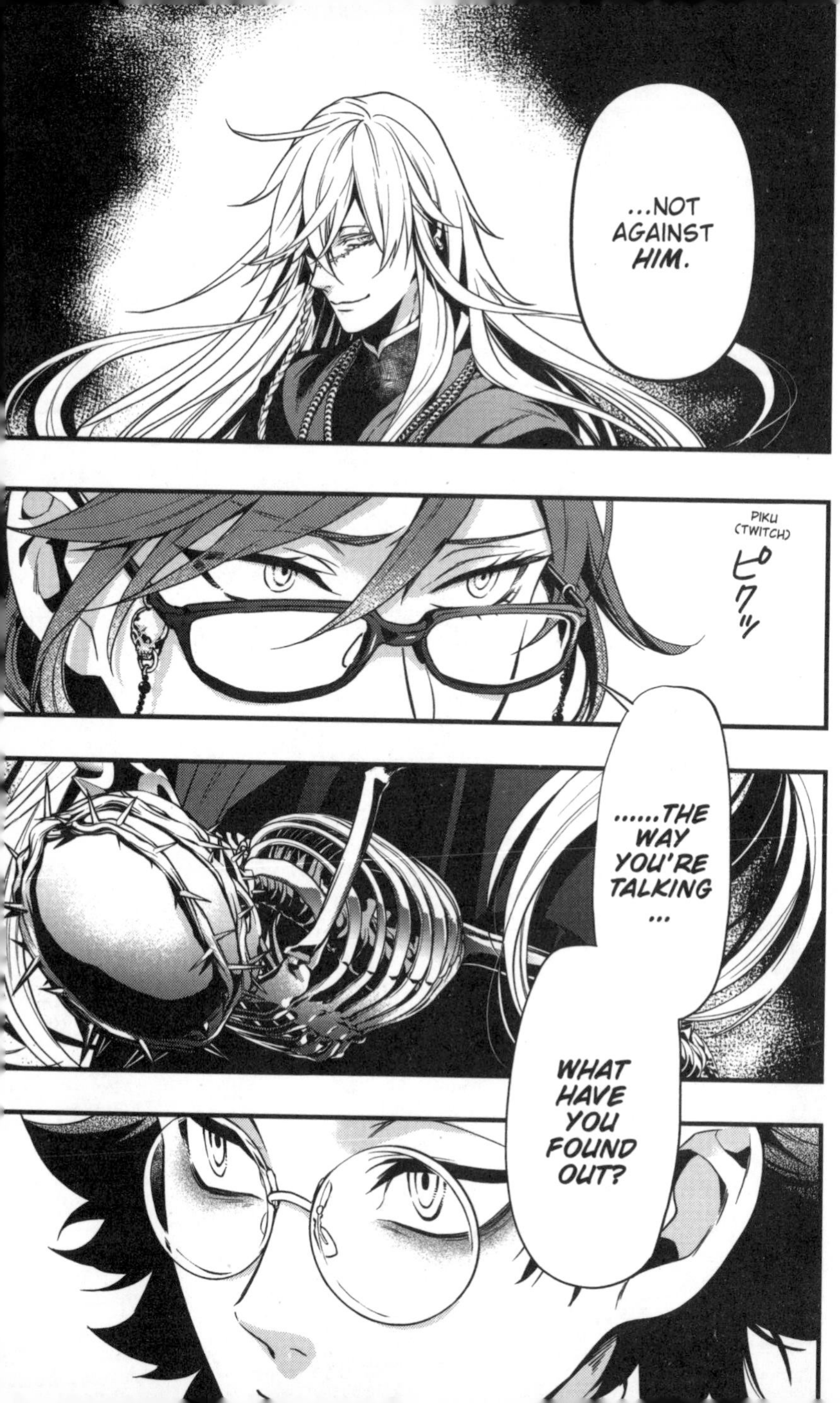
...NOT AGAINST HIM.
PIKU (TWITCH)
ピクッ
......THE WAY YOU'RE TALKING ...
WHAT HAVE YOU FOUND OUT?

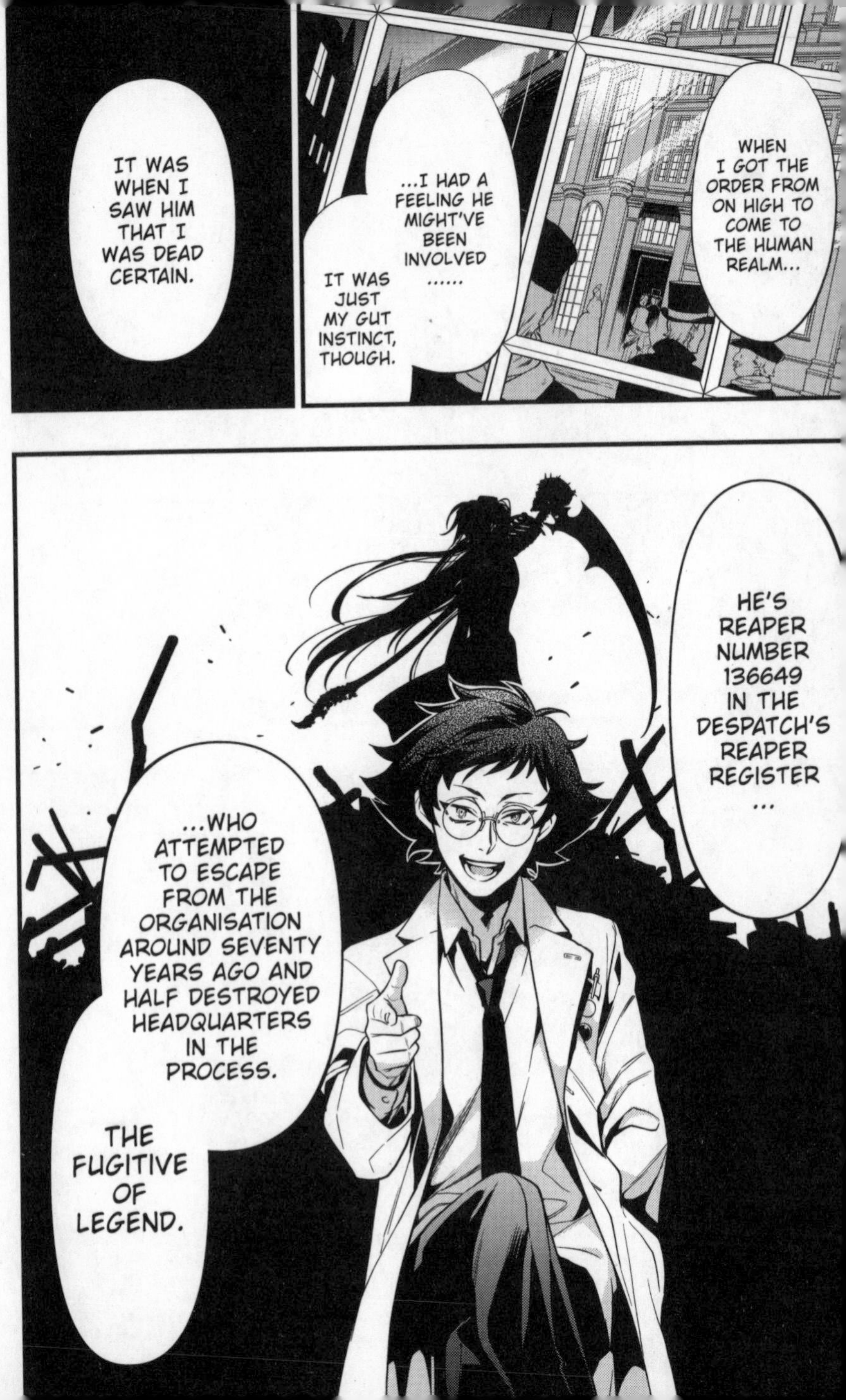
WHEN I GOT THE ORDER FROM ON HIGH TO COME TO THE HUMAN REALM...
...I HAD A FEELING HE MIGHT'VE BEEN INVOLVED ......
IT WAS JUST MY GUT INSTINCT, THOUGH.
IT WAS WHEN I SAW HIM THAT I WAS DEAD CERTAIN.
HE'S REAPER NUMBER 136649 IN THE DESPATCH'S REAPER REGISTER ...
...WHO ATTEMPTED TO ESCAPE FROM THE ORGANISATION AROUND SEVENTY YEARS AGO AND HALF DESTROYED HEADQUARTERS IN THE PROCESS.
THE FUGITIVE OF LEGEND.

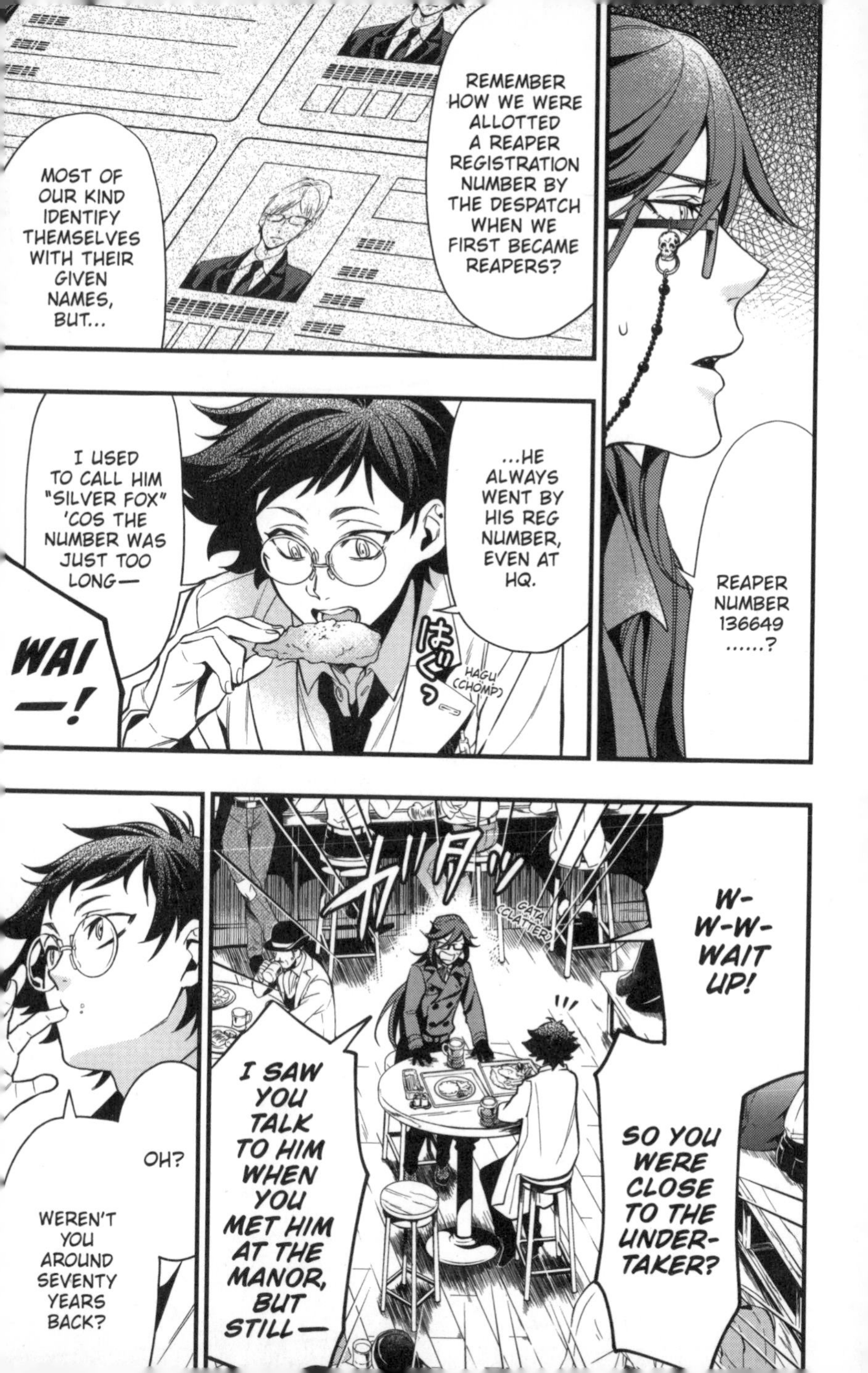
REAPER NUMBER 136649 ......?
REMEMBER HOW WE WERE ALLOTTED A REAPER REGISTRATION NUMBER BY THE DESPATCH WHEN WE FIRST BECAME REAPERS?
MOST OF OUR KIND IDENTIFY THEMSELVES WITH THEIR GIVEN NAMES, BUT...
...HE ALWAYS WENT BY HIS REG NUMBER, EVEN AT HQ.
はぐっ
HAGU (CHOMP)
I USED TO CALL HIM "SILVER FOX" 'COS THE NUMBER WAS JUST TOO LONG—
WAI —!
W-W-W-WAIT UP!
ガタッ
GATA (CLATTER)
SO YOU WERE CLOSE TO THE UNDER-TAKER?
I SAW YOU TALK TO HIM WHEN YOU MET HIM AT THE MANOR, BUT STILL—
OH?
WEREN'T YOU AROUND SEVENTY YEARS BACK?

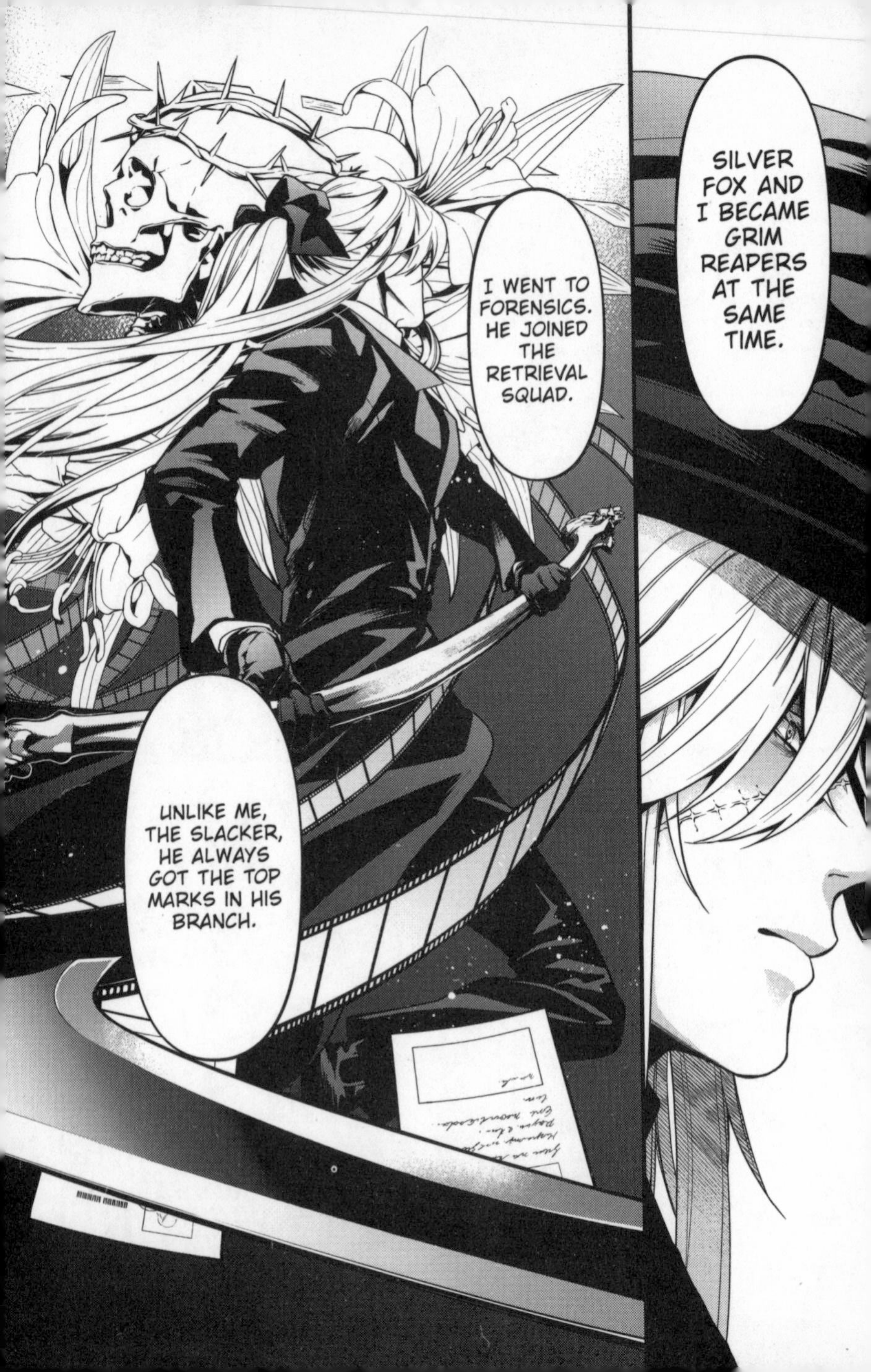
SILVER FOX AND I BECAME GRIM REAPERS AT THE SAME TIME.
I WENT TO FORENSICS. HE JOINED THE RETRIEVAL SQUAD.
UNLIKE ME, THE SLACKER, HE ALWAYS GOT THE TOP MARKS IN HIS BRANCH.

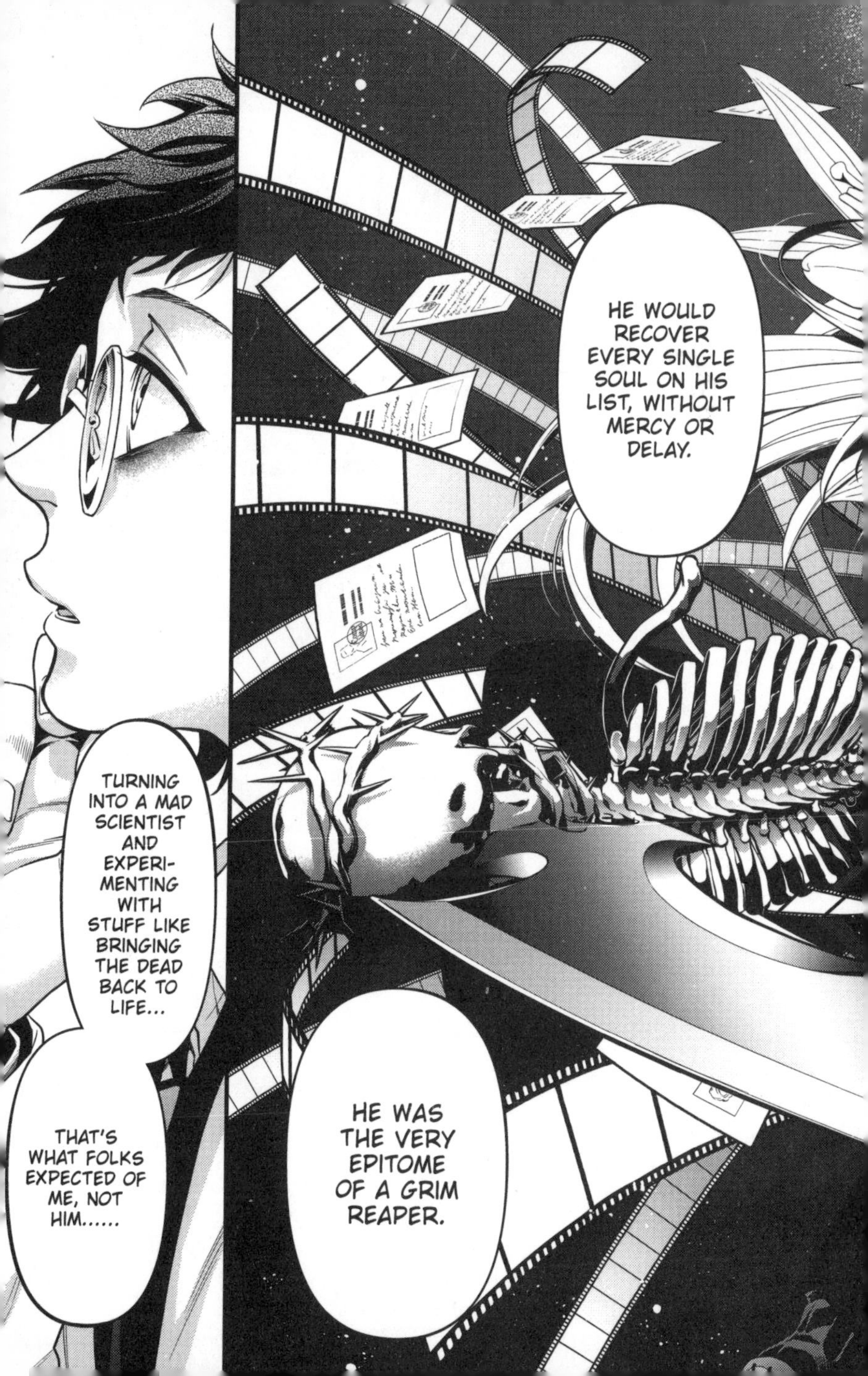
HE WOULD RECOVER EVERY SINGLE SOUL ON HIS LIST, WITHOUT MERCY OR DELAY.
HE WAS THE VERY EPITOME OF A GRIM REAPER.
TURNING INTO A MAD SCIENTIST AND EXPERI-MENTING WITH STUFF LIKE BRINGING THE DEAD BACK TO LIFE...
THAT'S WHAT FOLKS EXPECTED OF ME, NOT HIM......

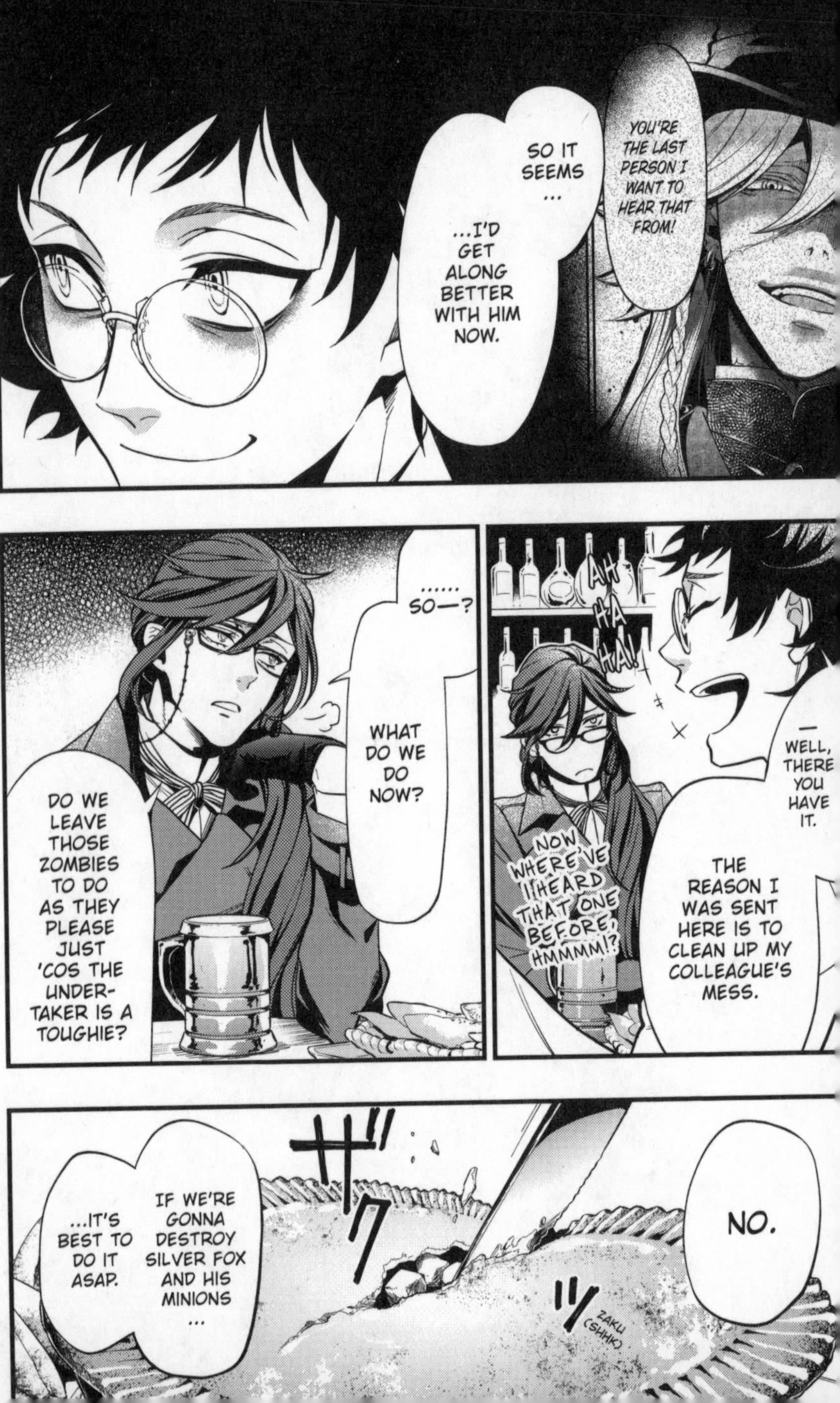
YOU'RE THE LAST PERSON I WANT TO HEAR THAT FROM!
SO IT SEEMS ...
...I'D GET ALONG BETTER WITH HIM NOW.
—WELL, THERE YOU HAVE IT.
THE REASON I WAS SENT HERE IS TO CLEAN UP MY COLLEAGUE'S MESS.
AH HA HA HA!
NOW WHERE'VE I HEARD THAT ONE BEFORE, HMMMM!?
...... SO—?
WHAT DO WE DO NOW?
DO WE LEAVE THOSE ZOMBIES TO DO AS THEY PLEASE JUST 'COS THE UNDER-TAKER IS A TOUGHIE?
NO.
ZAKU (SHHK)
IF WE'RE GONNA DESTROY SILVER FOX AND HIS MINIONS ...
...IT'S BEST TO DO IT ASAP.

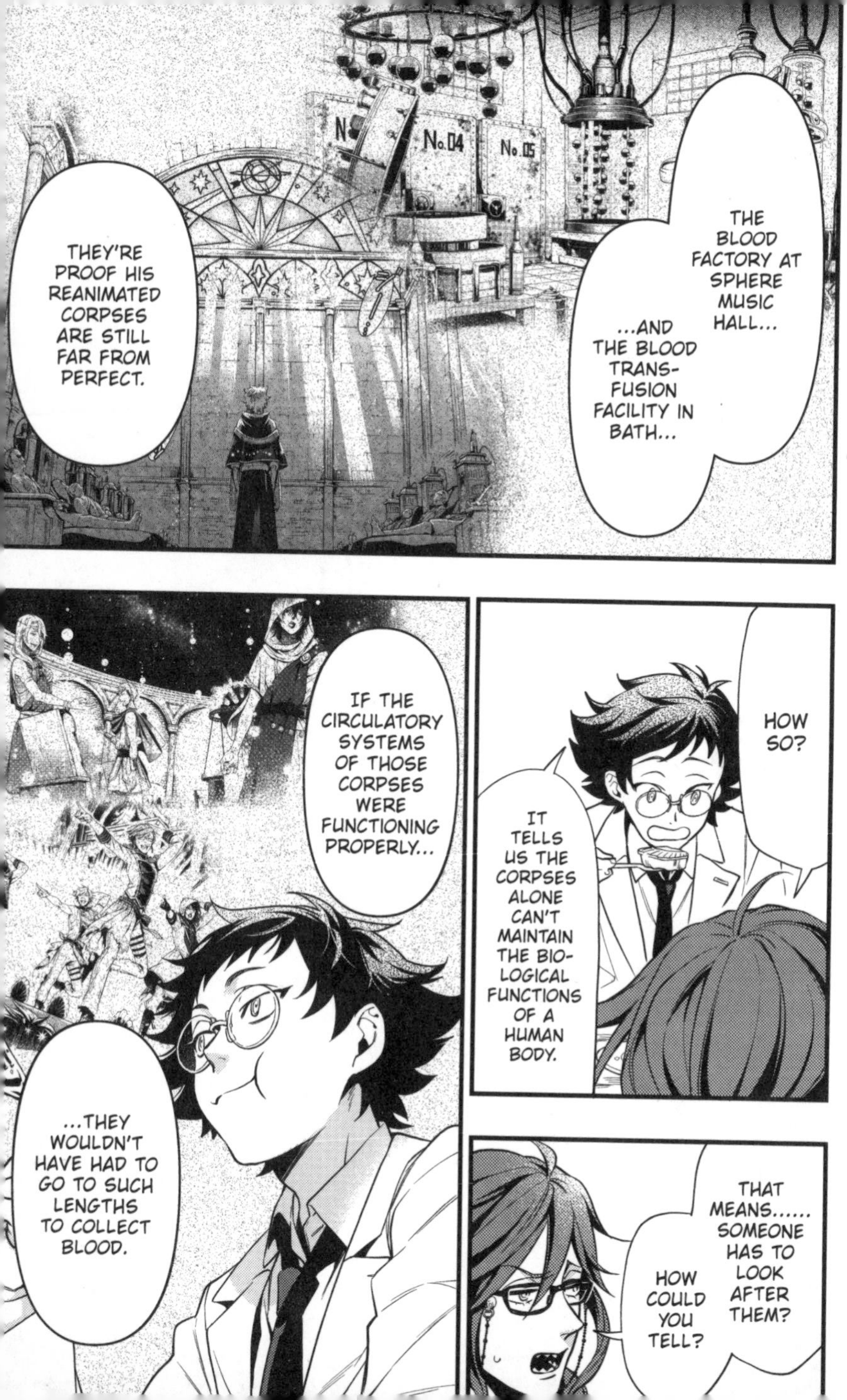
No.04
No.05
THE BLOOD FACTORY AT SPHERE MUSIC HALL...
...AND THE BLOOD TRANS-FUSION FACILITY IN BATH...
THEY'RE PROOF HIS REANIMATED CORPSES ARE STILL FAR FROM PERFECT.
HOW SO?
IT TELLS US THE CORPSES ALONE CAN'T MAINTAIN THE BIO-LOGICAL FUNCTIONS OF A HUMAN BODY.
THAT MEANS...... SOMEONE HAS TO LOOK AFTER THEM?
HOW COULD YOU TELL?
IF THE CIRCULATORY SYSTEMS OF THOSE CORPSES WERE FUNCTIONING PROPERLY...
...THEY WOULDN'T HAVE HAD TO GO TO SUCH LENGTHS TO COLLECT BLOOD.

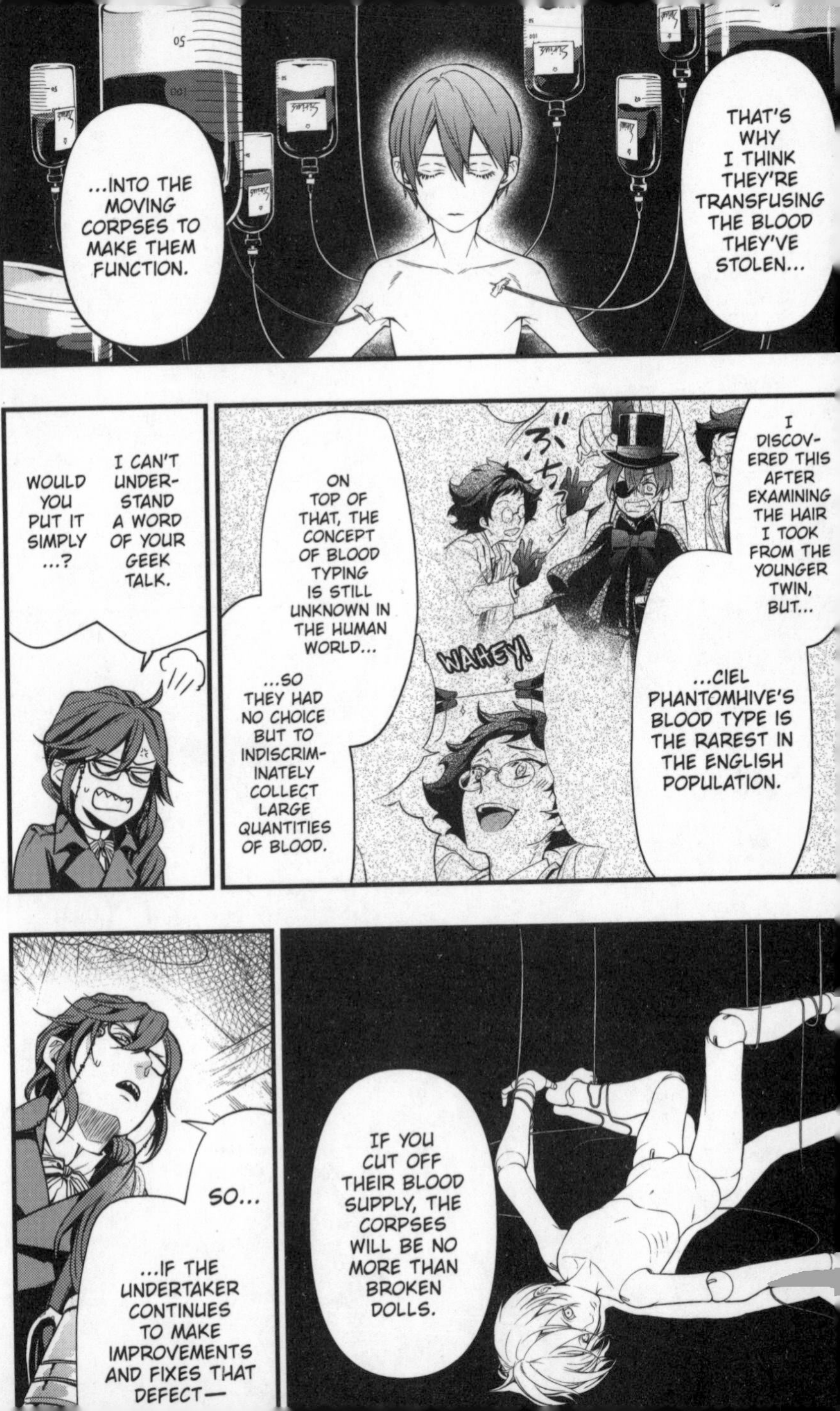
THAT'S WHY I THINK THEY'RE TRANSFUSING THE BLOOD THEY'VE STOLEN...
...INTO THE MOVING CORPSES TO MAKE THEM FUNCTION.
I DISCOVERED THIS AFTER EXAMINING THE HAIR I TOOK FROM THE YOUNGER TWIN, BUT...
ぶちっ
...CIEL PHANTOMHIVE'S BLOOD TYPE IS THE RAREST IN THE ENGLISH POPULATION.
WAHEY!
ON TOP OF THAT, THE CONCEPT OF BLOOD TYPING IS STILL UNKNOWN IN THE HUMAN WORLD...
...SO THEY HAD NO CHOICE BUT TO INDISCRIMINATELY COLLECT LARGE QUANTITIES OF BLOOD.
I CAN'T UNDERSTAND A WORD OF YOUR GEEK TALK.
WOULD YOU PUT IT SIMPLY...?
IF YOU CUT OFF THEIR BLOOD SUPPLY, THE CORPSES WILL BE NO MORE THAN BROKEN DOLLS.
SO...
...IF THE UNDERTAKER CONTINUES TO MAKE IMPROVEMENTS AND FIXES THAT DEFECT—

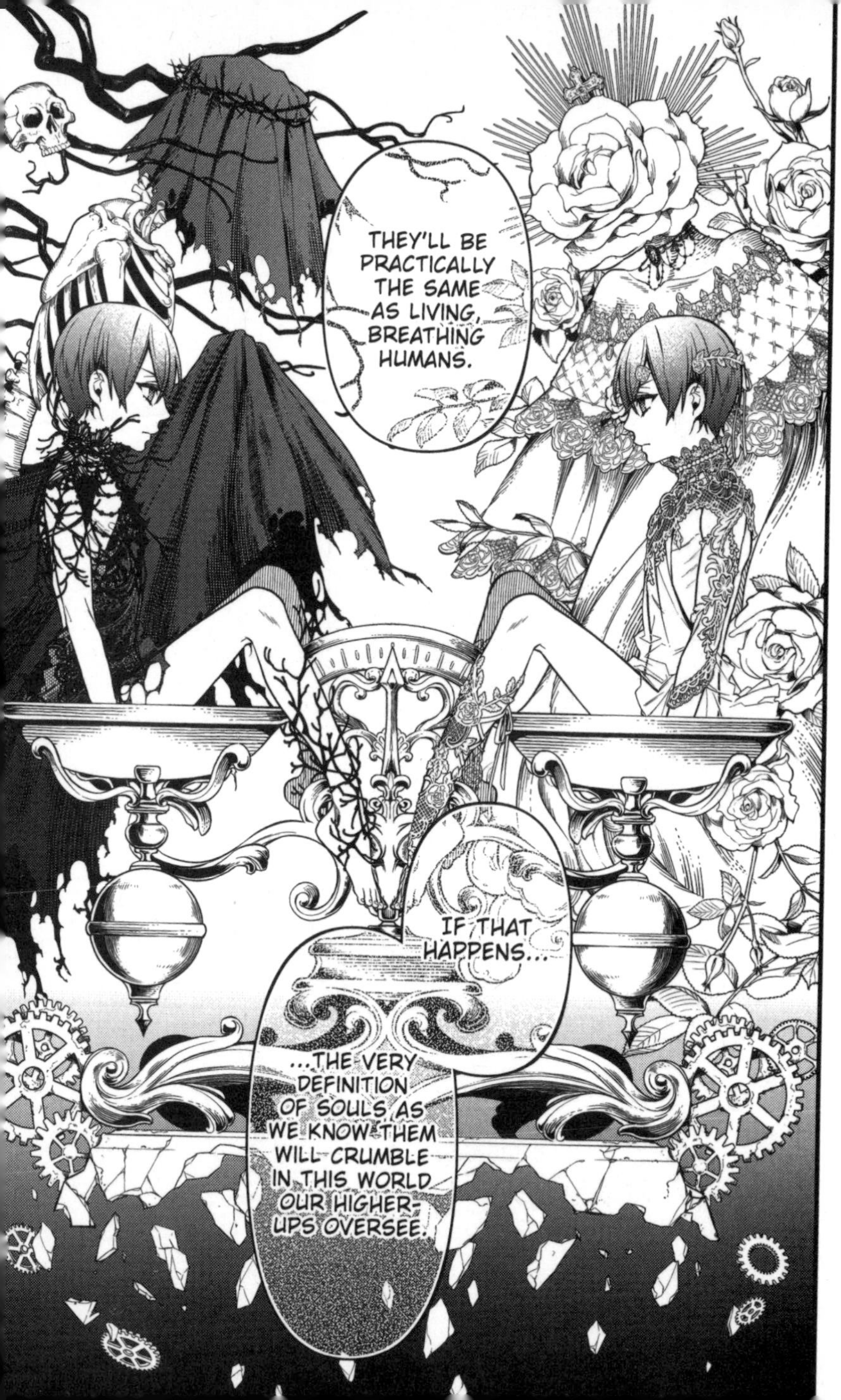
THEY'LL BE PRACTICALLY THE SAME AS LIVING, BREATHING HUMANS.
IF THAT HAPPENS...
...THE VERY DEFINITION OF SOULS AS WE KNOW THEM WILL CRUMBLE IN THIS WORLD OUR HIGHER-UPS OVERSEE.

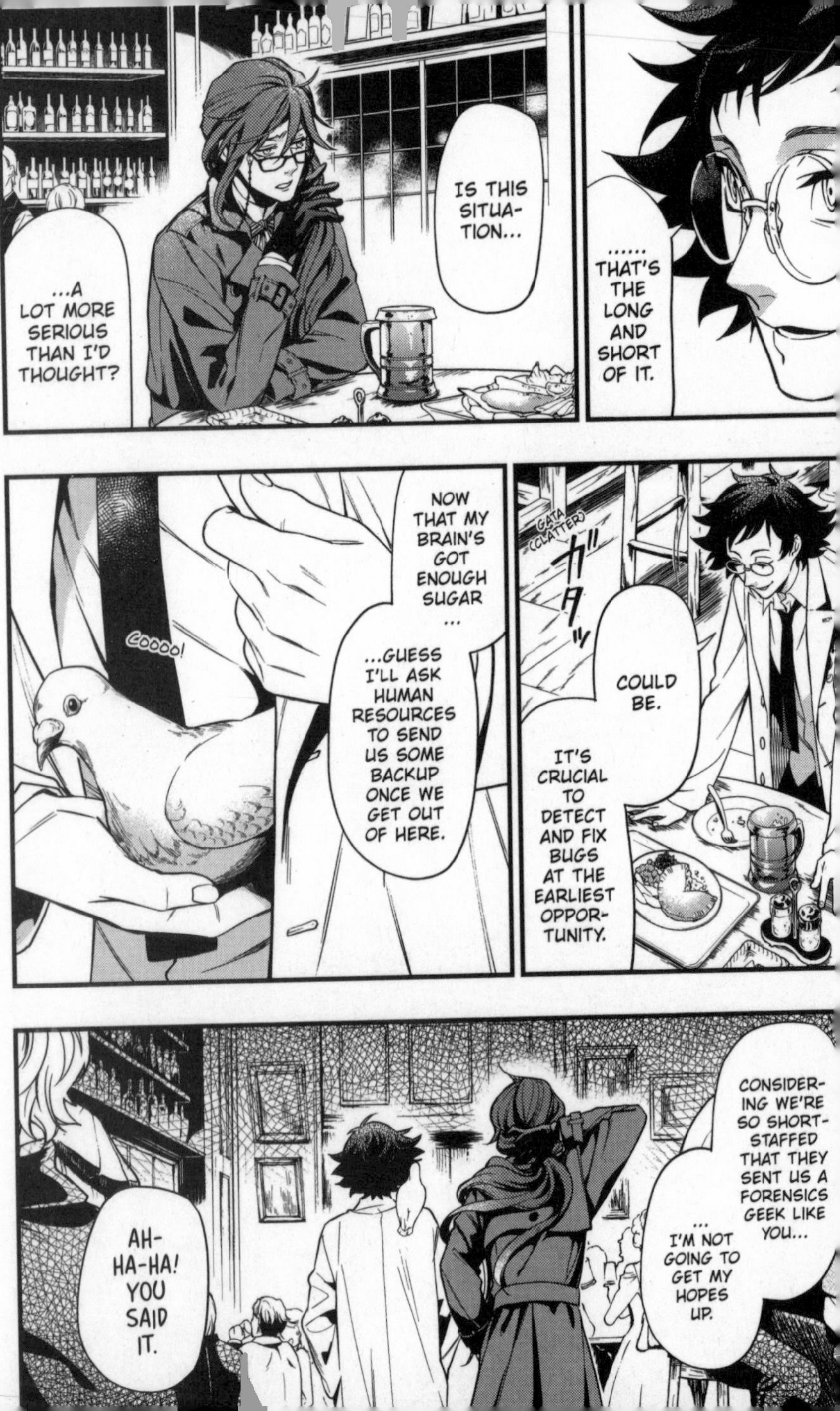

......THAT'S THE LONG AND SHORT OF IT.
IS THIS SITUATION...
...A LOT MORE SERIOUS THAN I'D THOUGHT?
GATA (CLATTER)
ガタッ
COULD BE.
IT'S CRUCIAL TO DETECT AND FIX BUGS AT THE EARLIEST OPPORTUNITY.
NOW THAT MY BRAIN'S GOT ENOUGH SUGAR...
...GUESS I'LL ASK HUMAN RESOURCES TO SEND US SOME BACKUP ONCE WE GET OUT OF HERE.
COOOOO!
CONSIDERING WE'RE SO SHORT-STAFFED THAT THEY SENT US A FORENSICS GEEK LIKE YOU...
...I'M NOT GOING TO GET MY HOPES UP.
AH-HA-HA! YOU SAID IT.

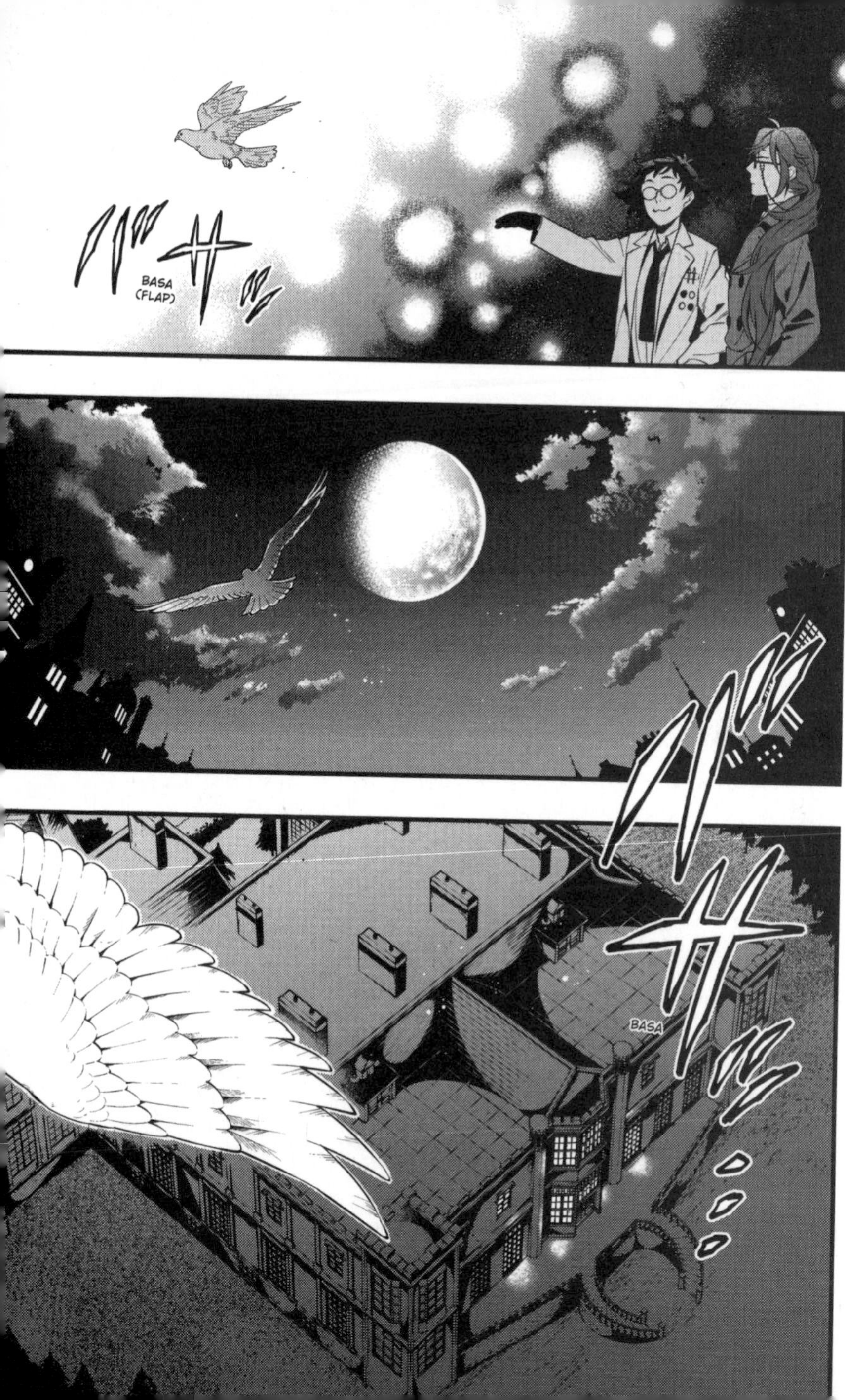
バサッ
BASA
(FLAP)
バサッ…
BASA

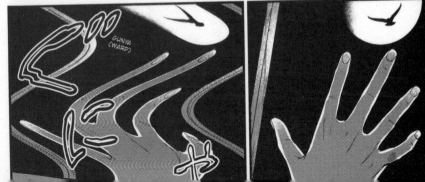

GUNYA
(WARP)

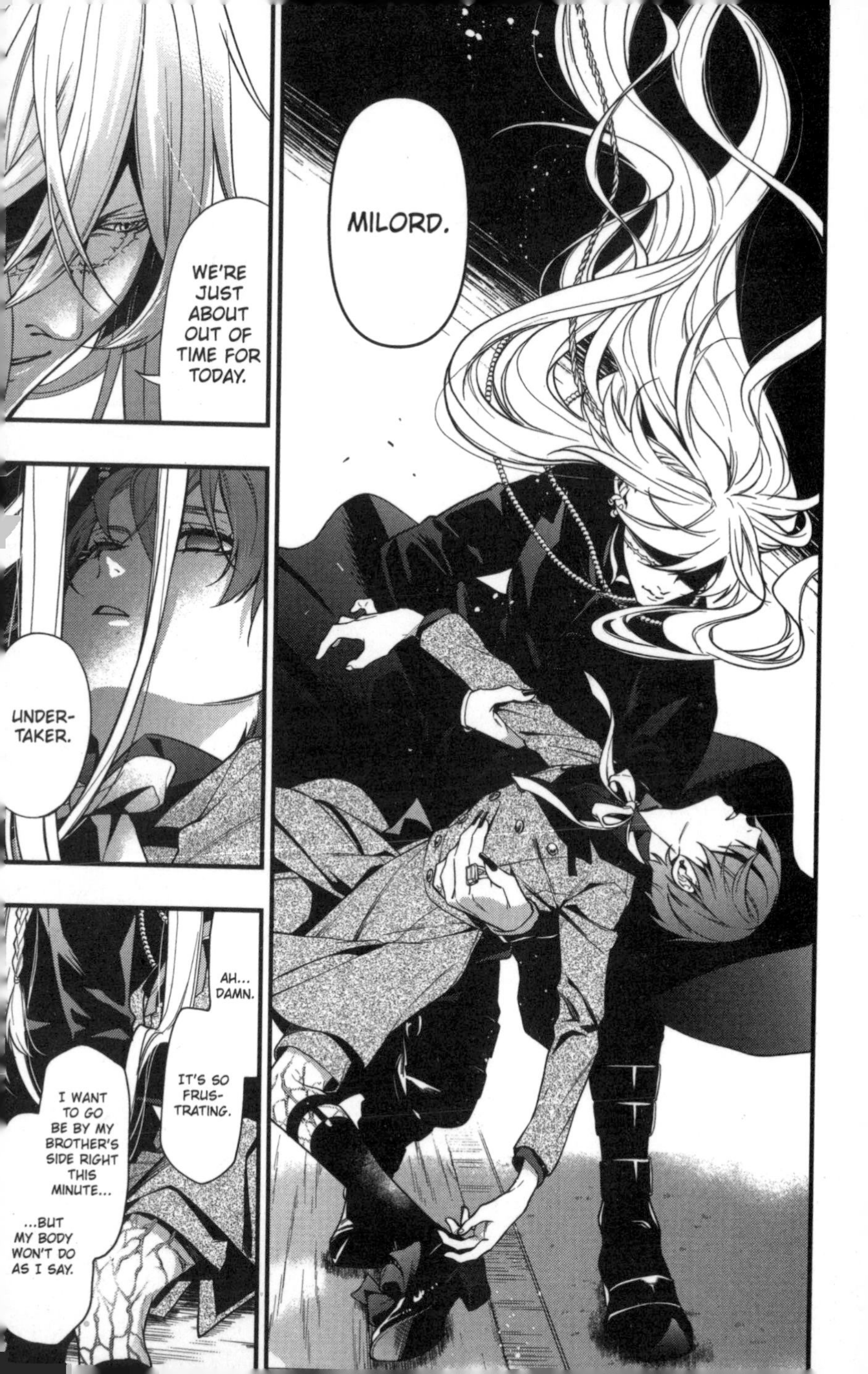
MILORD.
WE'RE JUST ABOUT OUT OF TIME FOR TODAY.
UNDER-TAKER.
AH... DAMN.
IT'S SO FRUS-TRATING.
I WANT TO GO BE BY MY BROTHER'S SIDE RIGHT THIS MINUTE...
...BUT MY BODY WON'T DO AS I SAY.

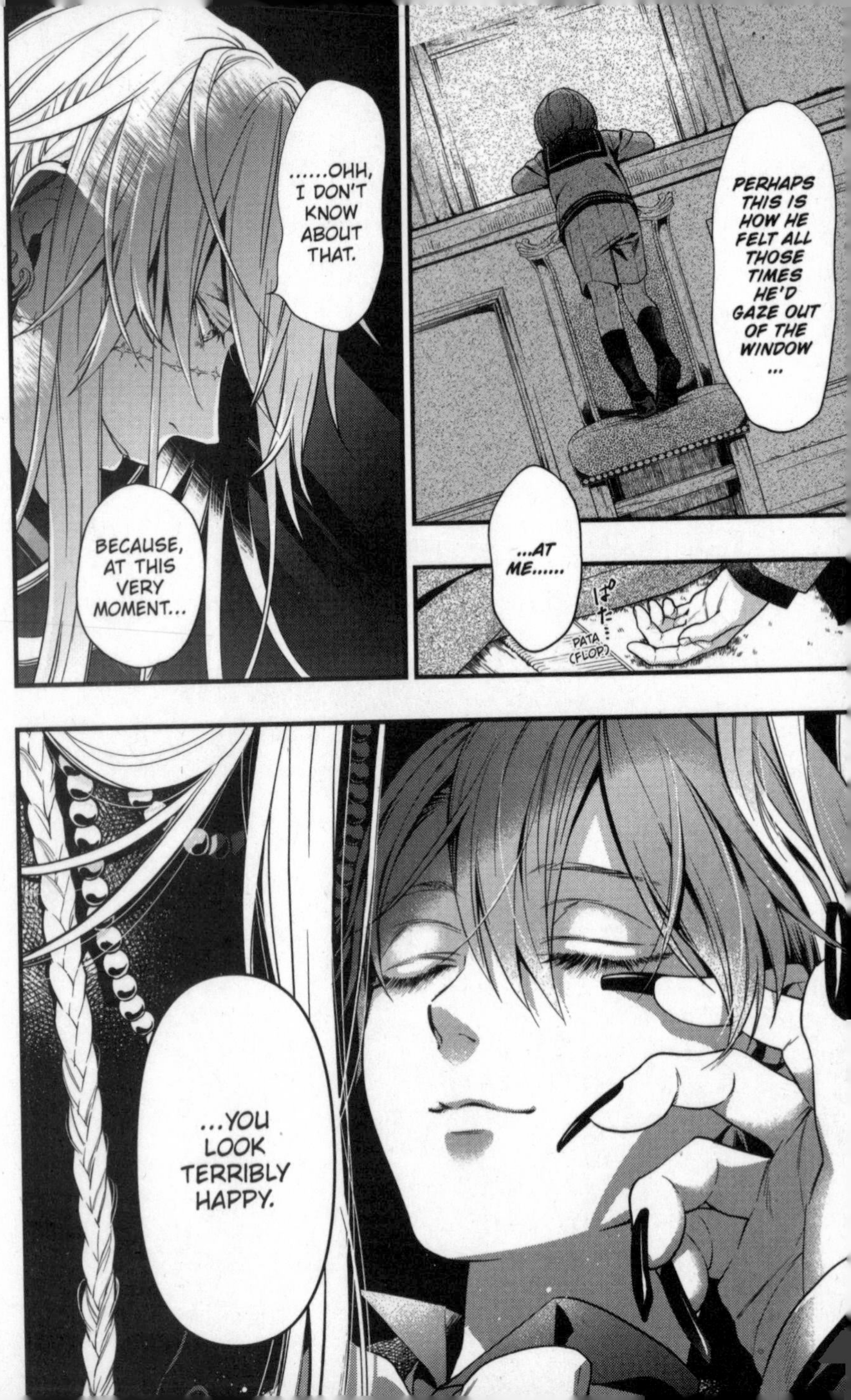
PERHAPS THIS IS HOW HE FELT ALL THOSE TIMES HE'D GAZE OUT OF THE WINDOW ...
...AT ME......
ぱた
PATA (FLOP)
......OHH, I DON'T KNOW ABOUT THAT.
BECAUSE, AT THIS VERY MOMENT...
...YOU LOOK TERRIBLY HAPPY.

Black Butler

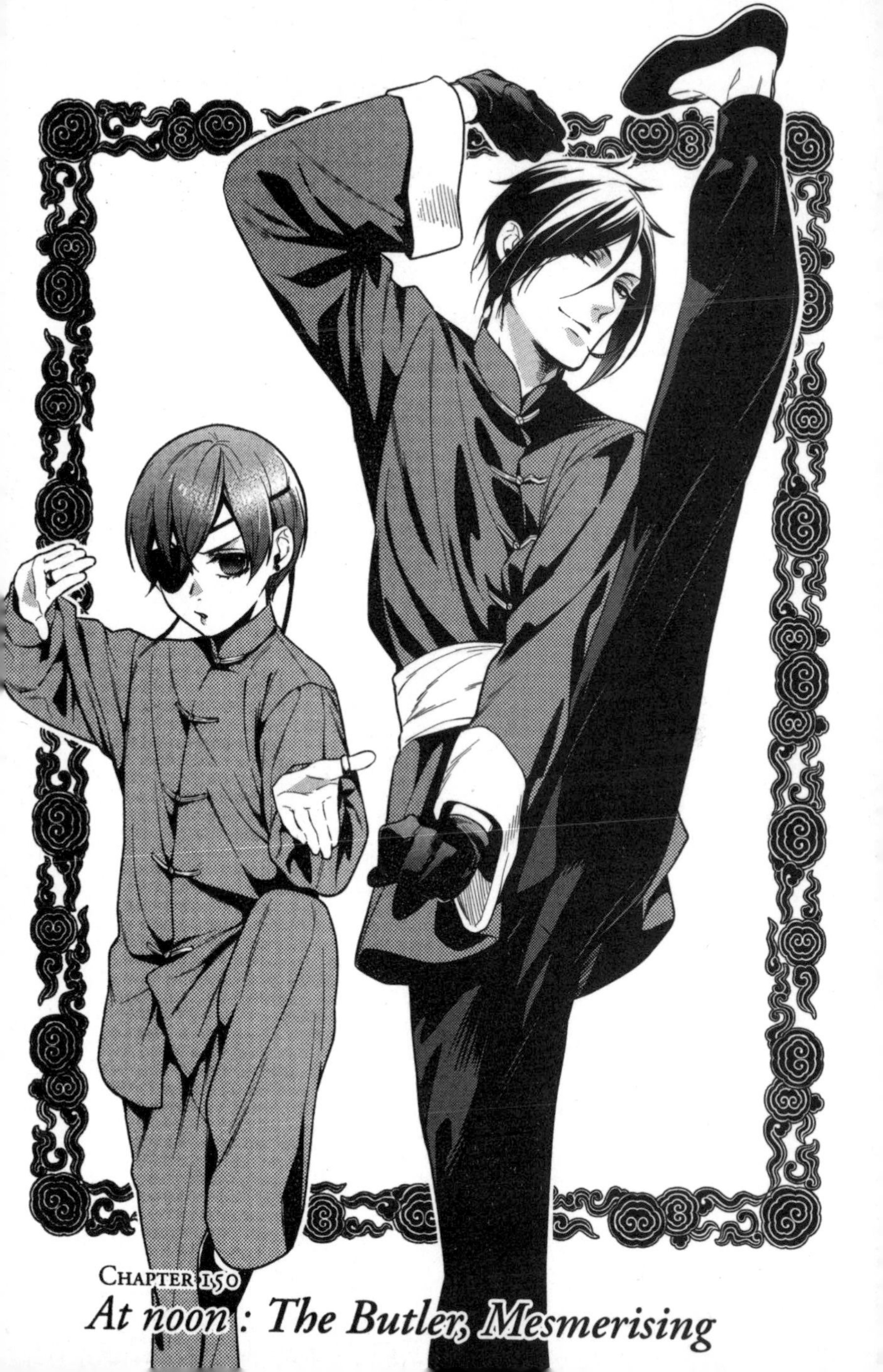

CHAPTER 150

At noon : The Butler, Mesmerising

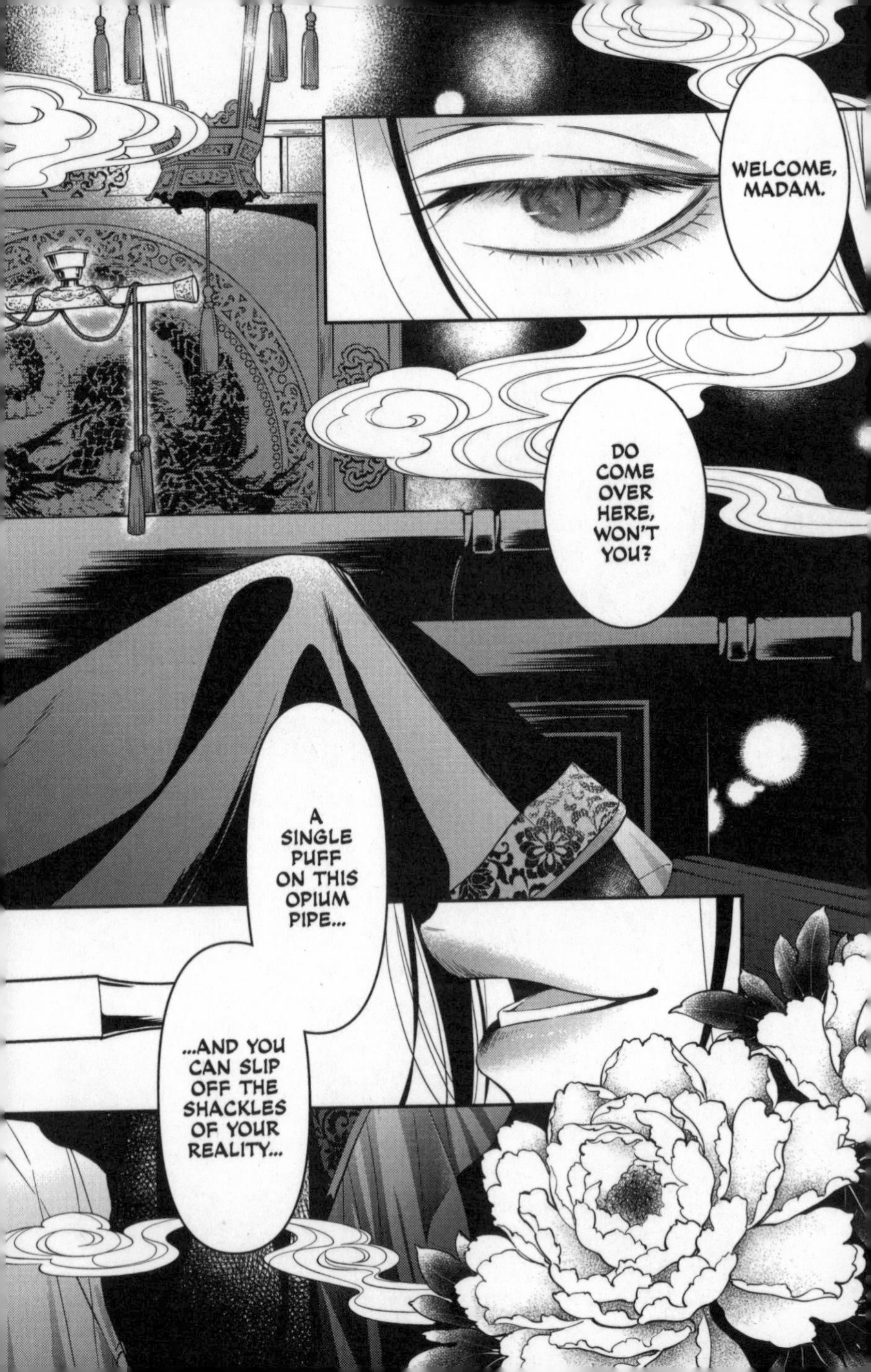
WELCOME, MADAM.
DO COME OVER HERE, WON'T YOU?
A SINGLE PUFF ON THIS OPIUM PIPE...
...AND YOU CAN SLIP OFF THE SHACKLES OF YOUR REALITY...

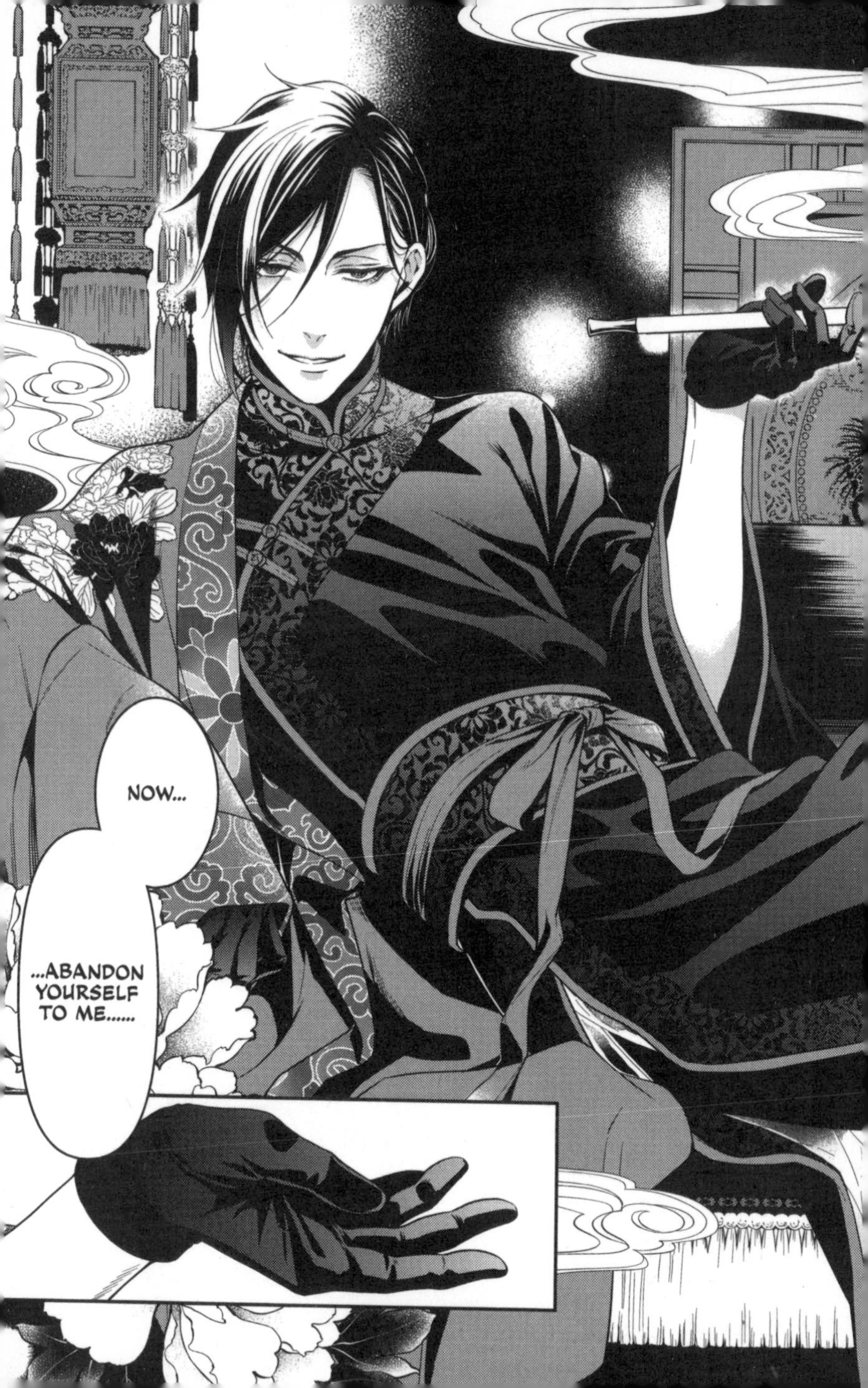
NOW...
...ABANDON YOURSELF TO ME......

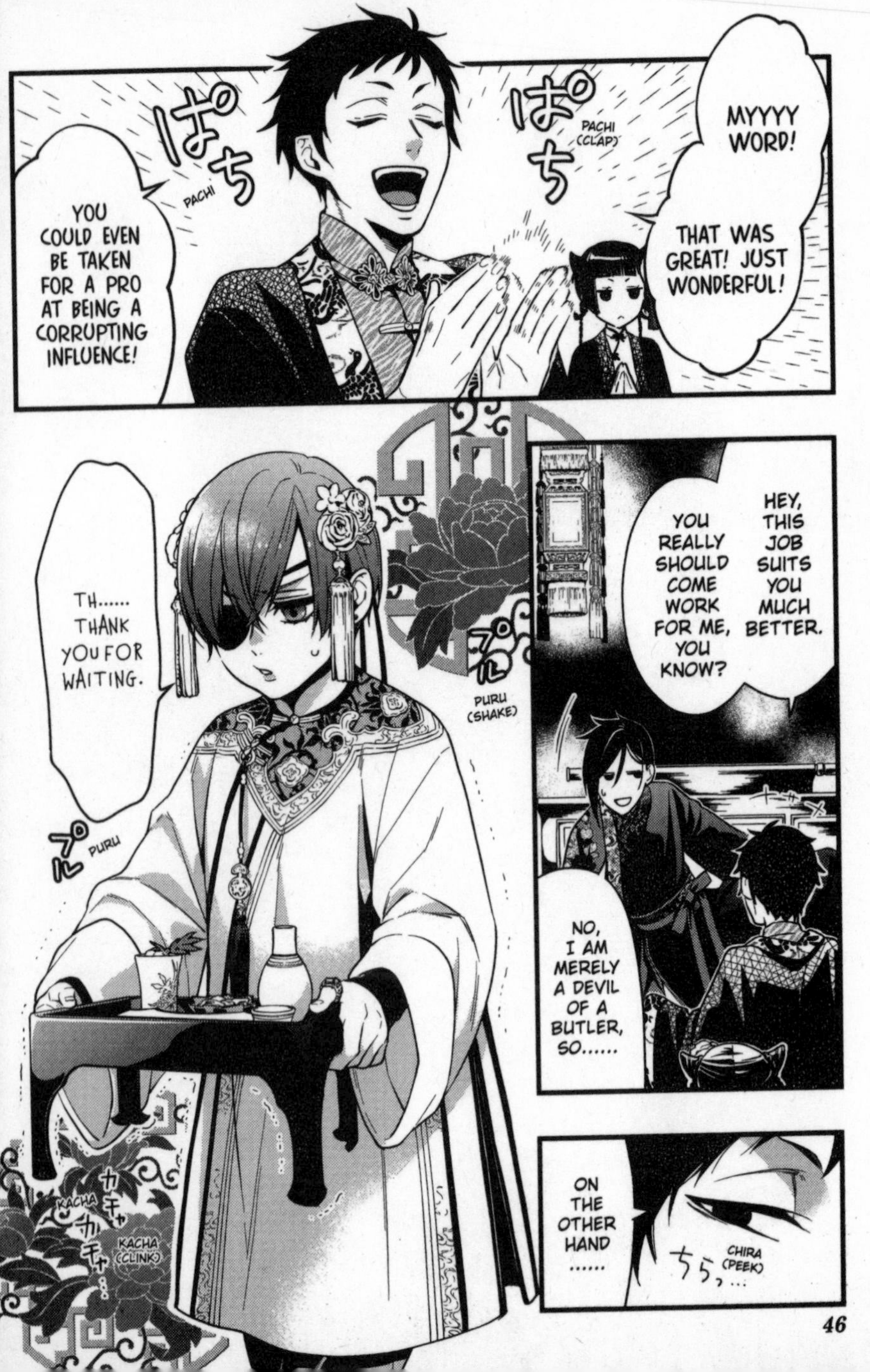
MYYYY WORD!
THAT WAS GREAT! JUST WONDERFUL!
ぱち
PACHI (CLAP)
ぱち
PACHI
YOU COULD EVEN BE TAKEN FOR A PRO AT BEING A CORRUPTING INFLUENCE!
HEY, THIS JOB SUITS YOU MUCH BETTER.
YOU REALLY SHOULD COME WORK FOR ME, YOU KNOW?
NO, I AM MERELY A DEVIL OF A BUTLER, SO......
ON THE OTHER HAND ......
ちら…
CHIRA (PEEK)
プル
PURU (SHAKE)
TH...... THANK YOU FOR WAITING.
プル
PURU
カチャ
KACHA
カチャ…
KACHA (CLINK)

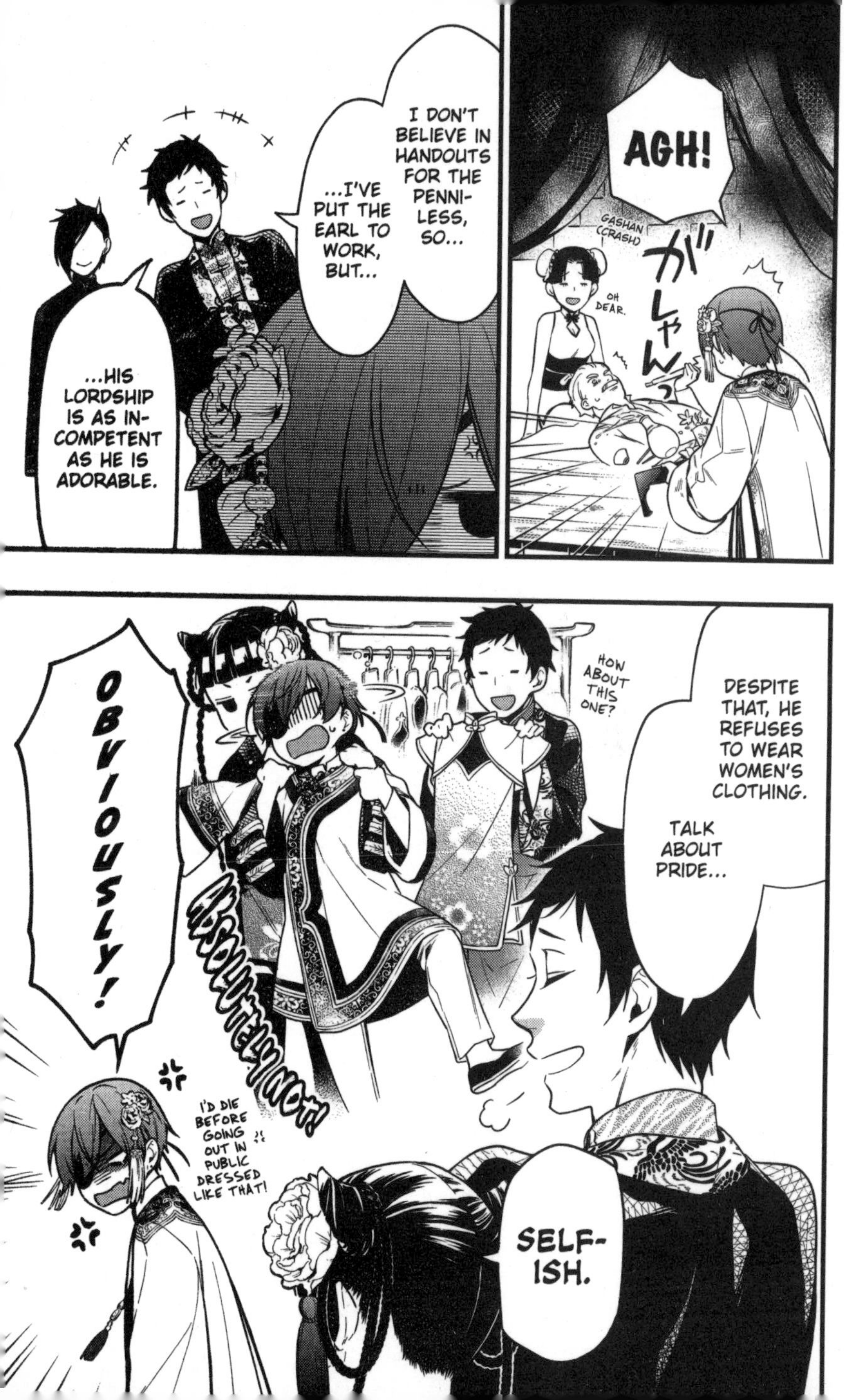
AGH!
GASHAN (CRASH)
がしゃんっ
OH DEAR.
I DON'T BELIEVE IN HANDOUTS FOR THE PENNI-LESS, SO...
...I'VE PUT THE EARL TO WORK, BUT...
...HIS LORDSHIP IS AS IN-COMPETENT AS HE IS ADORABLE.
DESPITE THAT, HE REFUSES TO WEAR WOMEN'S CLOTHING.
TALK ABOUT PRIDE...
HOW ABOUT THIS ONE?
ABSOLUTELY NOT!
OBVIOUSLY!
I'D DIE BEFORE GOING OUT IN PUBLIC DRESSED LIKE THAT!
SELF-ISH.

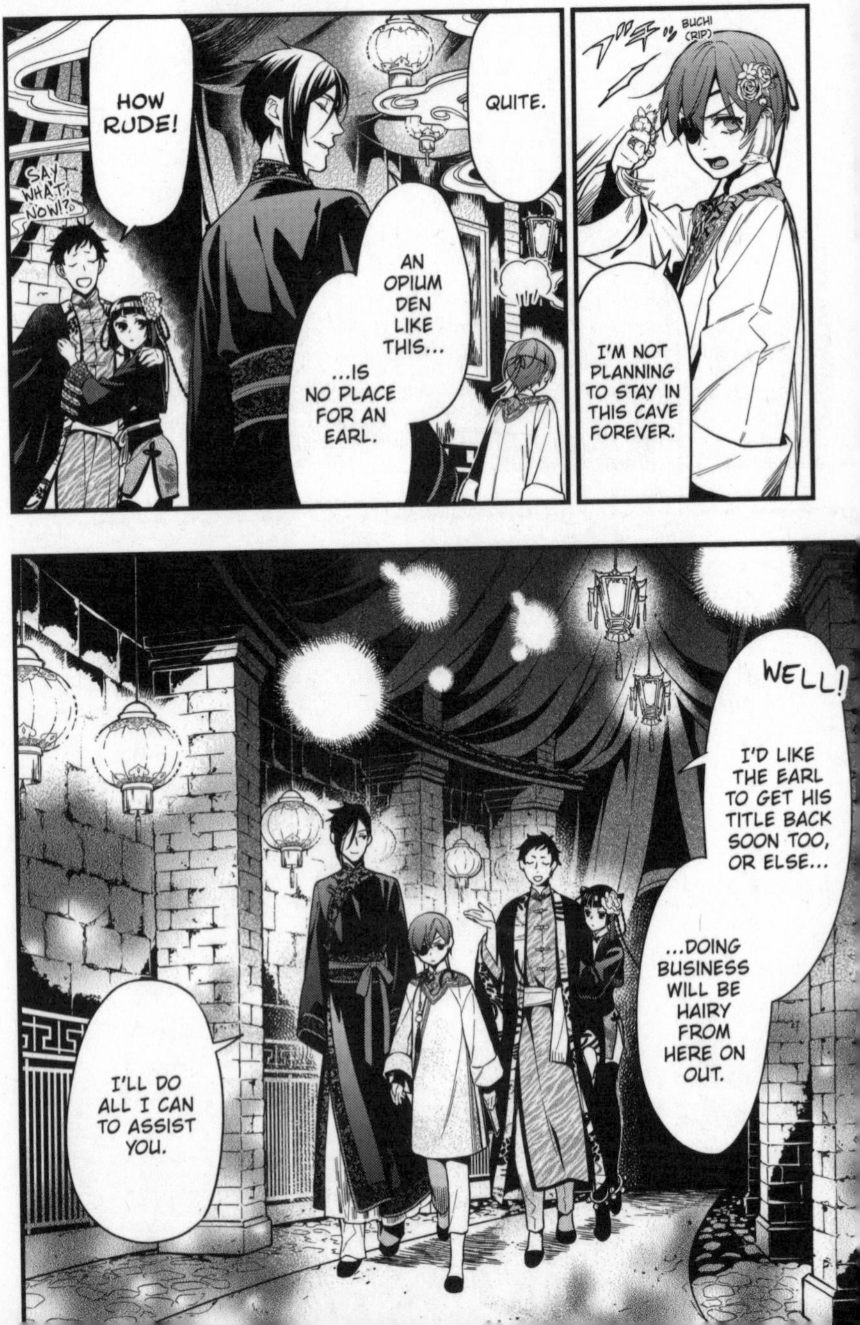
BUCHI (RIP)
I'M NOT PLANNING TO STAY IN THIS CAVE FOREVER.
QUITE.
AN OPIUM DEN LIKE THIS...
...IS NO PLACE FOR AN EARL.
HOW RUDE!
SAY WHAT, NOW!?
WELL!
I'D LIKE THE EARL TO GET HIS TITLE BACK SOON TOO, OR ELSE...
...DOING BUSINESS WILL BE HAIRY FROM HERE ON OUT.
I'LL DO ALL I CAN TO ASSIST YOU.

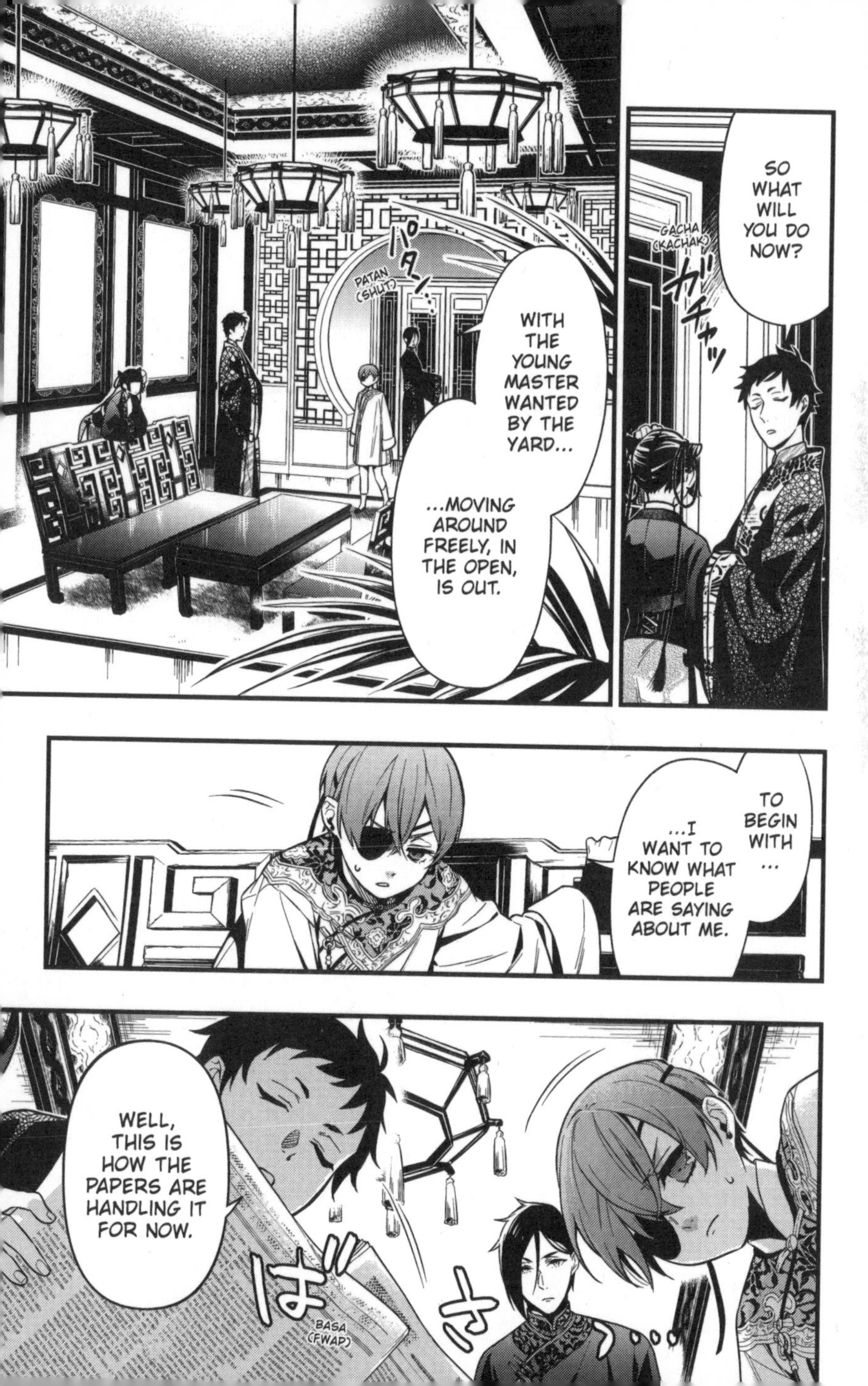
SO WHAT WILL YOU DO NOW?
ガチャッ
GACHA (KACHAK)
パタン…
PATAN (SHUT)
WITH THE YOUNG MASTER WANTED BY THE YARD...
...MOVING AROUND FREELY, IN THE OPEN, IS OUT.
TO BEGIN WITH...
...I WANT TO KNOW WHAT PEOPLE ARE SAYING ABOUT ME.
WELL, THIS IS HOW THE PAPERS ARE HANDLING IT FOR NOW.
ばさ
BASA (FWAP)

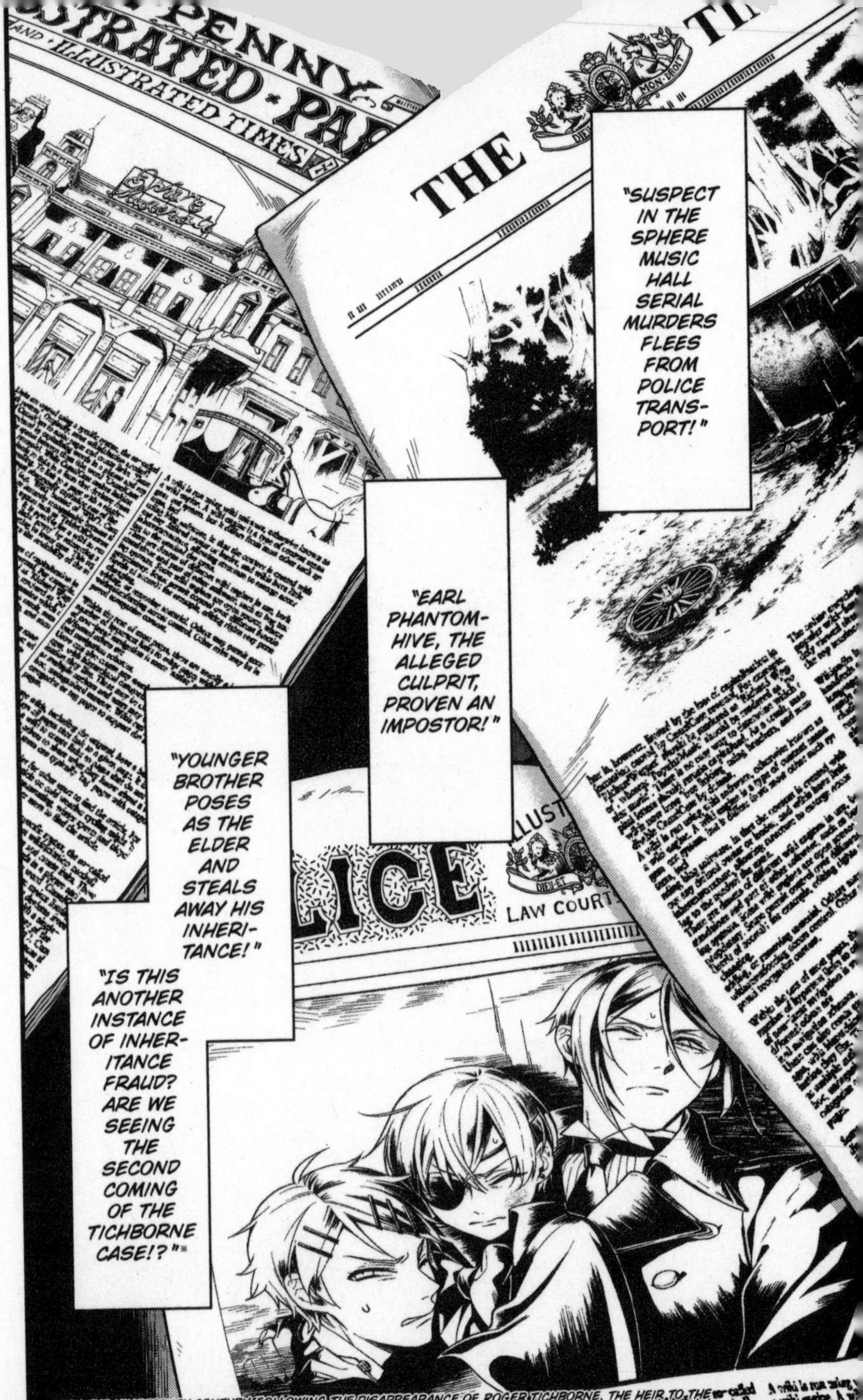
"SUSPECT IN THE SPHERE MUSIC HALL SERIAL MURDERS FLEES FROM POLICE TRANSPORT!"
"EARL PHANTOMHIVE, THE ALLEGED CULPRIT, PROVEN AN IMPOSTOR!"
"YOUNGER BROTHER POSES AS THE ELDER AND STEALS AWAY HIS INHERITANCE!"
"IS THIS ANOTHER INSTANCE OF INHERITANCE FRAUD? ARE WE SEEING THE SECOND COMING OF THE TICHBORNE CASE!?"※
THE
LAW COURTS

※IN THE NINETEENTH CENTURY, FOLLOWING THE DISAPPEARANCE OF ROGER TICHBORNE, THE HEIR TO THE

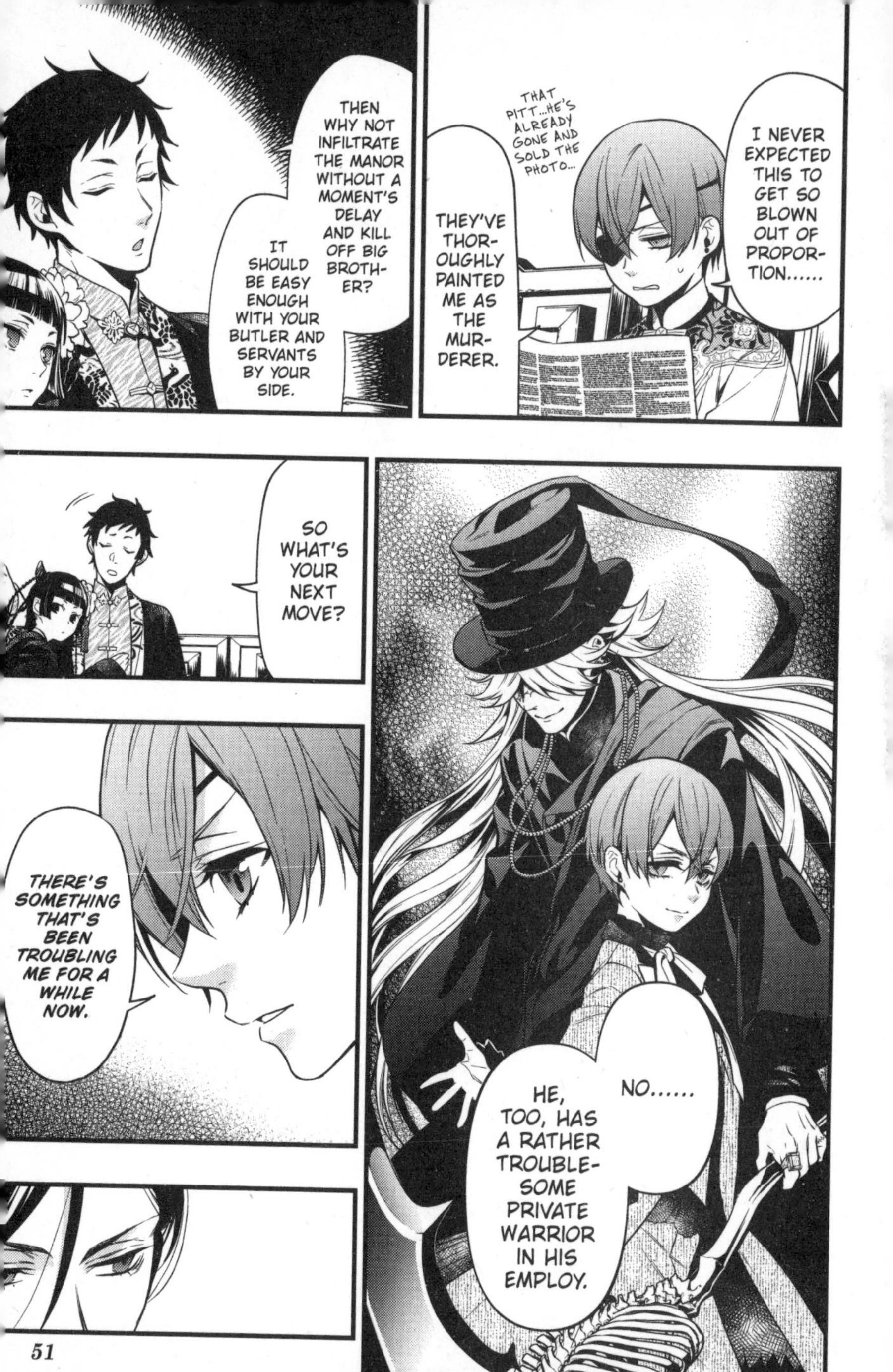
I NEVER EXPECTED THIS TO GET SO BLOWN OUT OF PROPORTION......
THAT PITT...HE'S ALREADY GONE AND SOLD THE PHOTO...
THEY'VE THOROUGHLY PAINTED ME AS THE MURDERER.
THEN WHY NOT INFILTRATE THE MANOR WITHOUT A MOMENT'S DELAY AND KILL OFF BIG BROTHER?
IT SHOULD BE EASY ENOUGH WITH YOUR BUTLER AND SERVANTS BY YOUR SIDE.
NO......
HE, TOO, HAS A RATHER TROUBLESOME PRIVATE WARRIOR IN HIS EMPLOY.
SO WHAT'S YOUR NEXT MOVE?
THERE'S SOMETHING THAT'S BEEN TROUBLING ME FOR A WHILE NOW.

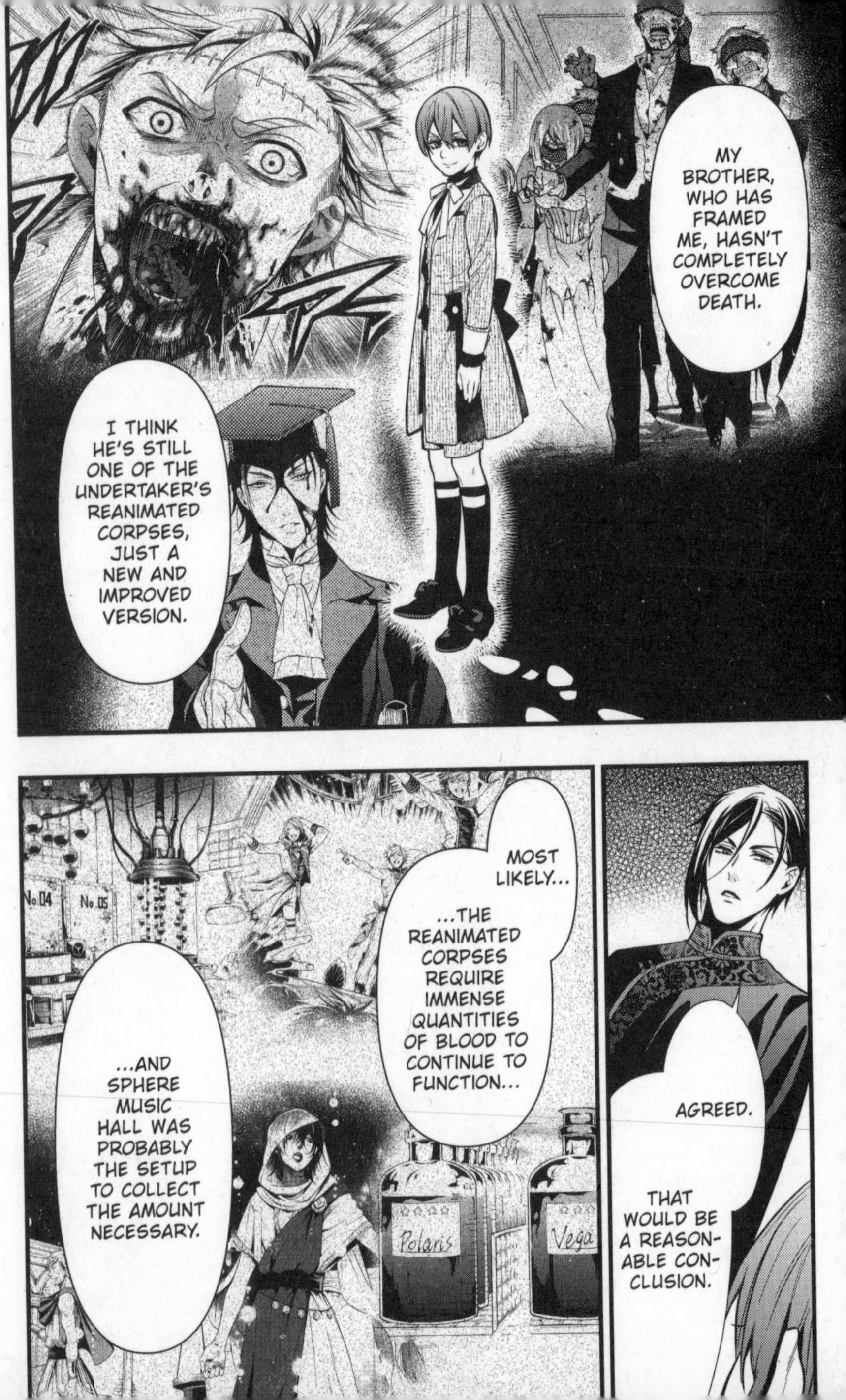
MY BROTHER, WHO HAS FRAMED ME, HASN'T COMPLETELY OVERCOME DEATH.
I THINK HE'S STILL ONE OF THE UNDERTAKER'S REANIMATED CORPSES, JUST A NEW AND IMPROVED VERSION.
AGREED.
THAT WOULD BE A REASON-ABLE CON-CLUSION.
MOST LIKELY...
...THE REANIMATED CORPSES REQUIRE IMMENSE QUANTITIES OF BLOOD TO CONTINUE TO FUNCTION...
No.04
No.05
...AND SPHERE MUSIC HALL WAS PROBABLY THE SETUP TO COLLECT THE AMOUNT NECESSARY.
Vega
Polaris

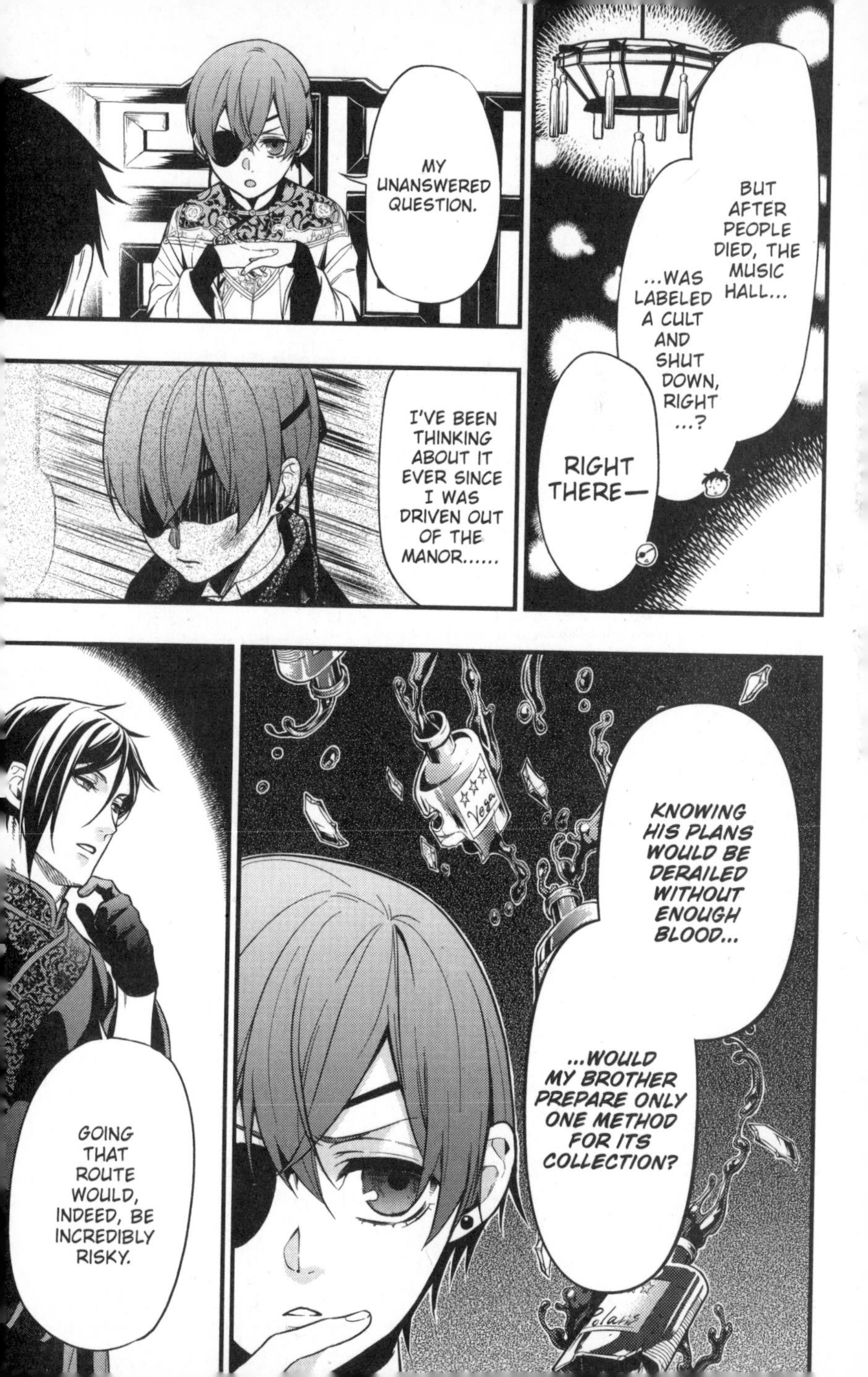
BUT AFTER PEOPLE DIED, THE MUSIC HALL...
...WAS LABELED A CULT AND SHUT DOWN, RIGHT ...?
RIGHT THERE—
MY UNANSWERED QUESTION.
I'VE BEEN THINKING ABOUT IT EVER SINCE I WAS DRIVEN OUT OF THE MANOR......
KNOWING HIS PLANS WOULD BE DERAILED WITHOUT ENOUGH BLOOD...
...WOULD MY BROTHER PREPARE ONLY ONE METHOD FOR ITS COLLECTION?
GOING THAT ROUTE WOULD, INDEED, BE INCREDIBLY RISKY.

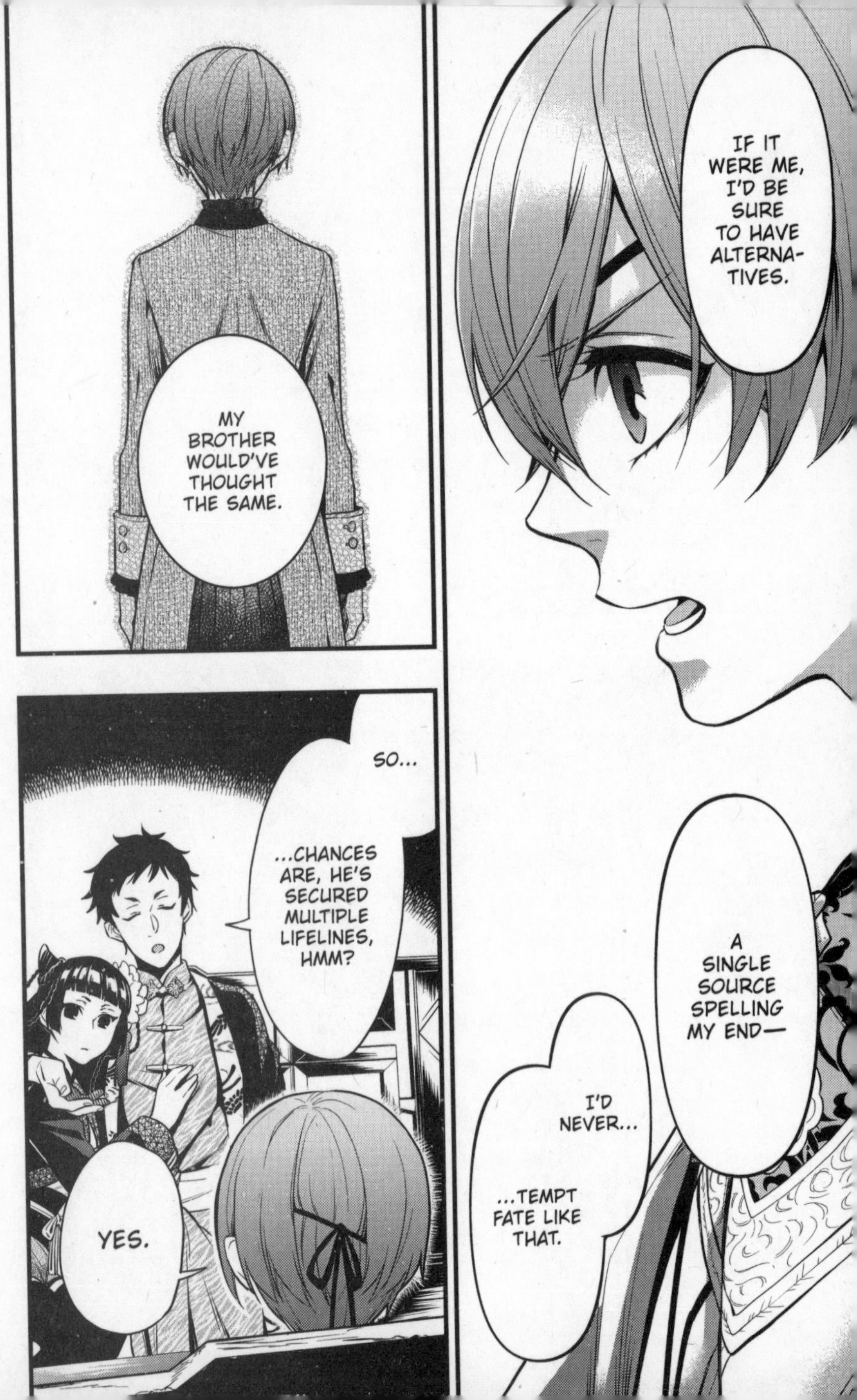
IF IT WERE ME, I'D BE SURE TO HAVE ALTERNATIVES.
A SINGLE SOURCE SPELLING MY END—
I'D NEVER...
...TEMPT FATE LIKE THAT.
MY BROTHER WOULD'VE THOUGHT THE SAME.
SO...
...CHANCES ARE, HE'S SECURED MULTIPLE LIFELINES, HMM?
YES.

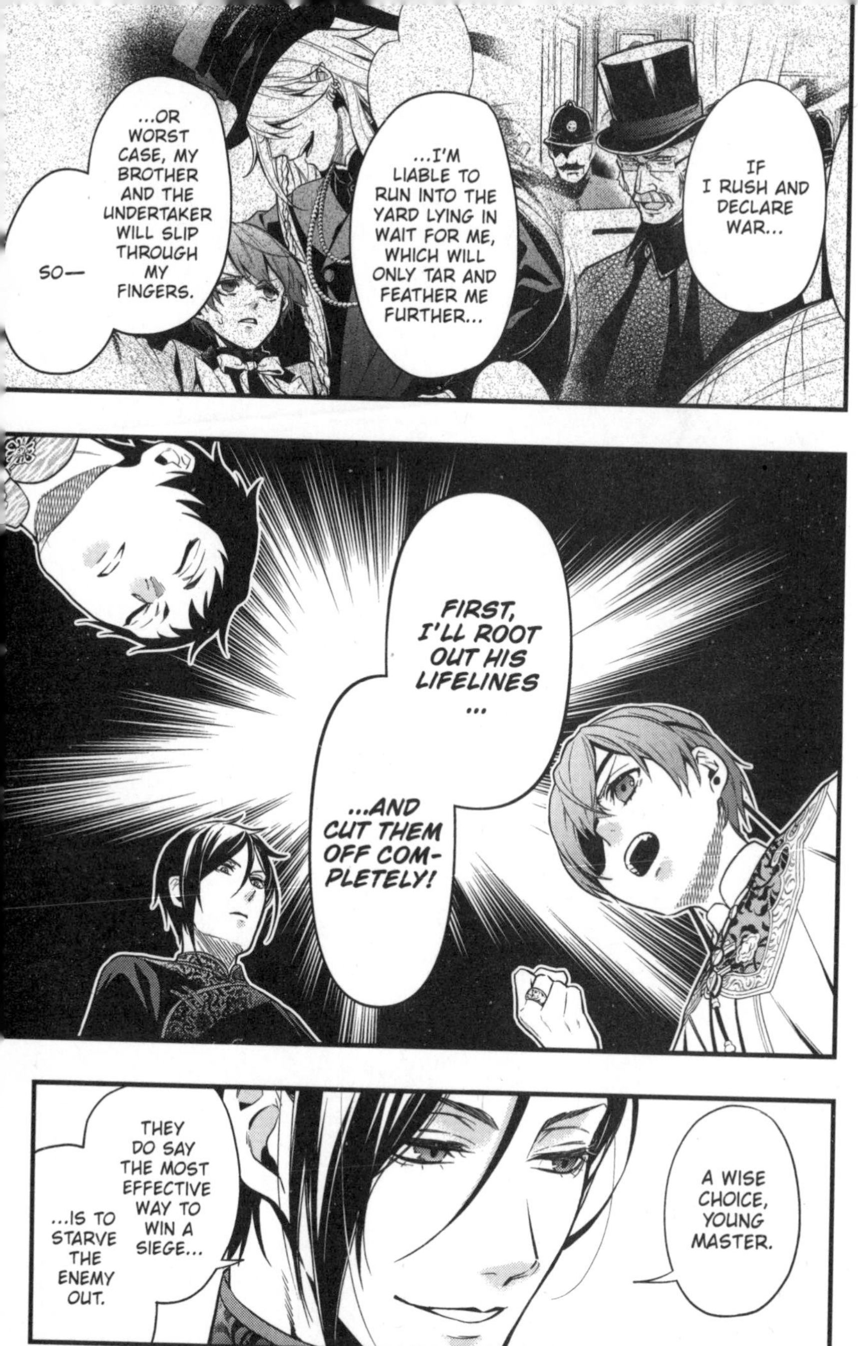
IF I RUSH AND DECLARE WAR...
...I'M LIABLE TO RUN INTO THE YARD LYING IN WAIT FOR ME, WHICH WILL ONLY TAR AND FEATHER ME FURTHER...
...OR WORST CASE, MY BROTHER AND THE UNDERTAKER WILL SLIP THROUGH MY FINGERS.
SO—
FIRST, I'LL ROOT OUT HIS LIFELINES...
...AND CUT THEM OFF COM-PLETELY!
A WISE CHOICE, YOUNG MASTER.
THEY DO SAY THE MOST EFFECTIVE WAY TO WIN A SIEGE...
...IS TO STARVE THE ENEMY OUT.

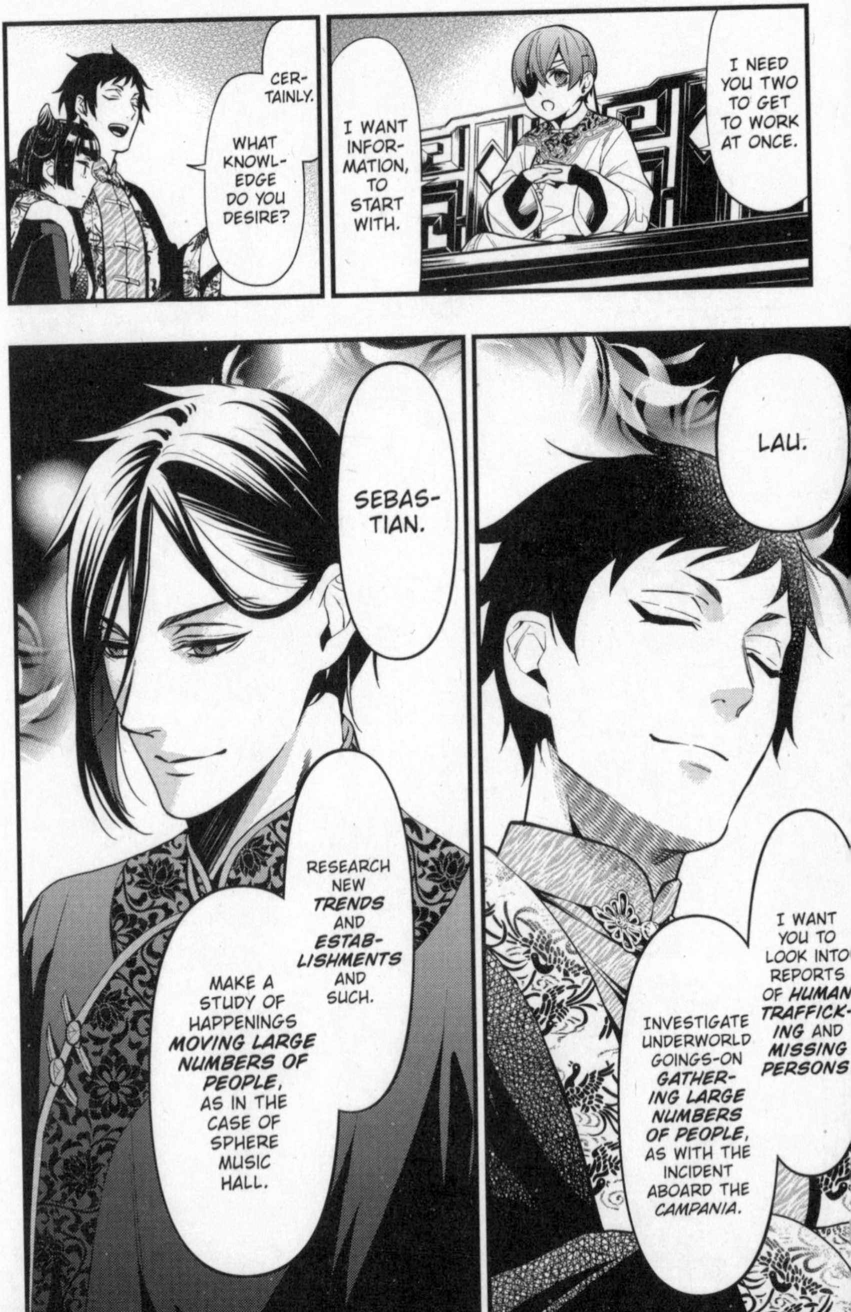
I NEED YOU TWO TO GET TO WORK AT ONCE.
I WANT INFORMATION, TO START WITH.
CERTAINLY.
WHAT KNOWLEDGE DO YOU DESIRE?
LAU.
I WANT YOU TO LOOK INTO REPORTS OF HUMAN TRAFFICKING AND MISSING PERSONS
INVESTIGATE UNDERWORLD GOINGS-ON GATHERING LARGE NUMBERS OF PEOPLE, AS WITH THE INCIDENT ABOARD THE CAMPANIA.
SEBASTIAN.
RESEARCH NEW TRENDS AND ESTABLISHMENTS AND SUCH.
MAKE A STUDY OF HAPPENINGS MOVING LARGE NUMBERS OF PEOPLE, AS IN THE CASE OF SPHERE MUSIC HALL.

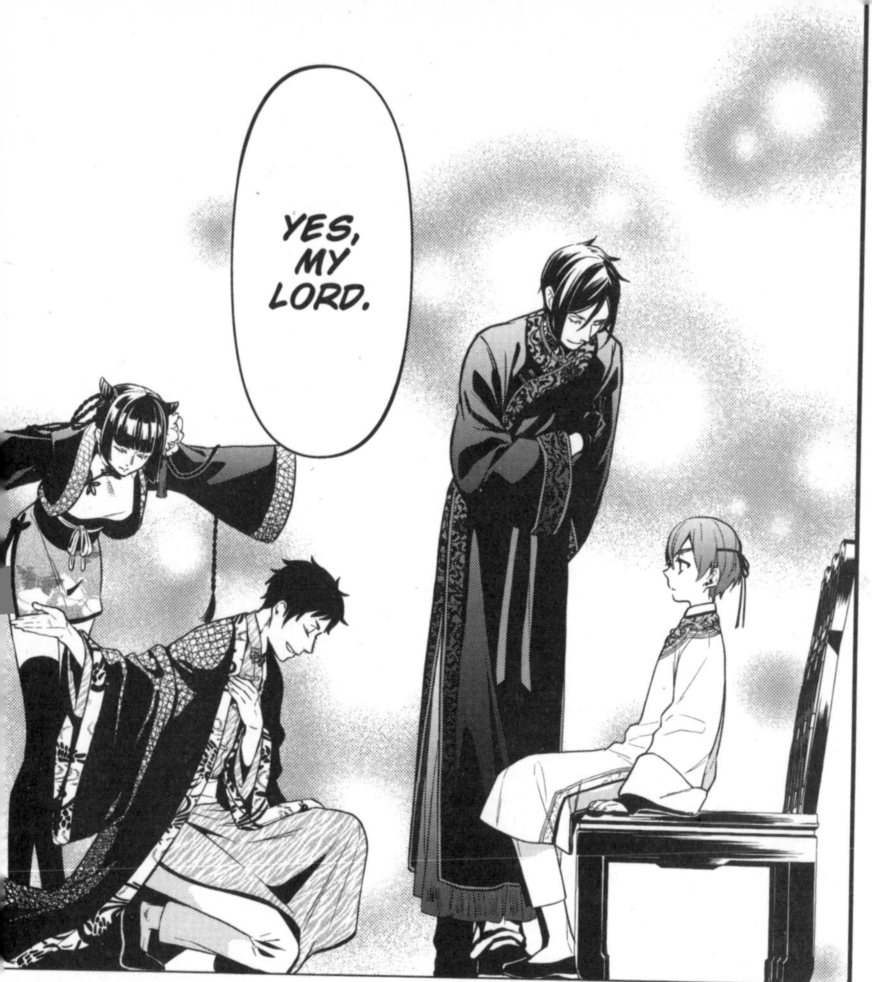
YES, MY LORD.
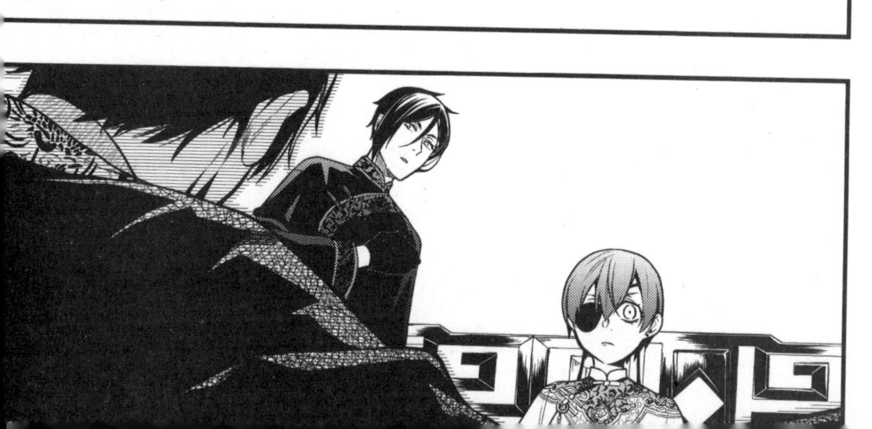

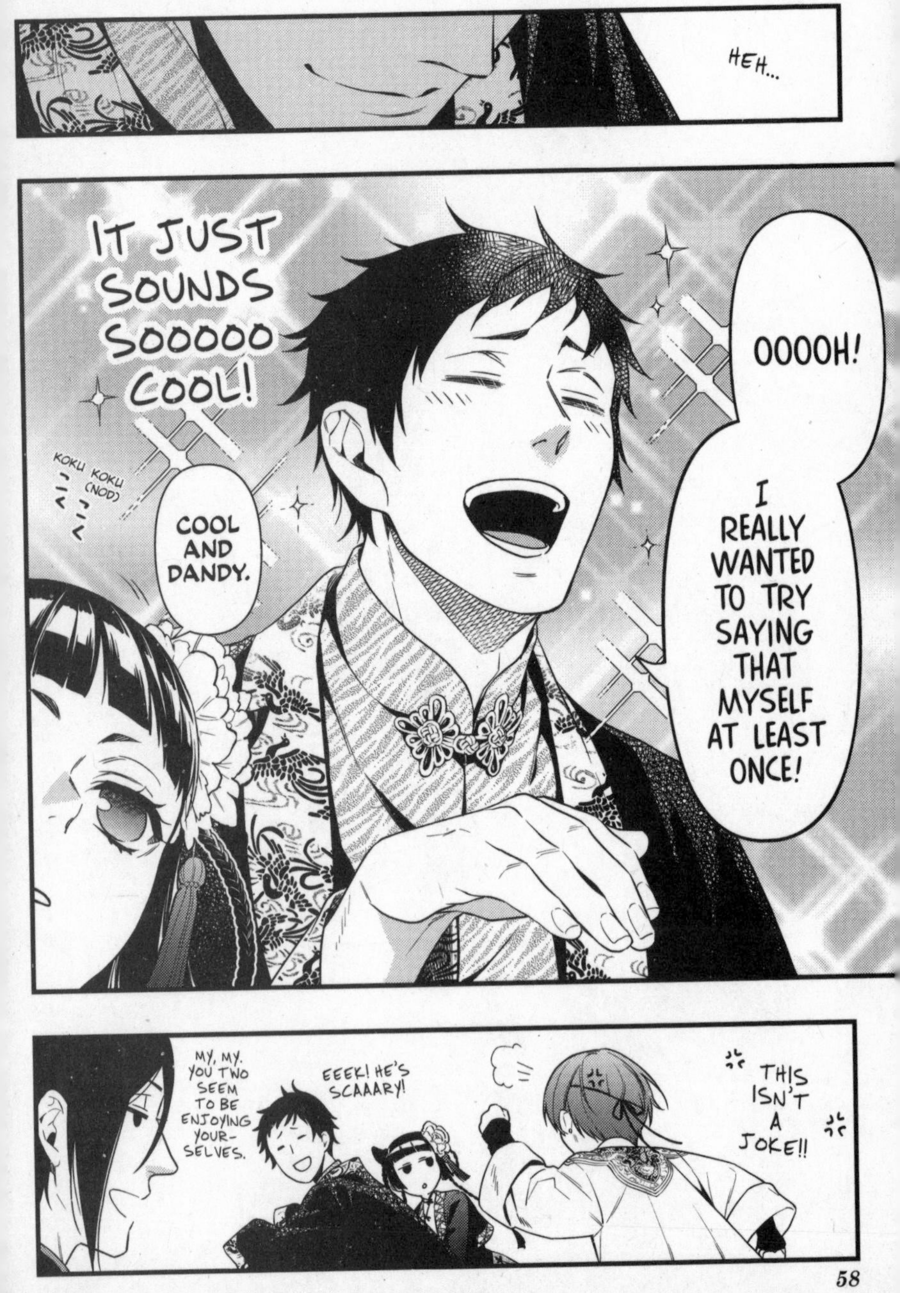
HEH...
OOOOH!
I REALLY WANTED TO TRY SAYING THAT MYSELF AT LEAST ONCE!
IT JUST SOUNDS SOOOOO COOL!
COOL AND DANDY.
KOKU KOKU (NOD)
THIS ISN'T A JOKE!!
EEEK! HE'S SCAAARY!
MY, MY. YOU TWO SEEM TO BE ENJOYING YOUR-SELVES.

Black Butler

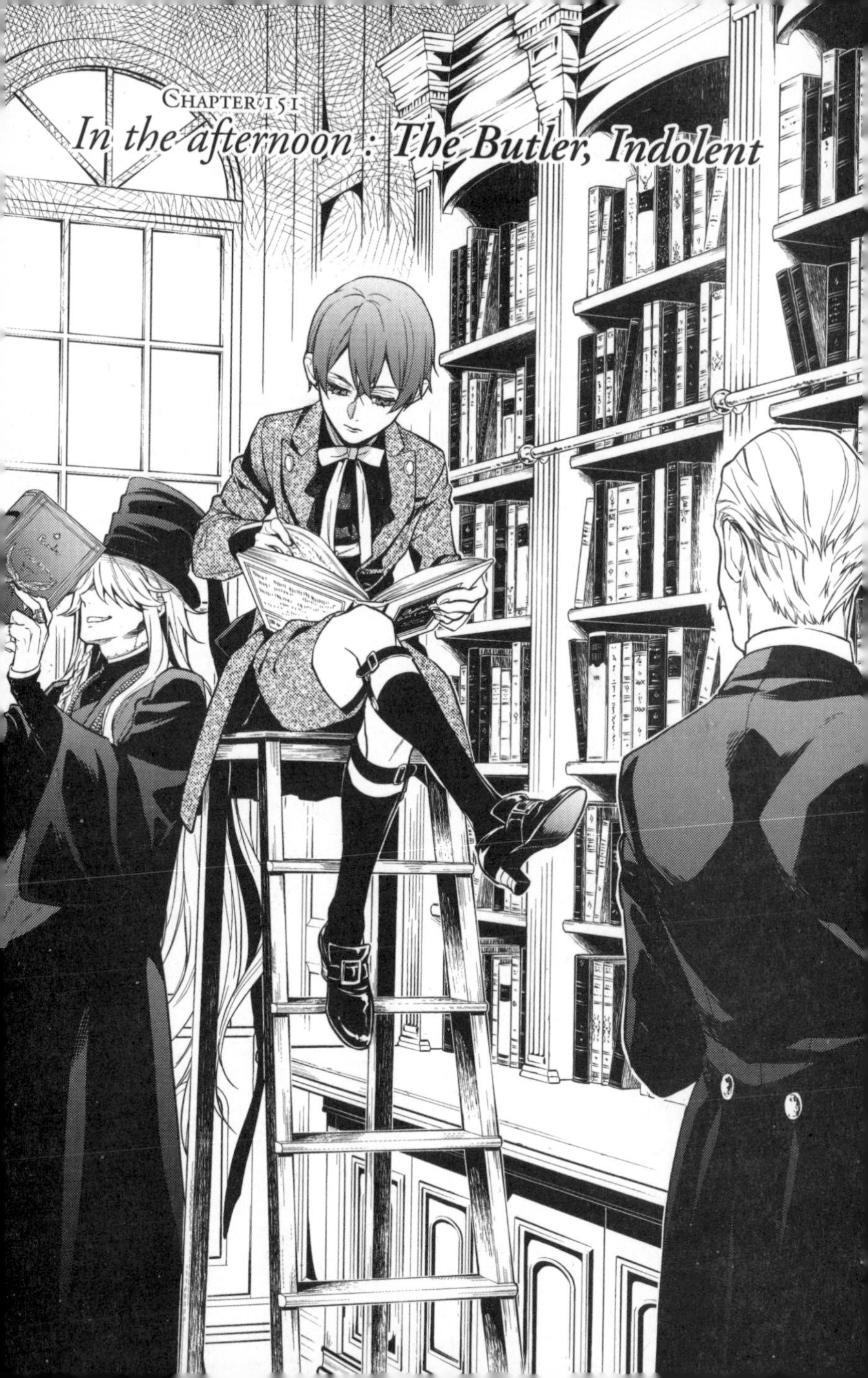
Chapter 151
In the afternoon : The Butler, Indolent

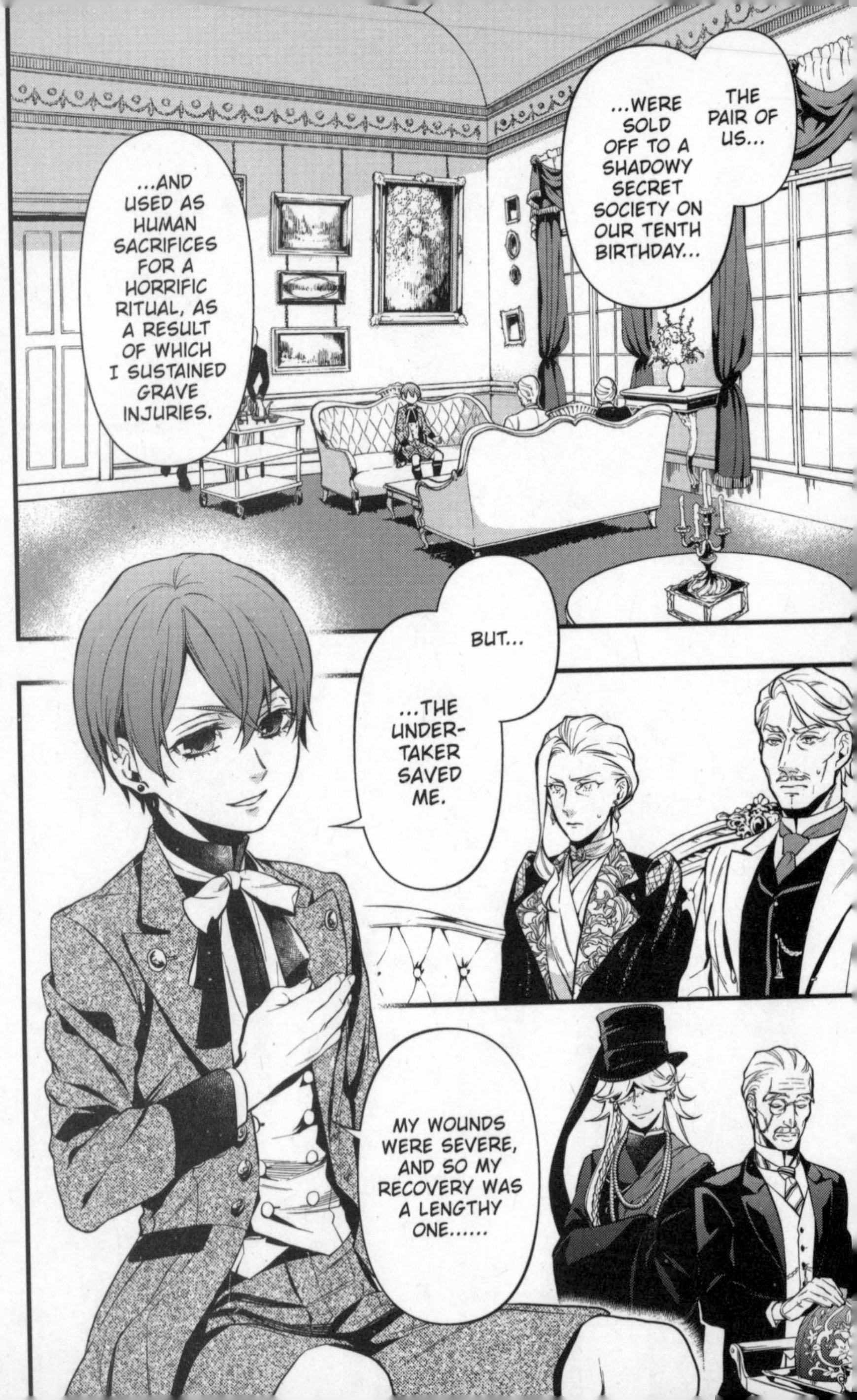
THE PAIR OF US...
...WERE SOLD OFF TO A SHADOWY SECRET SOCIETY ON OUR TENTH BIRTHDAY...
...AND USED AS HUMAN SACRIFICES FOR A HORRIFIC RITUAL, AS A RESULT OF WHICH I SUSTAINED GRAVE INJURIES.
BUT...
...THE UNDER-TAKER SAVED ME.
MY WOUNDS WERE SEVERE, AND SO MY RECOVERY WAS A LENGTHY ONE......

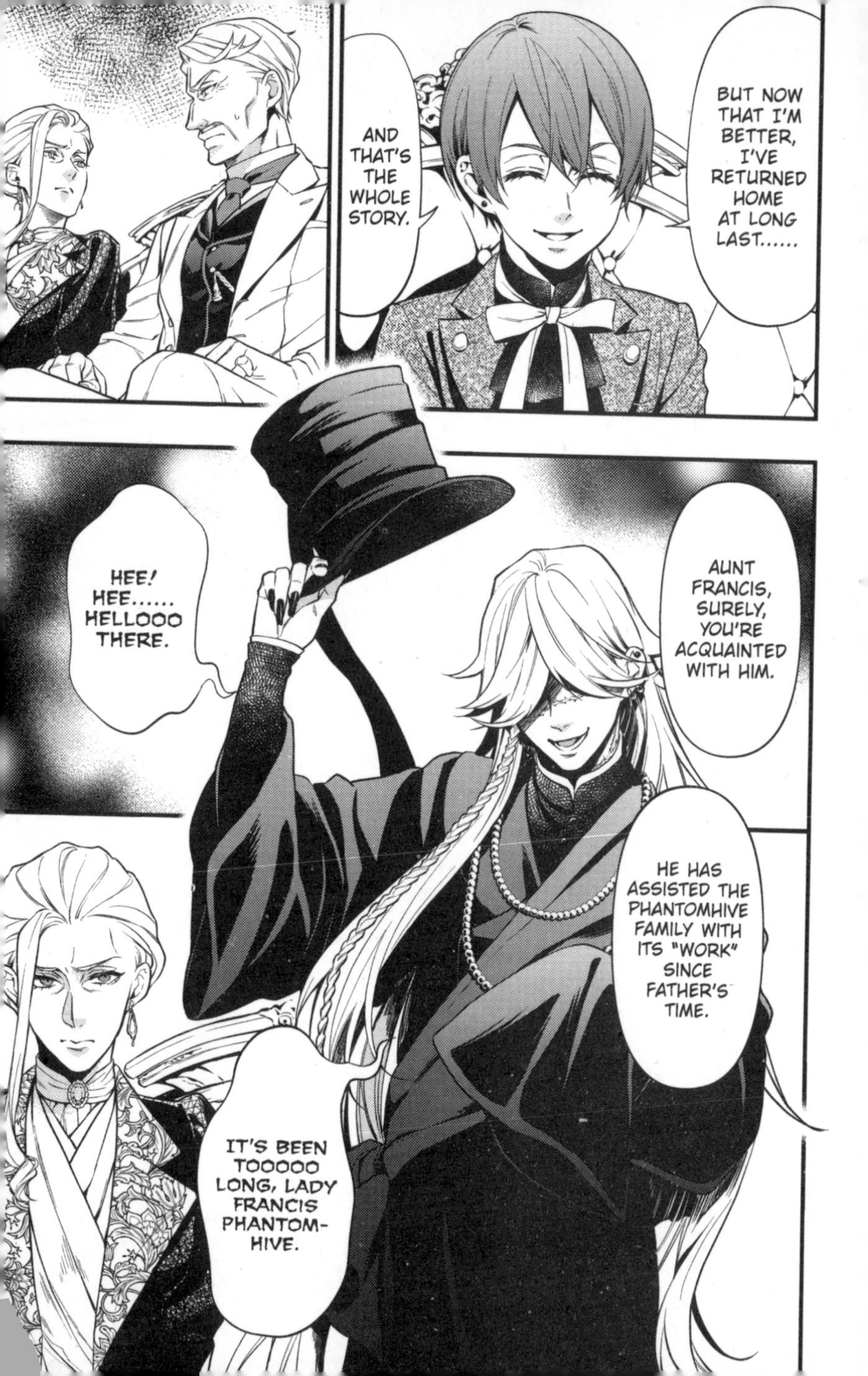
BUT NOW THAT I'M BETTER, I'VE RETURNED HOME AT LONG LAST......
AND THAT'S THE WHOLE STORY.
AUNT FRANCIS, SURELY, YOU'RE ACQUAINTED WITH HIM.
HEE! HEE...... HELLOOO THERE.
HE HAS ASSISTED THE PHANTOMHIVE FAMILY WITH ITS "WORK" SINCE FATHER'S TIME.
IT'S BEEN TOOOOO LONG, LADY FRANCIS PHANTOM-HIVE.

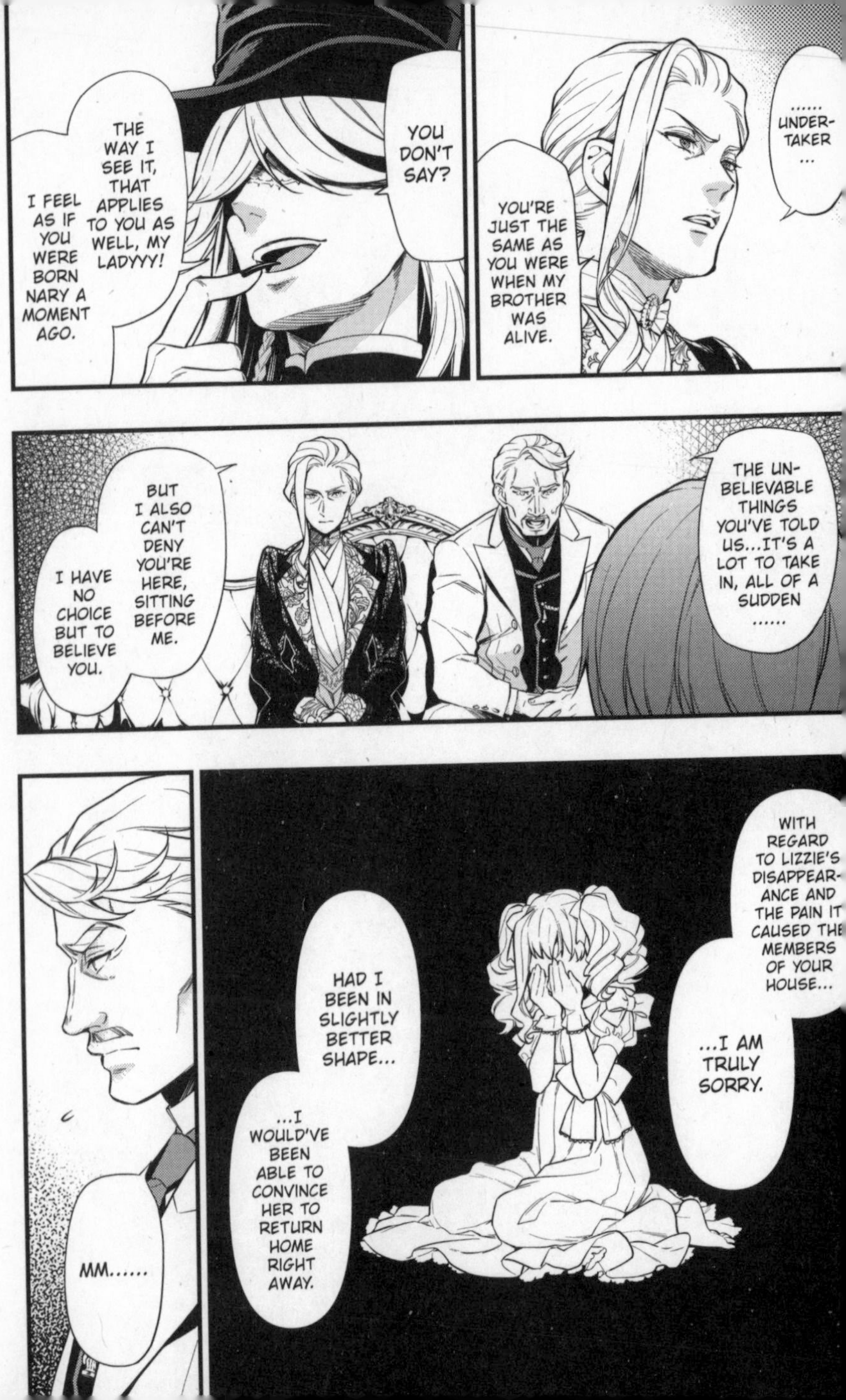

......UNDER-TAKER...
YOU'RE JUST THE SAME AS YOU WERE WHEN MY BROTHER WAS ALIVE.
YOU DON'T SAY?
THE WAY I SEE IT, THAT APPLIES TO YOU AS WELL, MY LADYYY!
I FEEL AS IF YOU WERE BORN NARY A MOMENT AGO.
THE UN-BELIEVABLE THINGS YOU'VE TOLD US...IT'S A LOT TO TAKE IN, ALL OF A SUDDEN......
BUT I ALSO CAN'T DENY YOU'RE HERE, SITTING BEFORE ME.
I HAVE NO CHOICE BUT TO BELIEVE YOU.
WITH REGARD TO LIZZIE'S DISAPPEAR-ANCE AND THE PAIN IT CAUSED THE MEMBERS OF YOUR HOUSE...
...I AM TRULY SORRY.
HAD I BEEN IN SLIGHTLY BETTER SHAPE...
...I WOULD'VE BEEN ABLE TO CONVINCE HER TO RETURN HOME RIGHT AWAY.
MM......

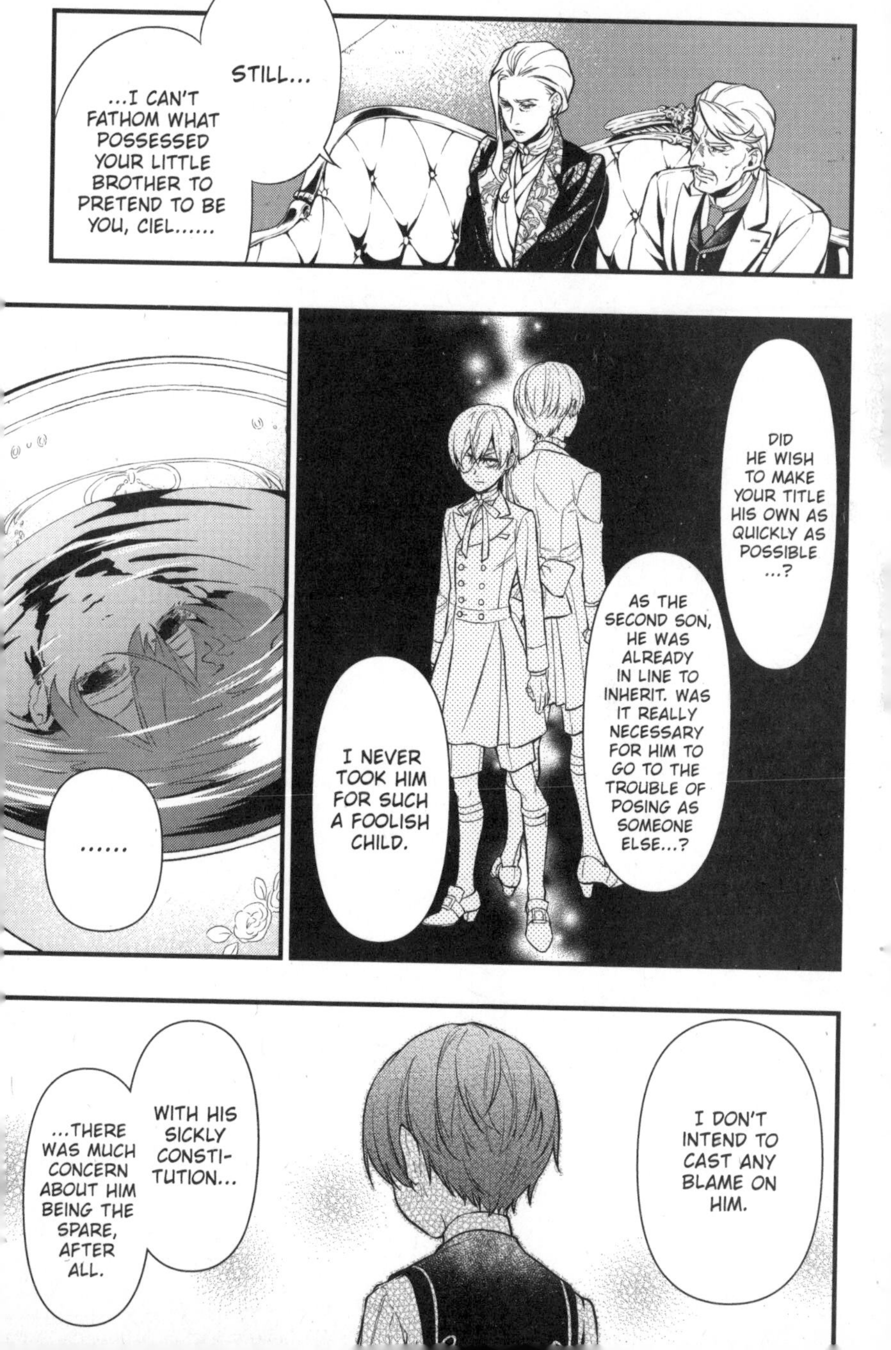
STILL...
...I CAN'T FATHOM WHAT POSSESSED YOUR LITTLE BROTHER TO PRETEND TO BE YOU, CIEL......
DID HE WISH TO MAKE YOUR TITLE HIS OWN AS QUICKLY AS POSSIBLE ...?
AS THE SECOND SON, HE WAS ALREADY IN LINE TO INHERIT. WAS IT REALLY NECESSARY FOR HIM TO GO TO THE TROUBLE OF POSING AS SOMEONE ELSE...?
I NEVER TOOK HIM FOR SUCH A FOOLISH CHILD.
......
I DON'T INTEND TO CAST ANY BLAME ON HIM.
WITH HIS SICKLY CONSTI-TUTION...
...THERE WAS MUCH CONCERN ABOUT HIM BEING THE SPARE, AFTER ALL.

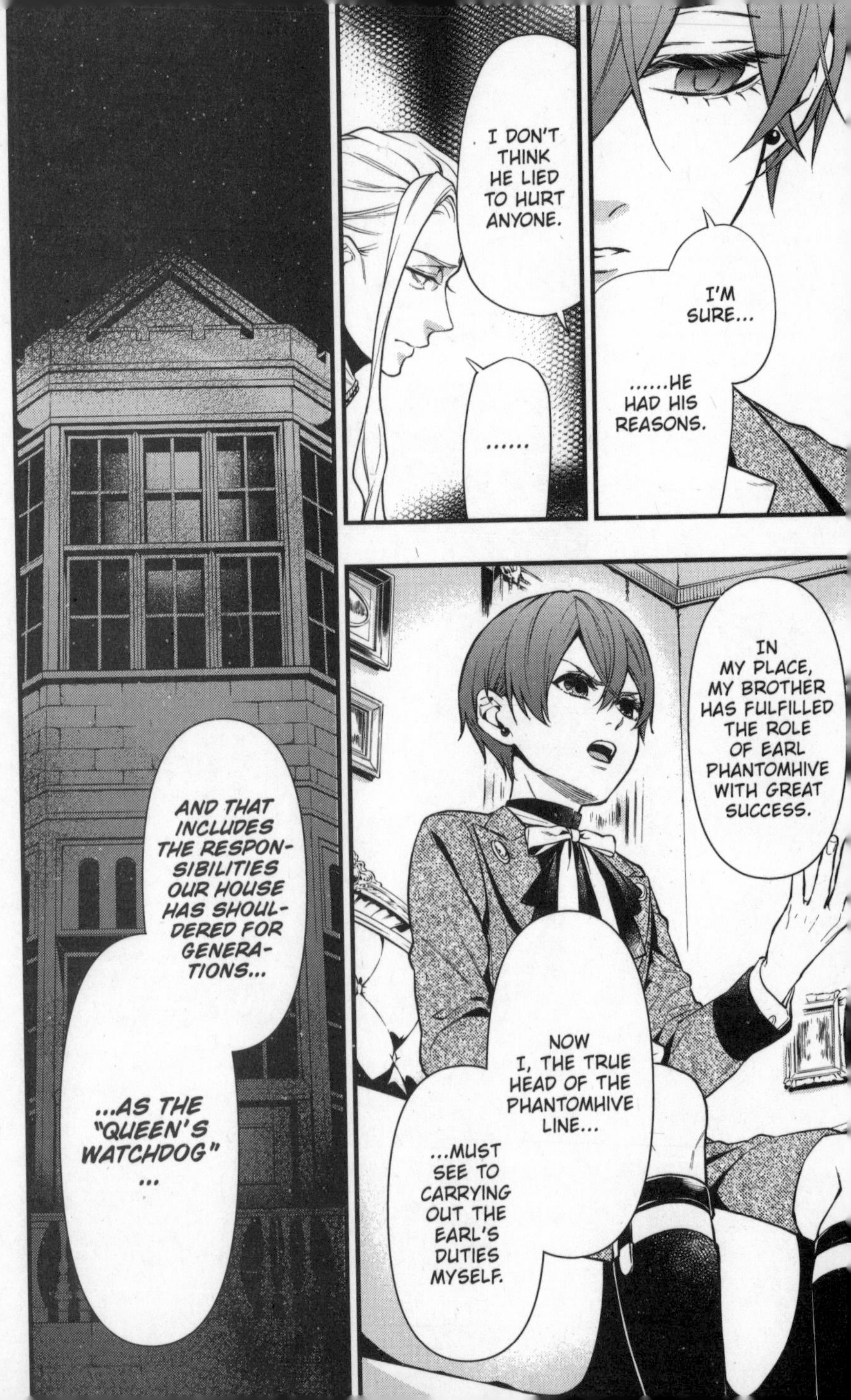
I'M SURE...
......HE HAD HIS REASONS.
I DON'T THINK HE LIED TO HURT ANYONE.
......
IN MY PLACE, MY BROTHER HAS FULFILLED THE ROLE OF EARL PHANTOMHIVE WITH GREAT SUCCESS.
NOW I, THE TRUE HEAD OF THE PHANTOMHIVE LINE...
...MUST SEE TO CARRYING OUT THE EARL'S DUTIES MYSELF.
AND THAT INCLUDES THE RESPONSIBILITIES OUR HOUSE HAS SHOULDERED FOR GENERATIONS...
...AS THE "QUEEN'S WATCHDOG"...

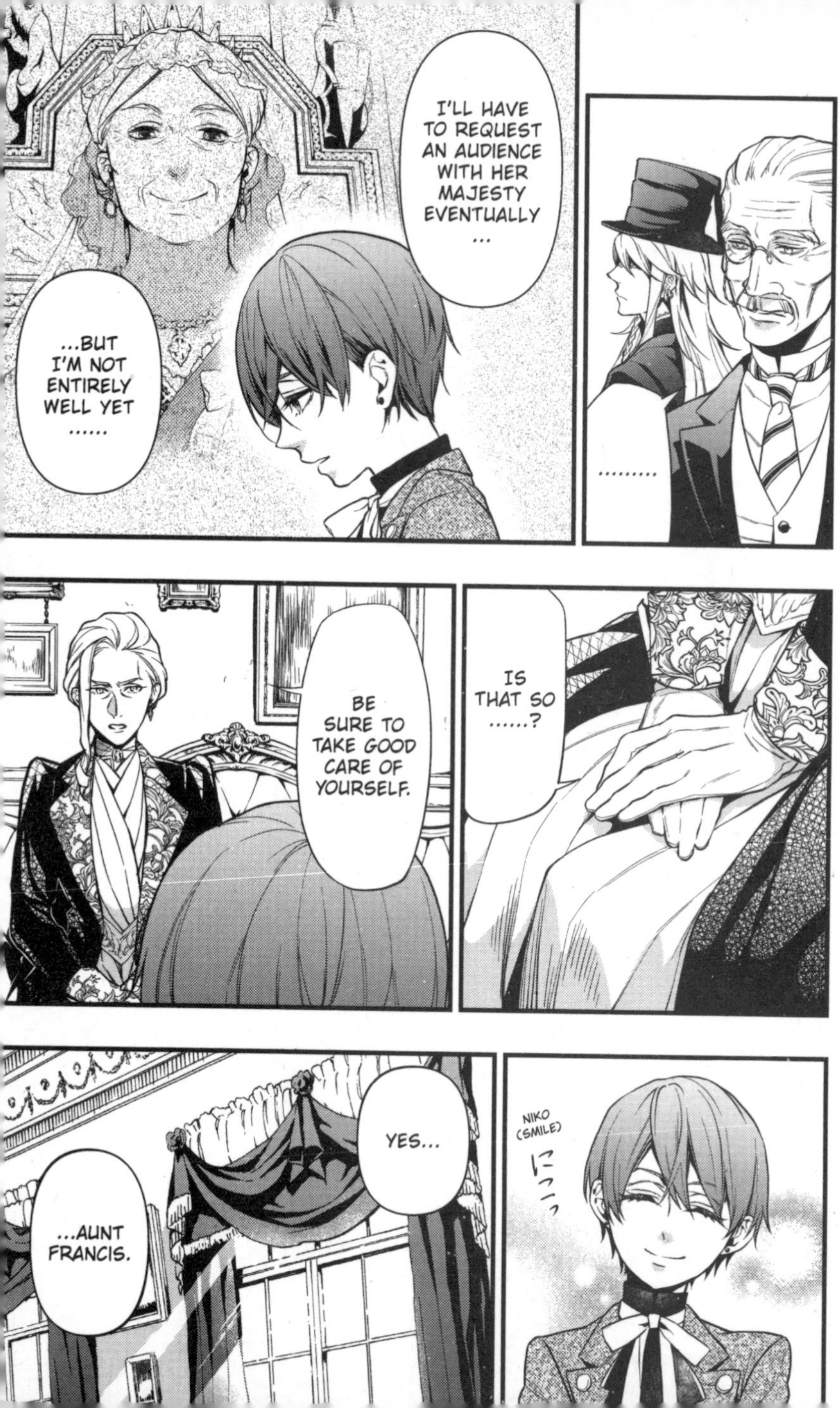
....
I'LL HAVE TO REQUEST AN AUDIENCE WITH HER MAJESTY EVENTUALLY ...
...BUT I'M NOT ENTIRELY WELL YET ......
IS THAT SO ......?
BE SURE TO TAKE GOOD CARE OF YOURSELF.
NIKO (SMILE)
にこっ
YES...
...AUNT FRANCIS.

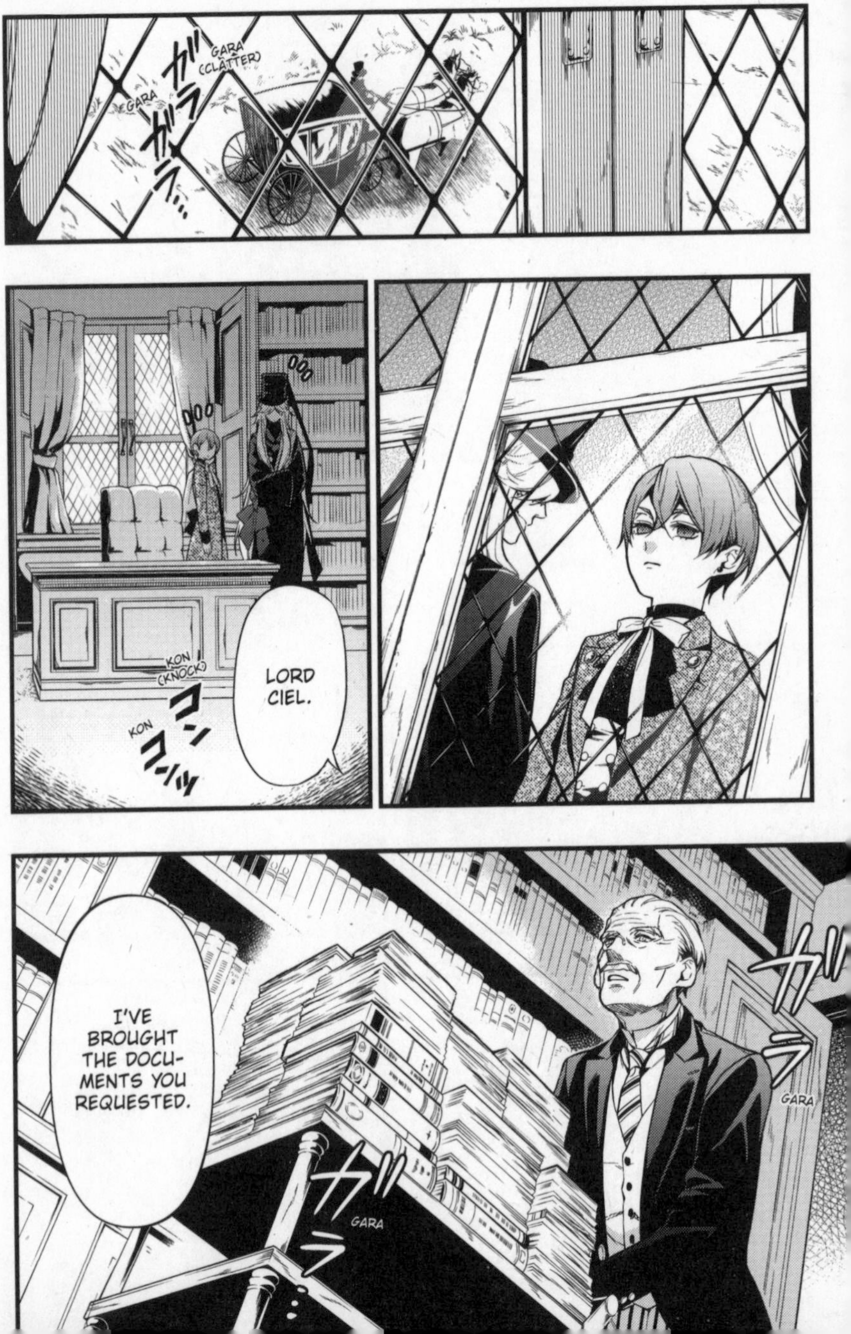
ガラガラ…
GARA (CLATTER)
GARA
LORD CIEL.
コンコンッ
KON (KNOCK)
KON
I'VE BROUGHT THE DOCU-MENTS YOU REQUESTED.
ガラ
GARA
ガラ
GARA

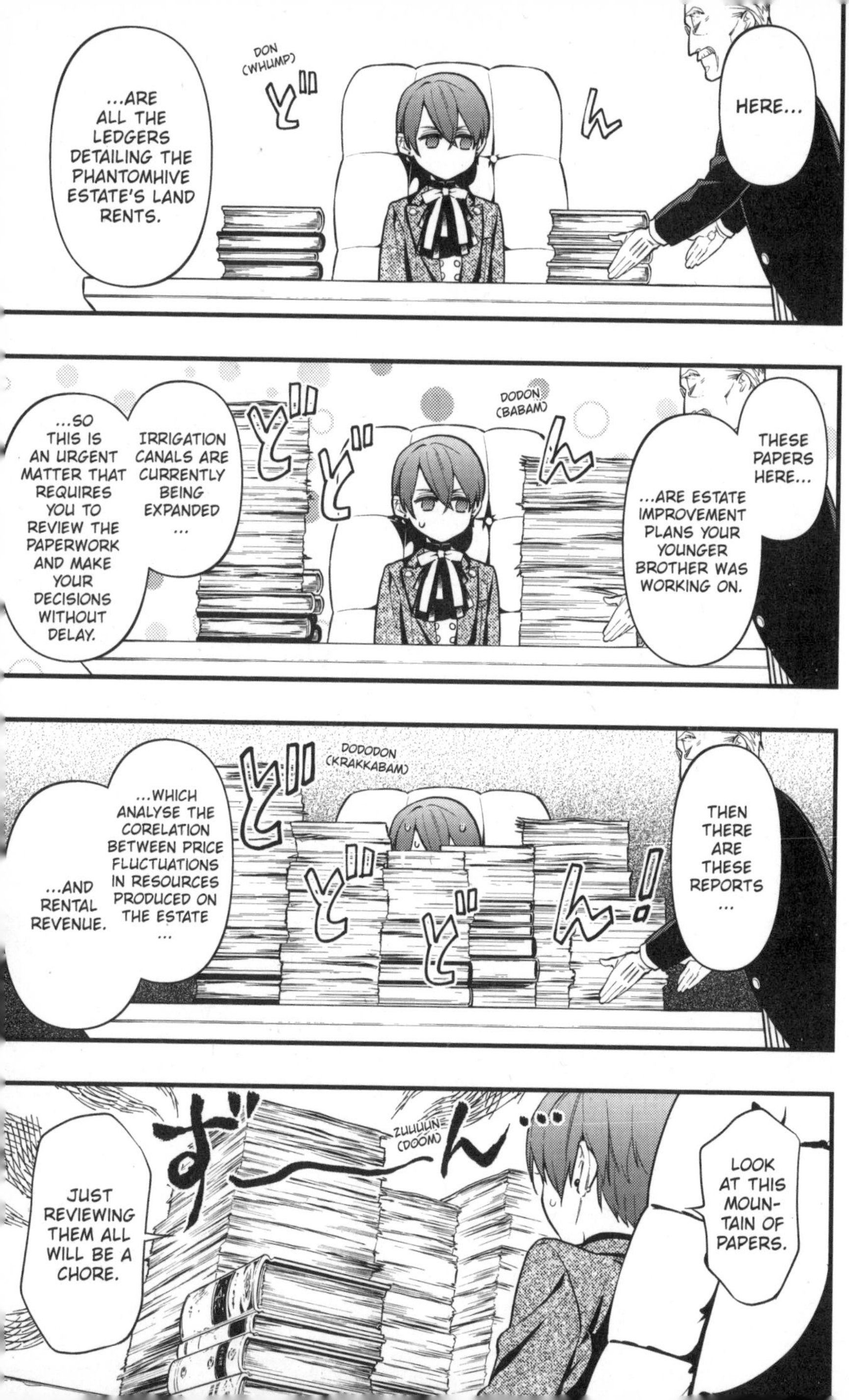
HERE...
DON (WHUMP)
...ARE ALL THE LEDGERS DETAILING THE PHANTOMHIVE ESTATE'S LAND RENTS.
THESE PAPERS HERE...
...ARE ESTATE IMPROVEMENT PLANS YOUR YOUNGER BROTHER WAS WORKING ON.
DODON (BABAM)
IRRIGATION CANALS ARE CURRENTLY BEING EXPANDED ...
...SO THIS IS AN URGENT MATTER THAT REQUIRES YOU TO REVIEW THE PAPERWORK AND MAKE YOUR DECISIONS WITHOUT DELAY.
THEN THERE ARE THESE REPORTS ...
DODODON (KRAKKABAM)
...WHICH ANALYSE THE CORELATION BETWEEN PRICE FLUCTUATIONS IN RESOURCES PRODUCED ON THE ESTATE ...
...AND RENTAL REVENUE.
LOOK AT THIS MOUN-TAIN OF PAPERS.
ZUUUUN (DOOM)
JUST REVIEWING THEM ALL WILL BE A CHORE.

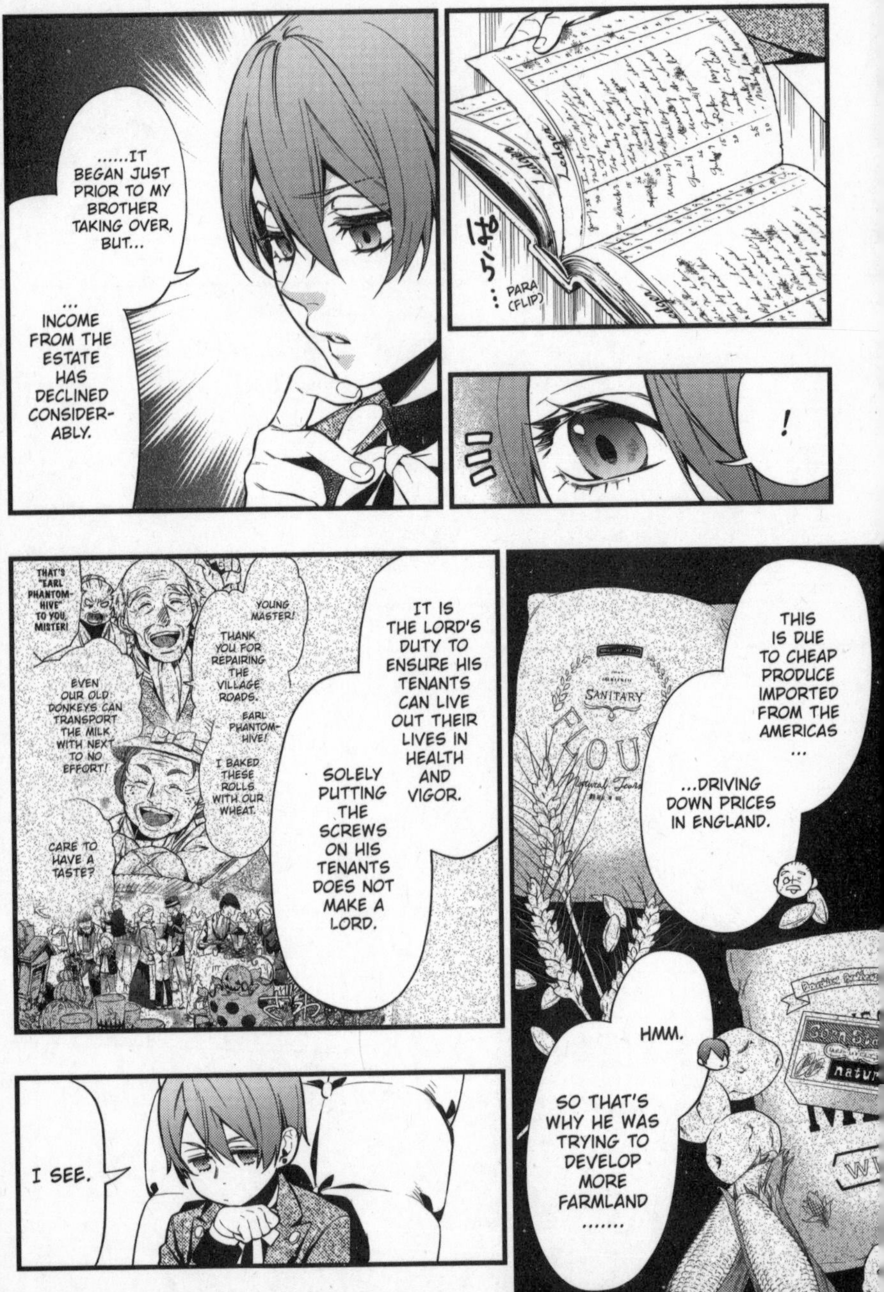
Ledger
ぱら…
PARA (FLIP)
!
......IT BEGAN JUST PRIOR TO MY BROTHER TAKING OVER, BUT...
... INCOME FROM THE ESTATE HAS DECLINED CONSIDERABLY.
SANITARY
THIS IS DUE TO CHEAP PRODUCE IMPORTED FROM THE AMERICAS ...
...DRIVING DOWN PRICES IN ENGLAND.
HMM.
SO THAT'S WHY HE WAS TRYING TO DEVELOP MORE FARMLAND ....
IT IS THE LORD'S DUTY TO ENSURE HIS TENANTS CAN LIVE OUT THEIR LIVES IN HEALTH AND VIGOR.
SOLELY PUTTING THE SCREWS ON HIS TENANTS DOES NOT MAKE A LORD.
YOUNG MASTER!
THANK YOU FOR REPAIRING THE VILLAGE ROADS.
THAT'S "EARL PHANTOM-HIVE" TO YOU, MISTER!
EARL PHANTOM-HIVE!
I BAKED THESE ROLLS WITH OUR WHEAT.
EVEN OUR OLD DONKEYS CAN TRANSPORT THE MILK WITH NEXT TO NO EFFORT!
CARE TO HAVE A TASTE?
I SEE.

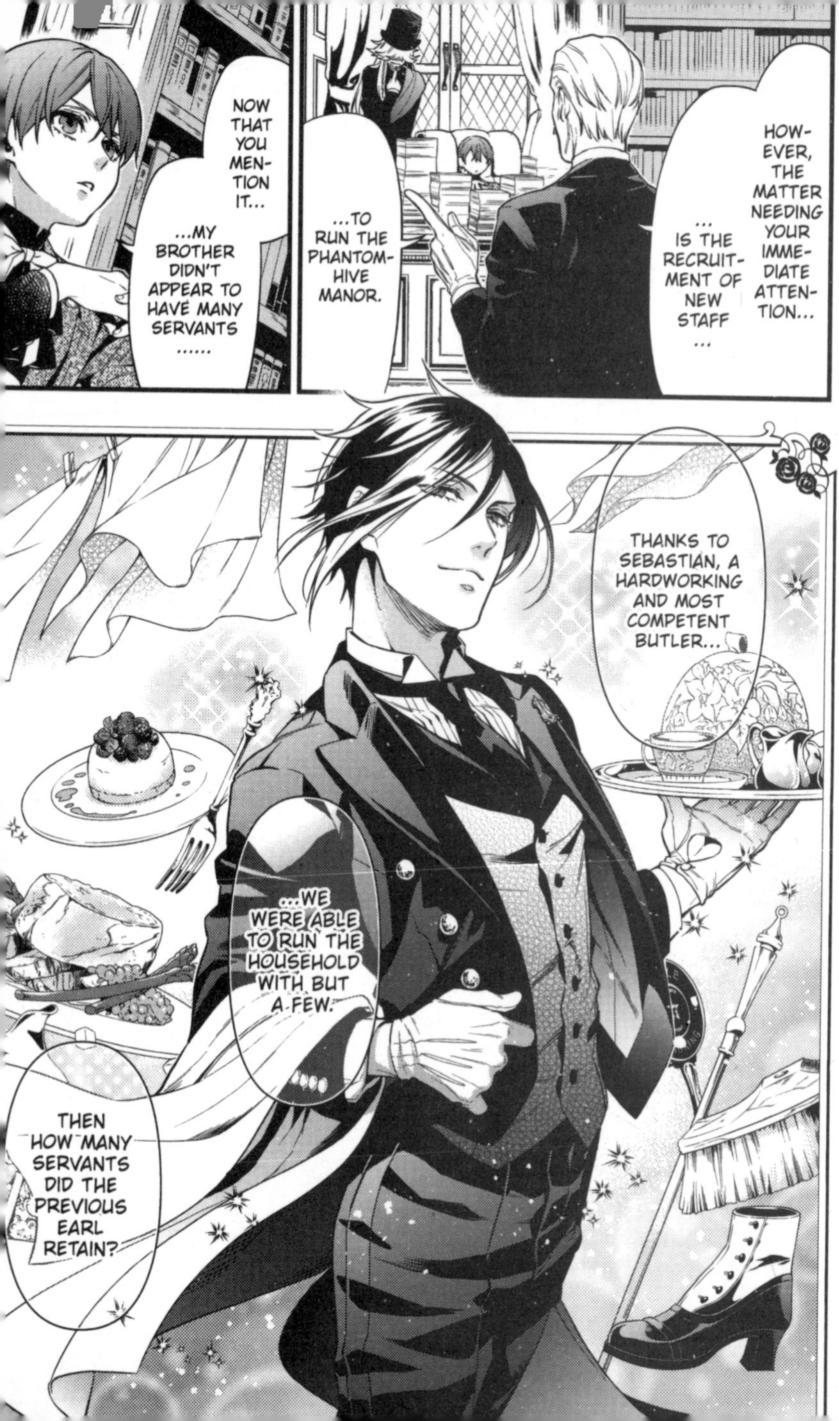
HOW-EVER, THE MATTER NEEDING YOUR IMME-DIATE ATTEN-TION...
...IS THE RECRUIT-MENT OF NEW STAFF...
...TO RUN THE PHANTOM-HIVE MANOR.
NOW THAT YOU MEN-TION IT...
...MY BROTHER DIDN'T APPEAR TO HAVE MANY SERVANTS......
THANKS TO SEBASTIAN, A HARDWORKING AND MOST COMPETENT BUTLER...
...WE WERE ABLE TO RUN THE HOUSEHOLD WITH BUT A FEW.
THEN HOW MANY SERVANTS DID THE PREVIOUS EARL RETAIN?

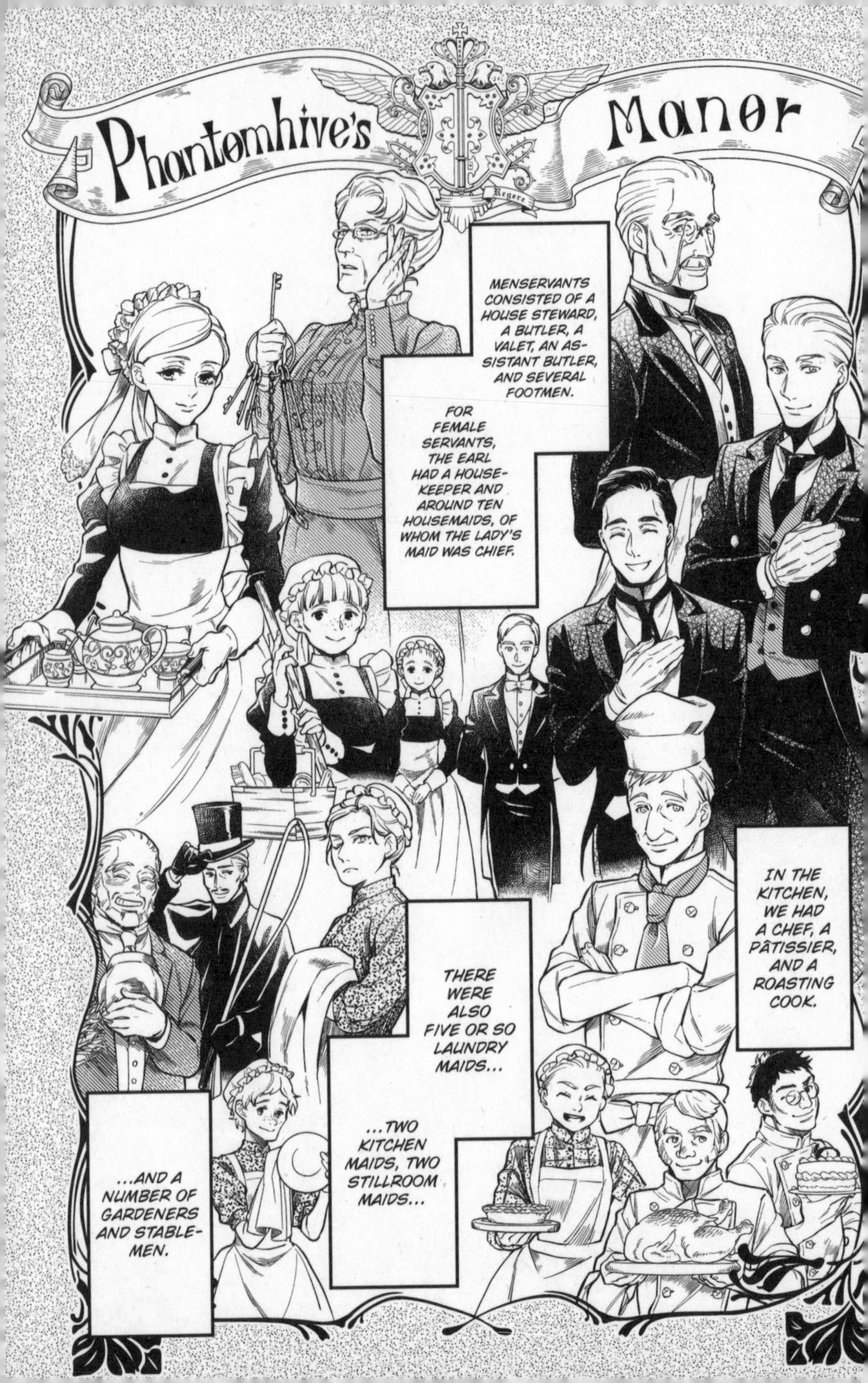
Phantomhive's Manor
Regere
MENSERVANTS CONSISTED OF A HOUSE STEWARD, A BUTLER, A VALET, AN ASSISTANT BUTLER, AND SEVERAL FOOTMEN.
FOR FEMALE SERVANTS, THE EARL HAD A HOUSEKEEPER AND AROUND TEN HOUSEMAIDS, OF WHOM THE LADY'S MAID WAS CHIEF.
IN THE KITCHEN, WE HAD A CHEF, A PÂTISSIER, AND A ROASTING COOK.
THERE WERE ALSO FIVE OR SO LAUNDRY MAIDS...
...TWO KITCHEN MAIDS, TWO STILLROOM MAIDS...
...AND A NUMBER OF GARDENERS AND STABLEMEN.

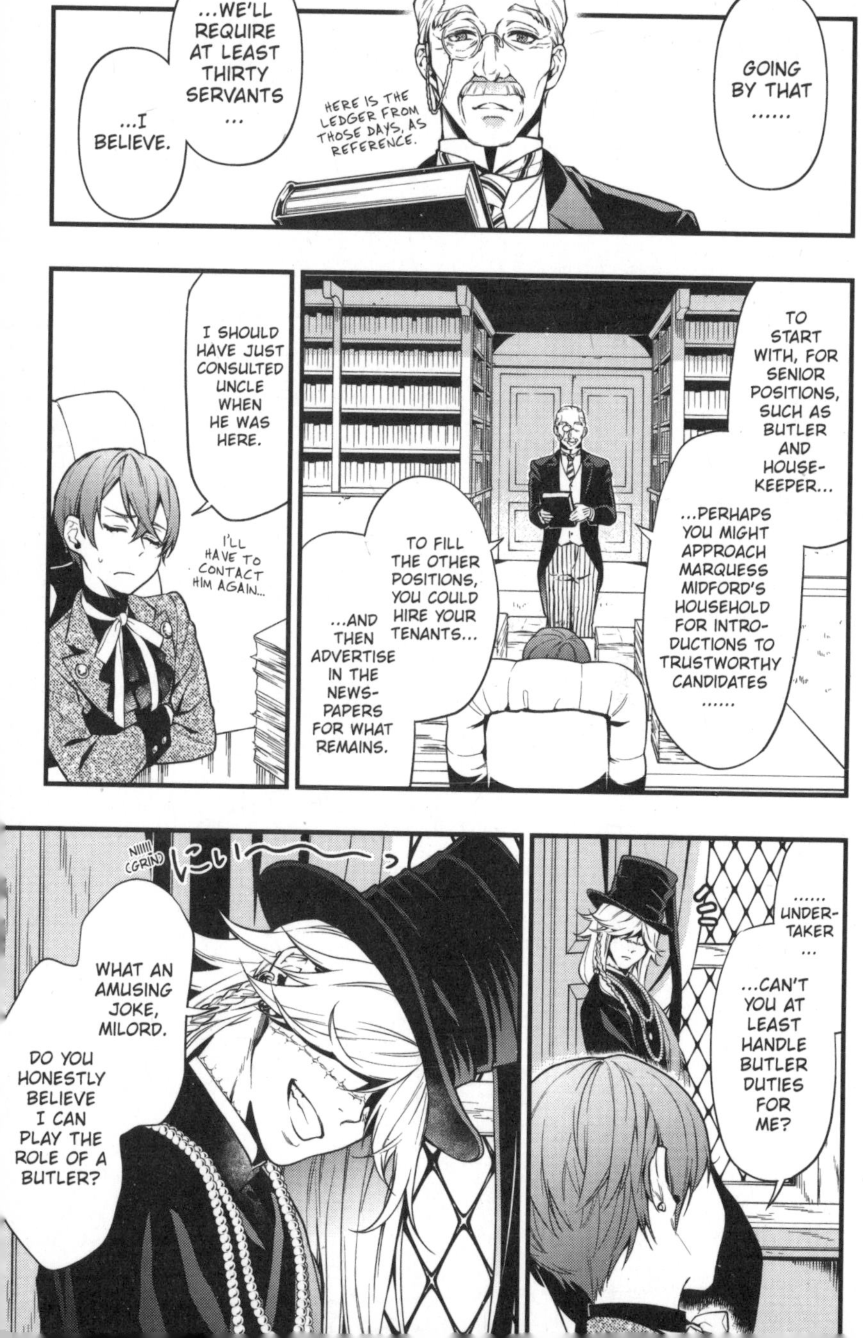
GOING BY THAT ......
...WE'LL REQUIRE AT LEAST THIRTY SERVANTS ...
HERE IS THE LEDGER FROM THOSE DAYS, AS REFERENCE.
...I BELIEVE.
TO START WITH, FOR SENIOR POSITIONS, SUCH AS BUTLER AND HOUSE-KEEPER...
...PERHAPS YOU MIGHT APPROACH MARQUESS MIDFORD'S HOUSEHOLD FOR INTRO-DUCTIONS TO TRUSTWORTHY CANDIDATES ......
TO FILL THE OTHER POSITIONS, YOU COULD HIRE YOUR TENANTS...
...AND THEN ADVERTISE IN THE NEWS-PAPERS FOR WHAT REMAINS.
I SHOULD HAVE JUST CONSULTED UNCLE WHEN HE WAS HERE.
I'LL HAVE TO CONTACT HIM AGAIN...
...... UNDER-TAKER ...
...CAN'T YOU AT LEAST HANDLE BUTLER DUTIES FOR ME?
NIIIII (GRIN)
にぃ――
WHAT AN AMUSING JOKE, MILORD.
DO YOU HONESTLY BELIEVE I CAN PLAY THE ROLE OF A BUTLER?

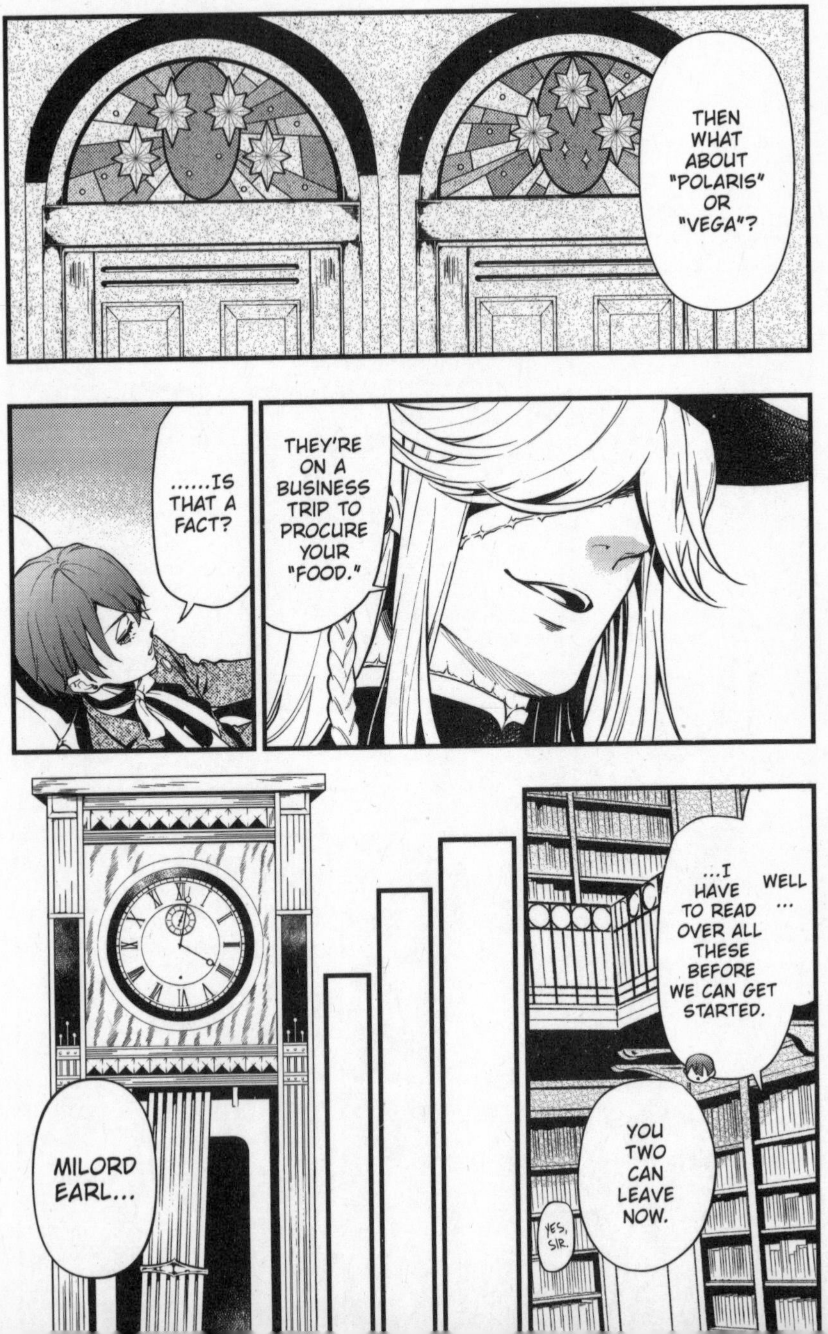
THEN WHAT ABOUT "POLARIS" OR "VEGA"?
THEY'RE ON A BUSINESS TRIP TO PROCURE YOUR "FOOD."
......IS THAT A FACT?
WELL...
...I HAVE TO READ OVER ALL THESE BEFORE WE CAN GET STARTED.
YOU TWO CAN LEAVE NOW.
YES, SIR.
MILORD EARL...

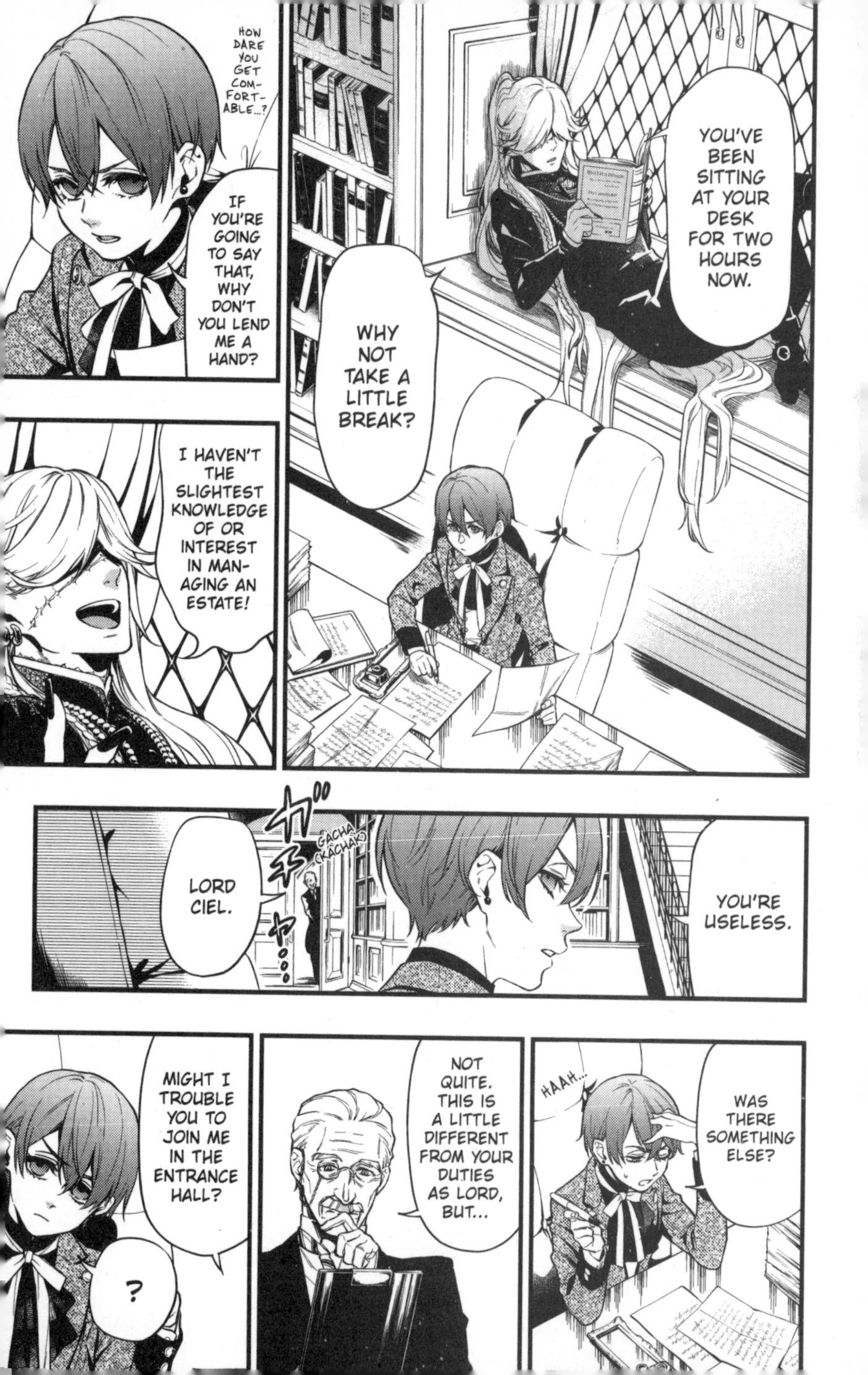
YOU'VE BEEN SITTING AT YOUR DESK FOR TWO HOURS NOW.
WHY NOT TAKE A LITTLE BREAK?
HOW DARE YOU GET COMFORTABLE...?
IF YOU'RE GOING TO SAY THAT, WHY DON'T YOU LEND ME A HAND?
I HAVEN'T THE SLIGHTEST KNOWLEDGE OF OR INTEREST IN MANAGING AN ESTATE!
YOU'RE USELESS.
GACHA (KACHAK)
LORD CIEL.
HAAH...
WAS THERE SOMETHING ELSE?
NOT QUITE. THIS IS A LITTLE DIFFERENT FROM YOUR DUTIES AS LORD, BUT...
MIGHT I TROUBLE YOU TO JOIN ME IN THE ENTRANCE HALL?
?

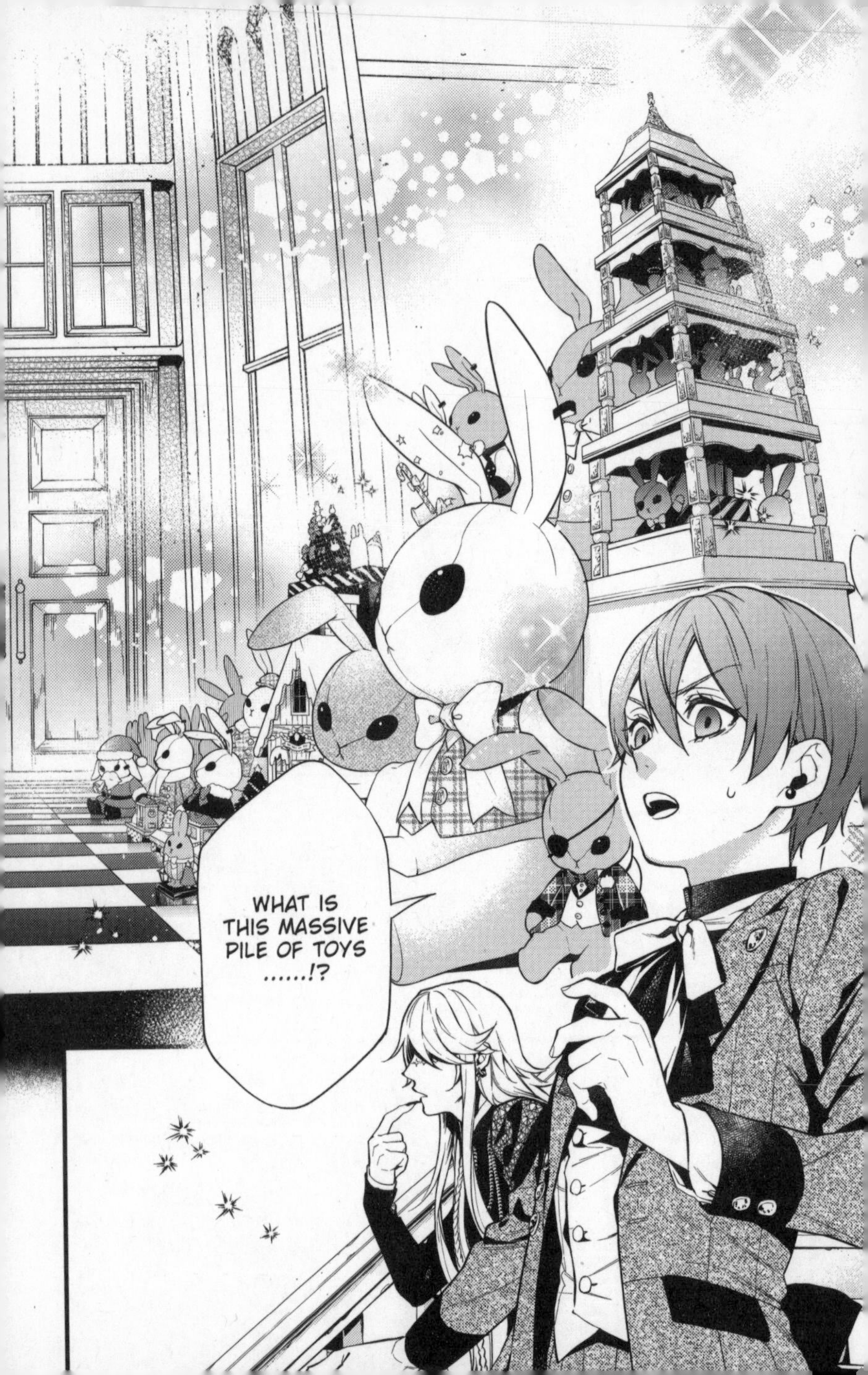
WHAT IS THIS MASSIVE PILE OF TOYS ......!?

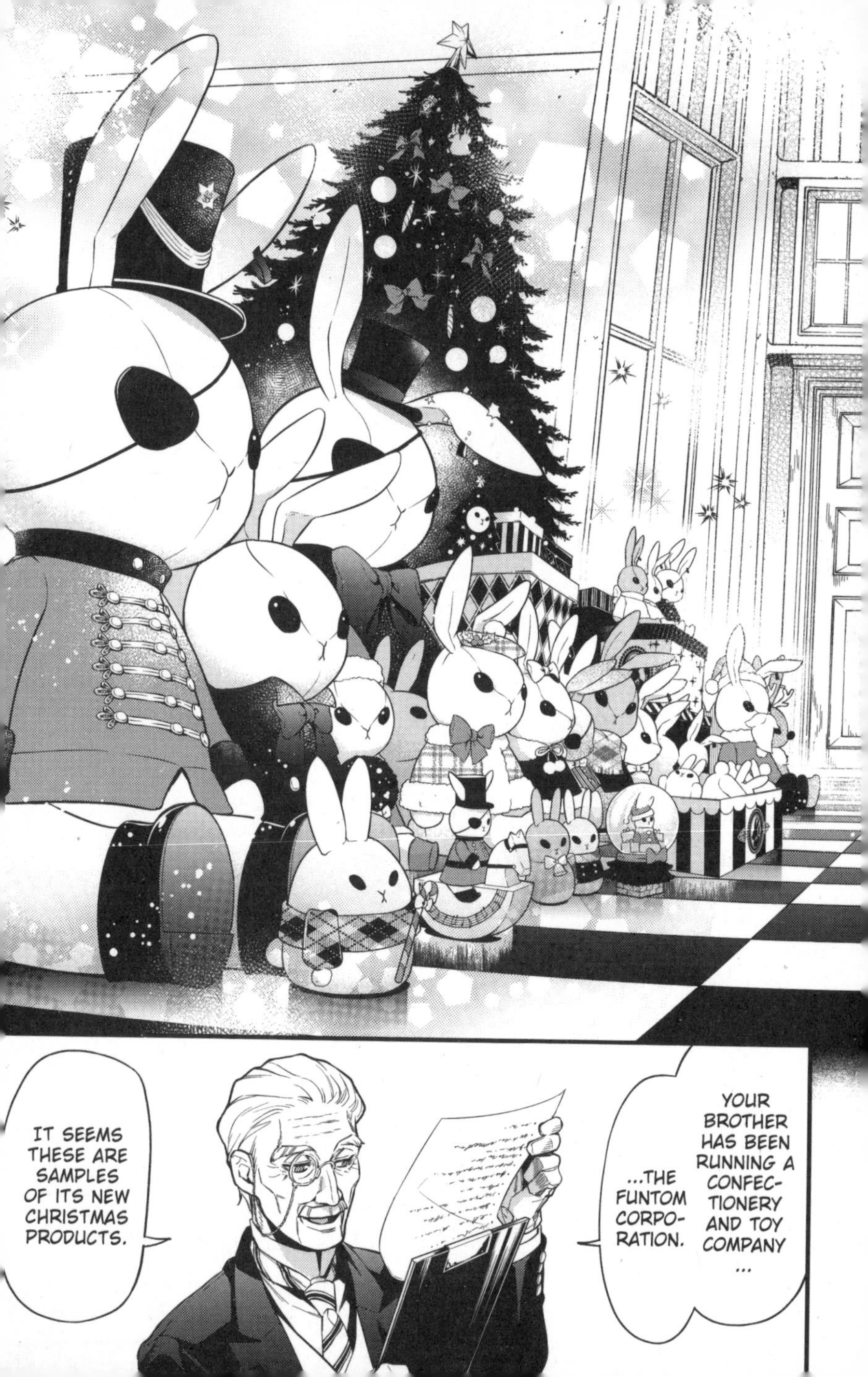
YOUR BROTHER HAS BEEN RUNNING A CONFEC-TIONERY AND TOY COMPANY ...
...THE FUNTOM CORPO-RATION.
IT SEEMS THESE ARE SAMPLES OF ITS NEW CHRISTMAS PRODUCTS.

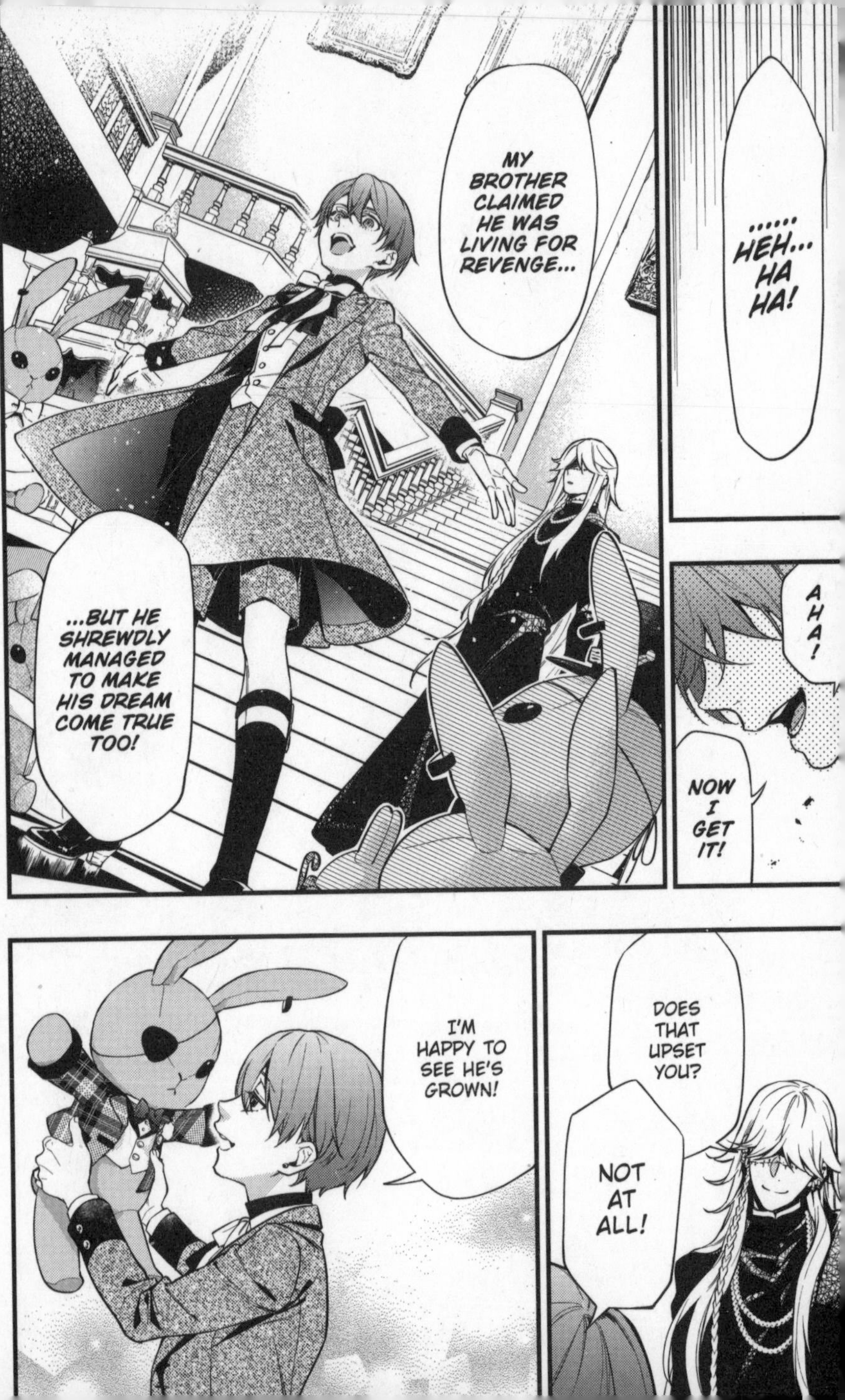
......HEH... HA HA!
AHA!
NOW I GET IT!
MY BROTHER CLAIMED HE WAS LIVING FOR REVENGE...
...BUT HE SHREWDLY MANAGED TO MAKE HIS DREAM COME TRUE TOO!
DOES THAT UPSET YOU?
NOT AT ALL!
I'M HAPPY TO SEE HE'S GROWN!

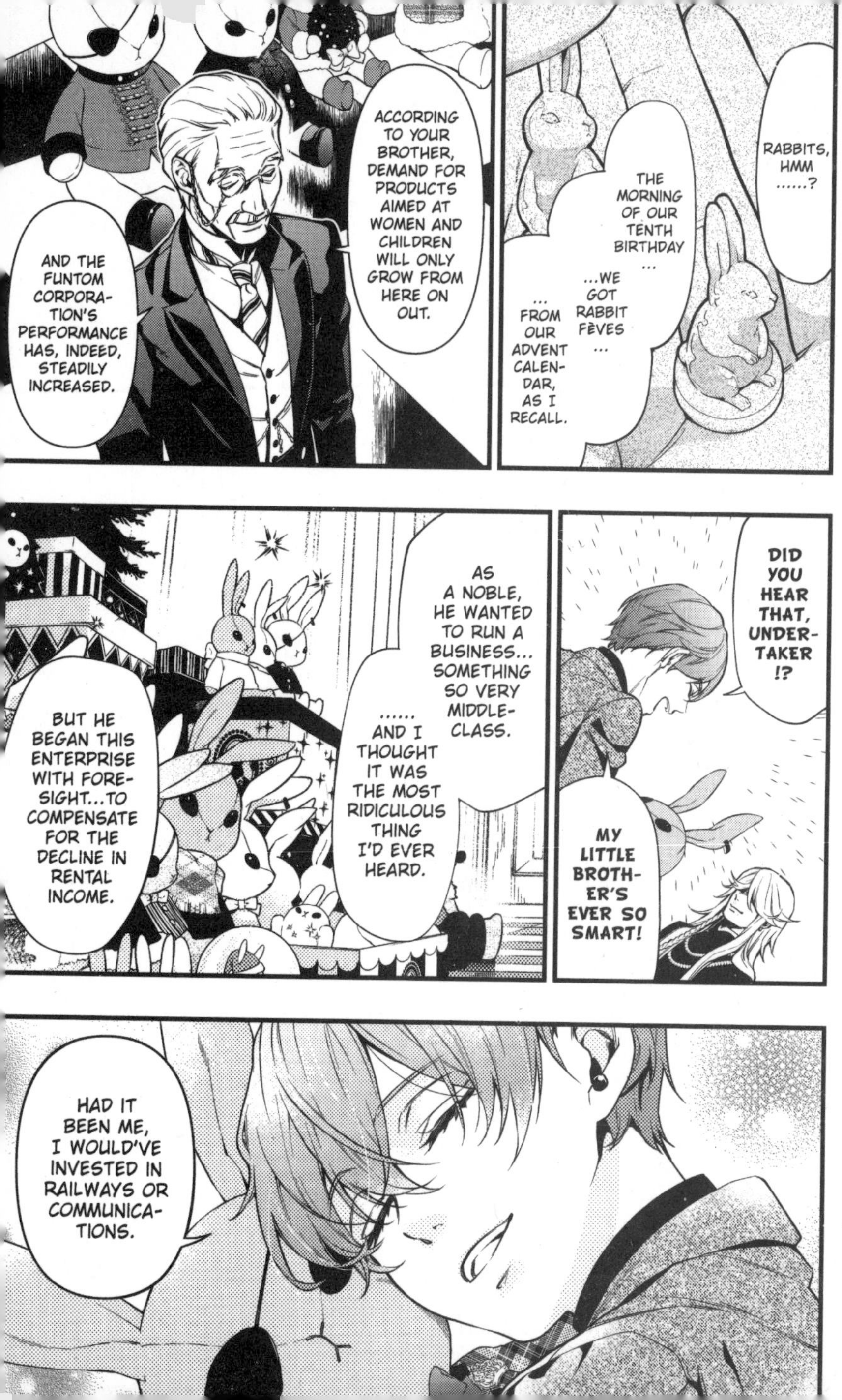
RABBITS, HMM ......?
THE MORNING OF OUR TENTH BIRTHDAY ...
...WE GOT RABBIT FÈVES ...
...FROM OUR ADVENT CALENDAR, AS I RECALL.
ACCORDING TO YOUR BROTHER, DEMAND FOR PRODUCTS AIMED AT WOMEN AND CHILDREN WILL ONLY GROW FROM HERE ON OUT.
AND THE FUNTOM CORPORATION'S PERFORMANCE HAS, INDEED, STEADILY INCREASED.
DID YOU HEAR THAT, UNDERTAKER!?
MY LITTLE BROTHER'S EVER SO SMART!
AS A NOBLE, HE WANTED TO RUN A BUSINESS... SOMETHING SO VERY MIDDLE-CLASS.
......AND I THOUGHT IT WAS THE MOST RIDICULOUS THING I'D EVER HEARD.
BUT HE BEGAN THIS ENTERPRISE WITH FORESIGHT...TO COMPENSATE FOR THE DECLINE IN RENTAL INCOME.
HAD IT BEEN ME, I WOULD'VE INVESTED IN RAILWAYS OR COMMUNICATIONS.

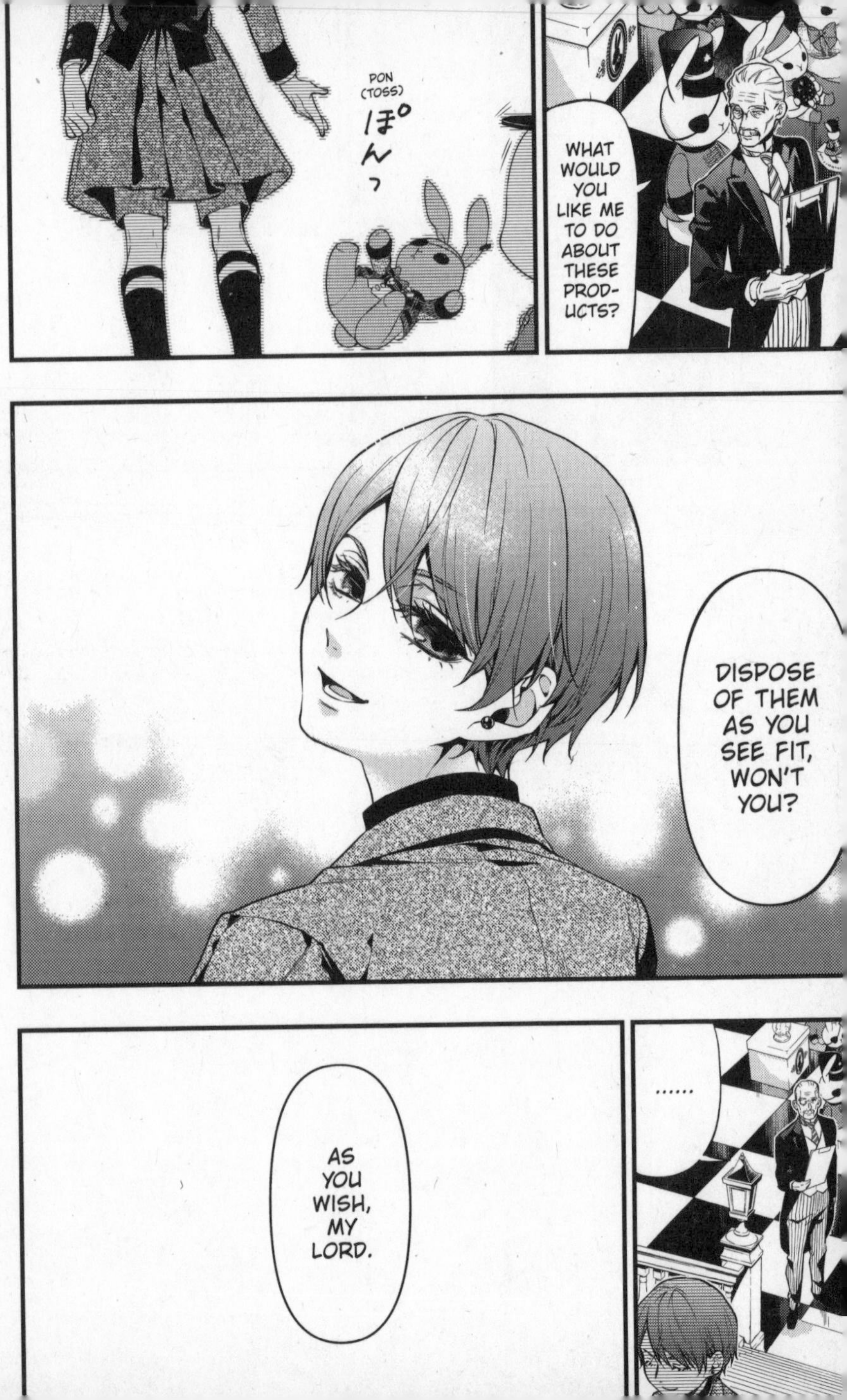
WHAT WOULD YOU LIKE ME TO DO ABOUT THESE PROD-UCTS?
PON (TOSS)
ぽんっ
DISPOSE OF THEM AS YOU SEE FIT, WON'T YOU?
......
AS YOU WISH, MY LORD.

Black Butler

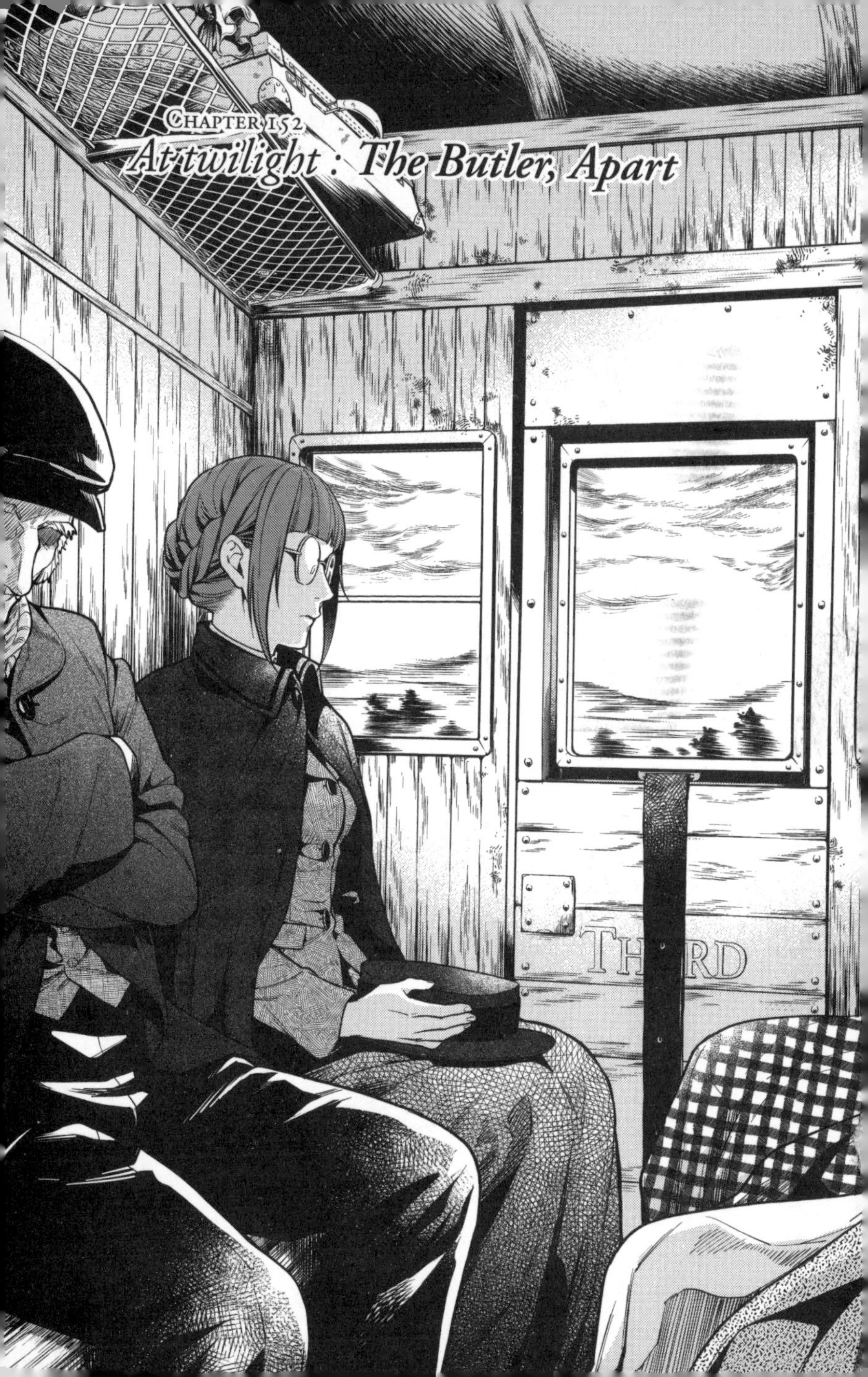
Chapter 152
At twilight : The Butler, Apart
THIRD

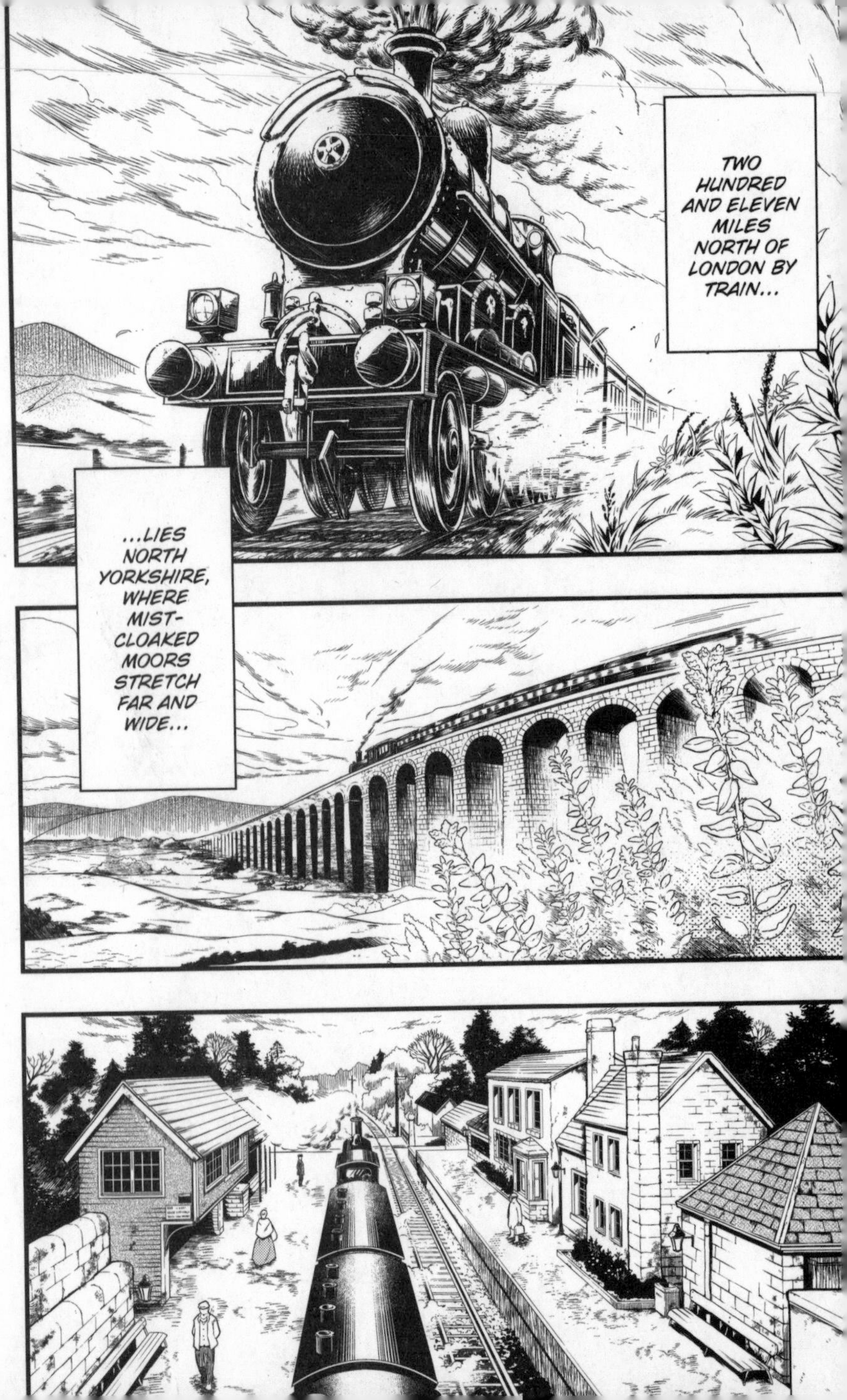
TWO HUNDRED AND ELEVEN MILES NORTH OF LONDON BY TRAIN...
...LIES NORTH YORKSHIRE, WHERE MIST-CLOAKED MOORS STRETCH FAR AND WIDE...

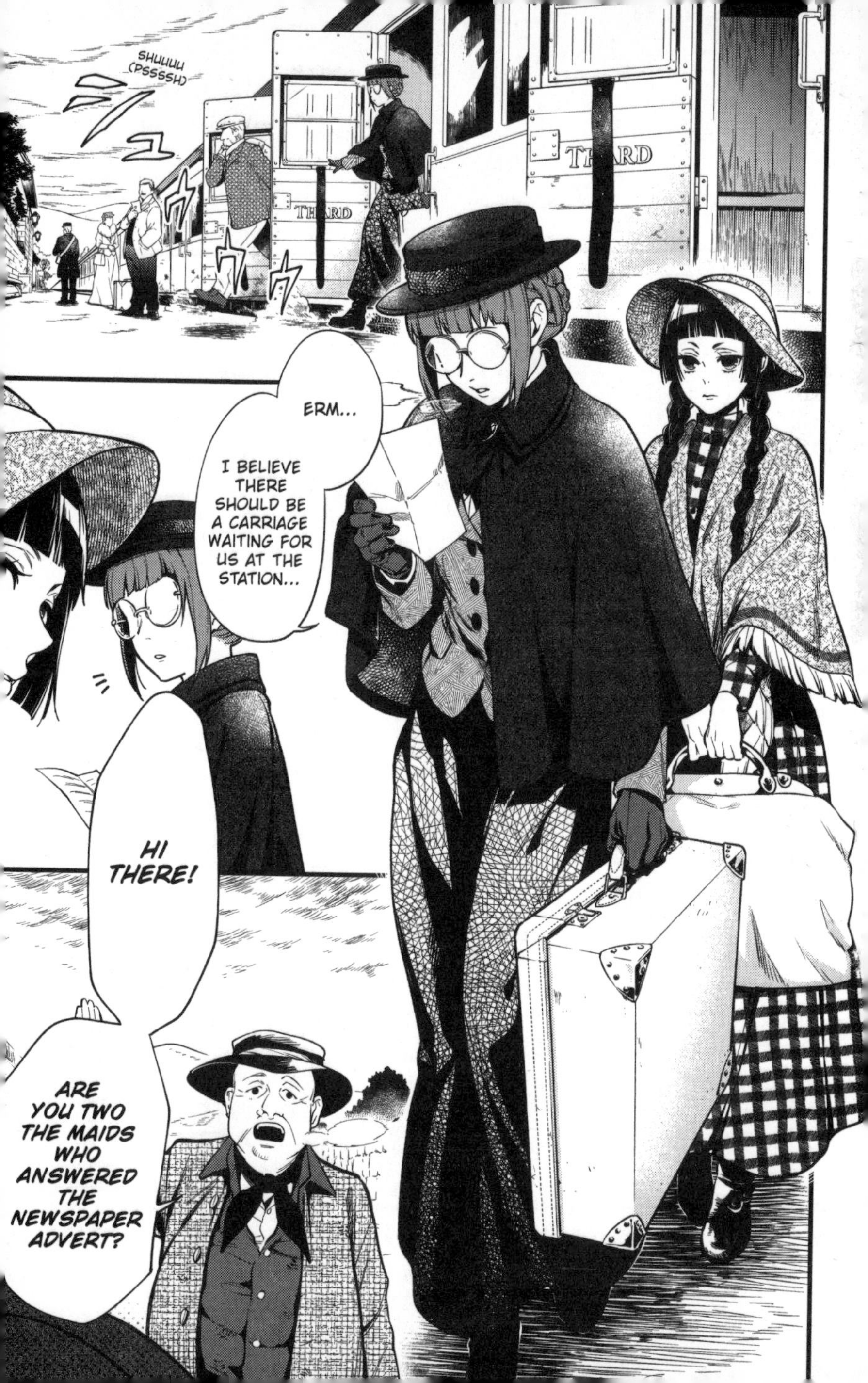

SHUUUU (PSSSSH)
THIRD
THIRD
ERM...
I BELIEVE THERE SHOULD BE A CARRIAGE WAITING FOR US AT THE STATION...
HI THERE!
ARE YOU TWO THE MAIDS WHO ANSWERED THE NEWSPAPER ADVERT?

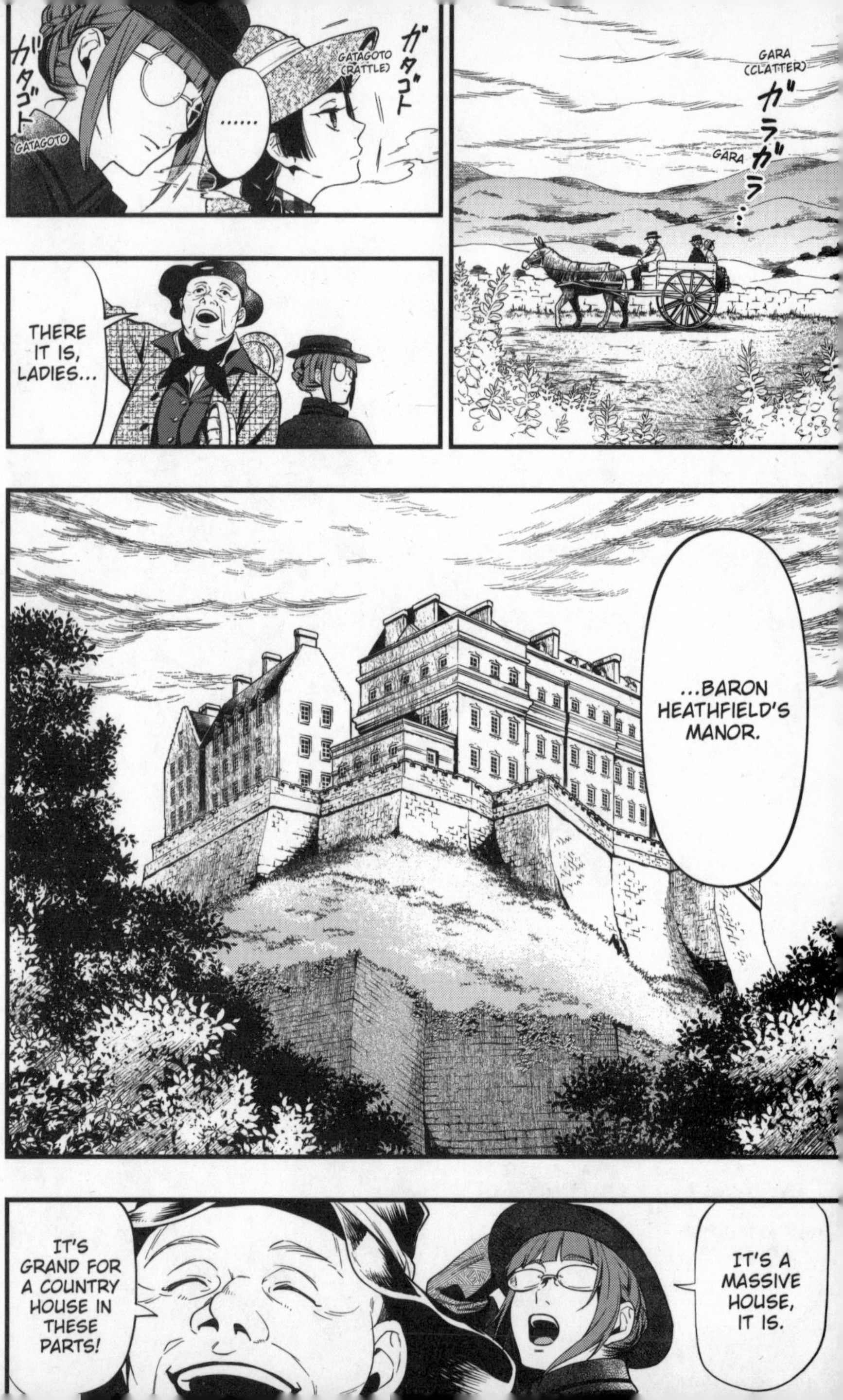
GARA (CLATTER)
ガラガラ…
GARA
ガタゴト
GATAGOTO (RATTLE)
......
ガタゴト
GATAGOTO
THERE IT IS, LADIES...
...BARON HEATHFIELD'S MANOR.
IT'S A MASSIVE HOUSE, IT IS.
IT'S GRAND FOR A COUNTRY HOUSE IN THESE PARTS!

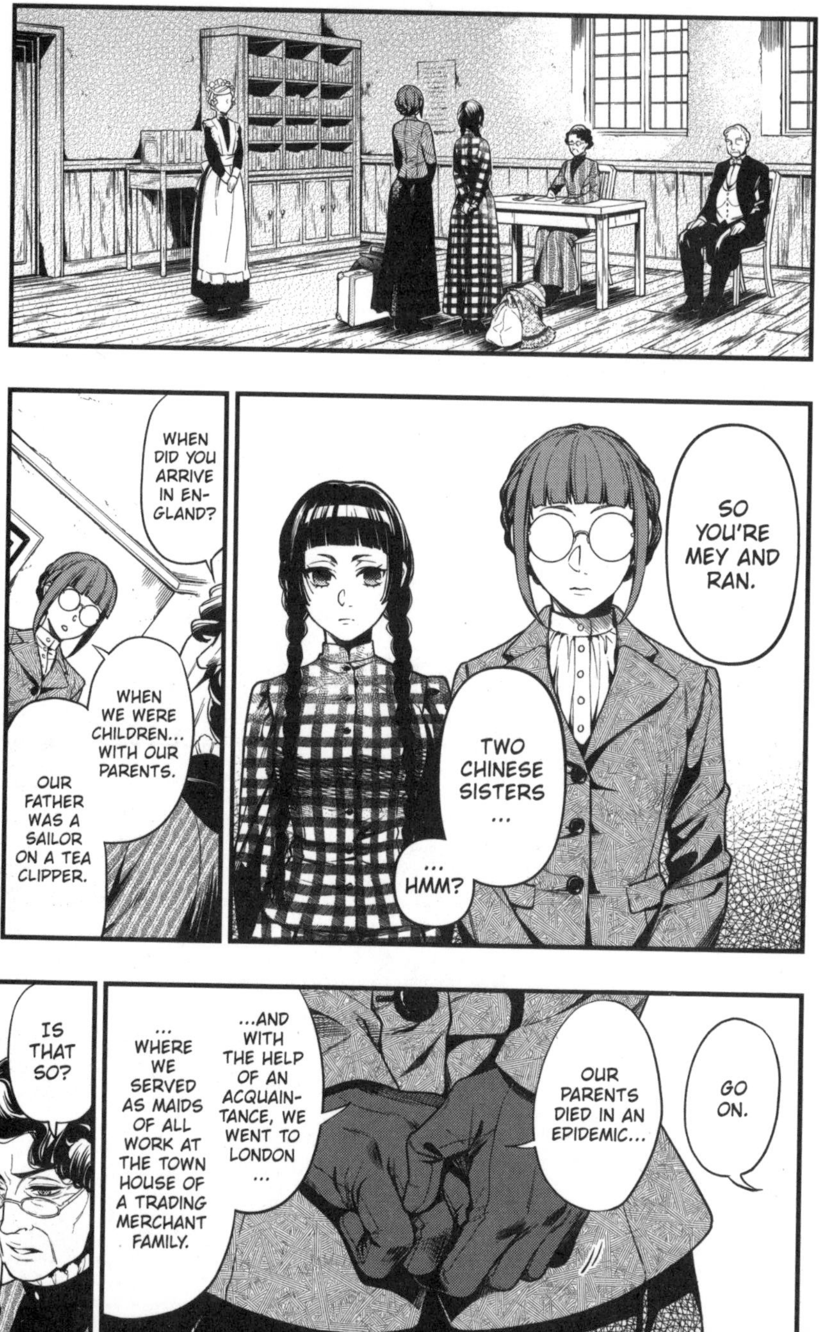
SO YOU'RE MEY AND RAN.
TWO CHINESE SISTERS...
...HMM?
WHEN DID YOU ARRIVE IN ENGLAND?
WHEN WE WERE CHILDREN... WITH OUR PARENTS.
OUR FATHER WAS A SAILOR ON A TEA CLIPPER.
GO ON.
OUR PARENTS DIED IN AN EPIDEMIC...
...AND WITH THE HELP OF AN ACQUAINTANCE, WE WENT TO LONDON...
...WHERE WE SERVED AS MAIDS OF ALL WORK AT THE TOWN HOUSE OF A TRADING MERCHANT FAMILY.
IS THAT SO?

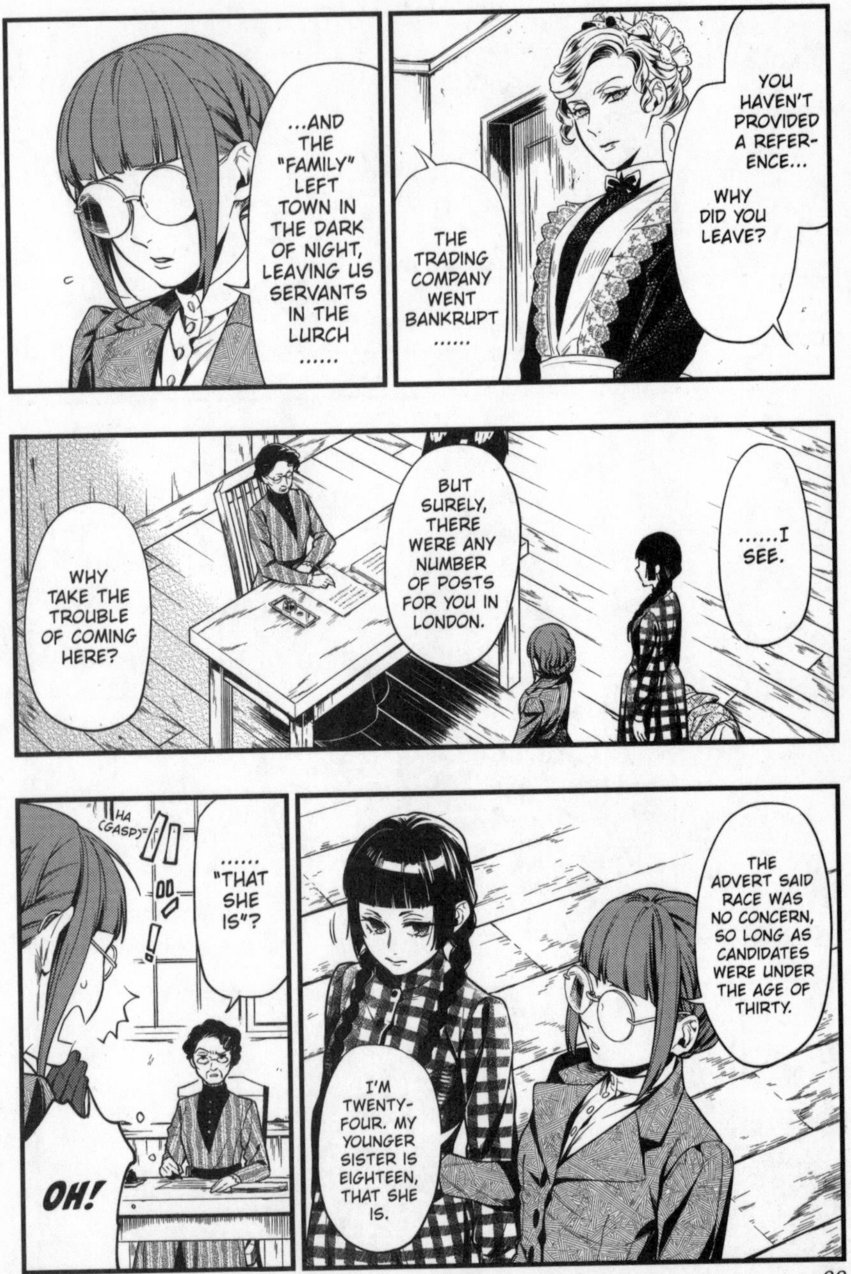
YOU HAVEN'T PROVIDED A REFERENCE... WHY DID YOU LEAVE?
THE TRADING COMPANY WENT BANKRUPT ......
...AND THE "FAMILY" LEFT TOWN IN THE DARK OF NIGHT, LEAVING US SERVANTS IN THE LURCH ......
......I SEE.
BUT SURELY, THERE WERE ANY NUMBER OF POSTS FOR YOU IN LONDON.
WHY TAKE THE TROUBLE OF COMING HERE?
THE ADVERT SAID RACE WAS NO CONCERN, SO LONG AS CANDIDATES WERE UNDER THE AGE OF THIRTY.
I'M TWENTY-FOUR. MY YOUNGER SISTER IS EIGHTEEN, THAT SHE IS.
...... "THAT SHE IS"?
HA (GASP)
OH!

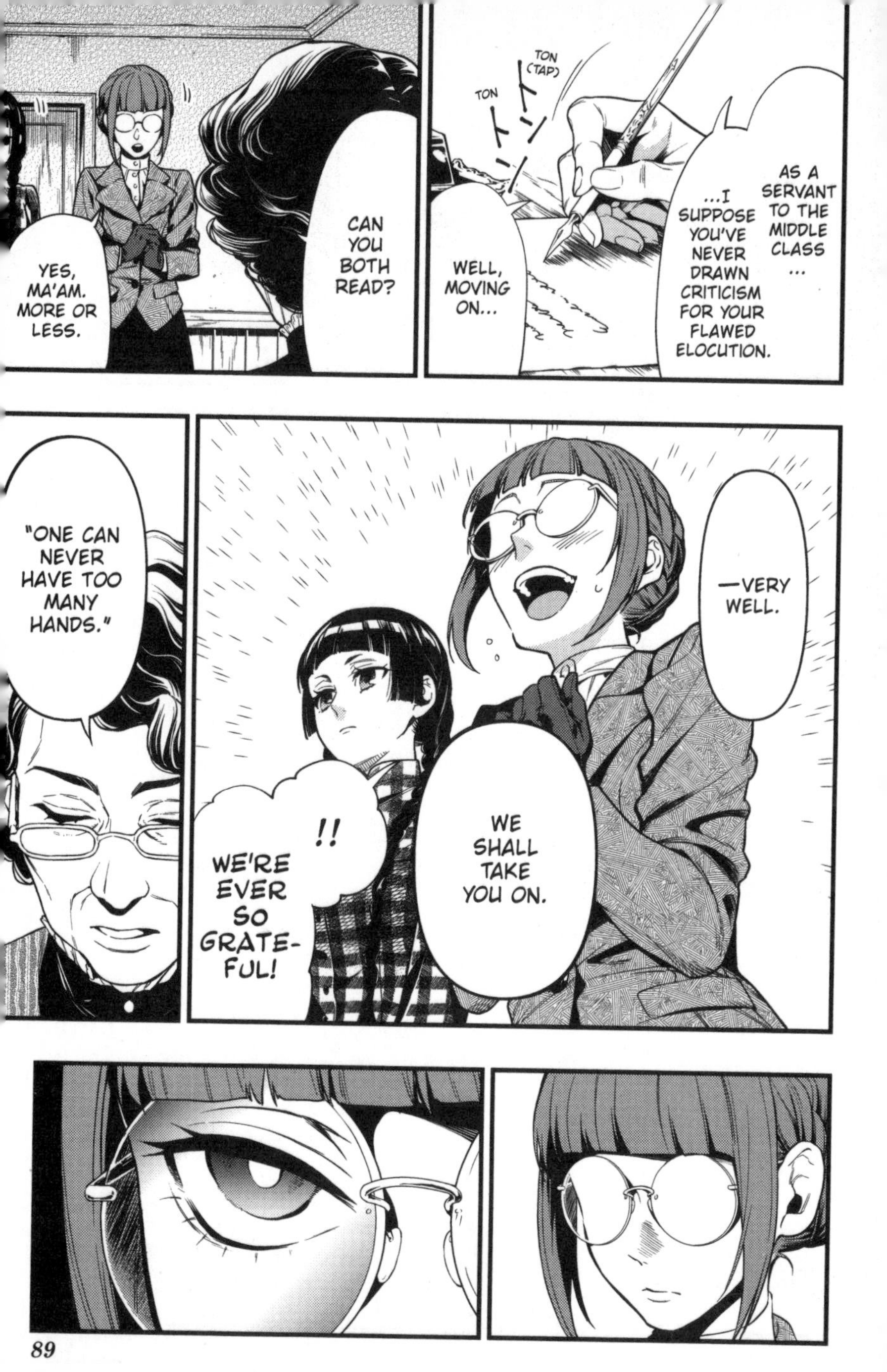
AS A SERVANT TO THE MIDDLE CLASS...
...I SUPPOSE YOU'VE NEVER DRAWN CRITICISM FOR YOUR FLAWED ELOCUTION.
TON (TAP)
TON
WELL, MOVING ON...
CAN YOU BOTH READ?
YES, MA'AM. MORE OR LESS.
—VERY WELL.
WE SHALL TAKE YOU ON.
!!
WE'RE EVER SO GRATE-FUL!
"ONE CAN NEVER HAVE TOO MANY HANDS."

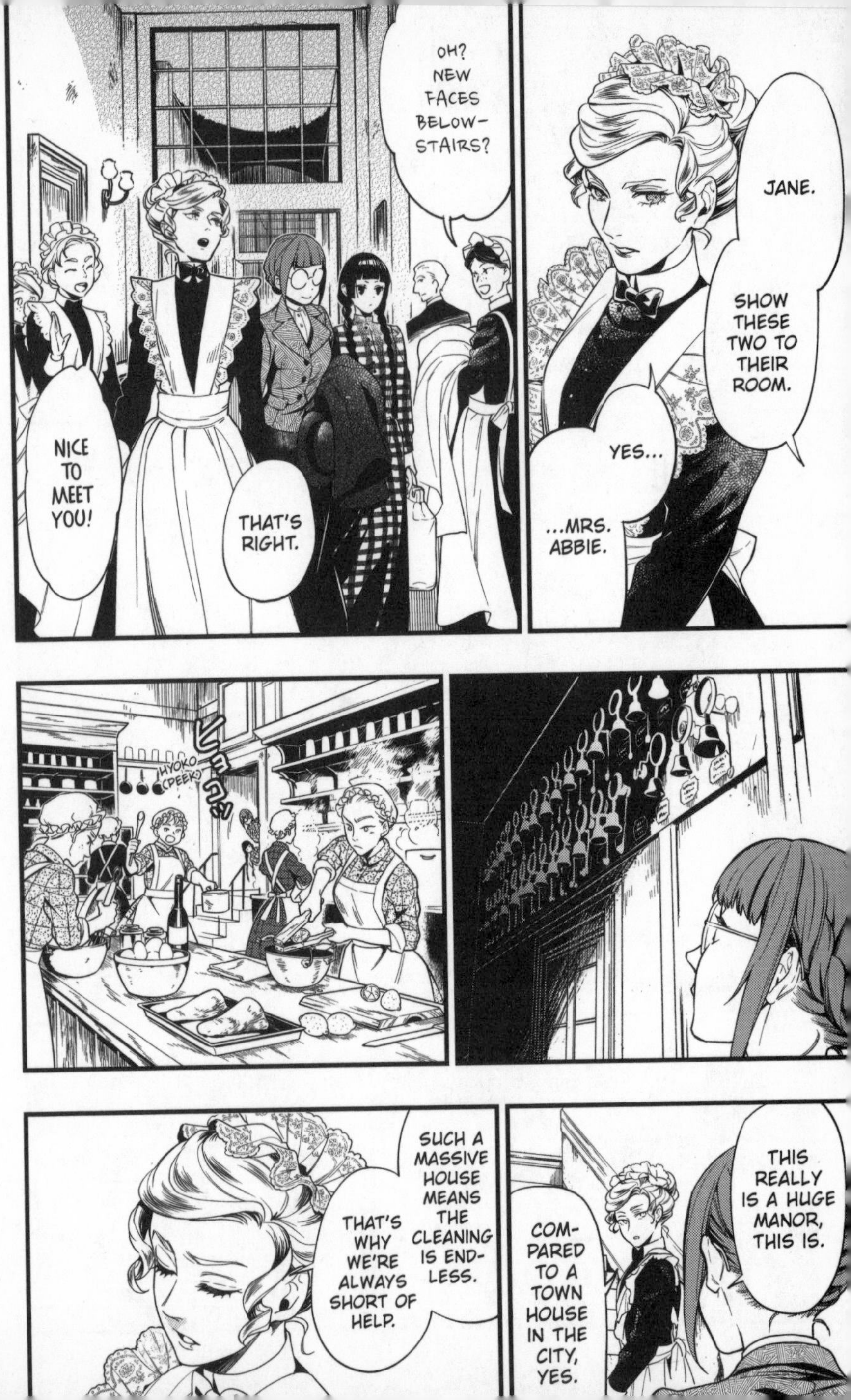
JANE.
SHOW THESE TWO TO THEIR ROOM.
YES... ...MRS. ABBIE.
OH? NEW FACES BELOW-STAIRS?
THAT'S RIGHT.
NICE TO MEET YOU!
HYOKO (PEEK)
THIS REALLY IS A HUGE MANOR, THIS IS.
COM-PARED TO A TOWN HOUSE IN THE CITY, YES.
SUCH A MASSIVE HOUSE MEANS THE CLEANING IS END-LESS.
THAT'S WHY WE'RE ALWAYS SHORT OF HELP.

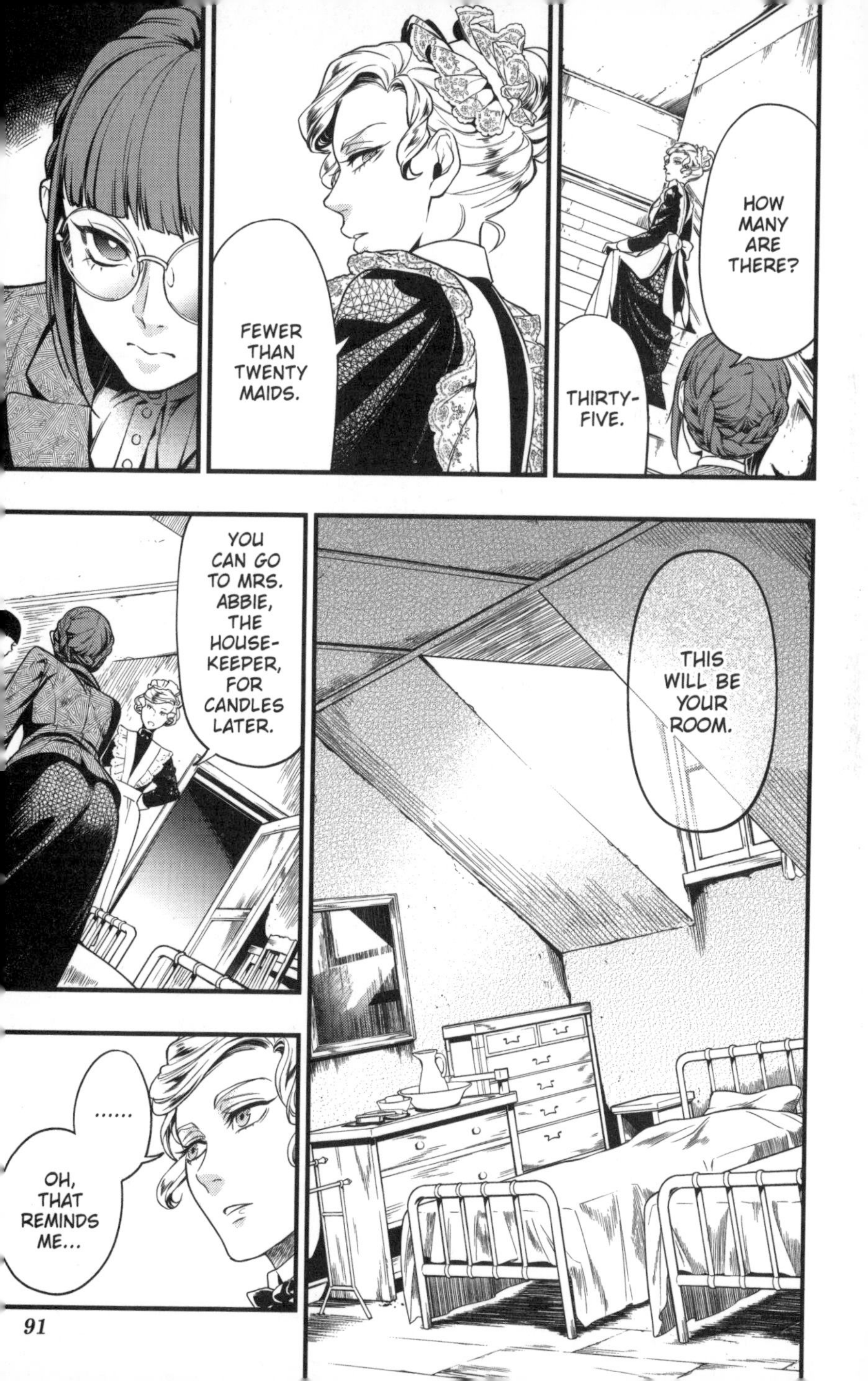
HOW MANY ARE THERE?
THIRTY-FIVE.
FEWER THAN TWENTY MAIDS.
THIS WILL BE YOUR ROOM.
YOU CAN GO TO MRS. ABBIE, THE HOUSE-KEEPER, FOR CANDLES LATER.
......
OH, THAT REMINDS ME...

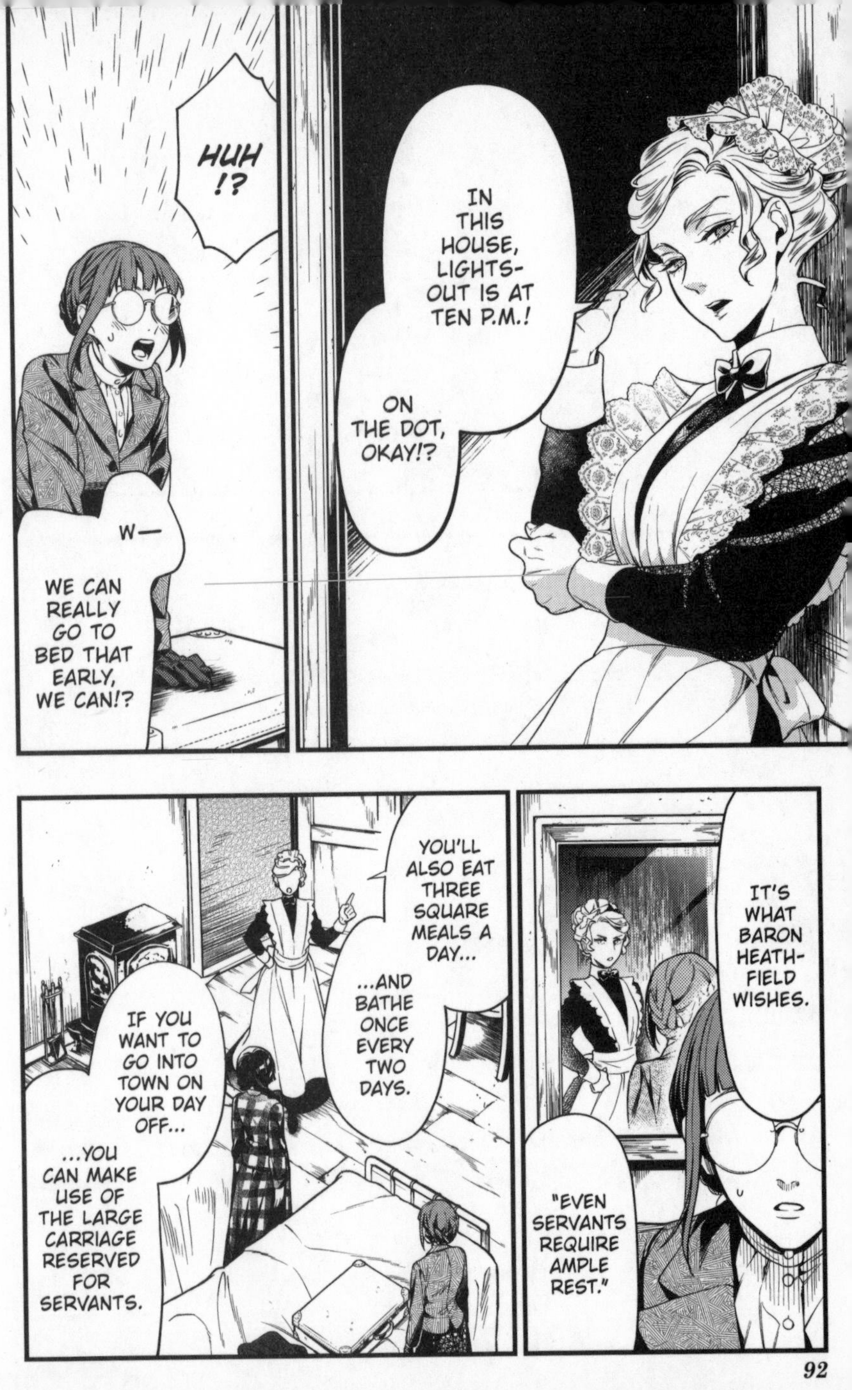
IN THIS HOUSE, LIGHTS-OUT IS AT TEN P.M.!
ON THE DOT, OKAY!?
HUH !?
W—
WE CAN REALLY GO TO BED THAT EARLY, WE CAN!?
IT'S WHAT BARON HEATHFIELD WISHES.
"EVEN SERVANTS REQUIRE AMPLE REST."
YOU'LL ALSO EAT THREE SQUARE MEALS A DAY...
...AND BATHE ONCE EVERY TWO DAYS.
IF YOU WANT TO GO INTO TOWN ON YOUR DAY OFF...
...YOU CAN MAKE USE OF THE LARGE CARRIAGE RESERVED FOR SERVANTS.

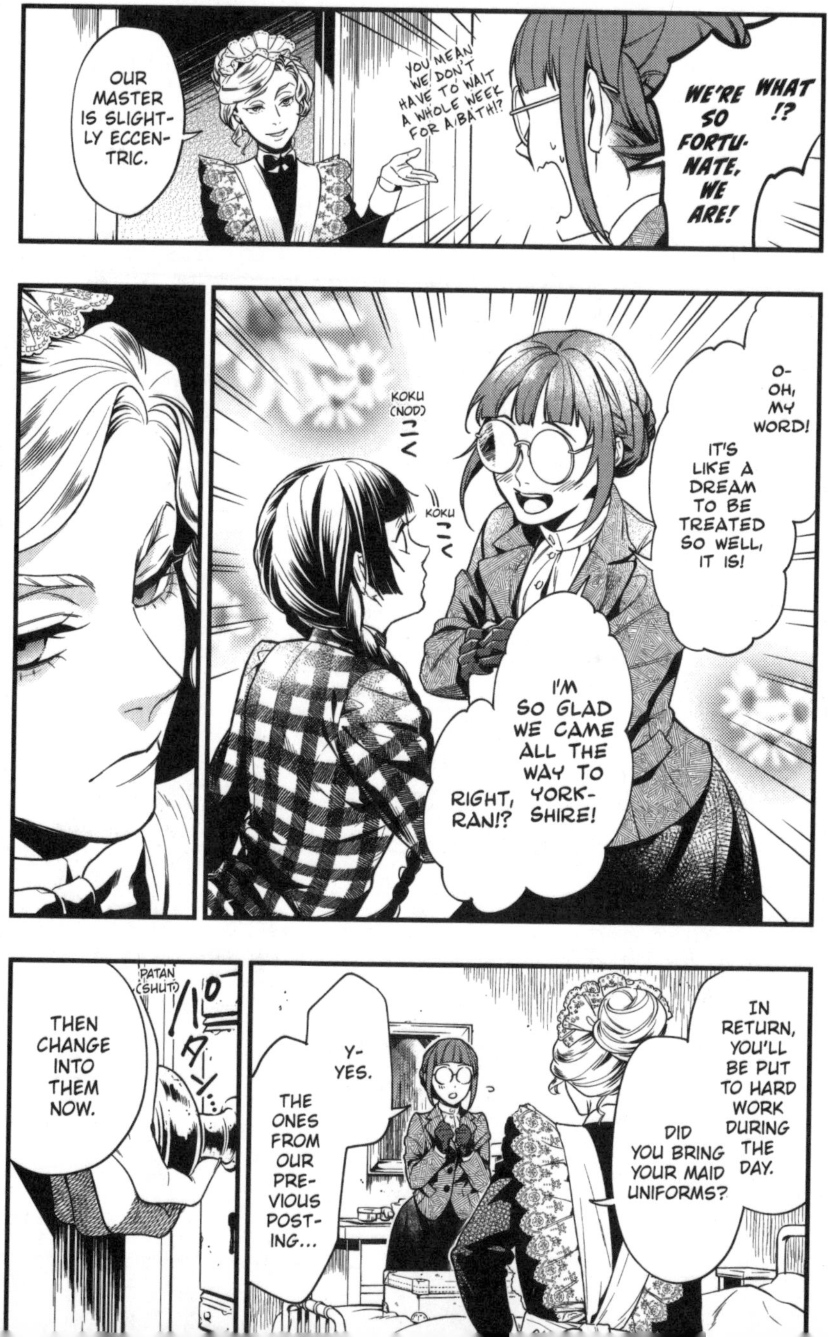
WHAT!?
WE'RE SO FORTUNATE, WE ARE!
YOU MEAN WE DON'T HAVE TO WAIT A WHOLE WEEK FOR A BATH!?
OUR MASTER IS SLIGHTLY ECCENTRIC.
O-OH, MY WORD!
IT'S LIKE A DREAM TO BE TREATED SO WELL, IT IS!
KOKU (NOD)
KOKU
I'M SO GLAD WE CAME ALL THE WAY TO YORKSHIRE!
RIGHT, RAN!?
IN RETURN, YOU'LL BE PUT TO HARD WORK DURING THE DAY.
DID YOU BRING YOUR MAID UNIFORMS?
Y-YES.
THE ONES FROM OUR PREVIOUS POSTING...
PATAN (SHUT)
THEN CHANGE INTO THEM NOW.

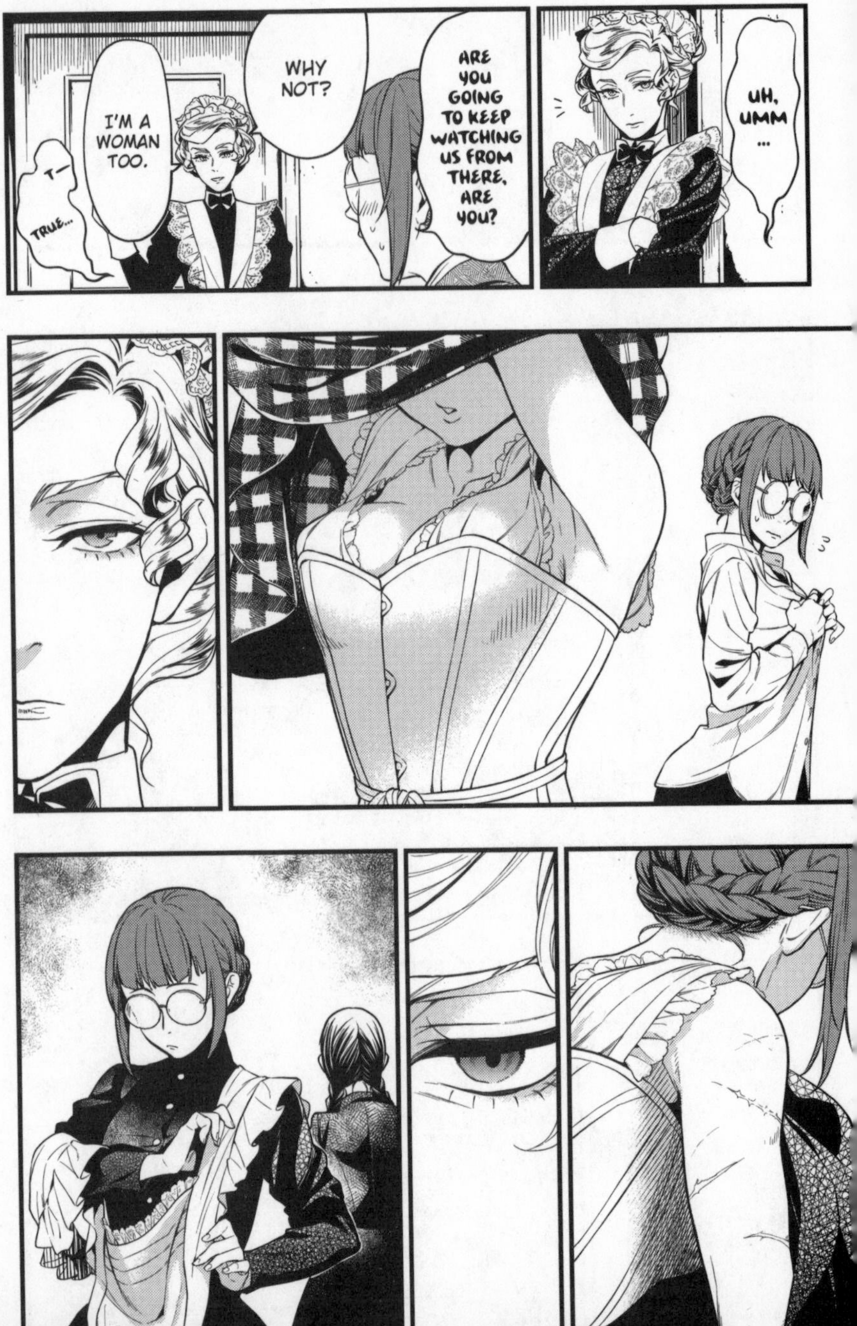
UH, UMM ...
ARE YOU GOING TO KEEP WATCHING US FROM THERE, ARE YOU?
WHY NOT?
I'M A WOMAN TOO.
T— TRUE...

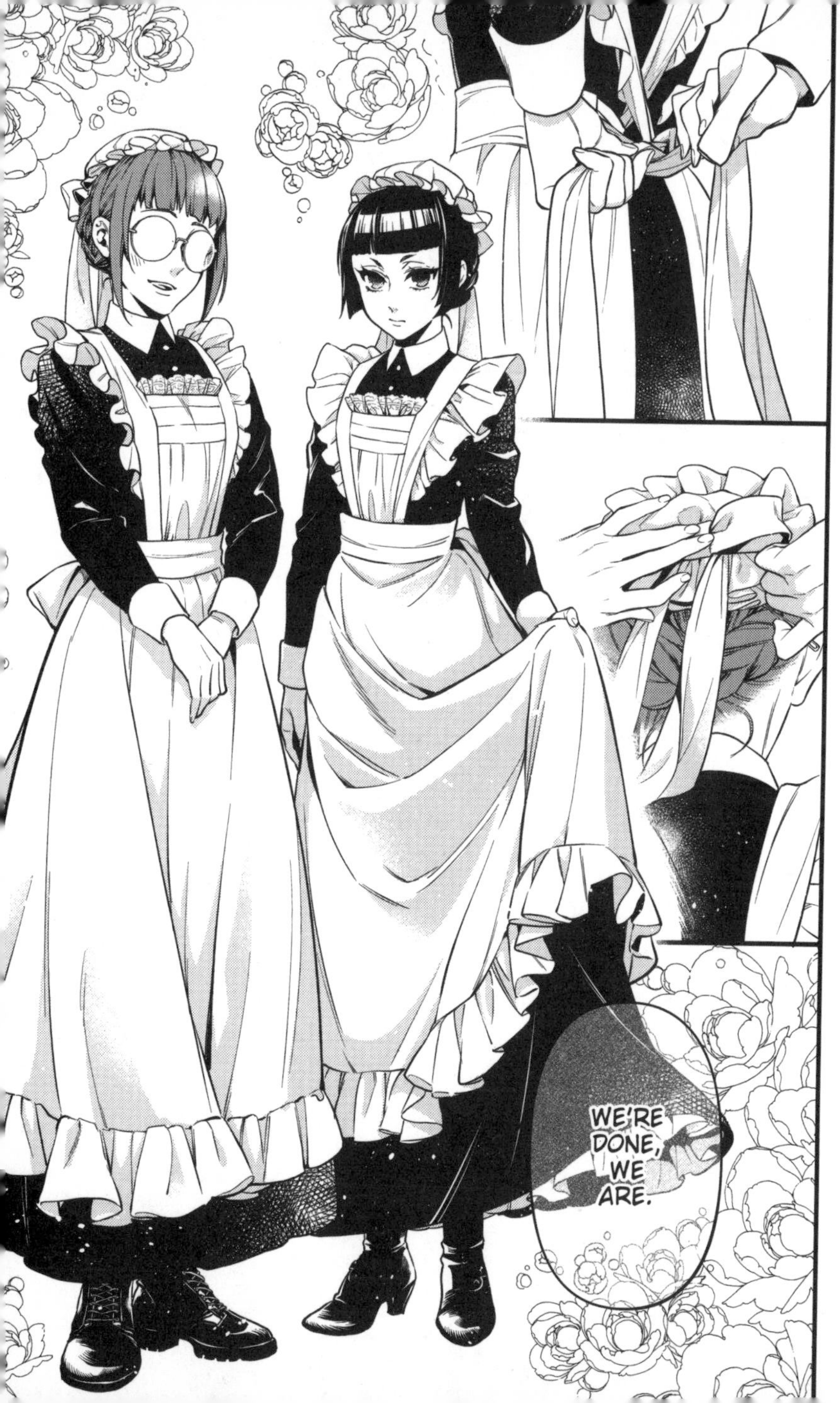
WE'RE DONE, WE ARE.

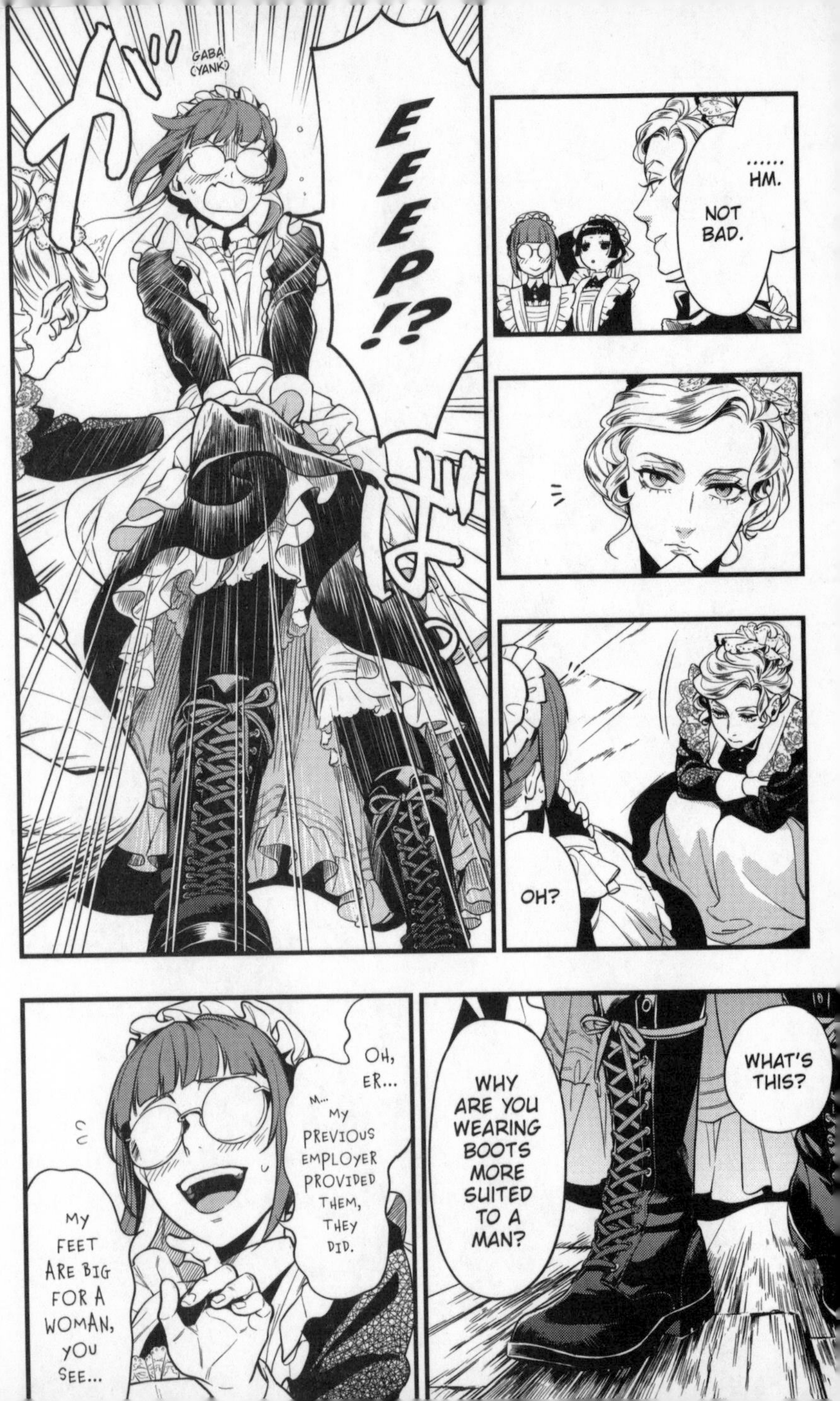

......
HM.
NOT BAD.
OH?
GABA (YANK)
EEEEP!?
WHAT'S THIS?
WHY ARE YOU WEARING BOOTS MORE SUITED TO A MAN?
OH, ER...
M... MY PREVIOUS EMPLOYER PROVIDED THEM, THEY DID.
MY FEET ARE BIG FOR A WOMAN, YOU SEE...

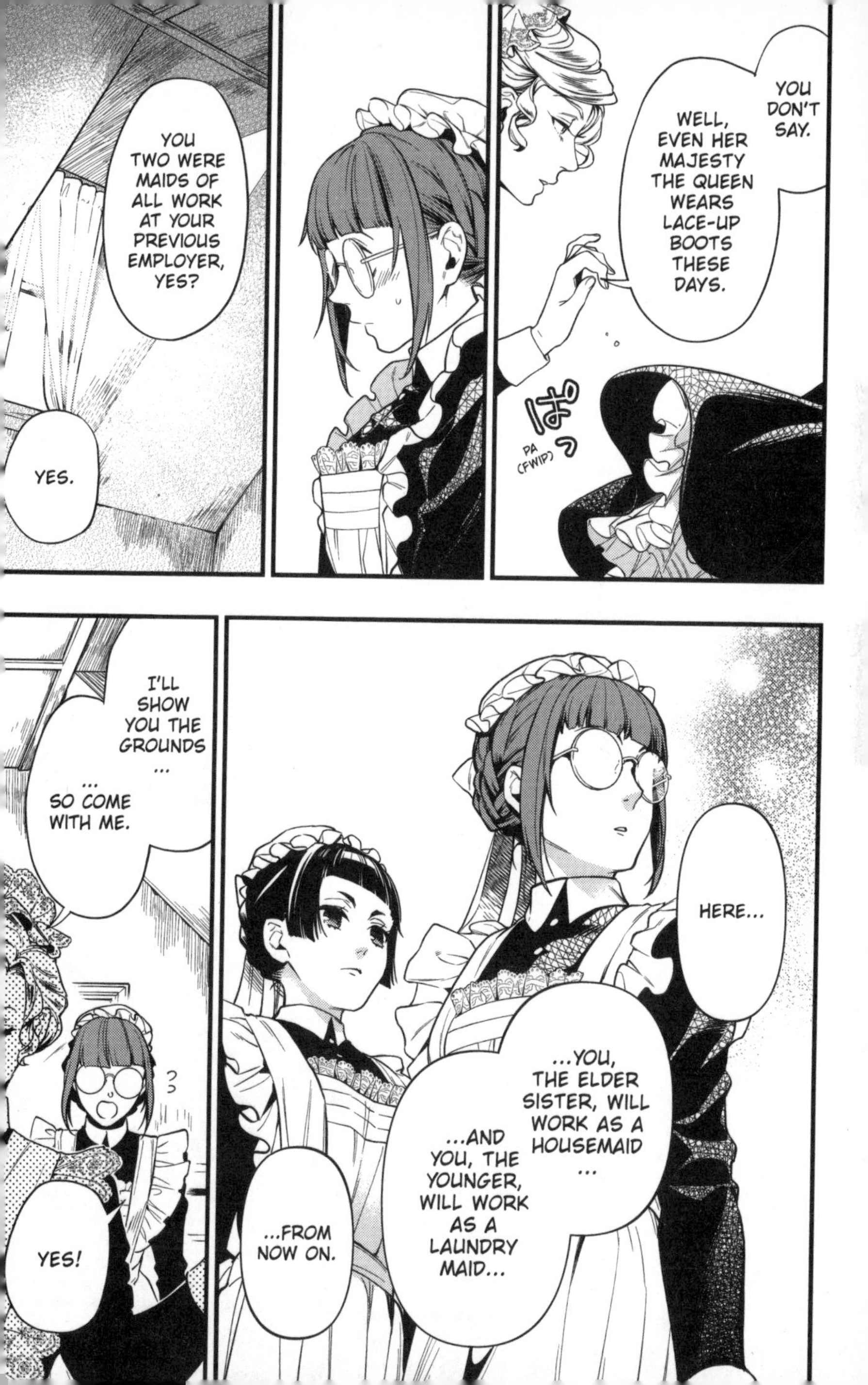
YOU DON'T SAY.
WELL, EVEN HER MAJESTY THE QUEEN WEARS LACE-UP BOOTS THESE DAYS.
ぱっ
PA (FWIP)
YOU TWO WERE MAIDS OF ALL WORK AT YOUR PREVIOUS EMPLOYER, YES?
YES.
HERE...
...YOU, THE ELDER SISTER, WILL WORK AS A HOUSEMAID...
...AND YOU, THE YOUNGER, WILL WORK AS A LAUNDRY MAID...
...FROM NOW ON.
I'LL SHOW YOU THE GROUNDS... ...SO COME WITH ME.
YES!

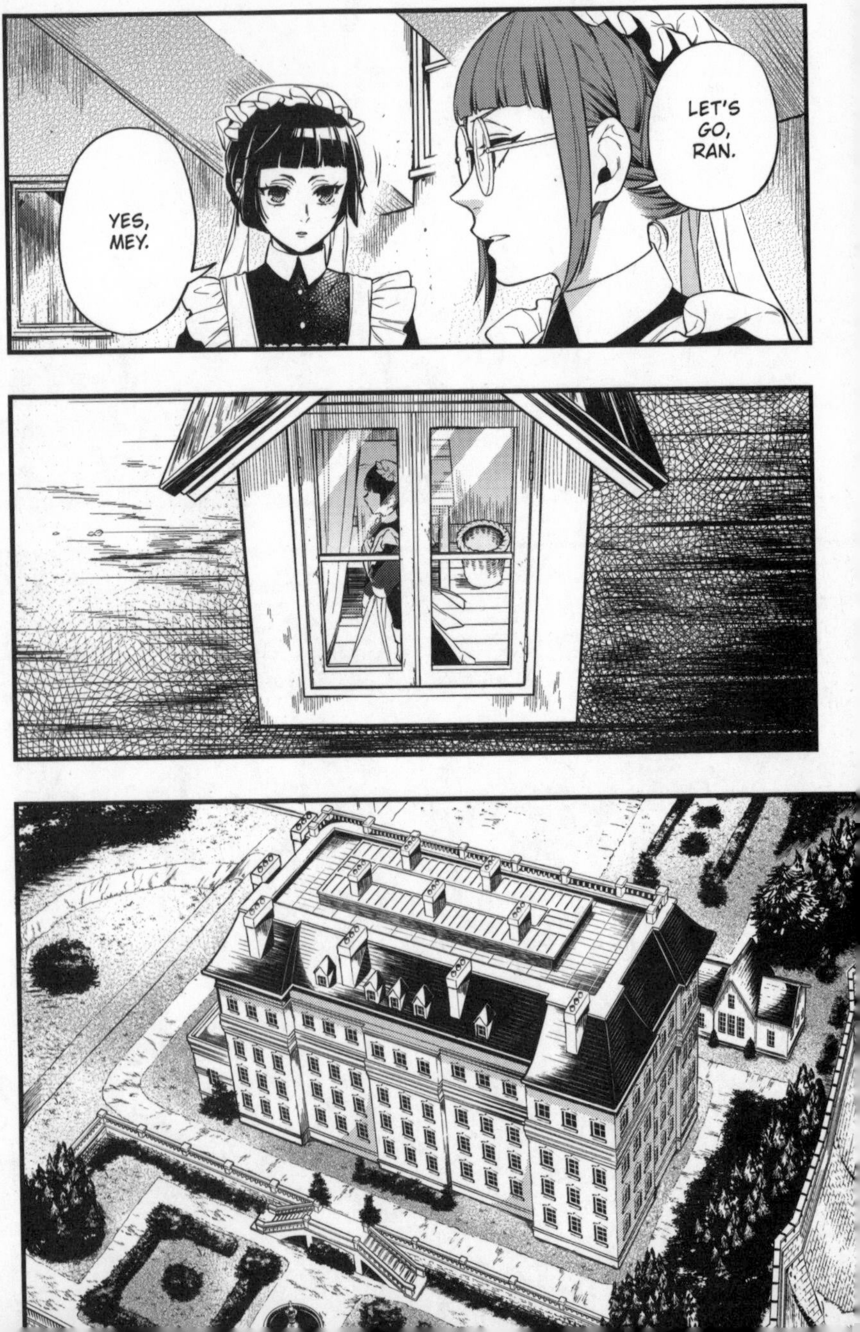
LET'S GO, RAN.
YES, MEY.

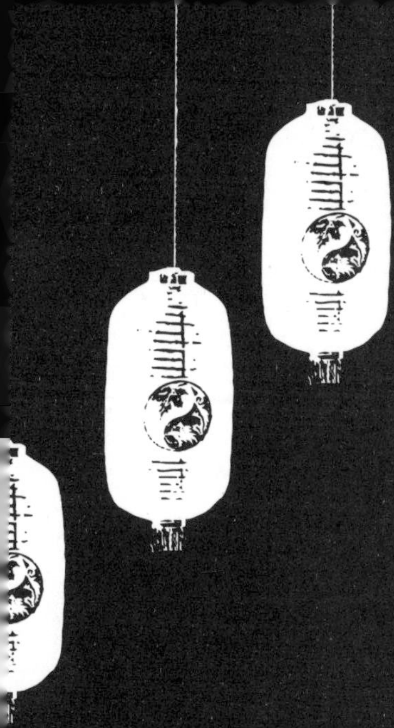

Black Butler

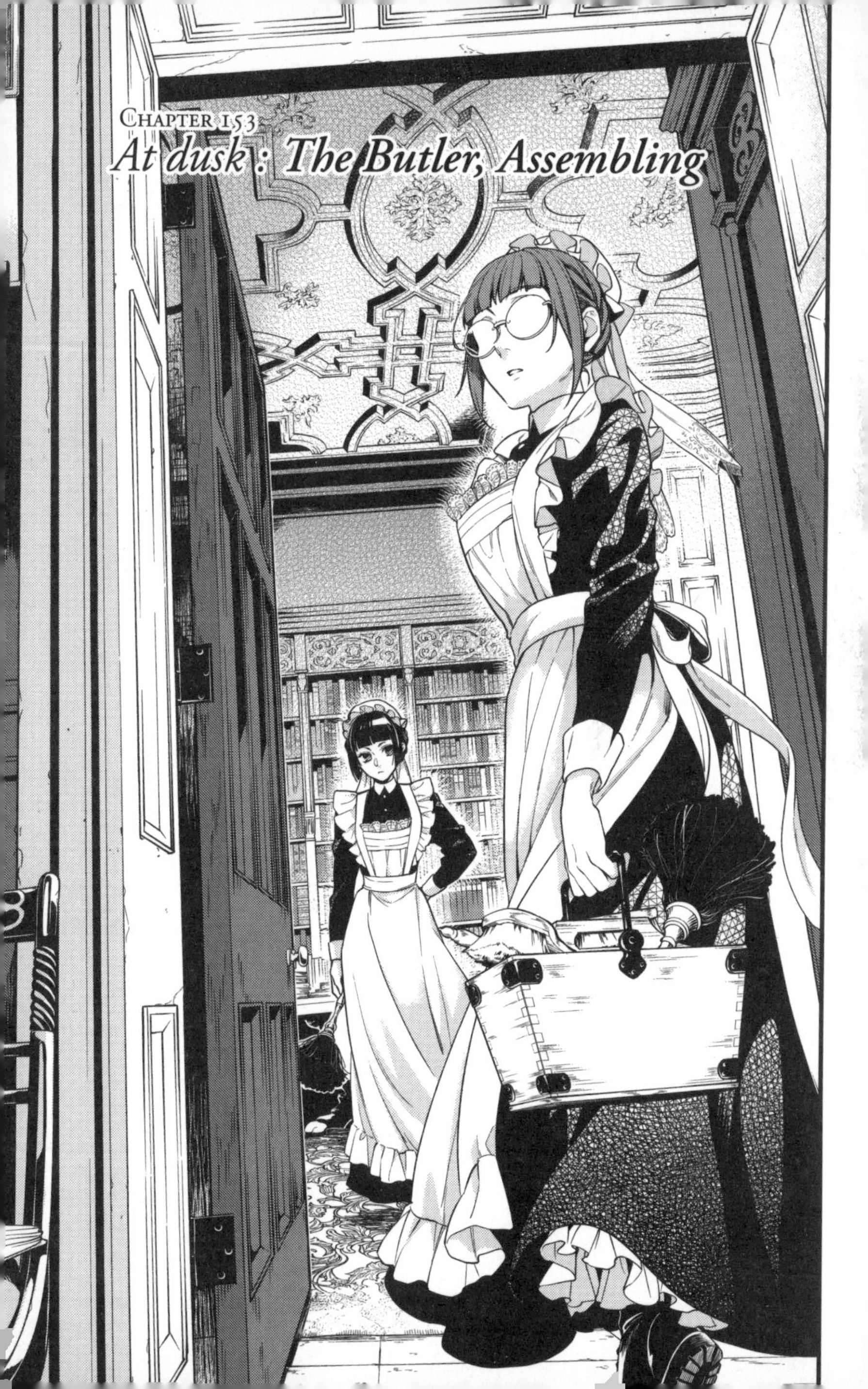
CHAPTER 153
At dusk : The Butler, Assembling

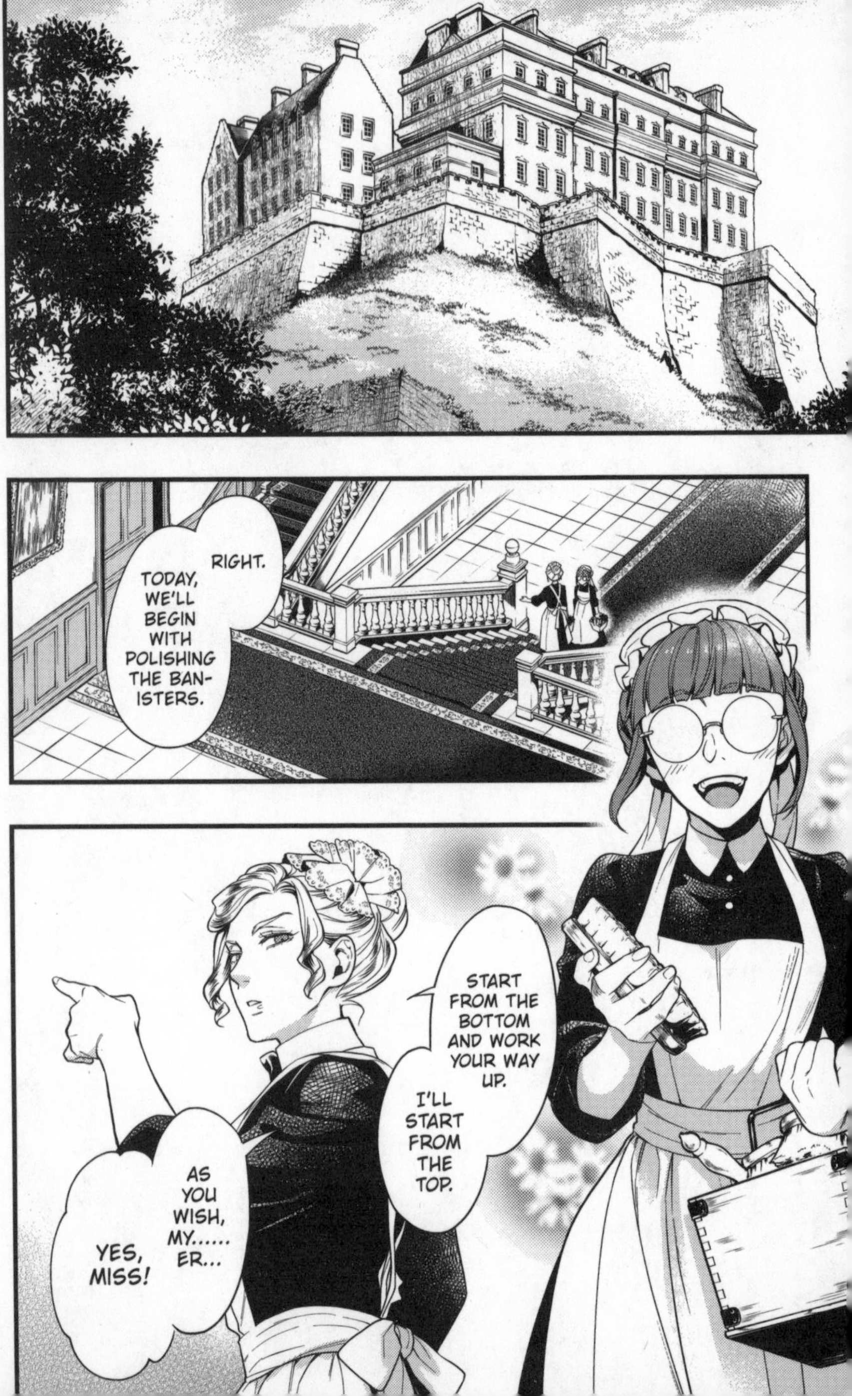
RIGHT. TODAY, WE'LL BEGIN WITH POLISHING THE BANISTERS.
START FROM THE BOTTOM AND WORK YOUR WAY UP.
I'LL START FROM THE TOP.
AS YOU WISH, MY...... ER...
YES, MISS!

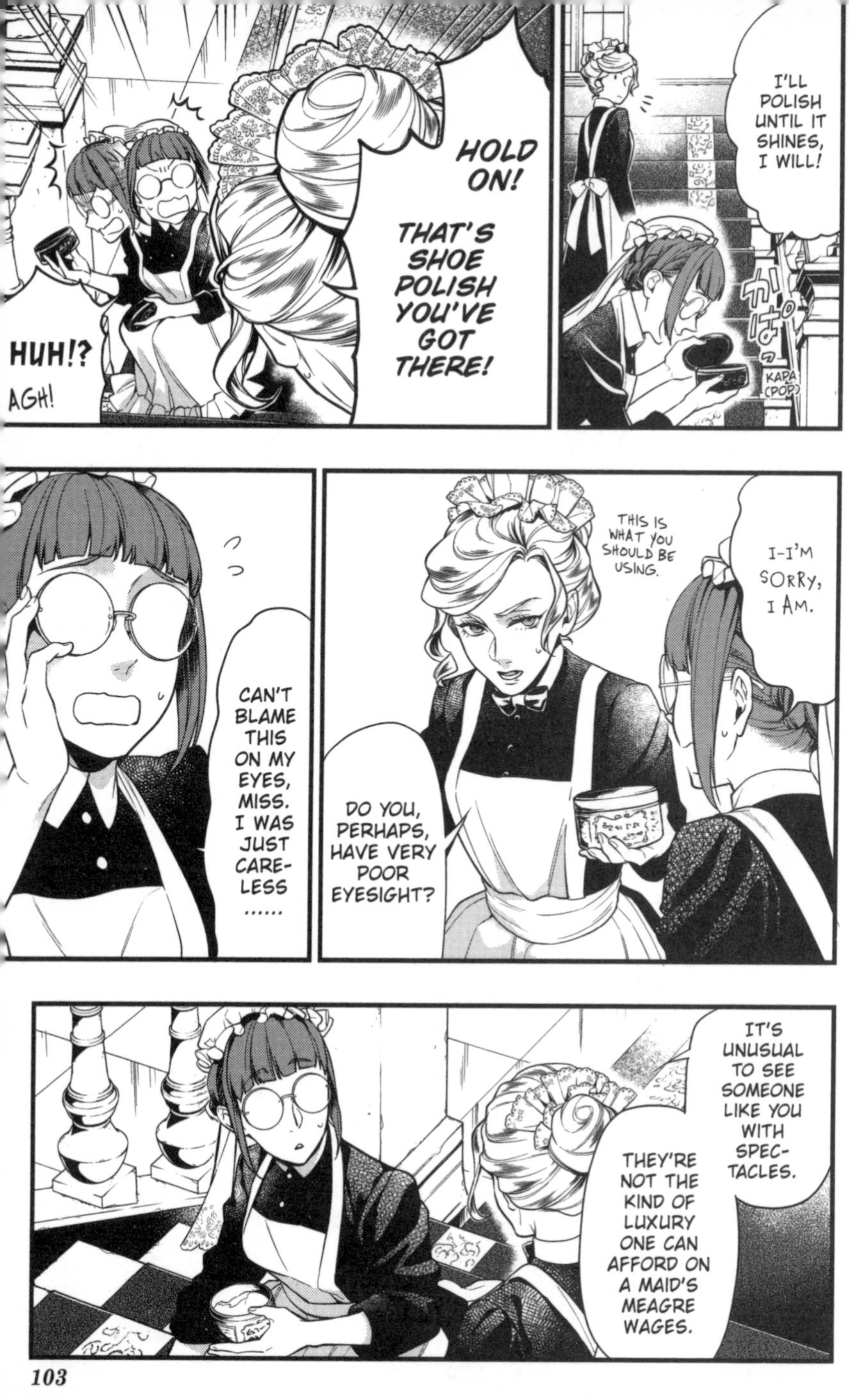
I'LL POLISH UNTIL IT SHINES, I WILL!
かぱっ
KAPA (POP)
HOLD ON!
THAT'S SHOE POLISH YOU'VE GOT THERE!
HUH!?
AGH!
I-I'M SORRY, I AM.
THIS IS WHAT YOU SHOULD BE USING.
DO YOU, PERHAPS, HAVE VERY POOR EYESIGHT?
CAN'T BLAME THIS ON MY EYES, MISS. I WAS JUST CARE-LESS ......
IT'S UNUSUAL TO SEE SOMEONE LIKE YOU WITH SPEC-TACLES.
THEY'RE NOT THE KIND OF LUXURY ONE CAN AFFORD ON A MAID'S MEAGRE WAGES.

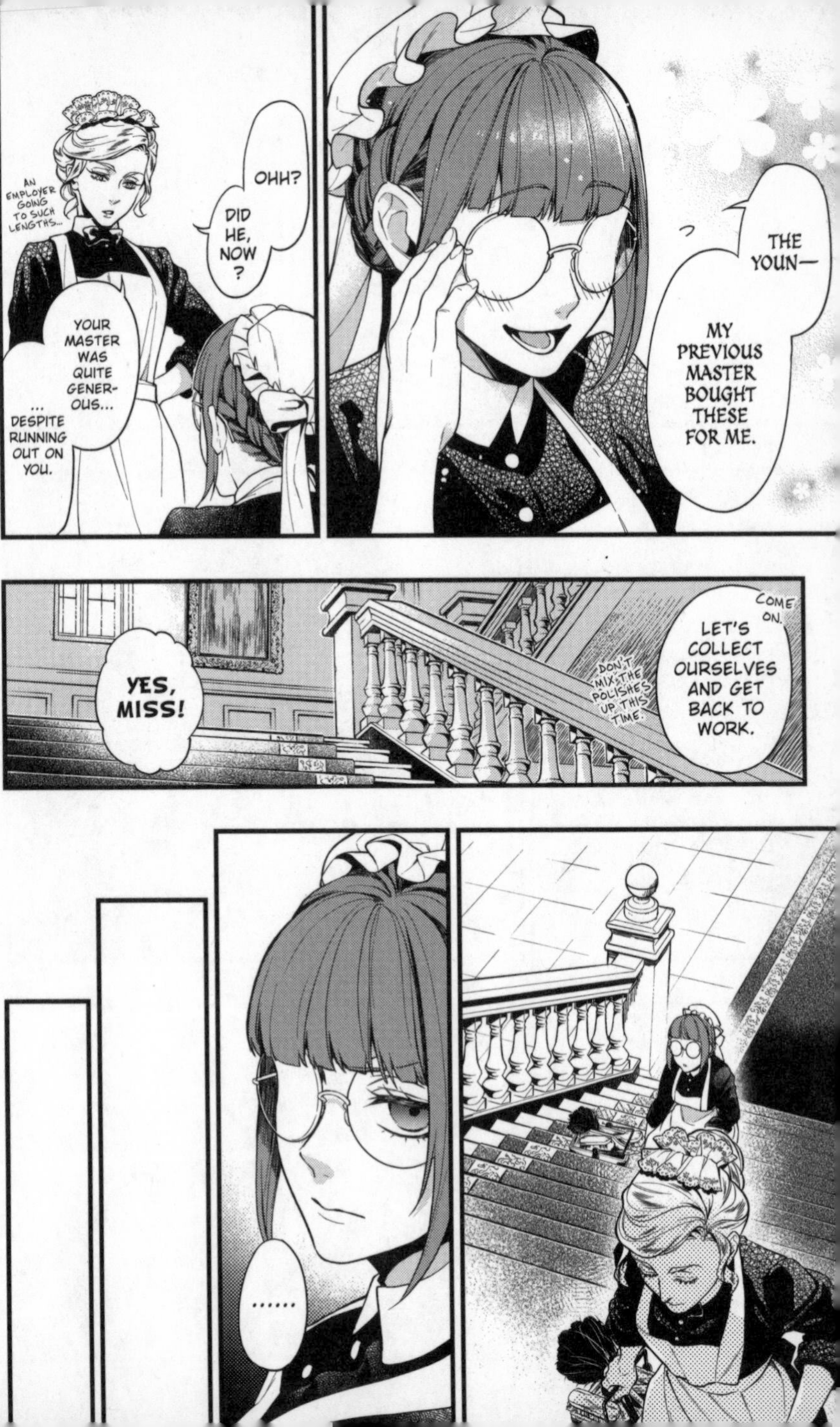
THE YOUN—
MY PREVIOUS MASTER BOUGHT THESE FOR ME.
OHH?
DID HE, NOW?
AN EMPLOYER GOING TO SUCH LENGTHS...
YOUR MASTER WAS QUITE GENEROUS...
...DESPITE RUNNING OUT ON YOU.
COME ON.
LET'S COLLECT OURSELVES AND GET BACK TO WORK.
DON'T MIX THE POLISHES UP THIS TIME.
YES, MISS!
....

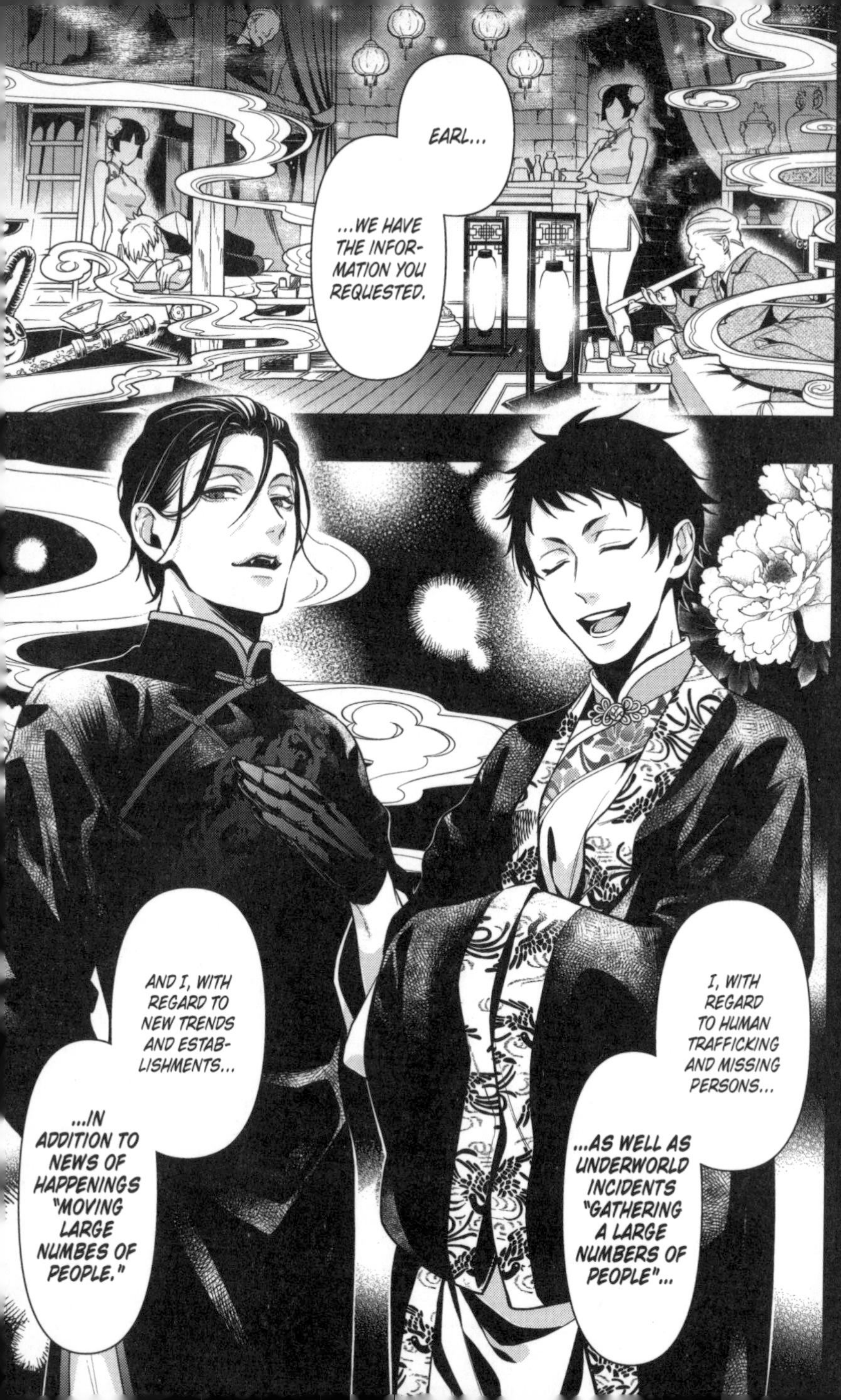
EARL...
...WE HAVE THE INFORMATION YOU REQUESTED.
I, WITH REGARD TO HUMAN TRAFFICKING AND MISSING PERSONS...
...AS WELL AS UNDERWORLD INCIDENTS "GATHERING A LARGE NUMBERS OF PEOPLE"...
AND I, WITH REGARD TO NEW TRENDS AND ESTABLISHMENTS...
...IN ADDITION TO NEWS OF HAPPENINGS "MOVING LARGE NUMBES OF PEOPLE."

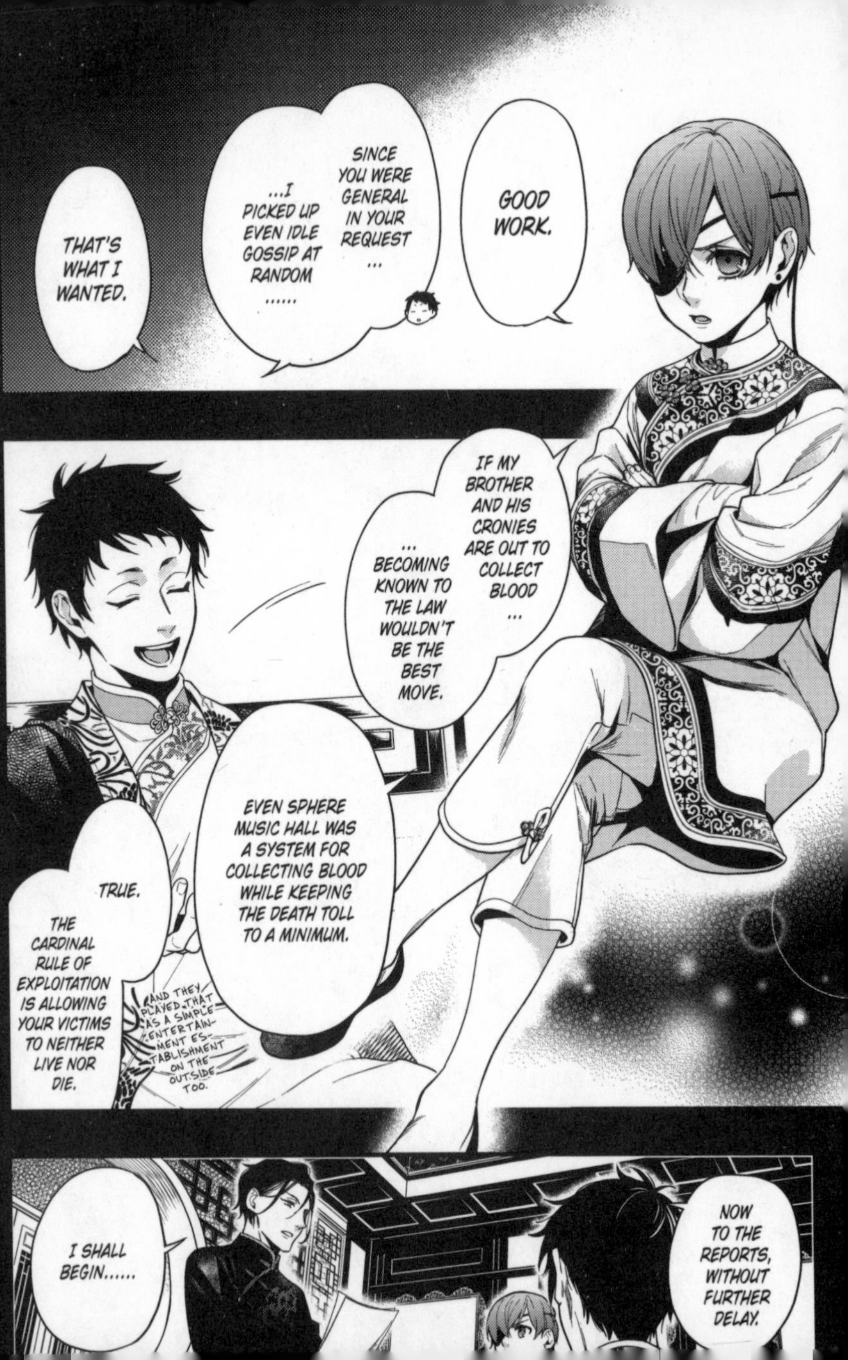
GOOD WORK.
SINCE YOU WERE GENERAL IN YOUR REQUEST...
...I PICKED UP EVEN IDLE GOSSIP AT RANDOM......
THAT'S WHAT I WANTED.
IF MY BROTHER AND HIS CRONIES ARE OUT TO COLLECT BLOOD...
...BECOMING KNOWN TO THE LAW WOULDN'T BE THE BEST MOVE.
EVEN SPHERE MUSIC HALL WAS A SYSTEM FOR COLLECTING BLOOD WHILE KEEPING THE DEATH TOLL TO A MINIMUM.
AND THEY PLAYED THAT AS A SIMPLE ENTERTAIN-MENT ES-TABLISHMENT ON THE OUTSIDE TOO.
TRUE. THE CARDINAL RULE OF EXPLOITATION IS ALLOWING YOUR VICTIMS TO NEITHER LIVE NOR DIE.
NOW TO THE REPORTS, WITHOUT FURTHER DELAY.
I SHALL BEGIN......

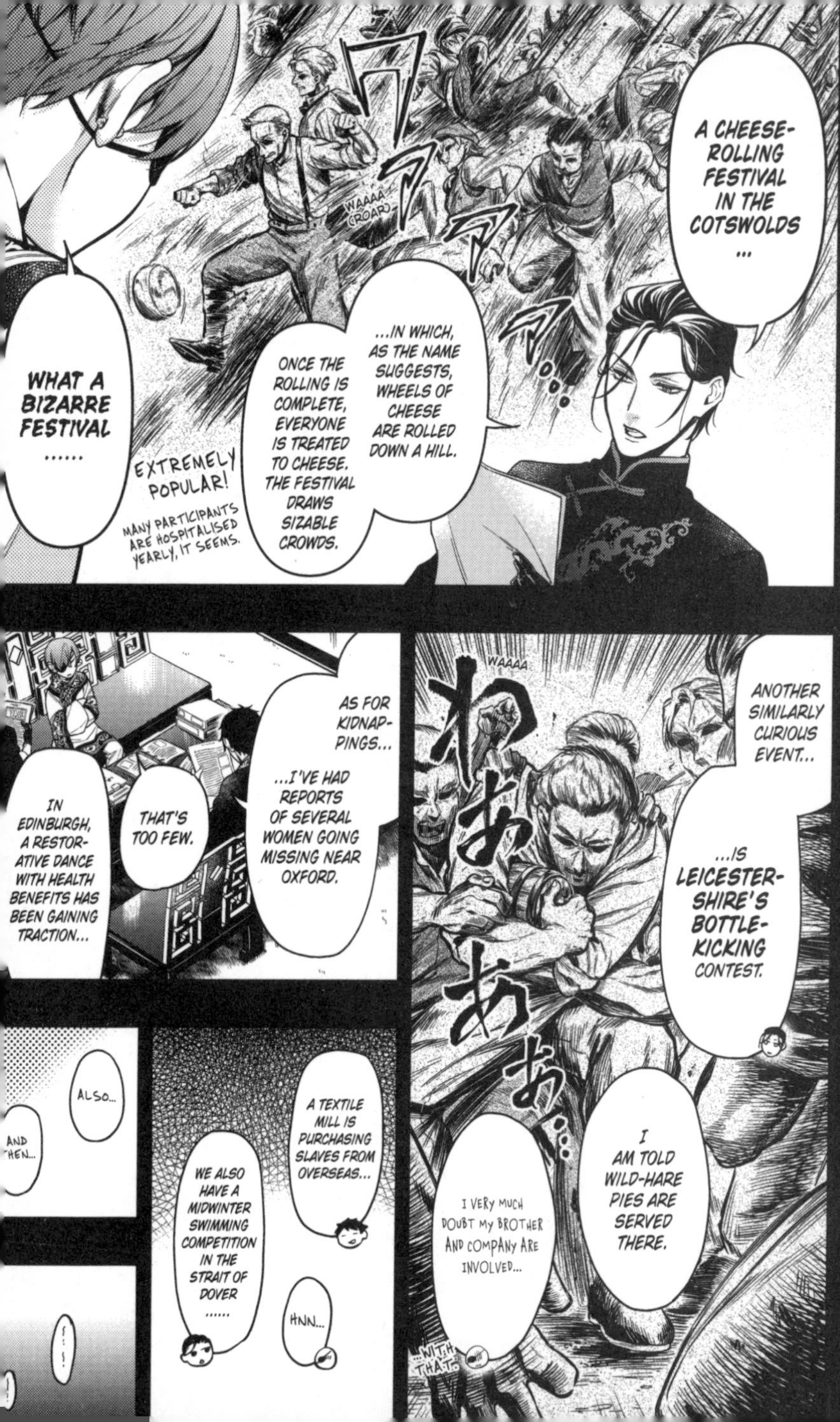
A CHEESE-ROLLING FESTIVAL IN THE COTSWOLDS ...
...IN WHICH, AS THE NAME SUGGESTS, WHEELS OF CHEESE ARE ROLLED DOWN A HILL.
ONCE THE ROLLING IS COMPLETE, EVERYONE IS TREATED TO CHEESE. THE FESTIVAL DRAWS SIZABLE CROWDS.
WAAAA (ROAR)
EXTREMELY POPULAR!
MANY PARTICIPANTS ARE HOSPITALISED YEARLY, IT SEEMS.
WHAT A BIZARRE FESTIVAL ......
ANOTHER SIMILARLY CURIOUS EVENT...
WAAAA
...IS LEICESTERSHIRE'S BOTTLE-KICKING CONTEST.
I AM TOLD WILD-HARE PIES ARE SERVED THERE.
I VERY MUCH DOUBT MY BROTHER AND COMPANY ARE INVOLVED...
...WITH THAT.
AS FOR KIDNAPPINGS...
...I'VE HAD REPORTS OF SEVERAL WOMEN GOING MISSING NEAR OXFORD.
THAT'S TOO FEW.
IN EDINBURGH, A RESTORATIVE DANCE WITH HEALTH BENEFITS HAS BEEN GAINING TRACTION...
A TEXTILE MILL IS PURCHASING SLAVES FROM OVERSEAS...
WE ALSO HAVE A MIDWINTER SWIMMING COMPETITION IN THE STRAIT OF DOVER ......
HNN...
ALSO...
AND THEN...

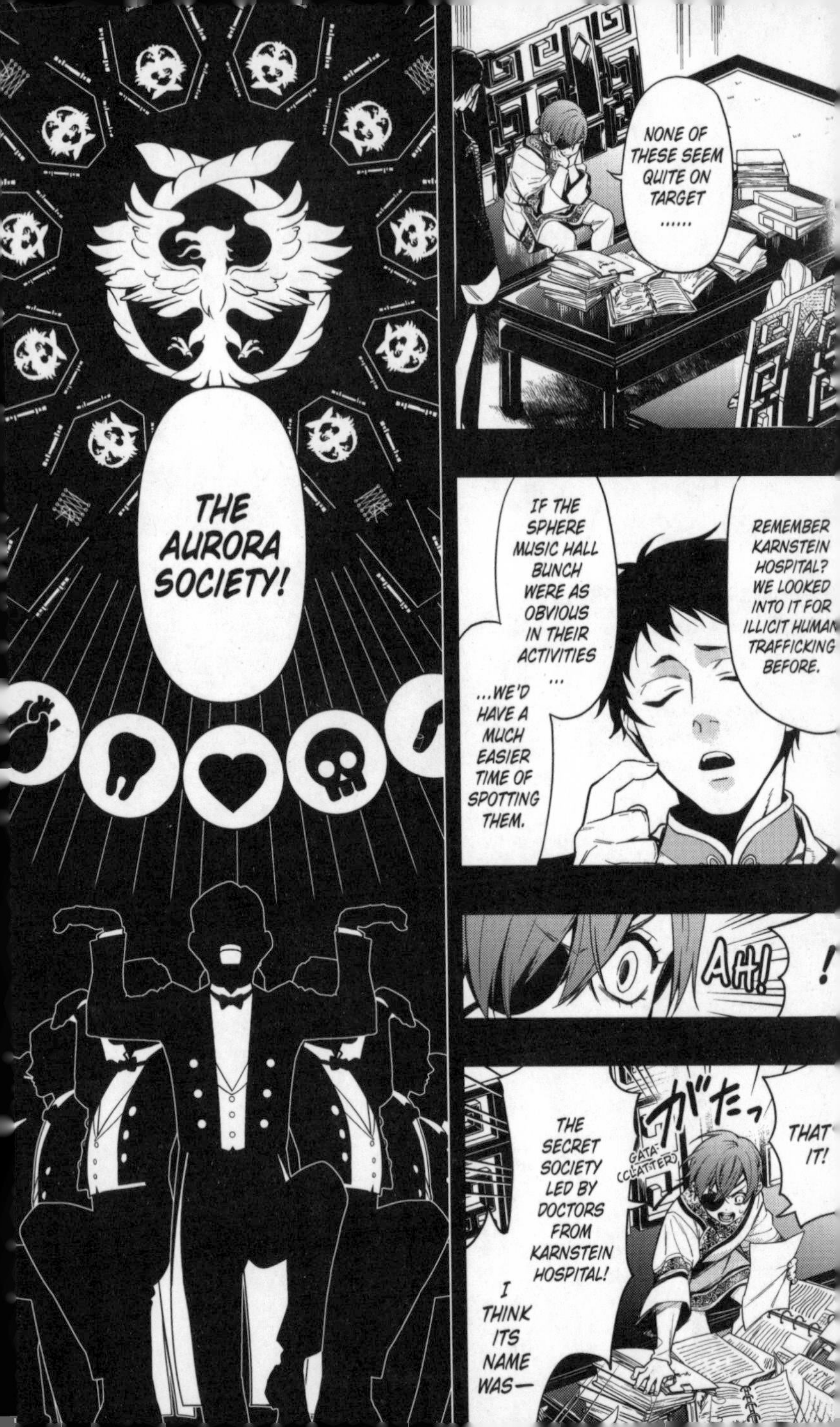
NONE OF THESE SEEM QUITE ON TARGET ......
REMEMBER KARNSTEIN HOSPITAL? WE LOOKED INTO IT FOR ILLICIT HUMAN TRAFFICKING BEFORE.
IF THE SPHERE MUSIC HALL BUNCH WERE AS OBVIOUS IN THEIR ACTIVITIES ...
...WE'D HAVE A MUCH EASIER TIME OF SPOTTING THEM.
AH!
!
がたっ
GATA (CLATTER)
THAT IT!
THE SECRET SOCIETY LED BY DOCTORS FROM KARNSTEIN HOSPITAL!
I THINK ITS NAME WAS—
THE AURORA SOCIETY!

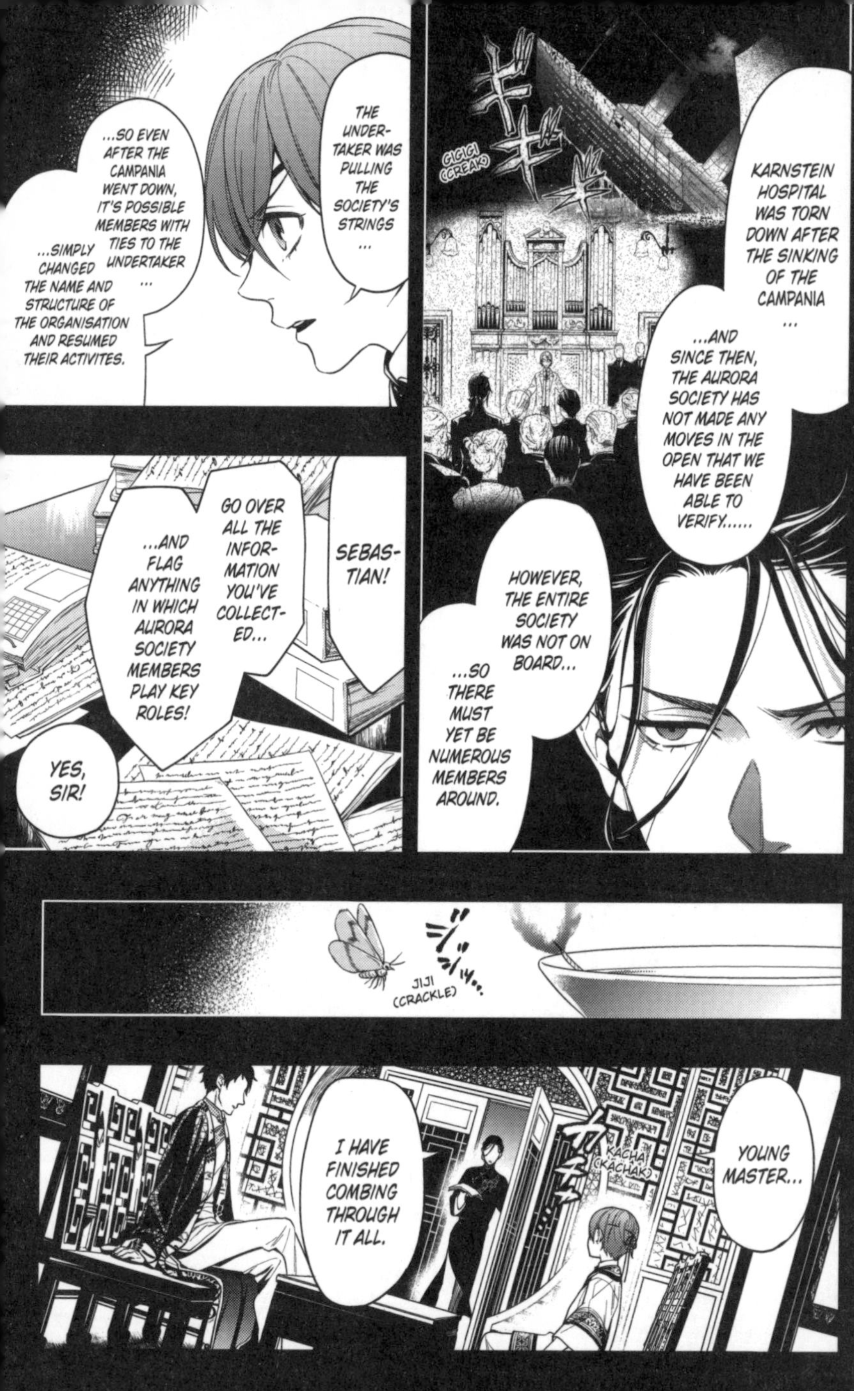

GIGIGI (CREAK)
KARNSTEIN HOSPITAL WAS TORN DOWN AFTER THE SINKING OF THE CAMPANIA...
...AND SINCE THEN, THE AURORA SOCIETY HAS NOT MADE ANY MOVES IN THE OPEN THAT WE HAVE BEEN ABLE TO VERIFY......
HOWEVER, THE ENTIRE SOCIETY WAS NOT ON BOARD...
...SO THERE MUST YET BE NUMEROUS MEMBERS AROUND.
THE UNDER-TAKER WAS PULLING THE SOCIETY'S STRINGS...
...SO EVEN AFTER THE CAMPANIA WENT DOWN, IT'S POSSIBLE MEMBERS WITH TIES TO THE UNDERTAKER...
...SIMPLY CHANGED THE NAME AND STRUCTURE OF THE ORGANISATION AND RESUMED THEIR ACTIVITES.
SEBAS-TIAN!
GO OVER ALL THE INFOR-MATION YOU'VE COLLECT-ED...
...AND FLAG ANYTHING IN WHICH AURORA SOCIETY MEMBERS PLAY KEY ROLES!
YES, SIR!
JIJI (CRACKLE)
YOUNG MASTER...
KACHA (KACHAK)
I HAVE FINISHED COMBING THROUGH IT ALL.

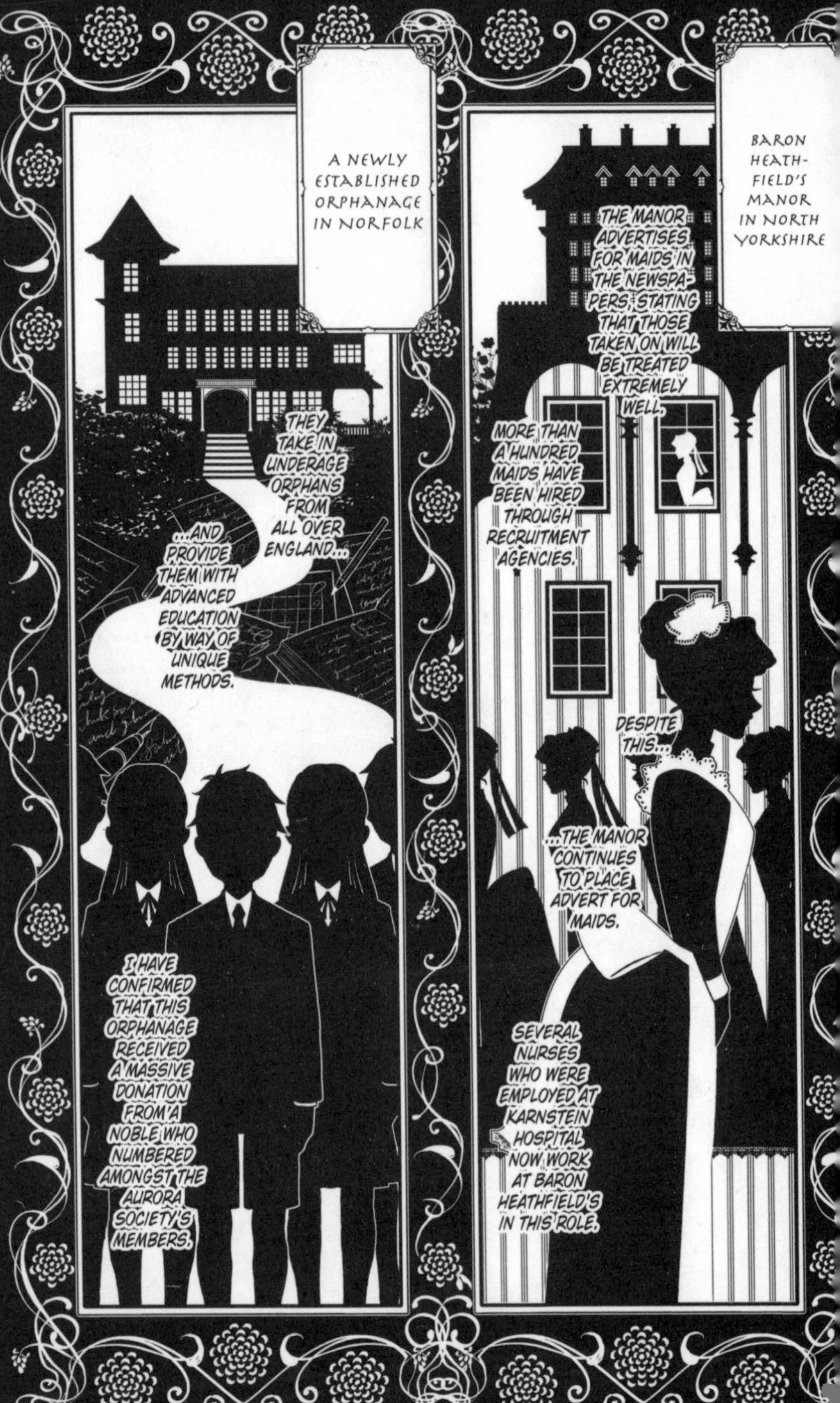
BARON HEATHFIELD'S MANOR IN NORTH YORKSHIRE
THE MANOR ADVERTISES FOR MAIDS IN THE NEWSPAPERS, STATING THAT THOSE TAKEN ON WILL BE TREATED EXTREMELY WELL.
MORE THAN A HUNDRED MAIDS HAVE BEEN HIRED THROUGH RECRUITMENT AGENCIES.
DESPITE THIS...
...THE MANOR CONTINUES TO PLACE ADVERT FOR MAIDS.
SEVERAL NURSES WHO WERE EMPLOYED AT KARNSTEIN HOSPITAL NOW WORK AT BARON HEATHFIELD'S IN THIS ROLE.
A NEWLY ESTABLISHED ORPHANAGE IN NORFOLK
THEY TAKE IN UNDERAGE ORPHANS FROM ALL OVER ENGLAND...
...AND PROVIDE THEM WITH ADVANCED EDUCATION BY WAY OF UNIQUE METHODS.
I HAVE CONFIRMED THAT THIS ORPHANAGE RECEIVED A MASSIVE DONATION FROM A NOBLE WHO NUMBERED AMONGST THE AURORA SOCIETY'S MEMBERS.

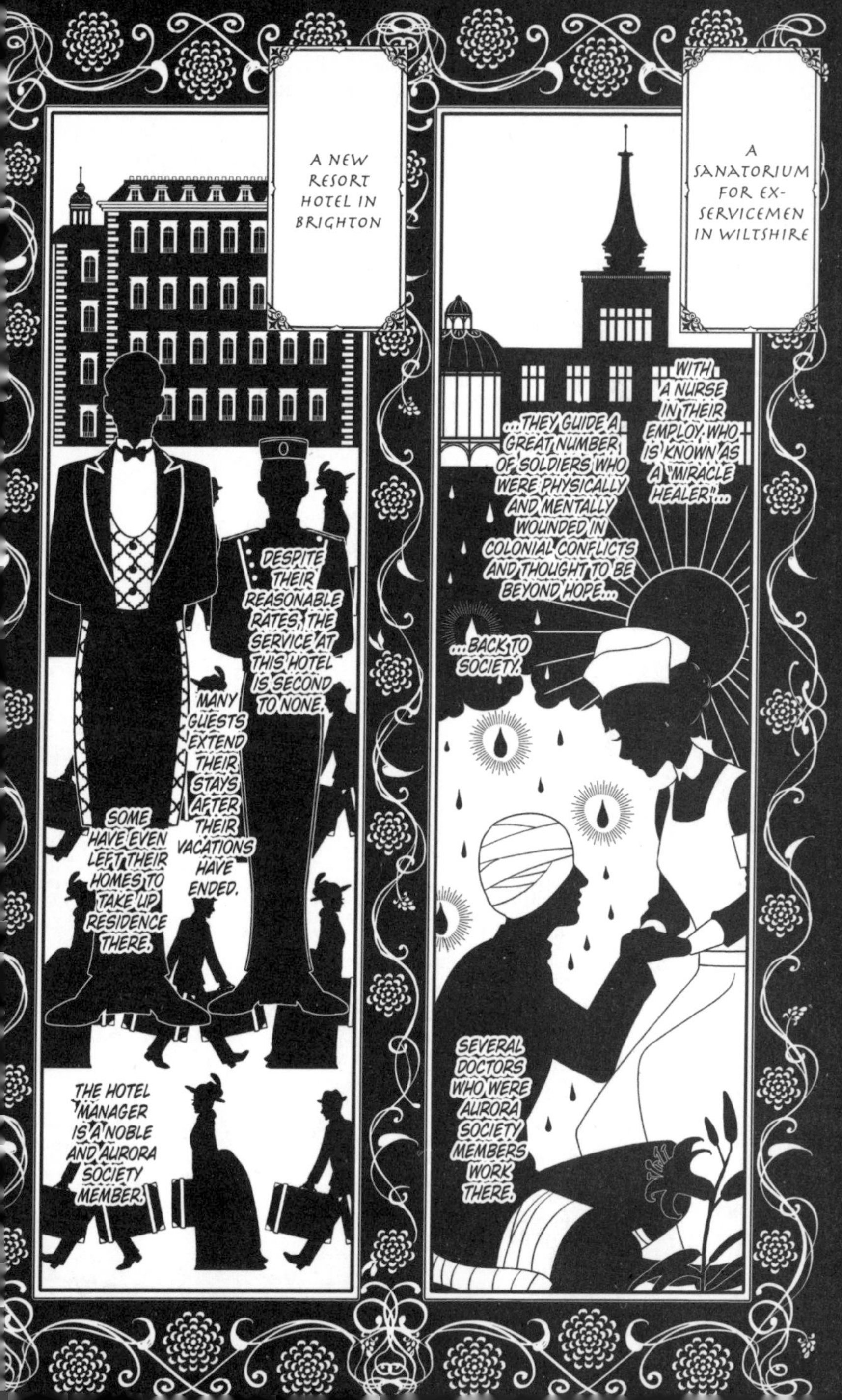
A SANATORIUM FOR EX-SERVICEMEN IN WILTSHIRE
WITH A NURSE IN THEIR EMPLOY WHO IS KNOWN AS A "MIRACLE HEALER"...
...THEY GUIDE A GREAT NUMBER OF SOLDIERS WHO WERE PHYSICALLY AND MENTALLY WOUNDED IN COLONIAL CONFLICTS AND THOUGHT TO BE BEYOND HOPE...
...BACK TO SOCIETY.
SEVERAL DOCTORS WHO WERE AURORA SOCIETY MEMBERS WORK THERE.
A NEW RESORT HOTEL IN BRIGHTON
DESPITE THEIR REASONABLE RATES, THE SERVICE AT THIS HOTEL IS SECOND TO NONE.
MANY GUESTS EXTEND THEIR STAYS AFTER THEIR VACATIONS HAVE ENDED.
SOME HAVE EVEN LEFT THEIR HOMES TO TAKE UP RESIDENCE THERE.
THE HOTEL MANAGER IS A NOBLE AND AURORA SOCIETY MEMBER.

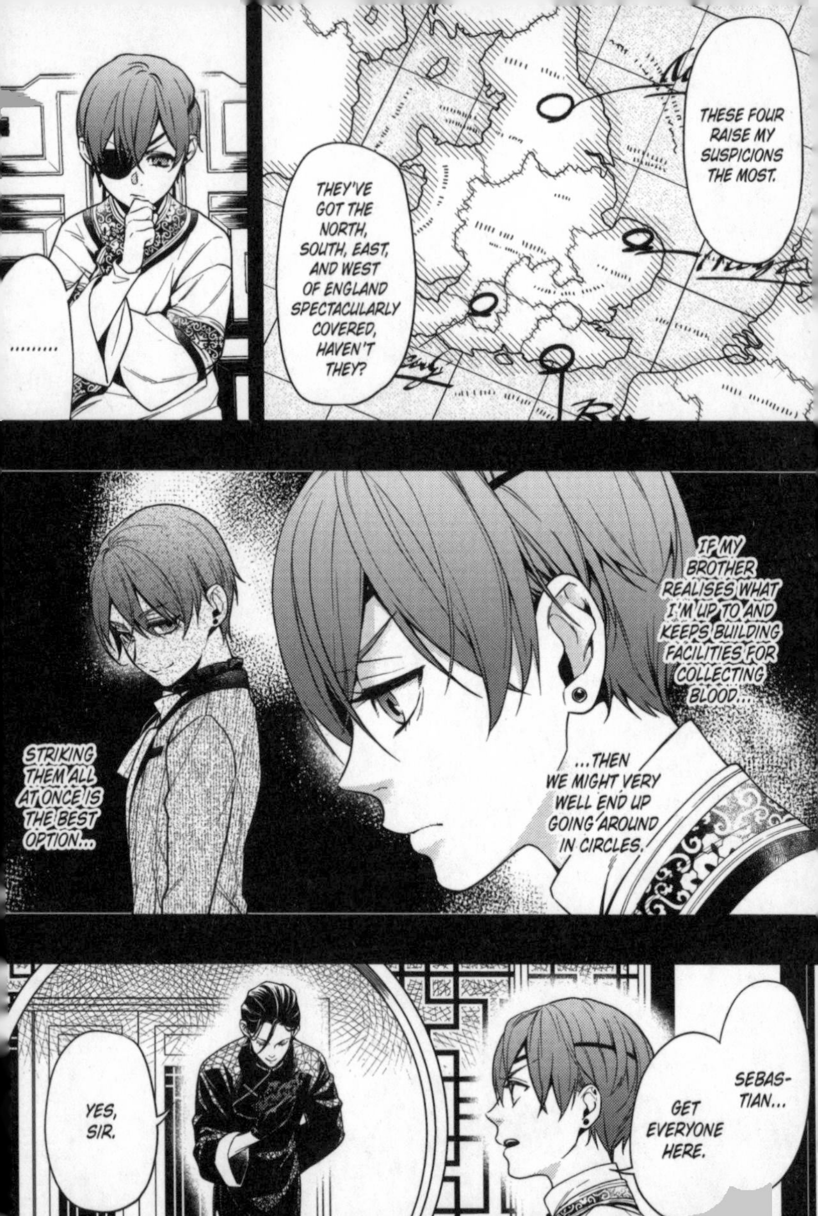
THESE FOUR RAISE MY SUSPICIONS THE MOST.
THEY'VE GOT THE NORTH, SOUTH, EAST, AND WEST OF ENGLAND SPECTACULARLY COVERED, HAVEN'T THEY?
....
IF MY BROTHER REALISES WHAT I'M UP TO AND KEEPS BUILDING FACILITIES FOR COLLECTING BLOOD...
...THEN WE MIGHT VERY WELL END UP GOING AROUND IN CIRCLES.
STRIKING THEM ALL AT ONCE IS THE BEST OPTION...
SEBAS-TIAN...
GET EVERYONE HERE.
YES, SIR.

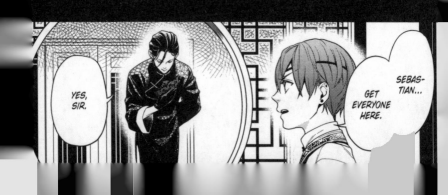

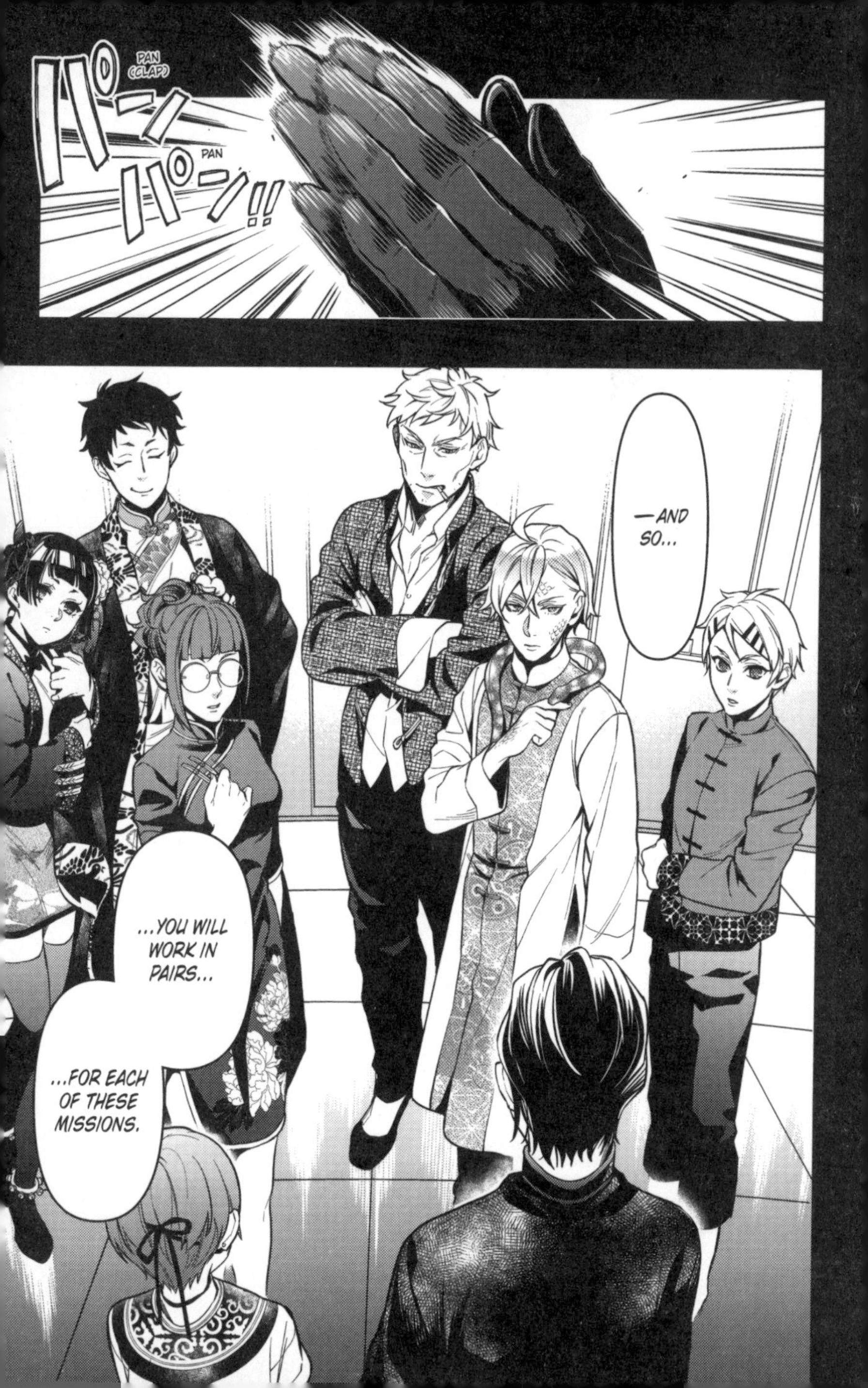
PAN (CLAP)
PAN
—AND SO...
...YOU WILL WORK IN PAIRS...
...FOR EACH OF THESE MISSIONS.

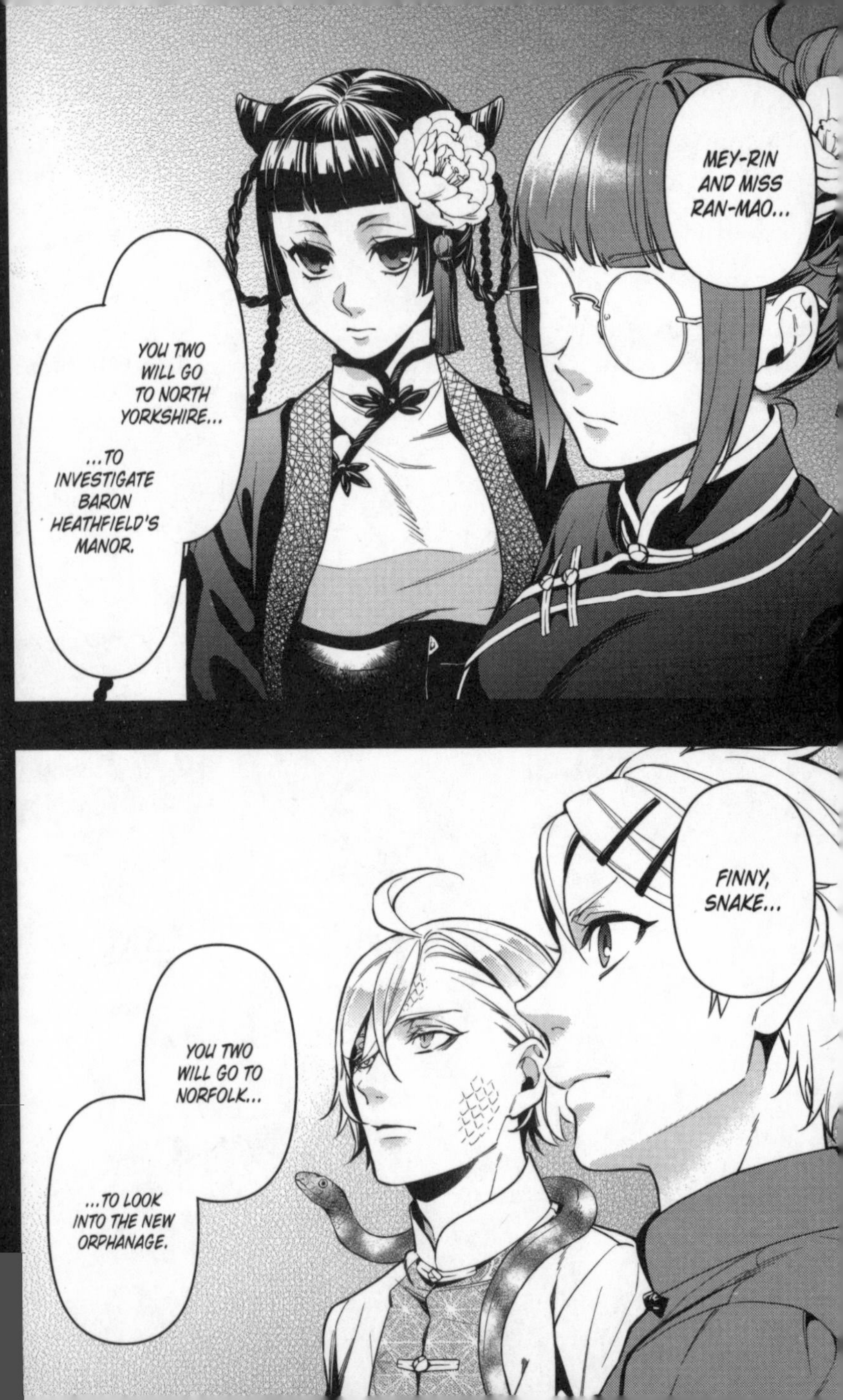
MEY-RIN AND MISS RAN-MAO...
YOU TWO WILL GO TO NORTH YORKSHIRE...
...TO INVESTIGATE BARON HEATHFIELD'S MANOR.
FINNY, SNAKE...
YOU TWO WILL GO TO NORFOLK...
...TO LOOK INTO THE NEW ORPHANAGE.

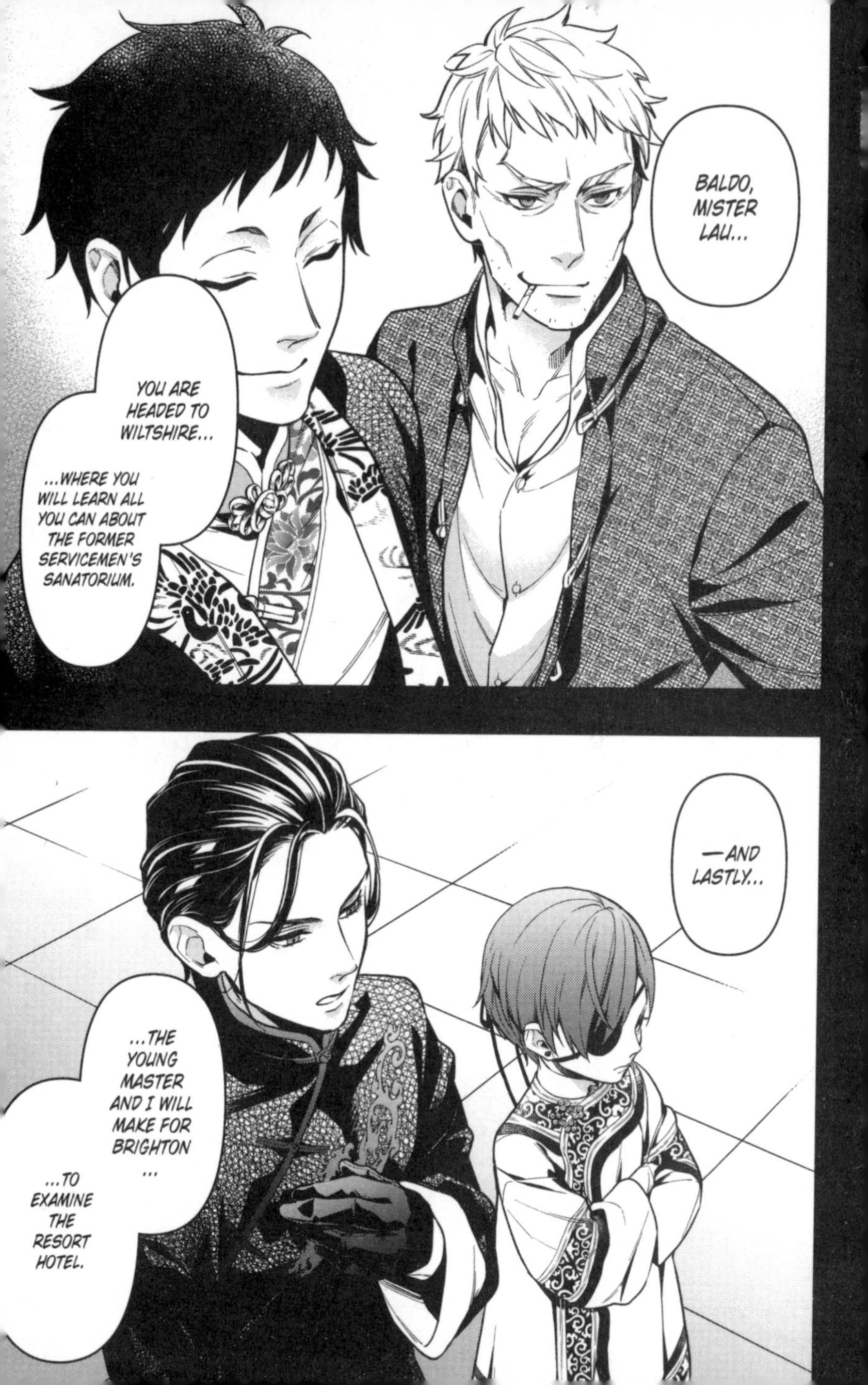
BALDO, MISTER LAU...
YOU ARE HEADED TO WILTSHIRE...
...WHERE YOU WILL LEARN ALL YOU CAN ABOUT THE FORMER SERVICEMEN'S SANATORIUM.
—AND LASTLY...
...THE YOUNG MASTER AND I WILL MAKE FOR BRIGHTON ...
...TO EXAMINE THE RESORT HOTEL.

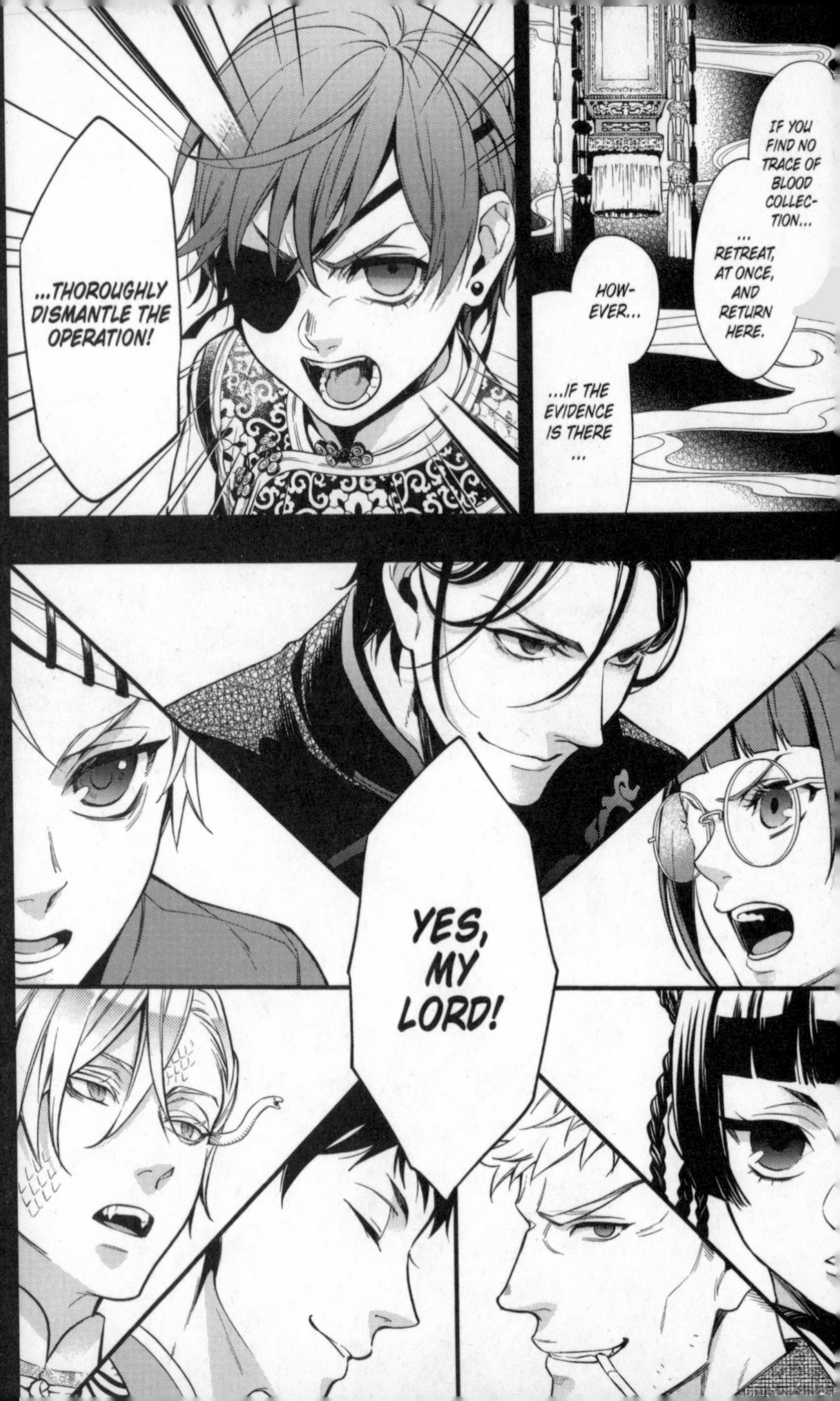
IF YOU FIND NO TRACE OF BLOOD COLLECTION...
...RETREAT, AT ONCE, AND RETURN HERE.
HOW-EVER...
...IF THE EVIDENCE IS THERE...
...THOROUGHLY DISMANTLE THE OPERATION!
YES, MY LORD!

Black Butler

Chapter 154
In the evening: The Butler, Far Away

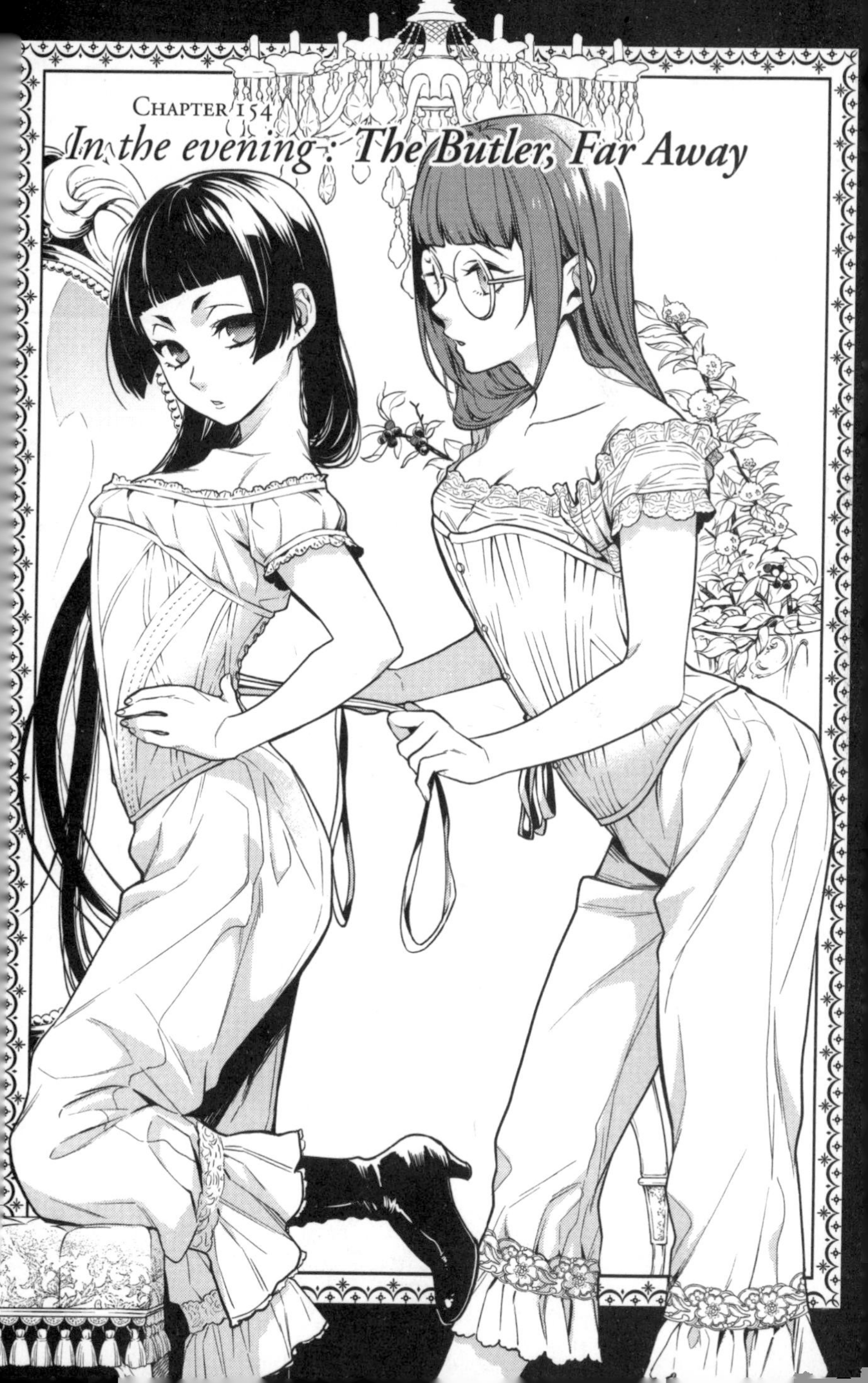

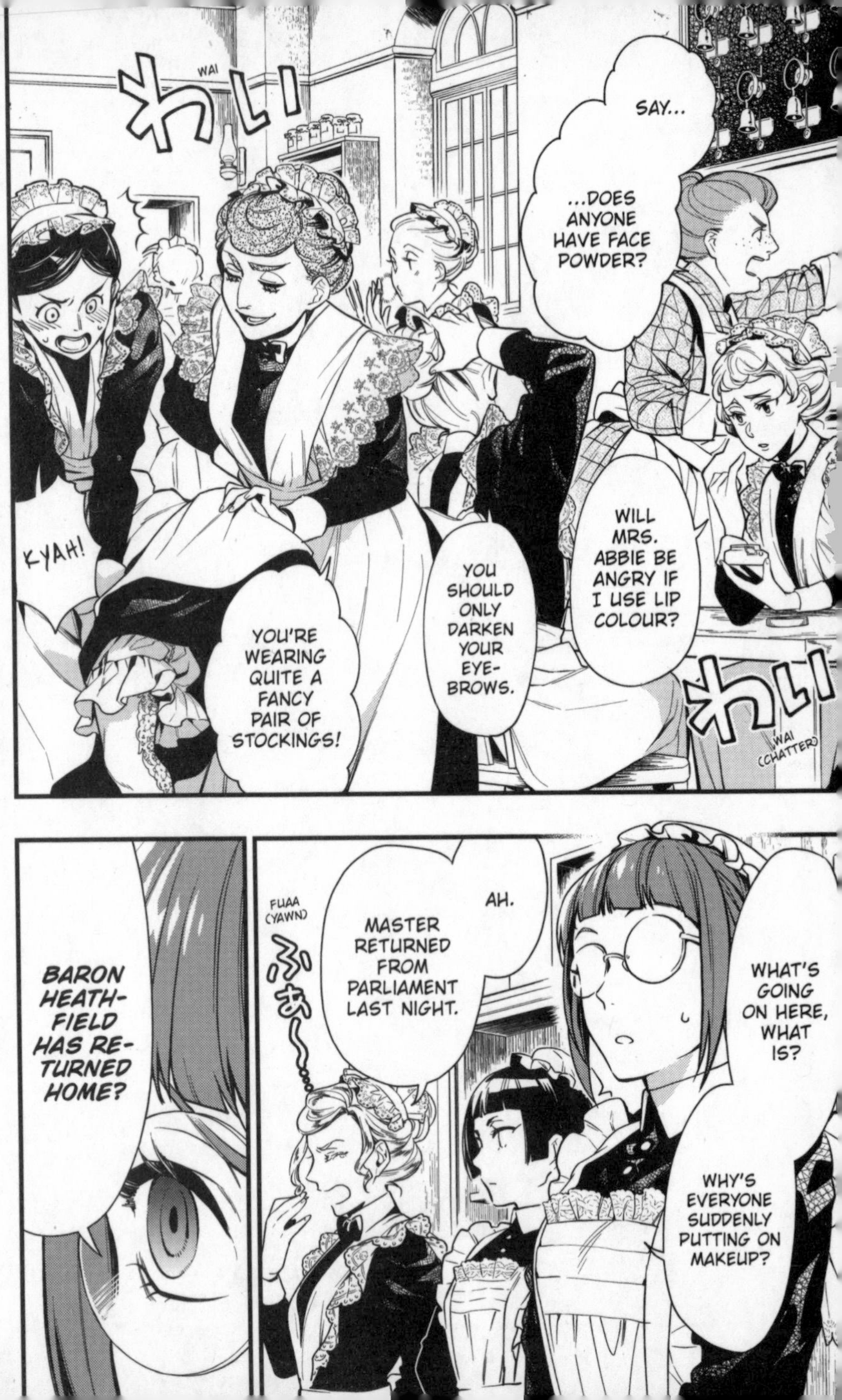
SAY...
...DOES ANYONE HAVE FACE POWDER?
WAI
WILL MRS. ABBIE BE ANGRY IF I USE LIP COLOUR?
WAI (CHATTER)
YOU SHOULD ONLY DARKEN YOUR EYE-BROWS.
YOU'RE WEARING QUITE A FANCY PAIR OF STOCKINGS!
KYAH!
WHAT'S GOING ON HERE, WHAT IS?
WHY'S EVERYONE SUDDENLY PUTTING ON MAKEUP?
AH.
MASTER RETURNED FROM PARLIAMENT LAST NIGHT.
FUAA (YAWN)
BARON HEATH-FIELD HAS RE-TURNED HOME?

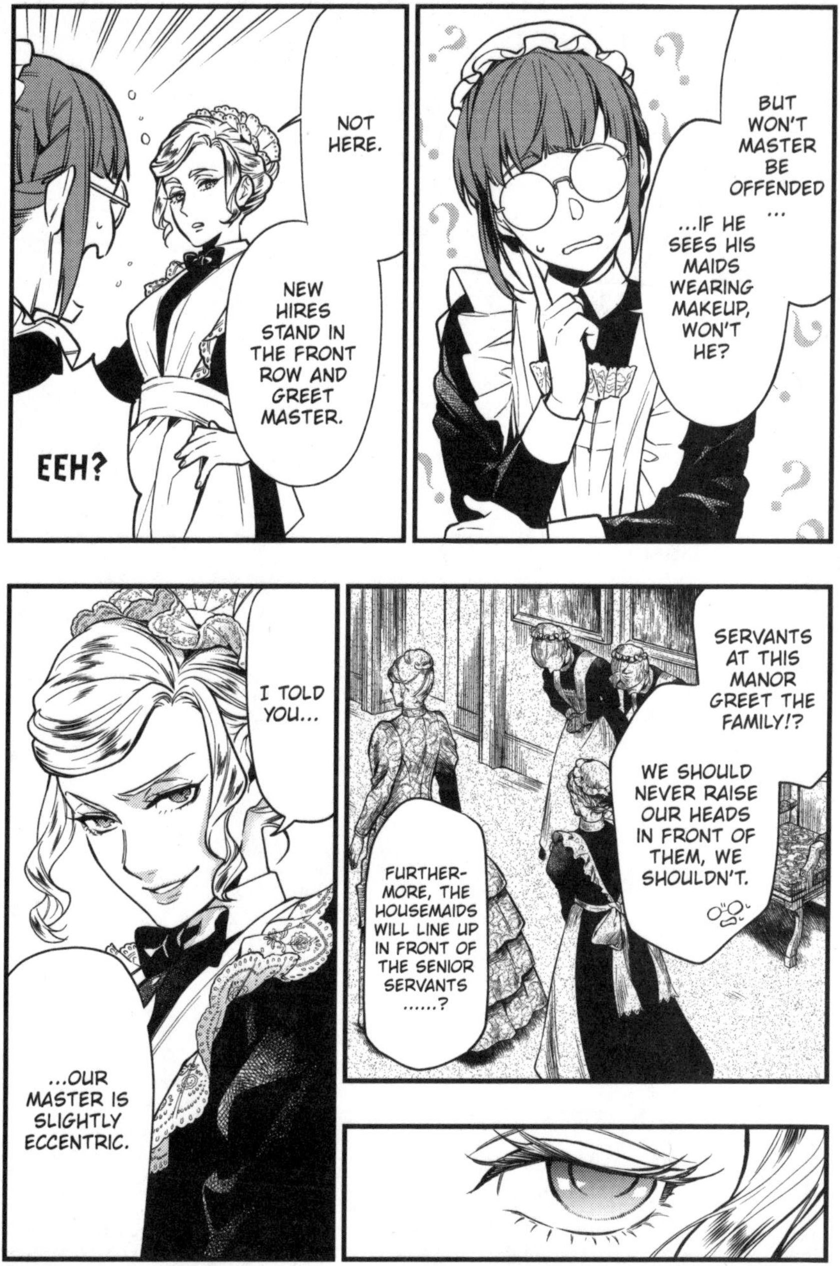
BUT WON'T MASTER BE OFFENDED...
...IF HE SEES HIS MAIDS WEARING MAKEUP, WON'T HE?
NOT HERE.
NEW HIRES STAND IN THE FRONT ROW AND GREET MASTER.
EEH?
SERVANTS AT THIS MANOR GREET THE FAMILY!?
WE SHOULD NEVER RAISE OUR HEADS IN FRONT OF THEM, WE SHOULDN'T.
FURTHER-MORE, THE HOUSEMAIDS WILL LINE UP IN FRONT OF THE SENIOR SERVANTS ......?
I TOLD YOU...
...OUR MASTER IS SLIGHTLY ECCENTRIC.

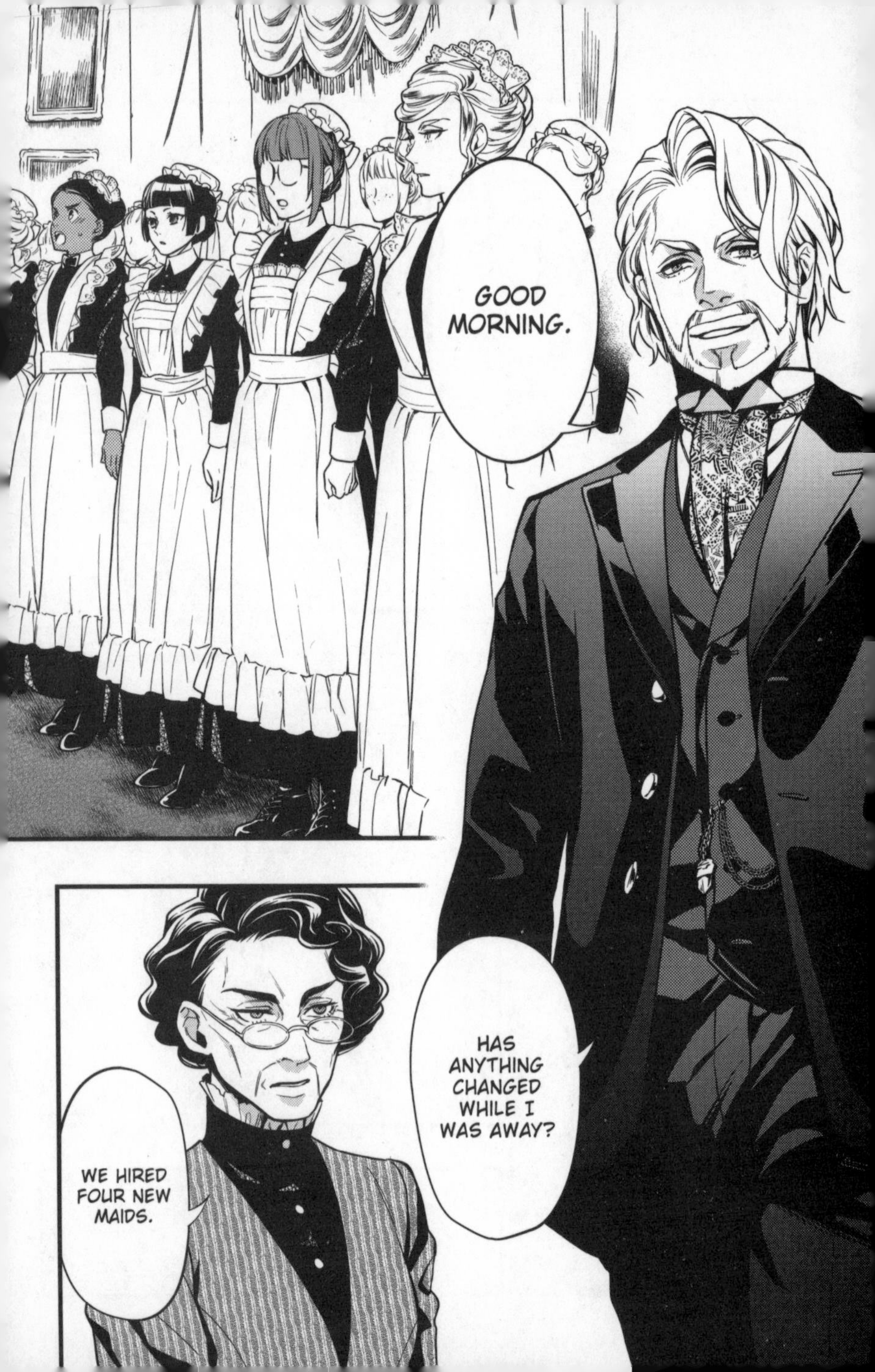
GOOD MORNING.
HAS ANYTHING CHANGED WHILE I WAS AWAY?
WE HIRED FOUR NEW MAIDS.

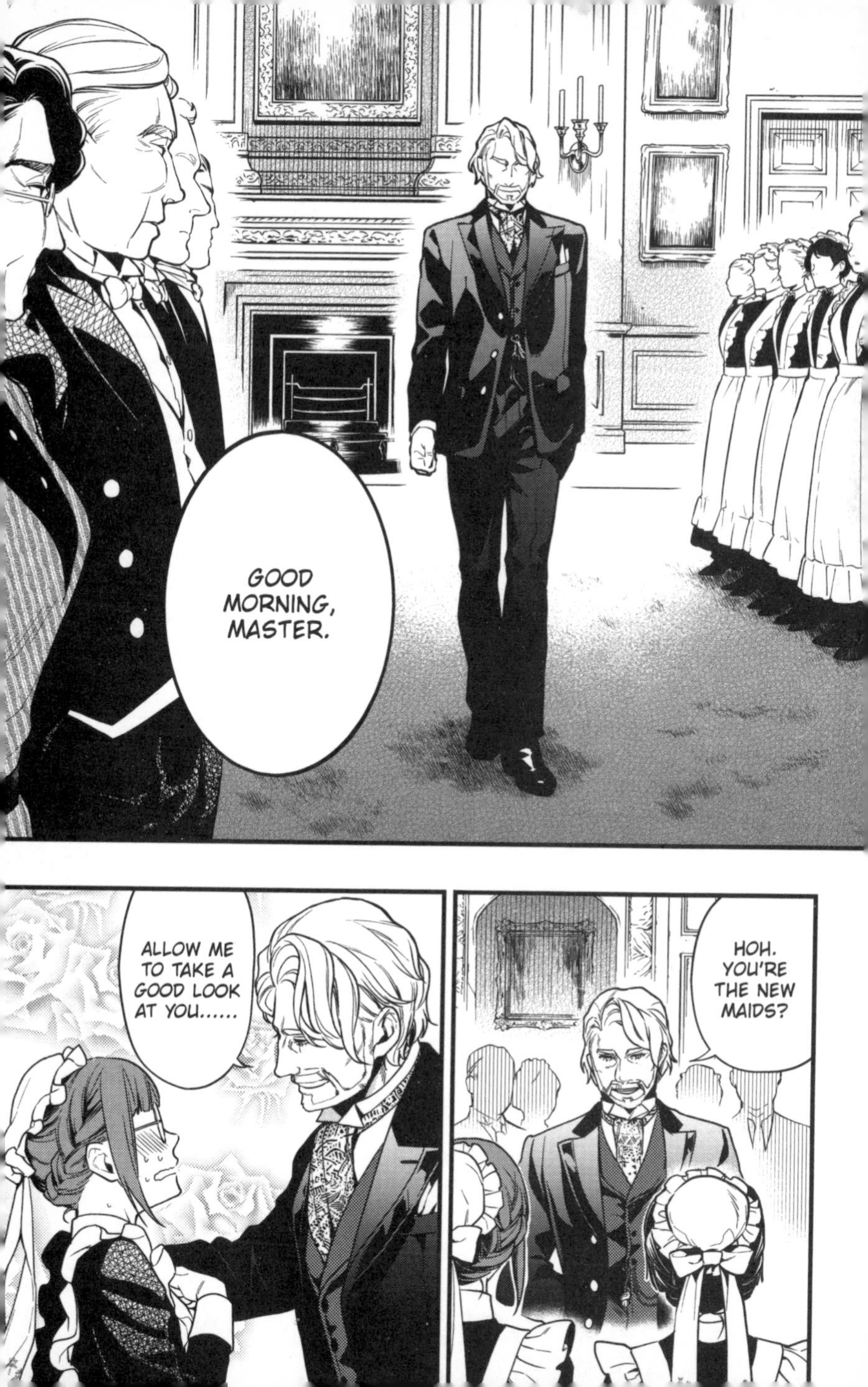
GOOD MORNING, MASTER.
HOH. YOU'RE THE NEW MAIDS?
ALLOW ME TO TAKE A GOOD LOOK AT YOU......

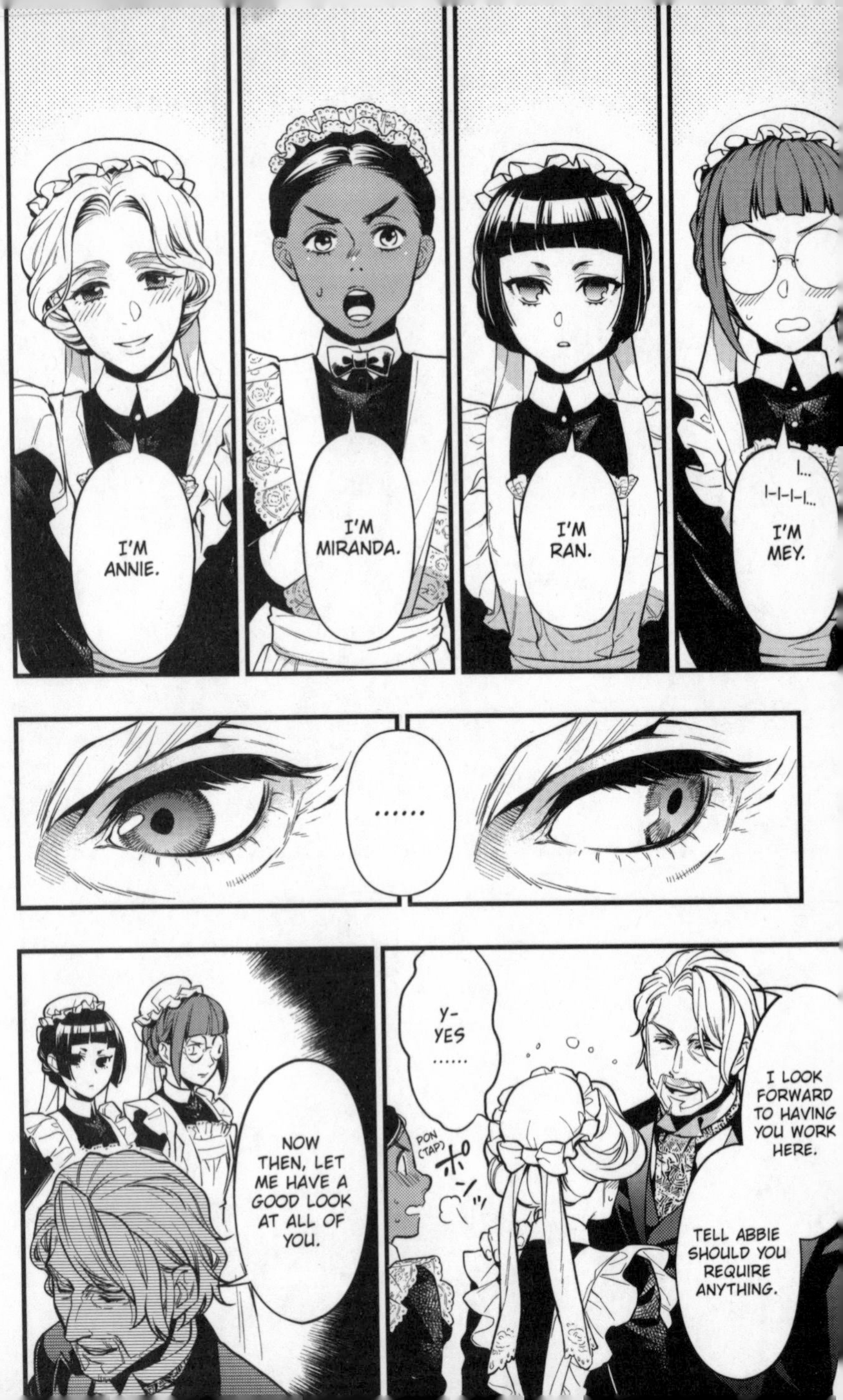
I... I-I-I-I... I'M MEY.
I'M RAN.
I'M MIRANDA.
I'M ANNIE.
......
I LOOK FORWARD TO HAVING YOU WORK HERE.
TELL ABBIE SHOULD YOU REQUIRE ANYTHING.
Y-YES ......
PON (TAP)
NOW THEN, LET ME HAVE A GOOD LOOK AT ALL OF YOU.

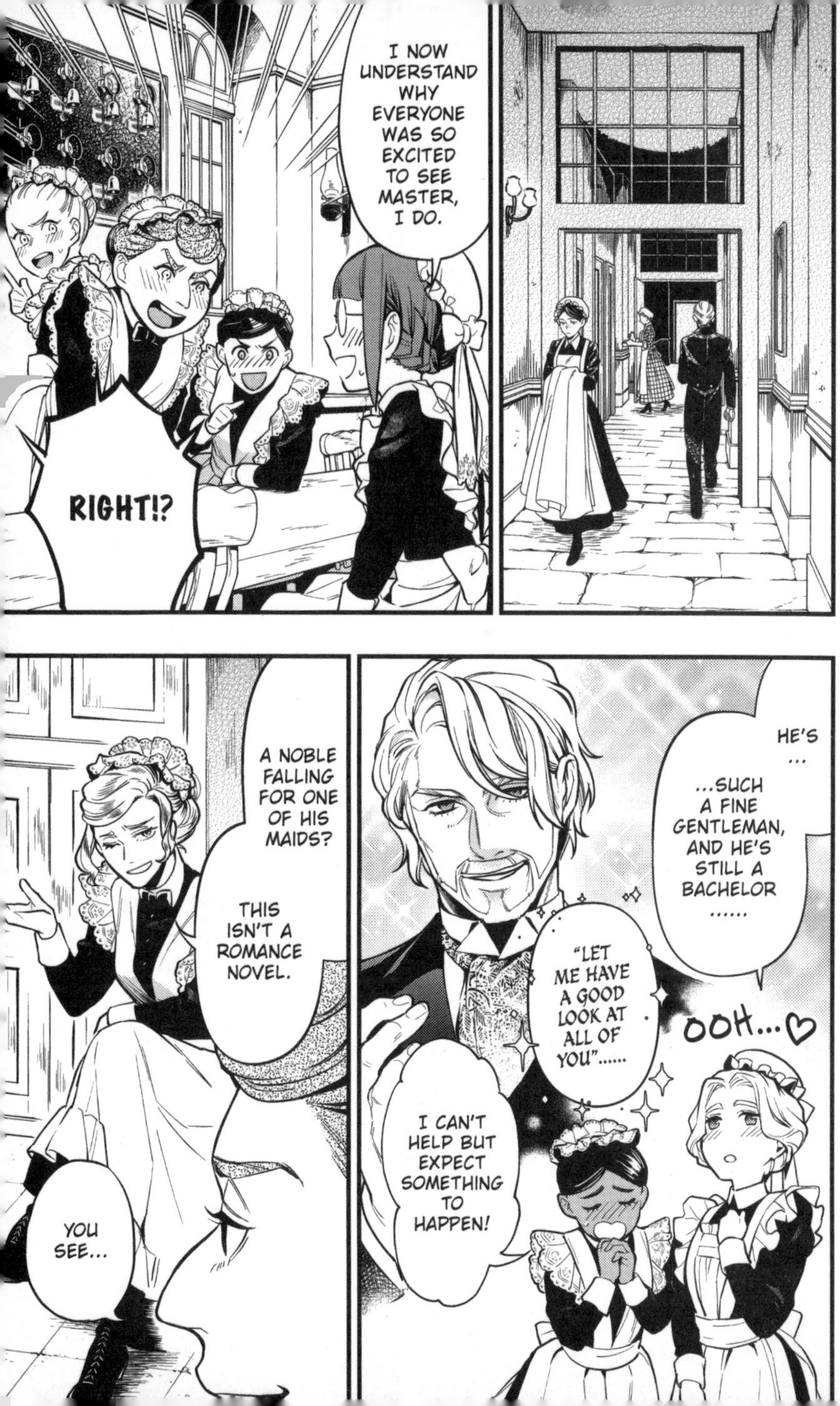
I NOW UNDERSTAND WHY EVERYONE WAS SO EXCITED TO SEE MASTER, I DO.
RIGHT!?
HE'S ...
...SUCH A FINE GENTLEMAN, AND HE'S STILL A BACHELOR ......
"LET ME HAVE A GOOD LOOK AT ALL OF YOU"......
OOH...♥
I CAN'T HELP BUT EXPECT SOMETHING TO HAPPEN!
A NOBLE FALLING FOR ONE OF HIS MAIDS?
THIS ISN'T A ROMANCE NOVEL.
YOU SEE...

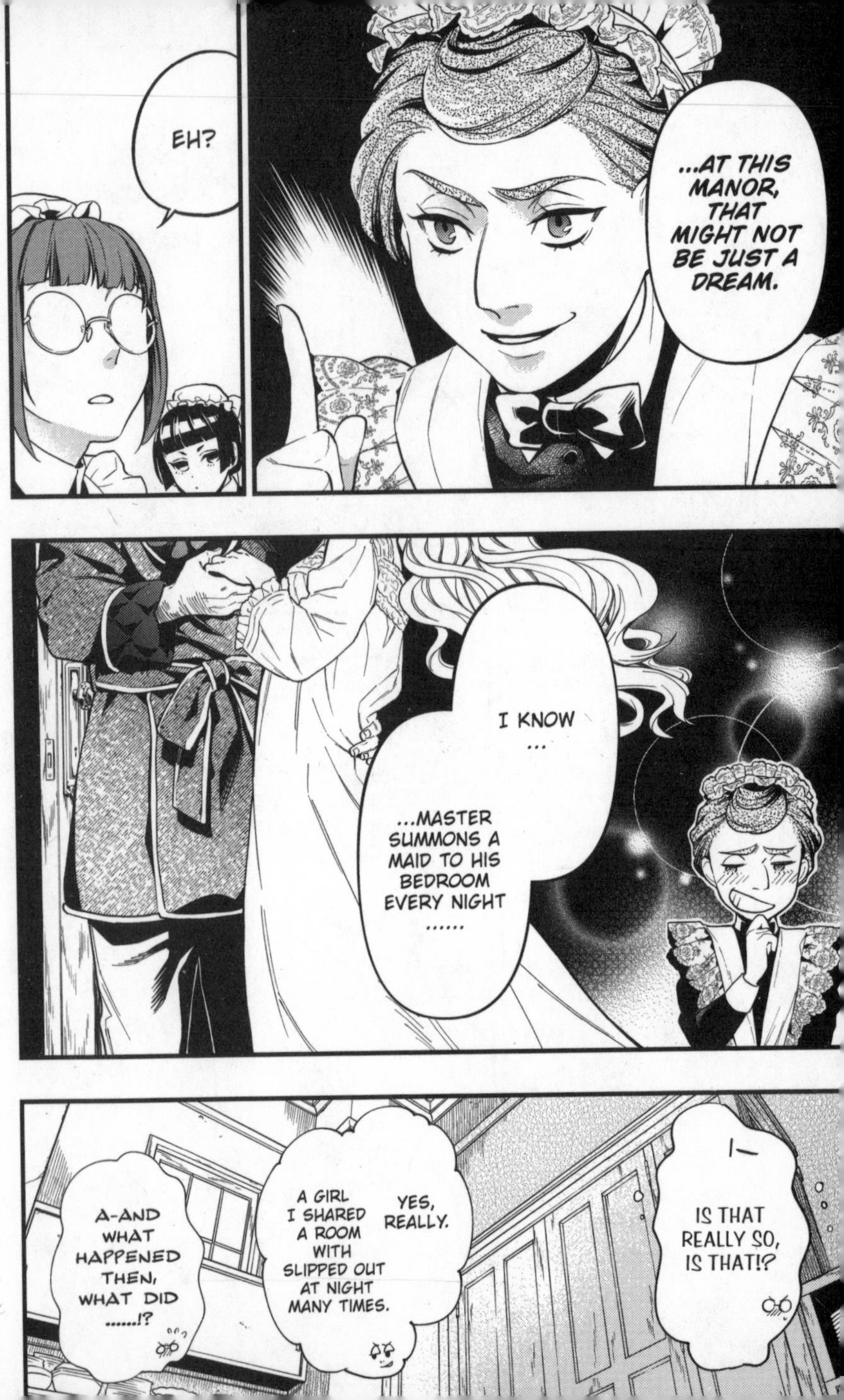
...AT THIS MANOR, THAT MIGHT NOT BE JUST A DREAM.
EH?
I KNOW ...
...MASTER SUMMONS A MAID TO HIS BEDROOM EVERY NIGHT ......
I—
IS THAT REALLY SO, IS THAT!?
YES, REALLY.
A GIRL I SHARED A ROOM WITH SLIPPED OUT AT NIGHT MANY TIMES.
A-AND WHAT HAPPENED THEN, WHAT DID ......!?

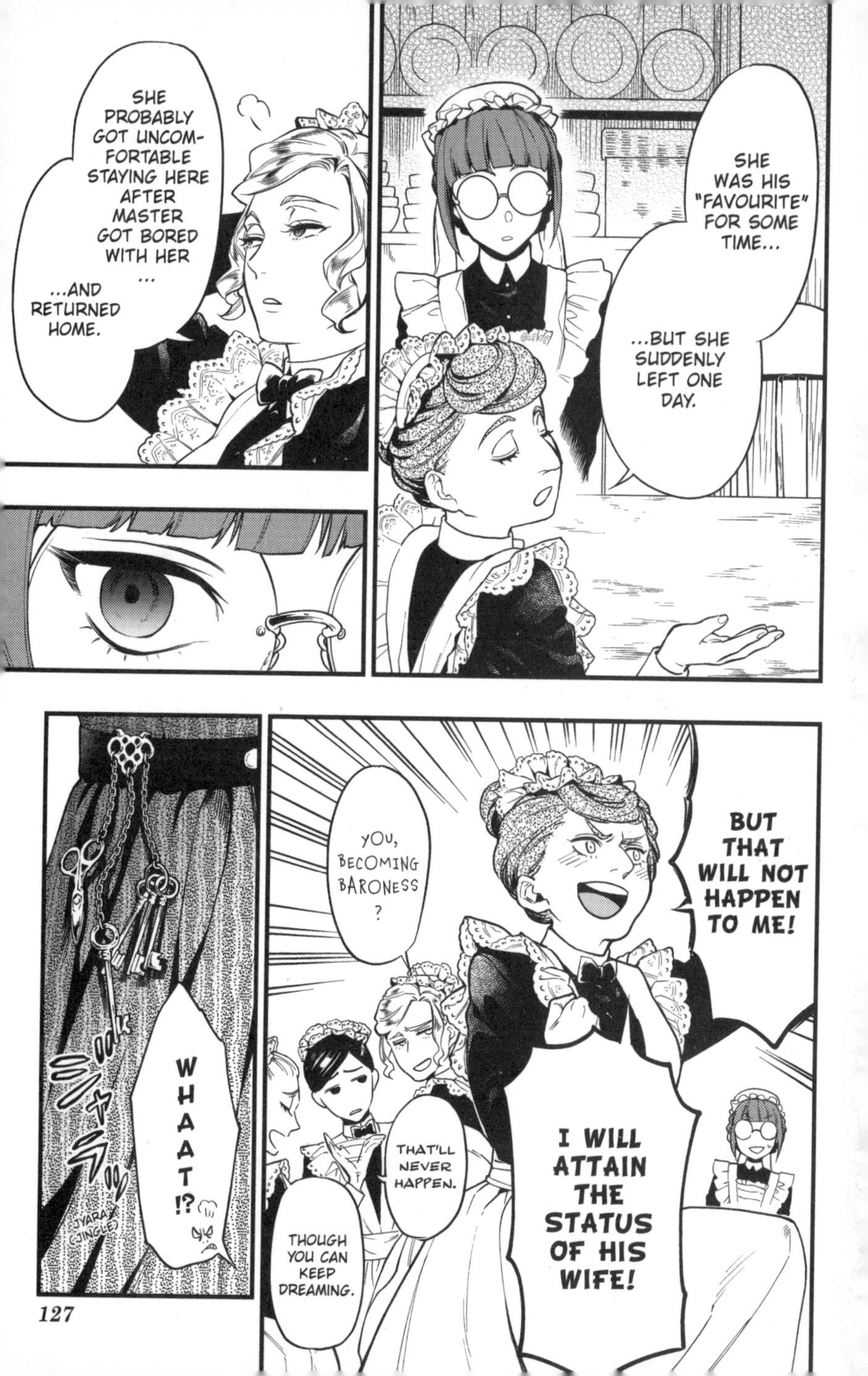
SHE WAS HIS "FAVOURITE" FOR SOME TIME...
...BUT SHE SUDDENLY LEFT ONE DAY.
SHE PROBABLY GOT UNCOM-FORTABLE STAYING HERE AFTER MASTER GOT BORED WITH HER ...
...AND RETURNED HOME.
BUT THAT WILL NOT HAPPEN TO ME!
I WILL ATTAIN THE STATUS OF HIS WIFE!
YOU, BECOMING BARONESS?
THAT'LL NEVER HAPPEN.
THOUGH YOU CAN KEEP DREAMING.
WHAAT!?
JYARA (JINGLE)

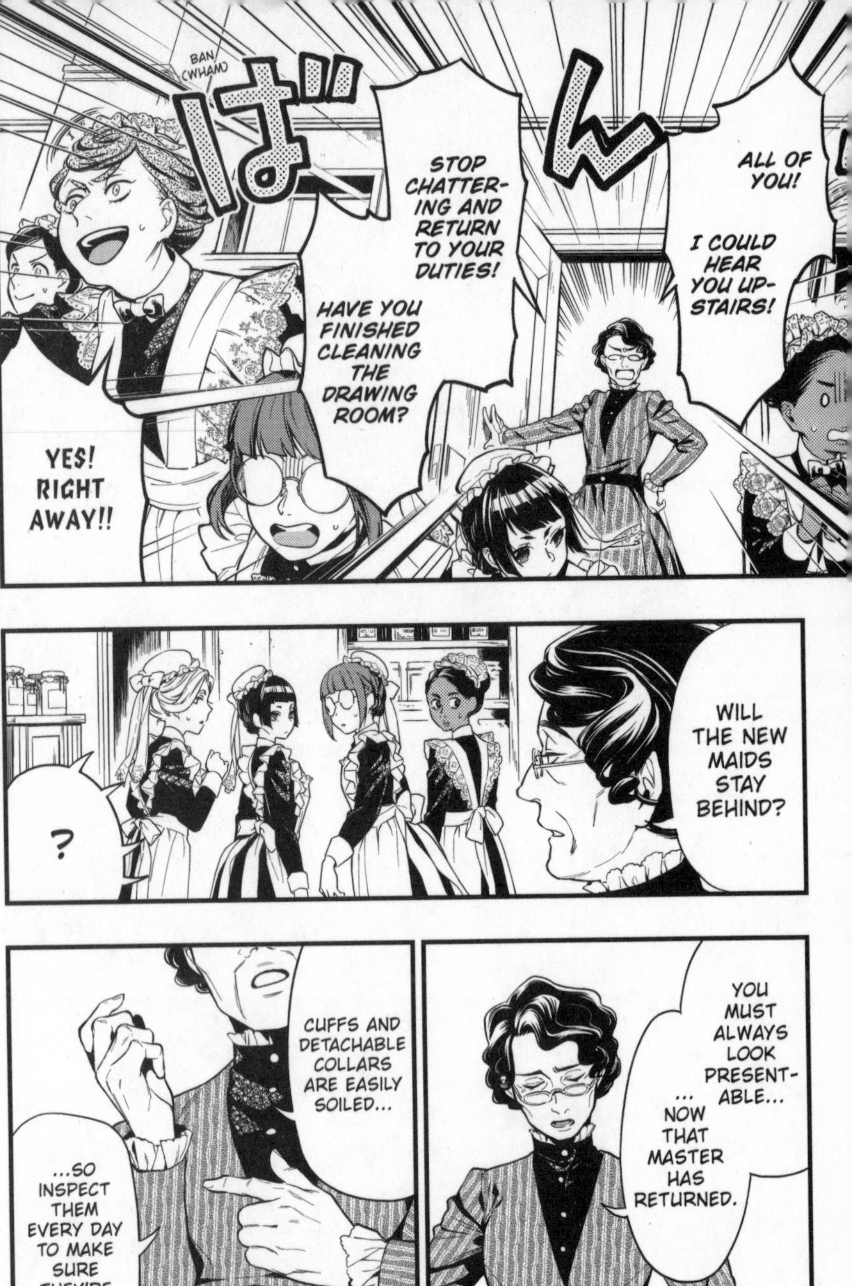
ALL OF YOU!
I COULD HEAR YOU UPSTAIRS!
STOP CHATTERING AND RETURN TO YOUR DUTIES!
ばん
BAN (WHAM)
HAVE YOU FINISHED CLEANING THE DRAWING ROOM?
YES! RIGHT AWAY!!
WILL THE NEW MAIDS STAY BEHIND?
?
YOU MUST ALWAYS LOOK PRESENTABLE...
...NOW THAT MASTER HAS RETURNED.
CUFFS AND DETACHABLE COLLARS ARE EASILY SOILED...
...SO INSPECT THEM EVERY DAY TO MAKE SURE THEY'RE SPOTLESS.

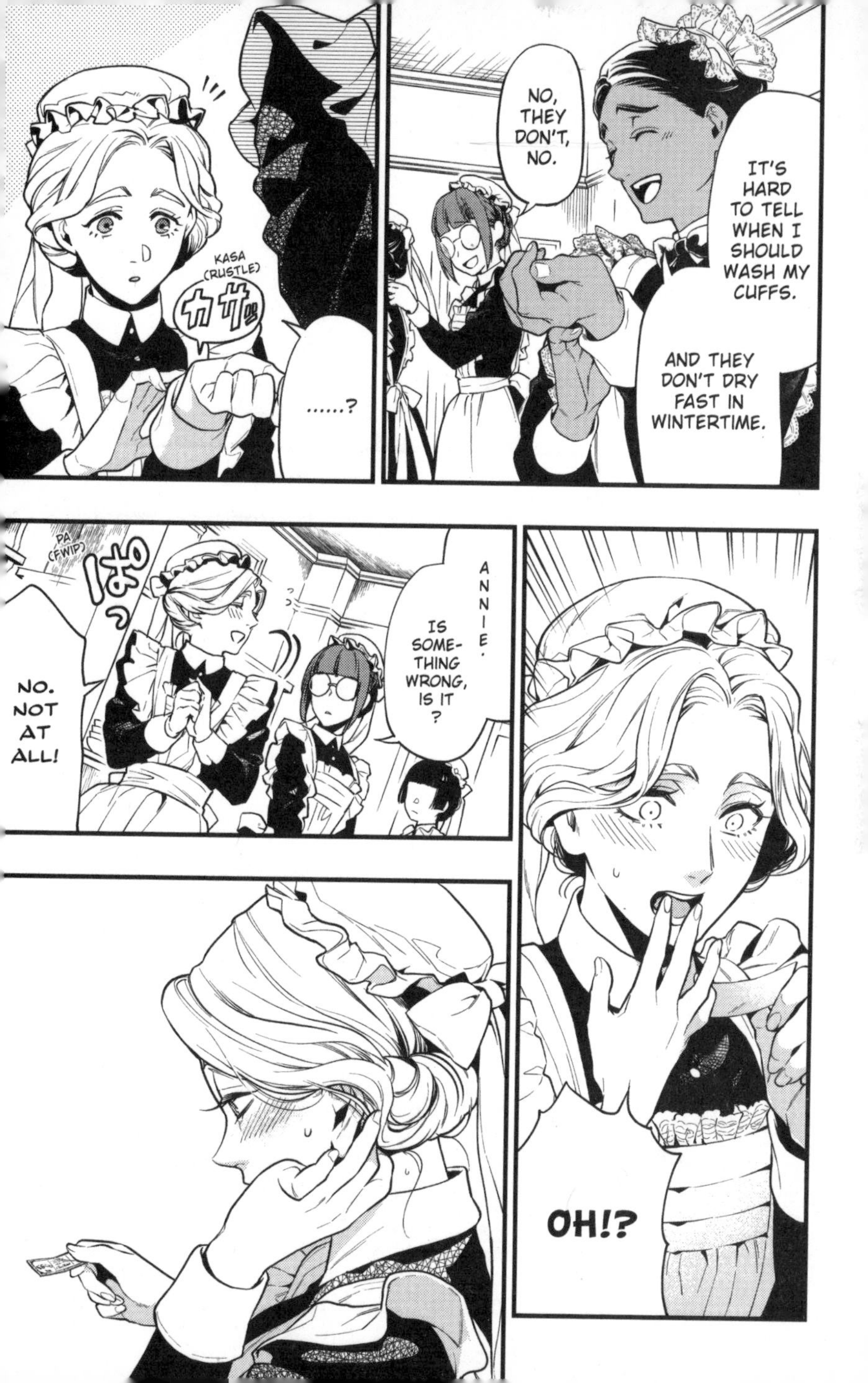
IT'S HARD TO TELL WHEN I SHOULD WASH MY CUFFS.
AND THEY DON'T DRY FAST IN WINTERTIME.
NO, THEY DON'T, NO.
KASA (RUSTLE)
カサッ
......?
OH!?
ANNIE.
IS SOMETHING WRONG, IS IT?
PA (FWIP)
ぱっ
NO. NOT AT ALL!

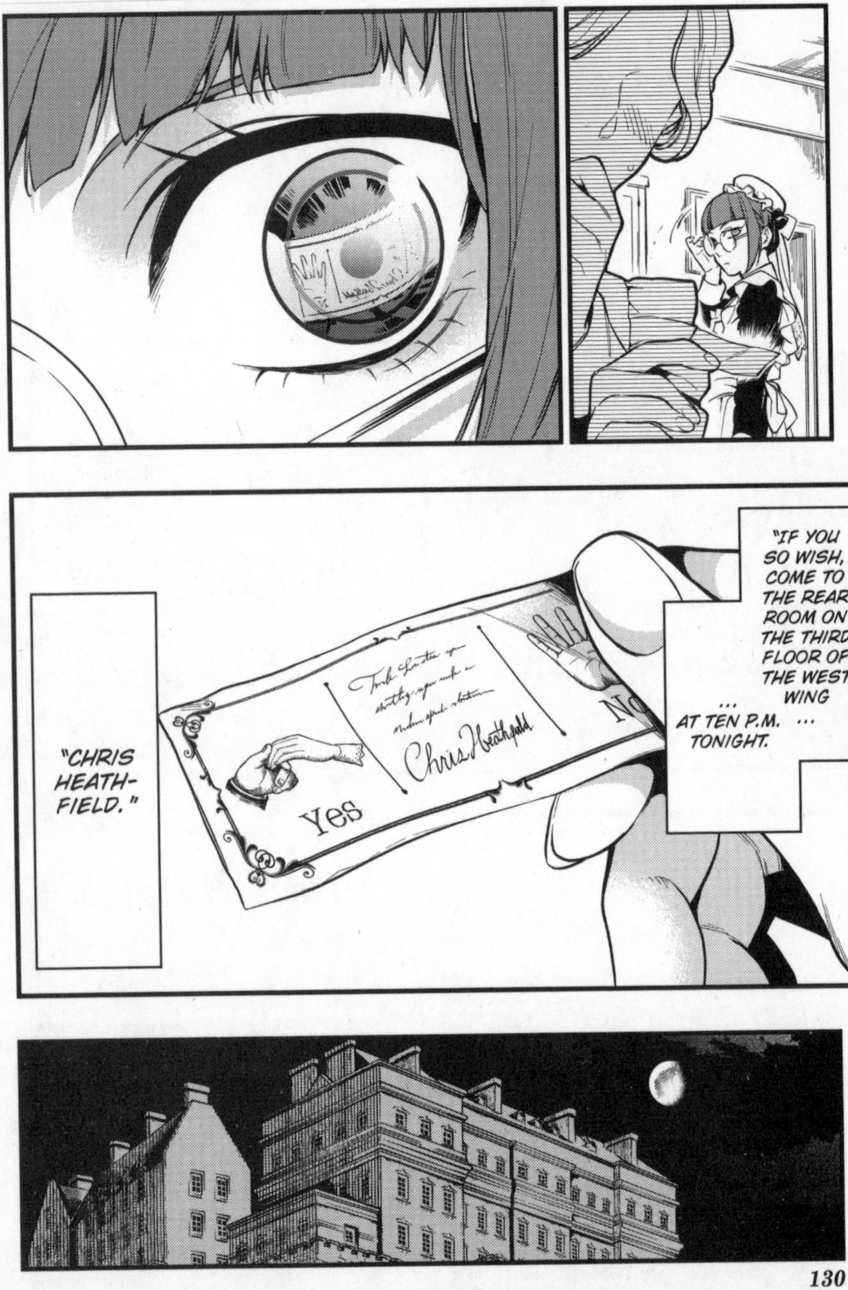
"IF YOU SO WISH, COME TO THE REAR ROOM ON THE THIRD FLOOR OF THE WEST WING ... AT TEN P.M. TONIGHT. ...
Yes
"CHRIS HEATH-FIELD."

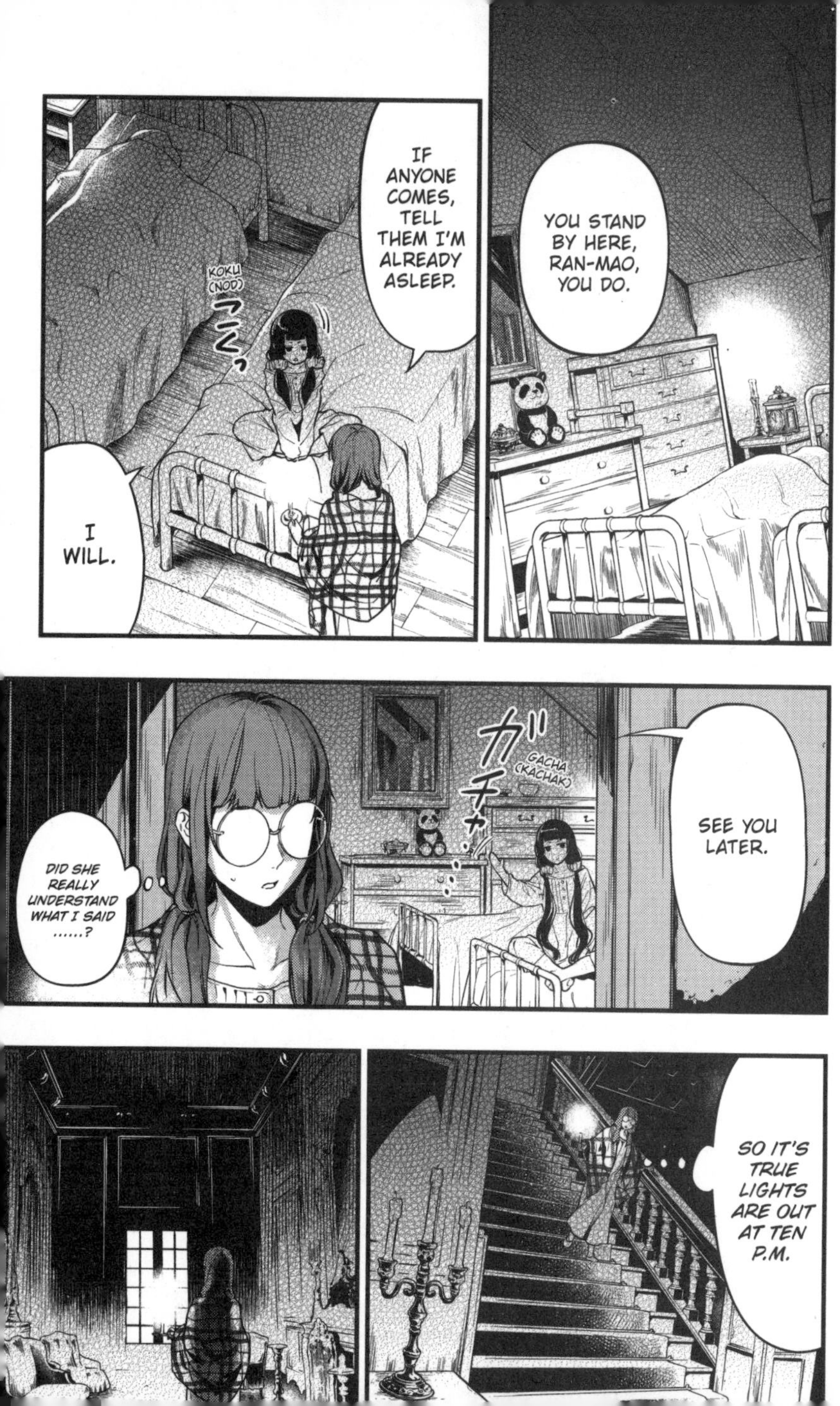
YOU STAND BY HERE, RAN-MAO, YOU DO.
IF ANYONE COMES, TELL THEM I'M ALREADY ASLEEP.
KOKU (NOD)
I WILL.
SEE YOU LATER.
GACHA (KACHAK)
DID SHE REALLY UNDERSTAND WHAT I SAID ......?
SO IT'S TRUE LIGHTS ARE OUT AT TEN P.M.

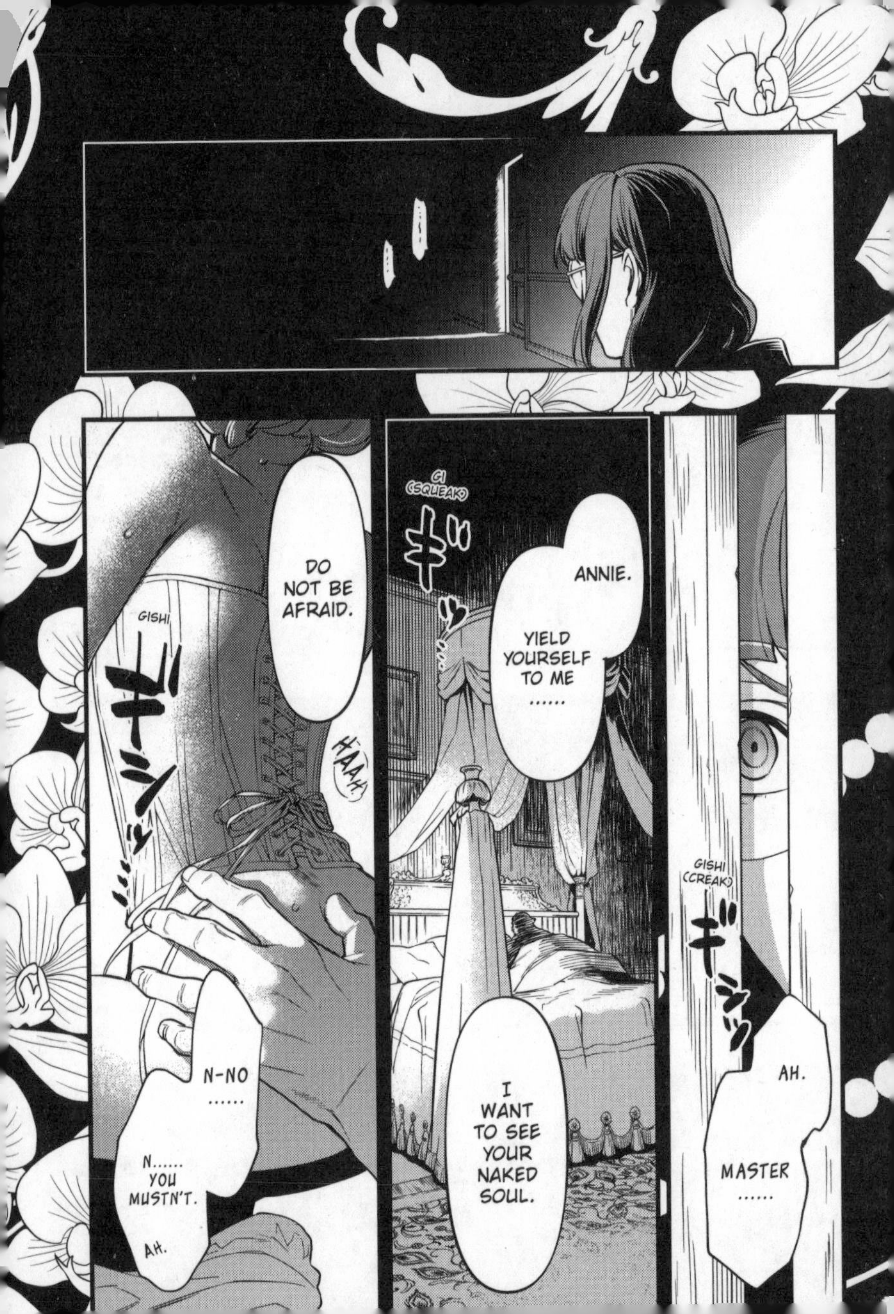
GISHI (CREAK)
AH.
MASTER ......
GI (SQUEAK)
ANNIE.
YIELD YOURSELF TO ME ......
I WANT TO SEE YOUR NAKED SOUL.
DO NOT BE AFRAID.
GISHI
HAAH
N-NO ......
N...... YOU MUSTN'T.
AH.

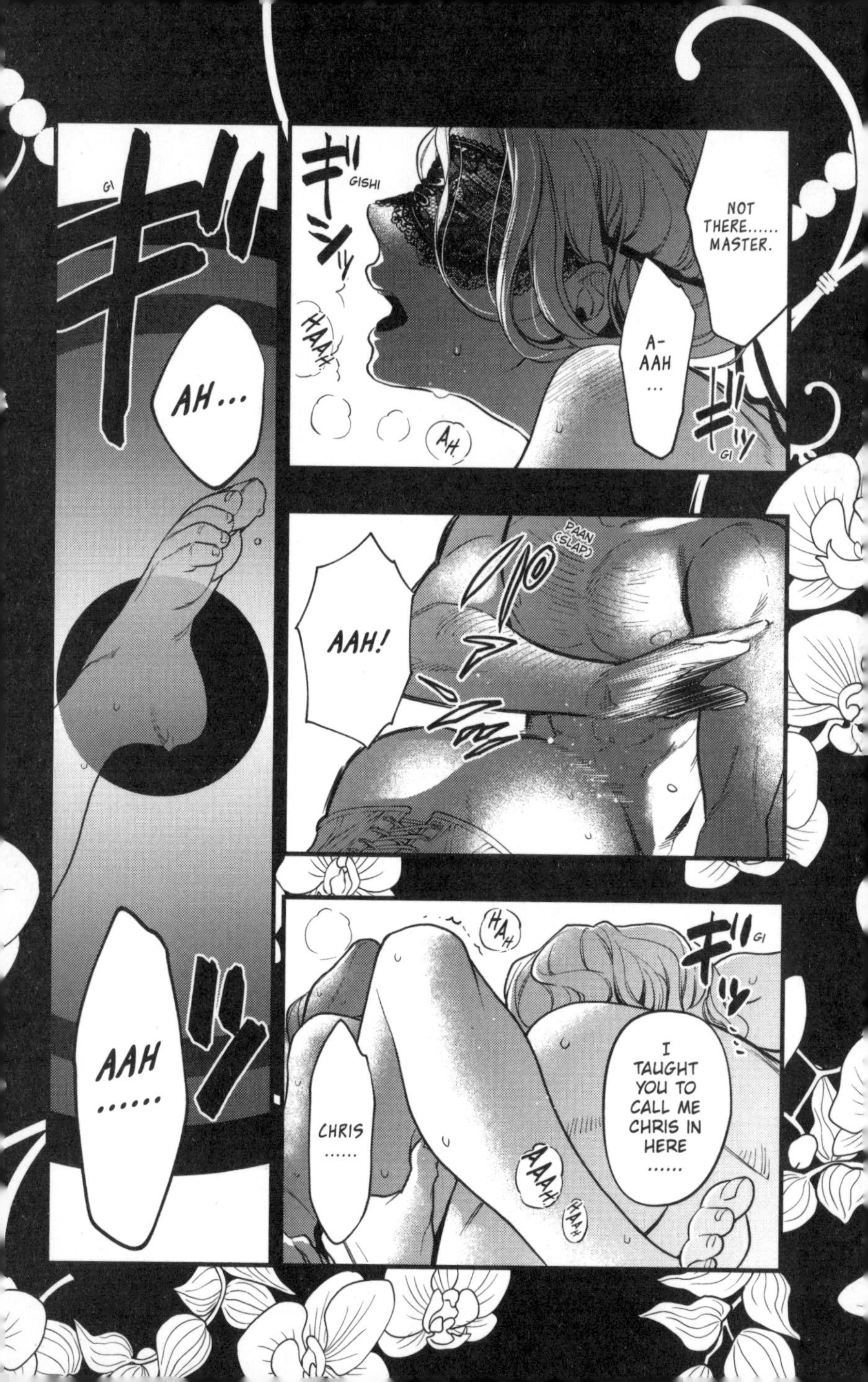
NOT THERE...... MASTER.
A- AAH ...
GI
GISHI
HAAA
AH
PAAN (SLAP)
AAH!
GI
I TAUGHT YOU TO CALL ME CHRIS IN HERE ......
HAH
AAAH
HAAA
CHRIS ......
GI
AH...
AAH ......

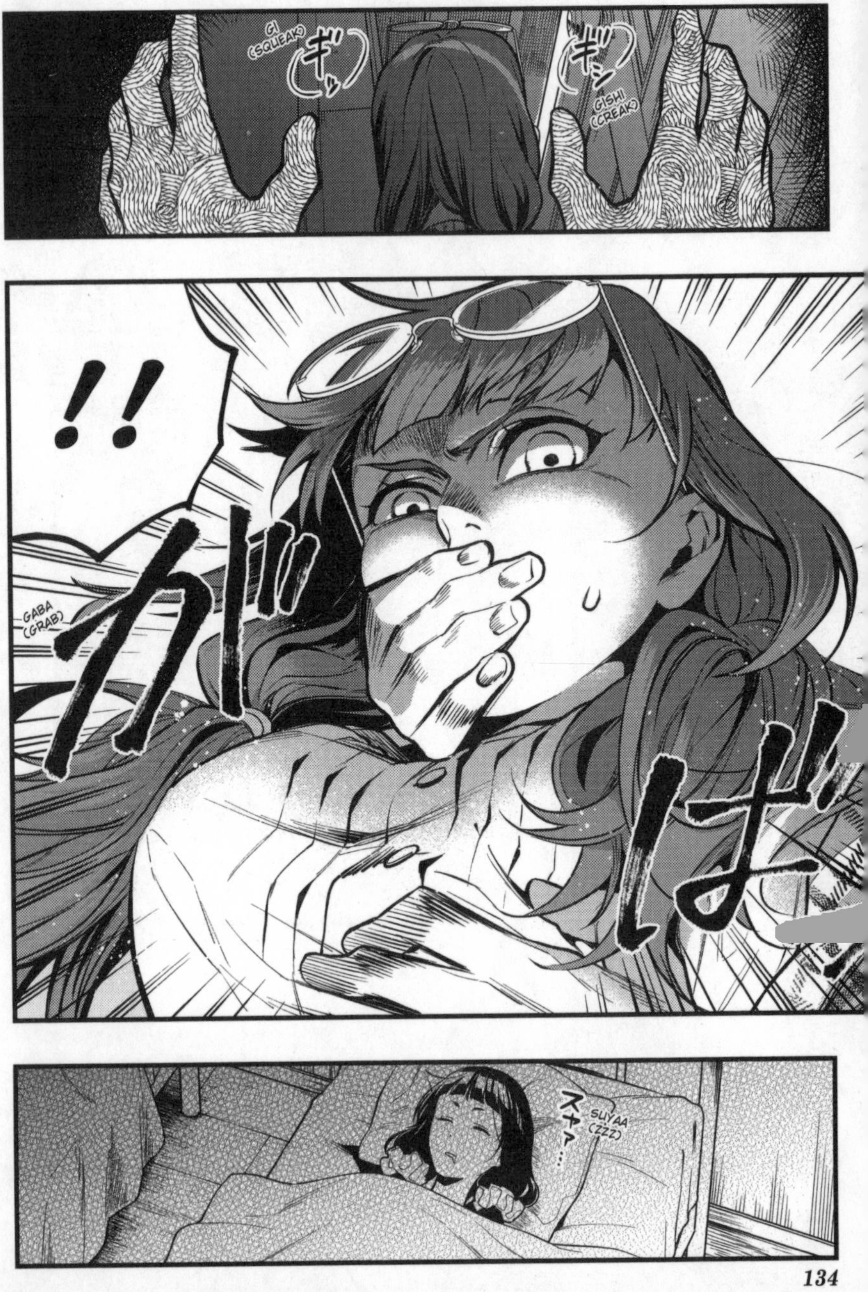

ギシ
GISHI (CREAK)
ギッ
GI (SQUEAK)
!!
ガばっ
GABA (GRAB)
スャァ…
SUYAA (ZZZ)

Black Butler

Chapter 155

At night : The Butler, Absent

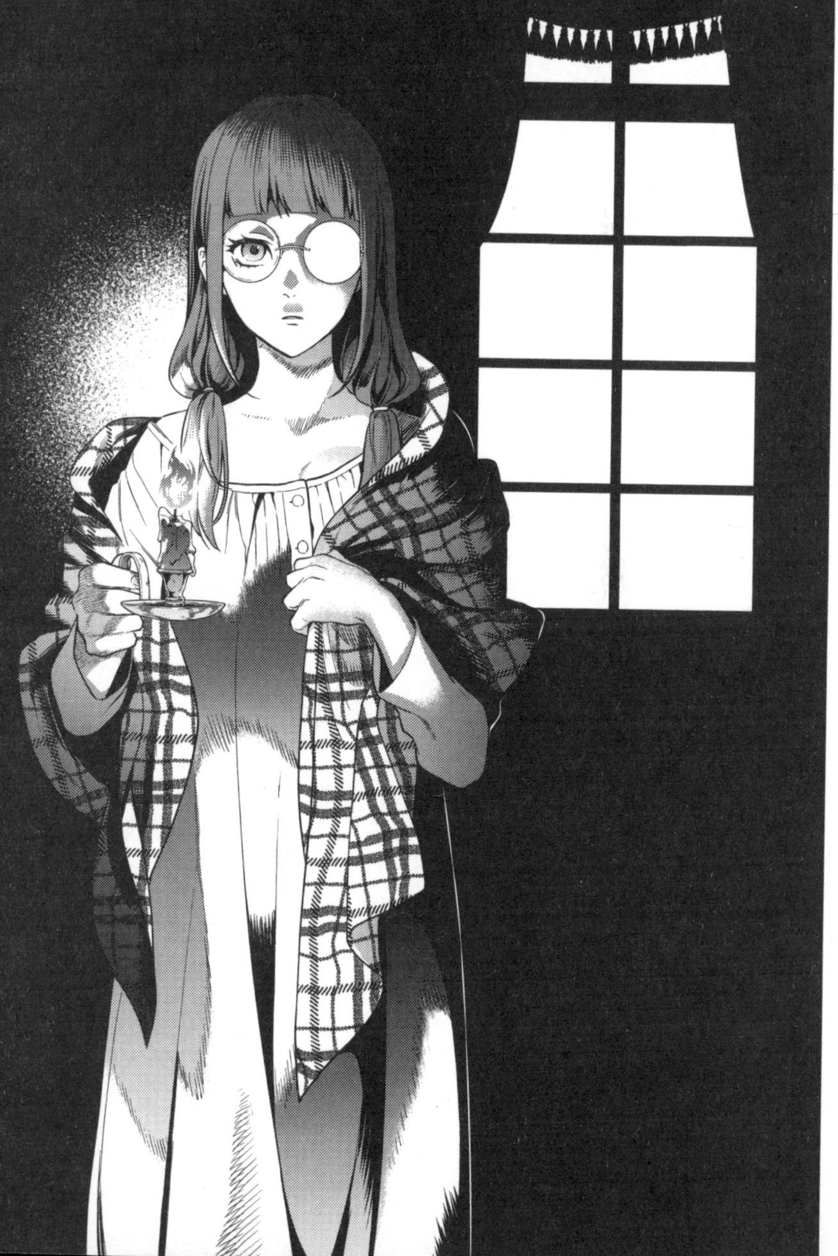

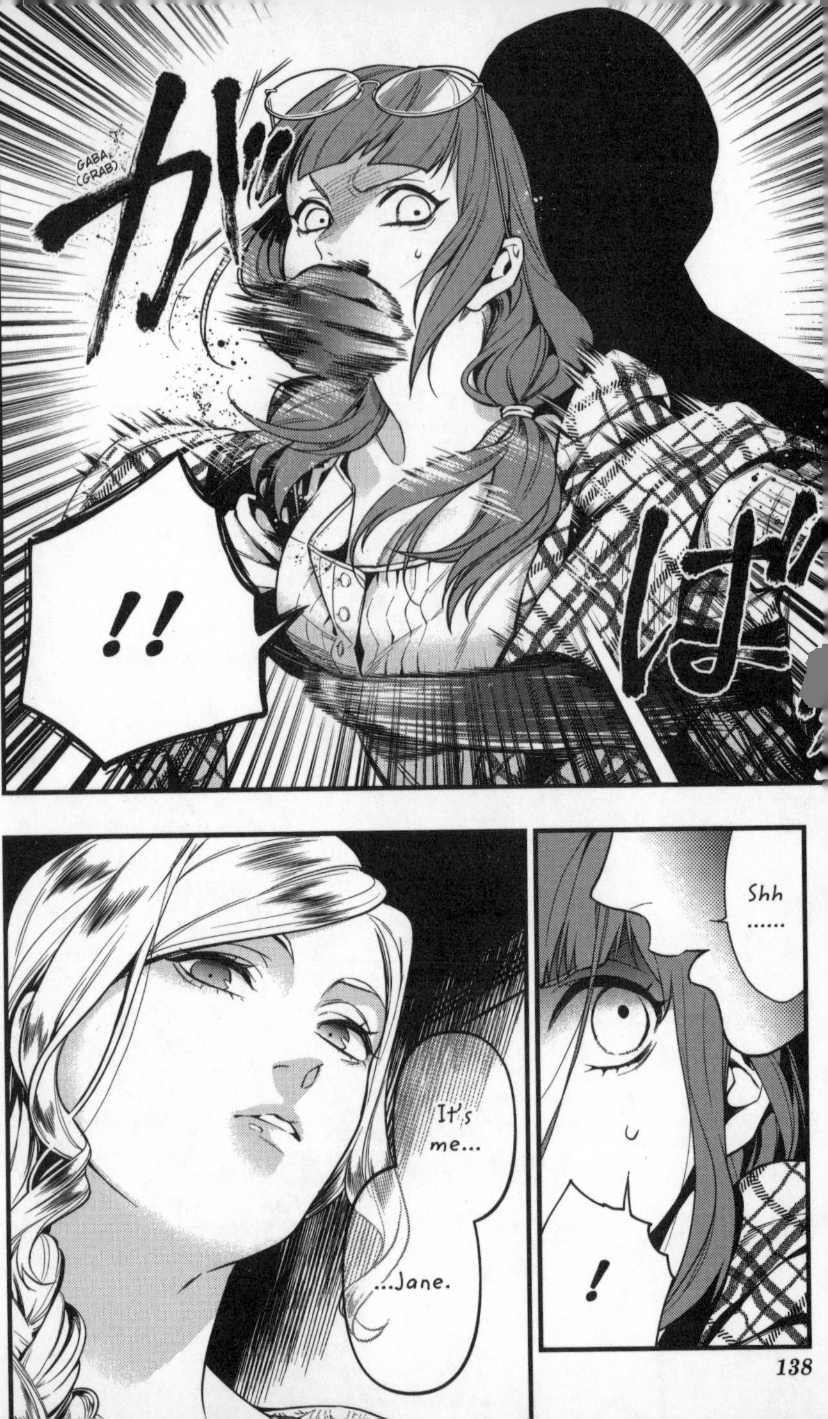

GABA (GRAB)
!!
Shh ......
!
It's me...
...Jane.

GI (SQUEAK)

AH. AAH ......

GISHI (CREAK)

AAH...

This way.

Jane !?

Quiet, Mey.

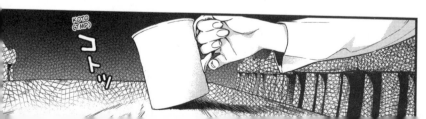

KOTO (TMP)

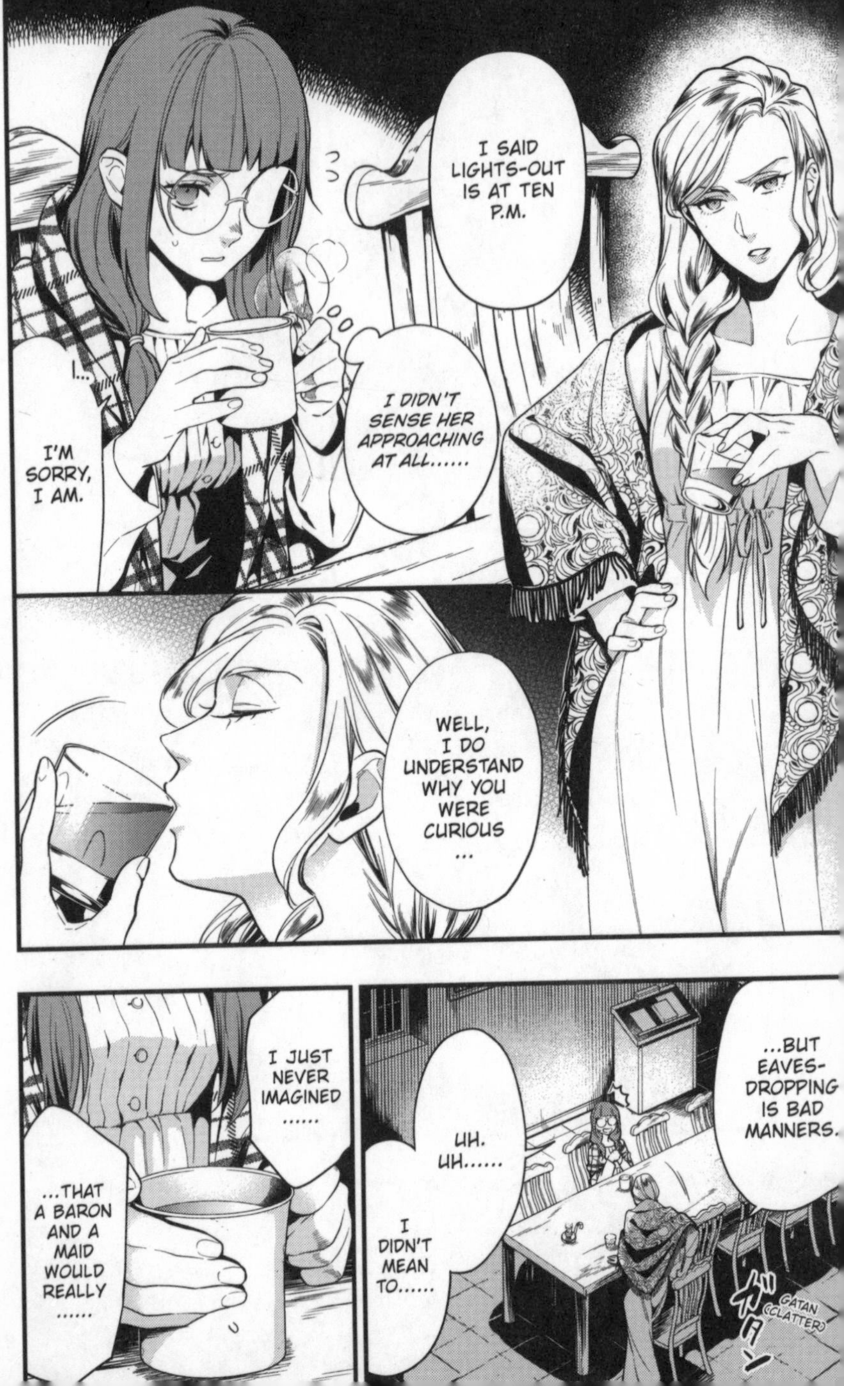
I SAID LIGHTS-OUT IS AT TEN P.M.
I DIDN'T SENSE HER APPROACHING AT ALL......
I...
I'M SORRY, I AM.
WELL, I DO UNDERSTAND WHY YOU WERE CURIOUS ...
...BUT EAVES-DROPPING IS BAD MANNERS.
GATAN (CLATTER)
UH. UH......
I DIDN'T MEAN TO......
I JUST NEVER IMAGINED ......
...THAT A BARON AND A MAID WOULD REALLY ......

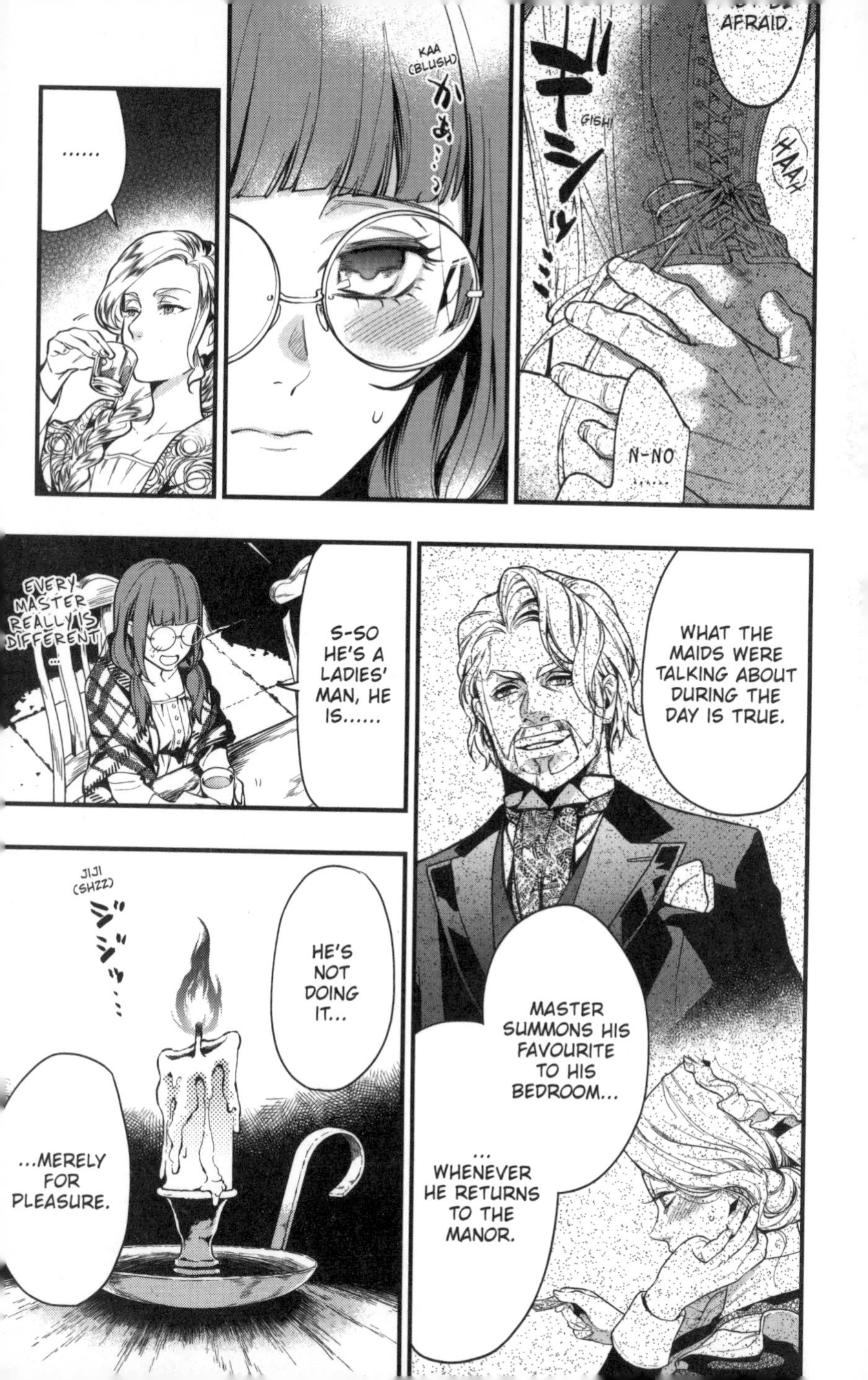
AFRAID.
GISHI
HAAH
N-NO......
KAA (BLUSH)
......
WHAT THE MAIDS WERE TALKING ABOUT DURING THE DAY IS TRUE.
MASTER SUMMONS HIS FAVOURITE TO HIS BEDROOM...
... WHENEVER HE RETURNS TO THE MANOR.
S-SO HE'S A LADIES' MAN, HE IS......
EVERY MASTER REALLY IS DIFFERENT...
JIJI (SHZZ)
HE'S NOT DOING IT...
...MERELY FOR PLEASURE.

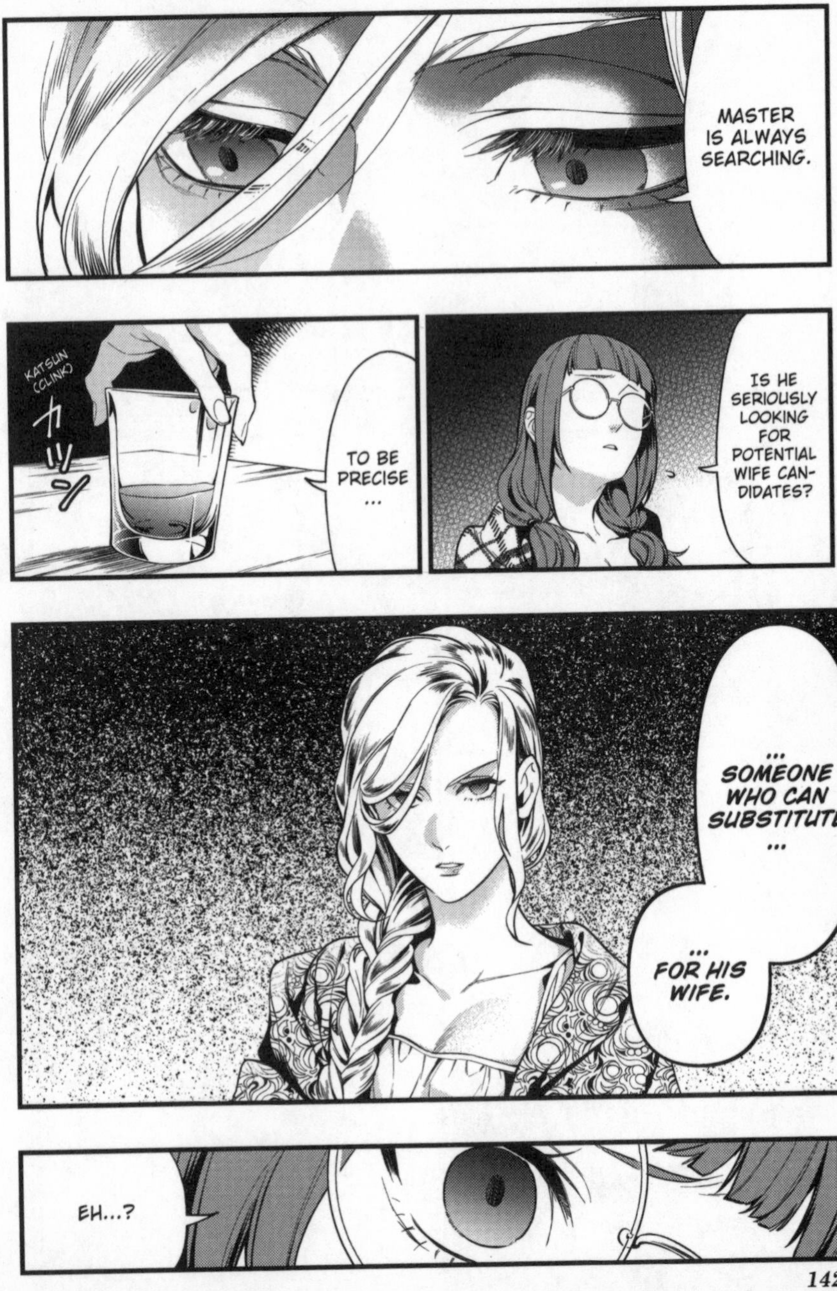
MASTER IS ALWAYS SEARCHING.
IS HE SERIOUSLY LOOKING FOR POTENTIAL WIFE CAN-DIDATES?
TO BE PRECISE ...
KATSUN (CLINK)
カツン
... SOMEONE WHO CAN SUBSTITUTE ...
... FOR HIS WIFE.
EH...?

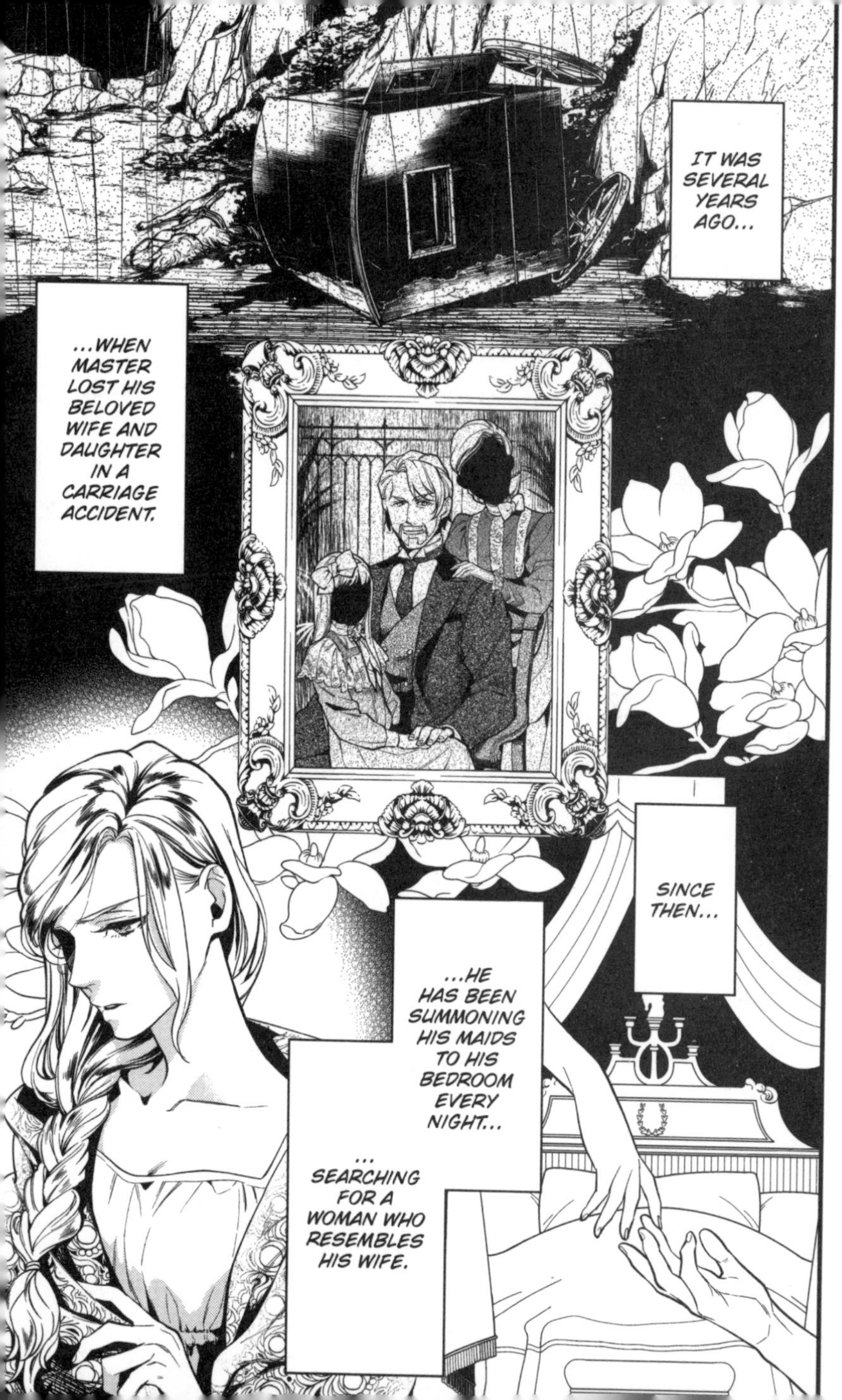
IT WAS SEVERAL YEARS AGO...
...WHEN MASTER LOST HIS BELOVED WIFE AND DAUGHTER IN A CARRIAGE ACCIDENT.
SINCE THEN...
...HE HAS BEEN SUMMONING HIS MAIDS TO HIS BEDROOM EVERY NIGHT...
...SEARCHING FOR A WOMAN WHO RESEMBLES HIS WIFE.

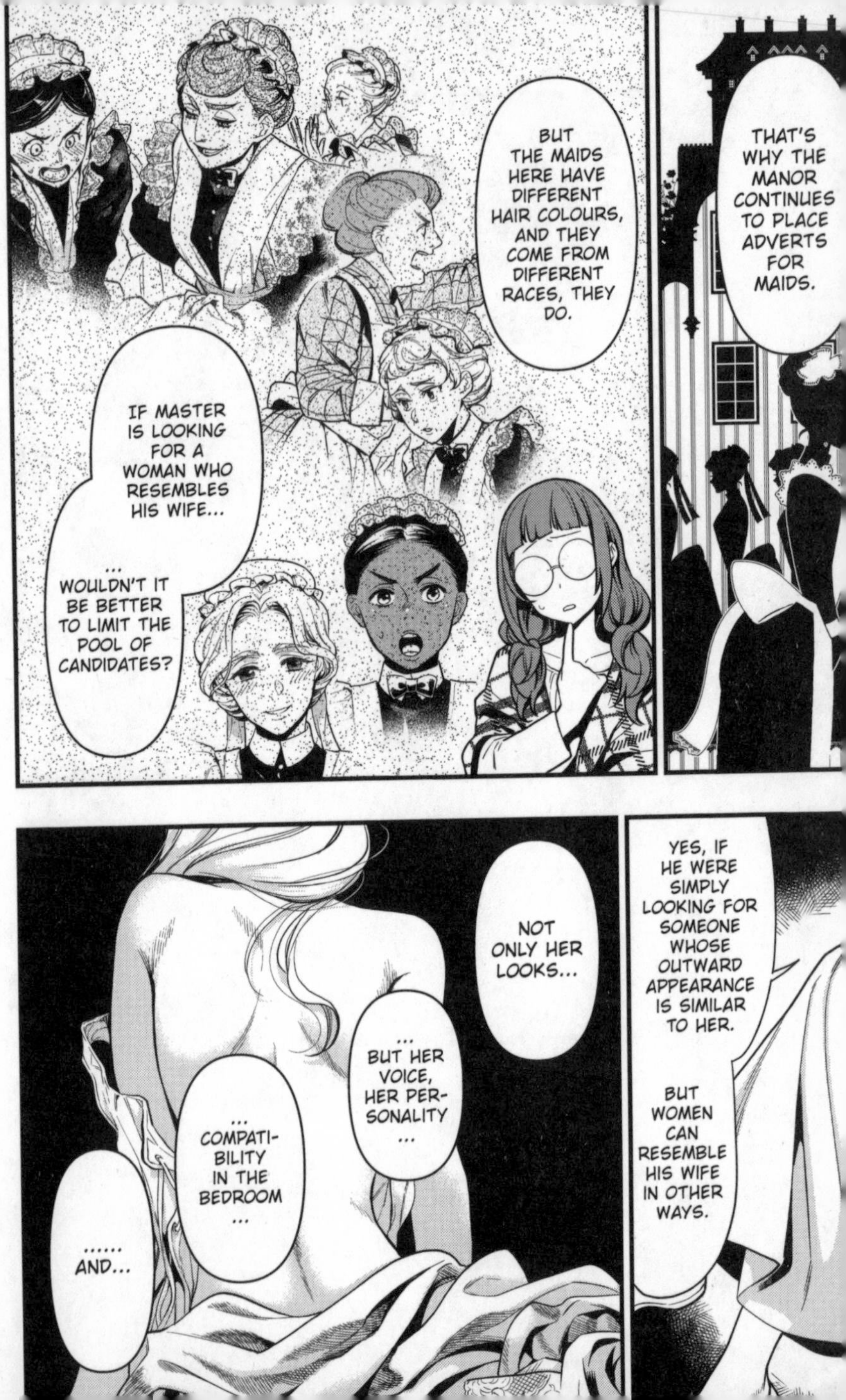
THAT'S WHY THE MANOR CONTINUES TO PLACE ADVERTS FOR MAIDS.
BUT THE MAIDS HERE HAVE DIFFERENT HAIR COLOURS, AND THEY COME FROM DIFFERENT RACES, THEY DO.
IF MASTER IS LOOKING FOR A WOMAN WHO RESEMBLES HIS WIFE...
...WOULDN'T IT BE BETTER TO LIMIT THE POOL OF CANDIDATES?
YES, IF HE WERE SIMPLY LOOKING FOR SOMEONE WHOSE OUTWARD APPEARANCE IS SIMILAR TO HER.
BUT WOMEN CAN RESEMBLE HIS WIFE IN OTHER WAYS.
NOT ONLY HER LOOKS...
...BUT HER VOICE, HER PERSONALITY...
...COMPATIBILITY IN THE BEDROOM...
......AND...

—AND THE LIKE.

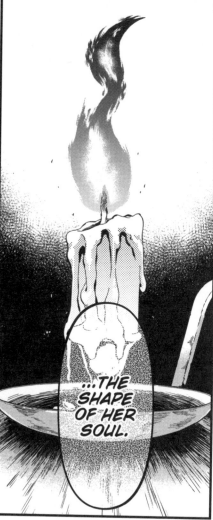

HER SOUL ......

...THE SHAPE OF HER SOUL.

... OUR MASTER IS SLIGHTLY ECCENTRIC.

I TOLD YOU...

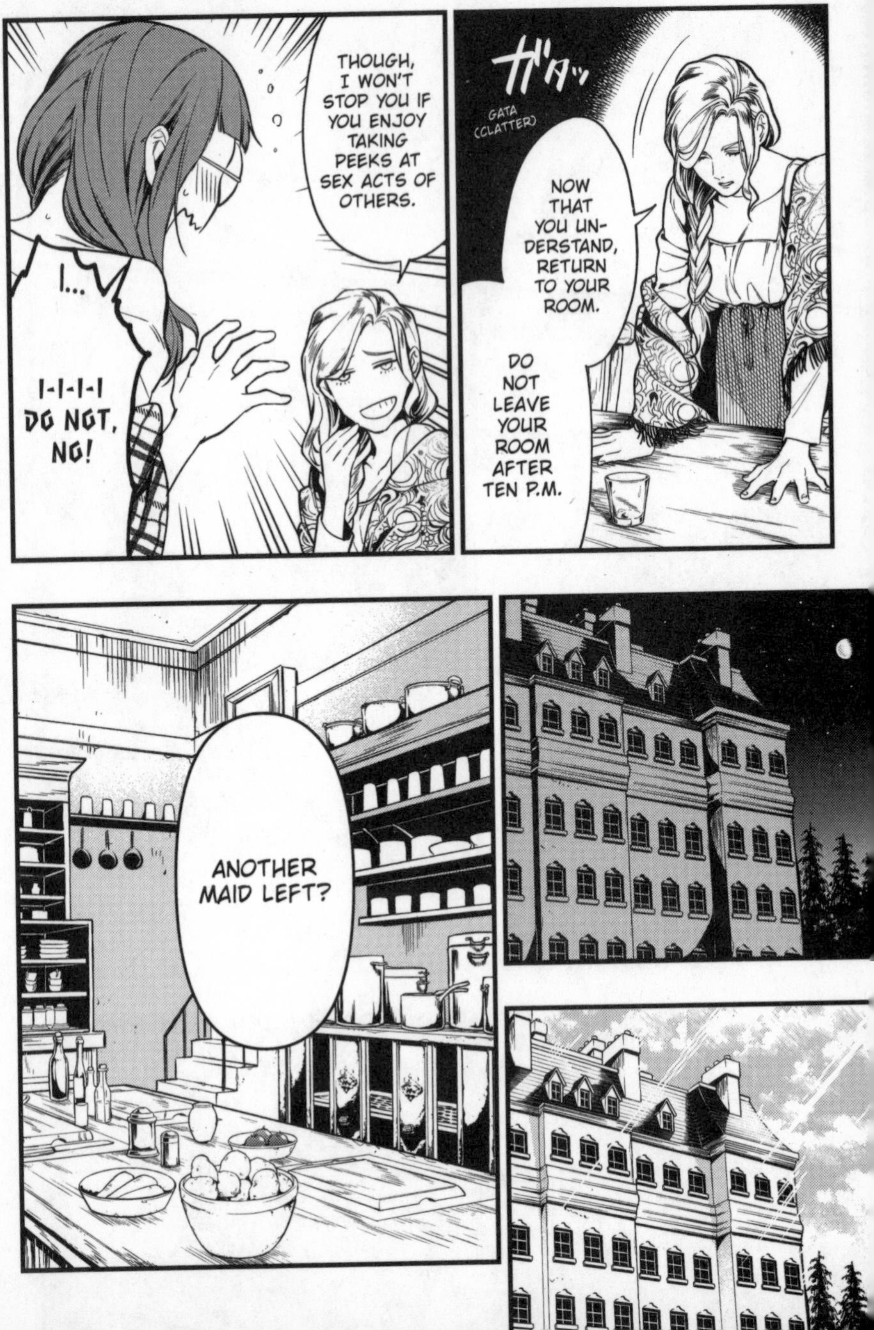
ガタッ
GATA (CLATTER)
NOW THAT YOU UN- DERSTAND, RETURN TO YOUR ROOM.
DO NOT LEAVE YOUR ROOM AFTER TEN P.M.
THOUGH, I WON'T STOP YOU IF YOU ENJOY TAKING PEEKS AT SEX ACTS OF OTHERS.
I...
I-I-I-I DO NOT, NO!
ANOTHER MAID LEFT?

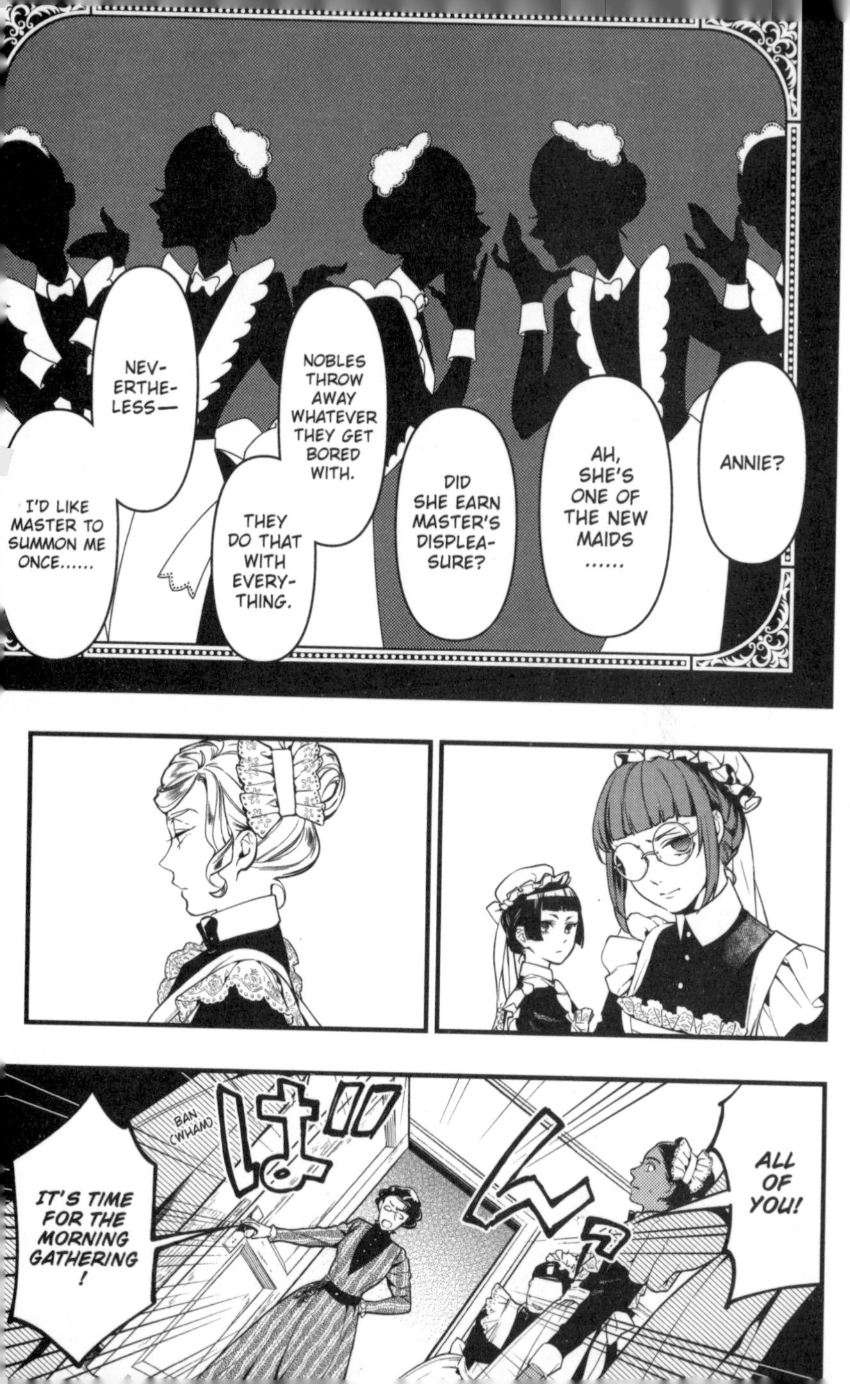
ANNIE?
AH, SHE'S ONE OF THE NEW MAIDS ......
DID SHE EARN MASTER'S DISPLEA-SURE?
NOBLES THROW AWAY WHATEVER THEY GET BORED WITH.
THEY DO THAT WITH EVERY-THING.
NEV-ERTHE-LESS—
I'D LIKE MASTER TO SUMMON ME ONCE......
ALL OF YOU!
BAN (WHAM)
IT'S TIME FOR THE MORNING GATHERING!

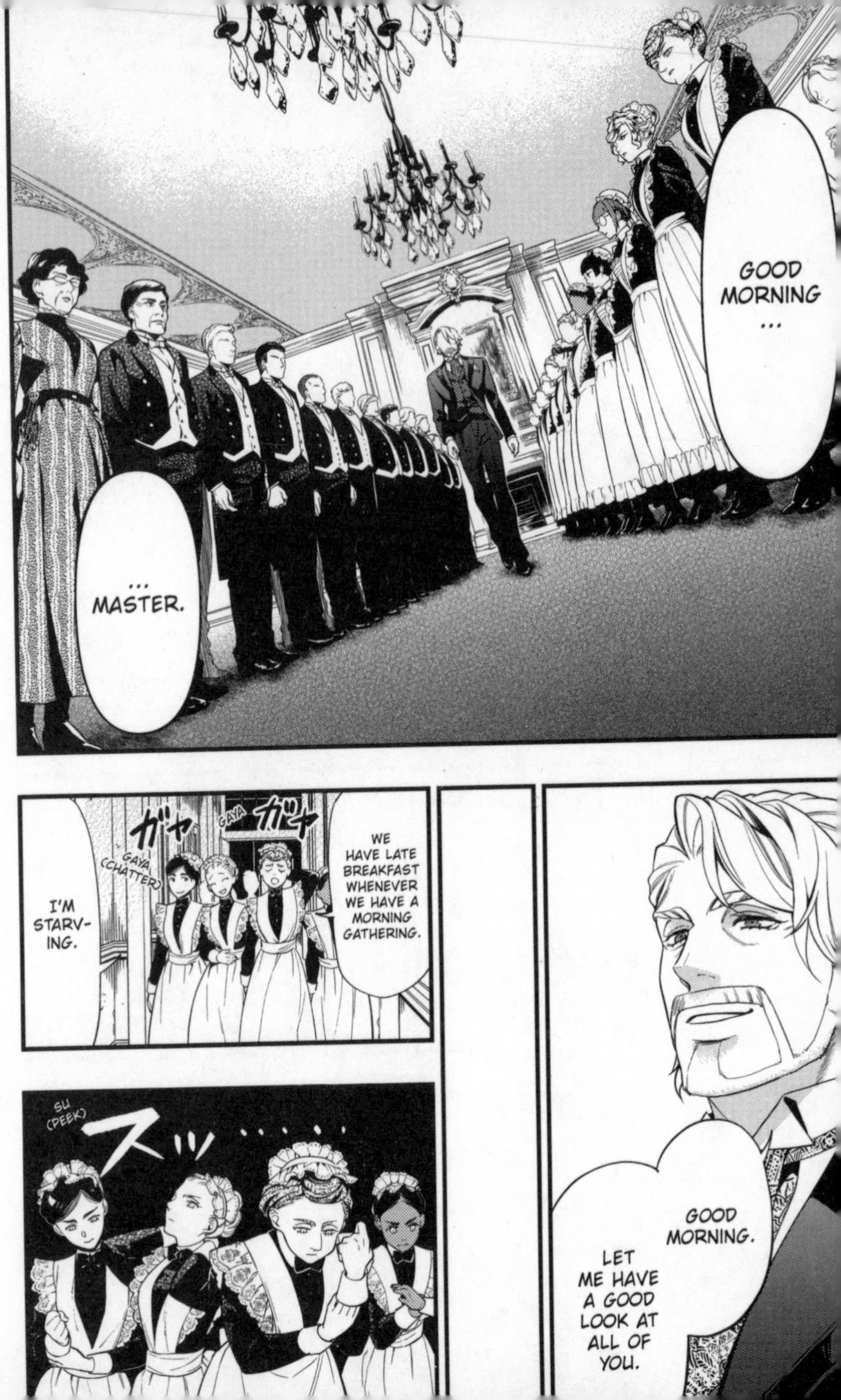
GOOD MORNING ...
... MASTER.
GOOD MORNING.
LET ME HAVE A GOOD LOOK AT ALL OF YOU.
ガヤ
GAYA
ガヤ
GAYA (CHATTER)
WE HAVE LATE BREAKFAST WHENEVER WE HAVE A MORNING GATHERING.
I'M STARV-ING.
SU (PEEK)
スッ

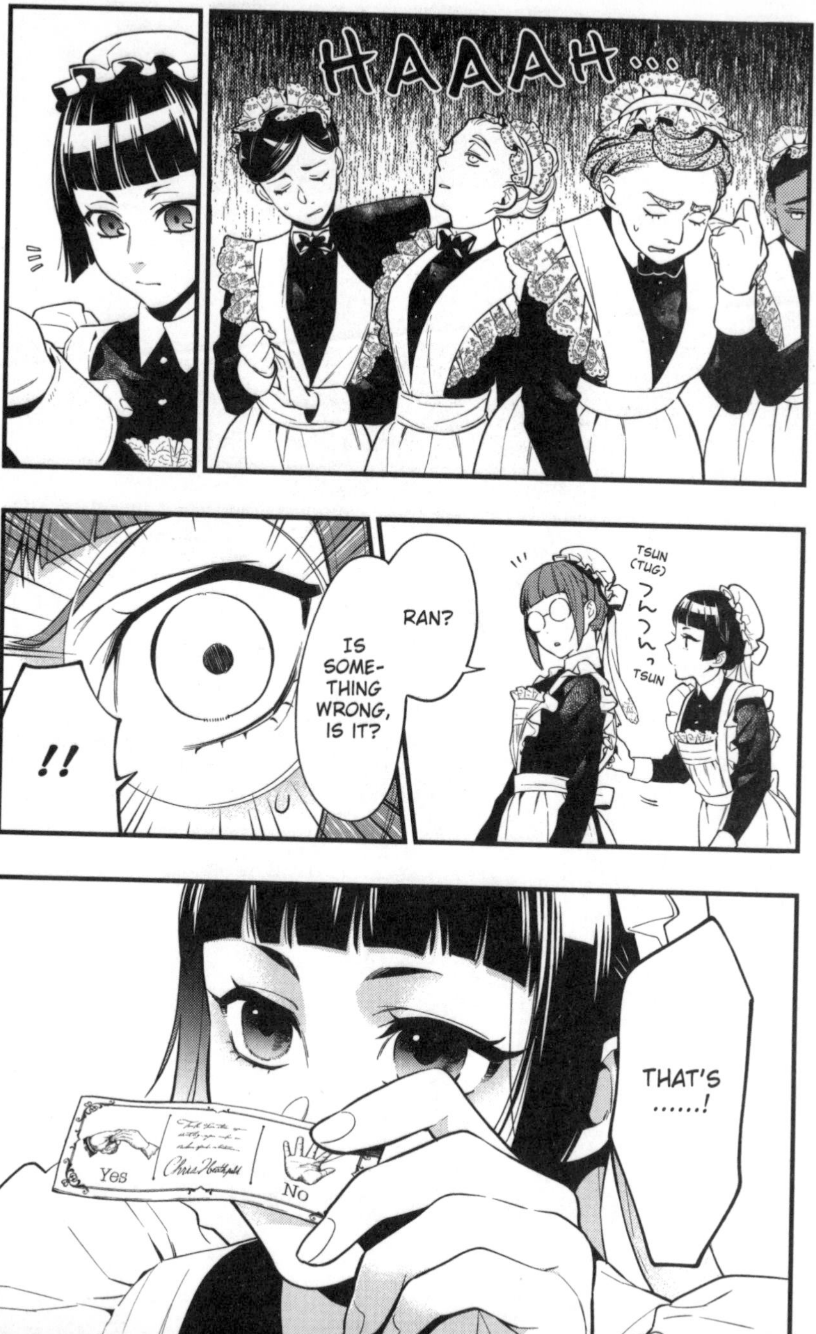
HAAAH...
TSUN (TUG)
つんつん、
TSUN
RAN?
IS SOMETHING WRONG, IS IT?
!!
THAT'S ......!
Yes
No

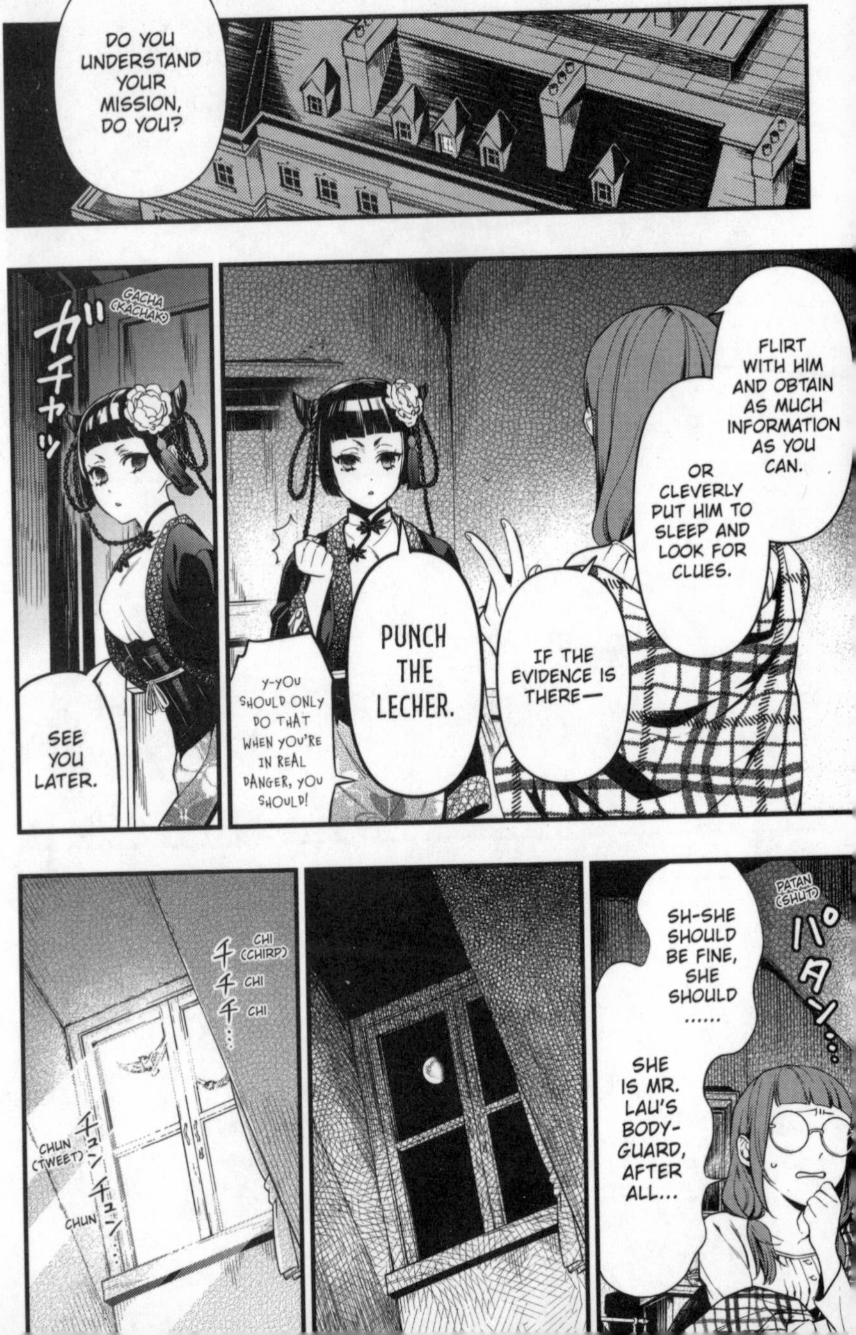
DO YOU UNDERSTAND YOUR MISSION, DO YOU?
FLIRT WITH HIM AND OBTAIN AS MUCH INFORMATION AS YOU CAN.
OR CLEVERLY PUT HIM TO SLEEP AND LOOK FOR CLUES.
IF THE EVIDENCE IS THERE—
PUNCH THE LECHER.
Y-YOU SHOULD ONLY DO THAT WHEN YOU'RE IN REAL DANGER, YOU SHOULD!
ガチャッ
GACHA (KACHAK)
SEE YOU LATER.
パタン…
PATAN (SHUT)
SH-SHE SHOULD BE FINE, SHE SHOULD ......
SHE IS MR. LAU'S BODY-GUARD, AFTER ALL...
チチチ…
CHI (CHIRP) CHI CHI
チュン チュン
CHUN (TWEET) CHUN

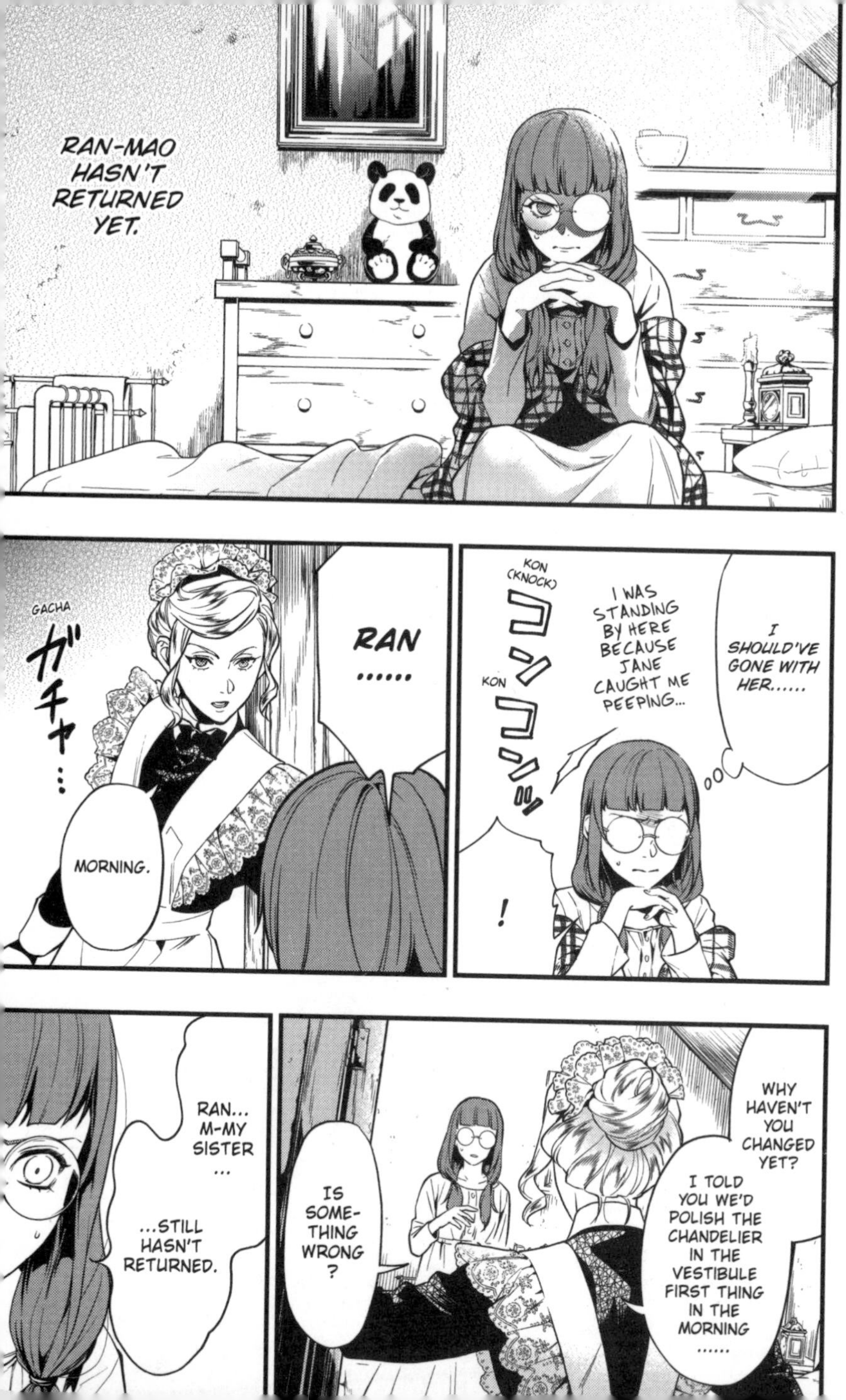
RAN-MAO HASN'T RETURNED YET.
I SHOULD'VE GONE WITH HER......
I WAS STANDING BY HERE BECAUSE JANE CAUGHT ME PEEPING...
KON (KNOCK)
コン
KON
コンッ
!
RAN ......
GACHA
ガチャ…
MORNING.
WHY HAVEN'T YOU CHANGED YET?
I TOLD YOU WE'D POLISH THE CHANDELIER IN THE VESTIBULE FIRST THING IN THE MORNING ......
IS SOME-THING WRONG?
RAN... M-MY SISTER ...
...STILL HASN'T RETURNED.

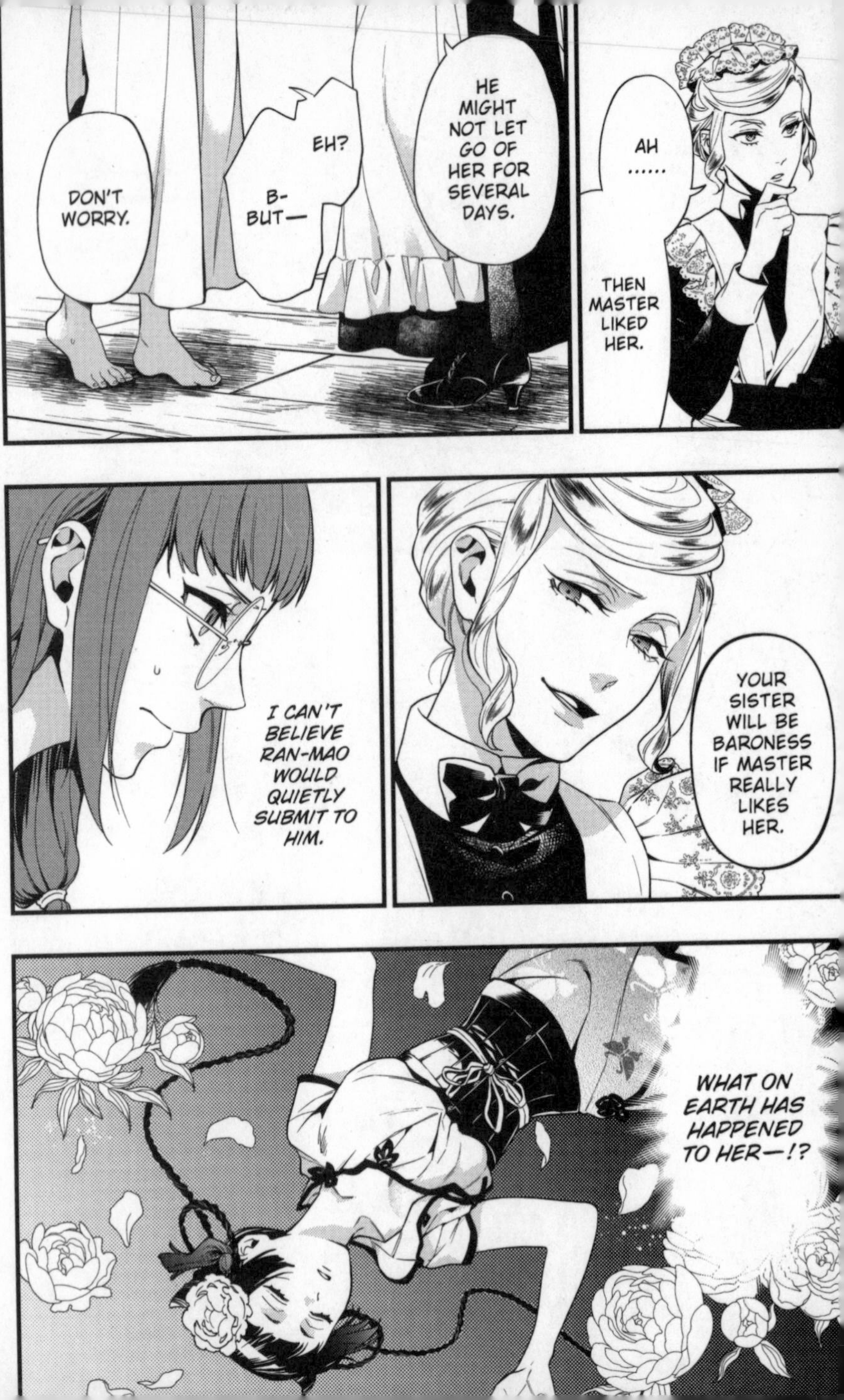
AH ......
THEN MASTER LIKED HER.
HE MIGHT NOT LET GO OF HER FOR SEVERAL DAYS.
EH?
B- BUT—
DON'T WORRY.
YOUR SISTER WILL BE BARONESS IF MASTER REALLY LIKES HER.
I CAN'T BELIEVE RAN-MAO WOULD QUIETLY SUBMIT TO HIM.
WHAT ON EARTH HAS HAPPENED TO HER—!?

Black Butler

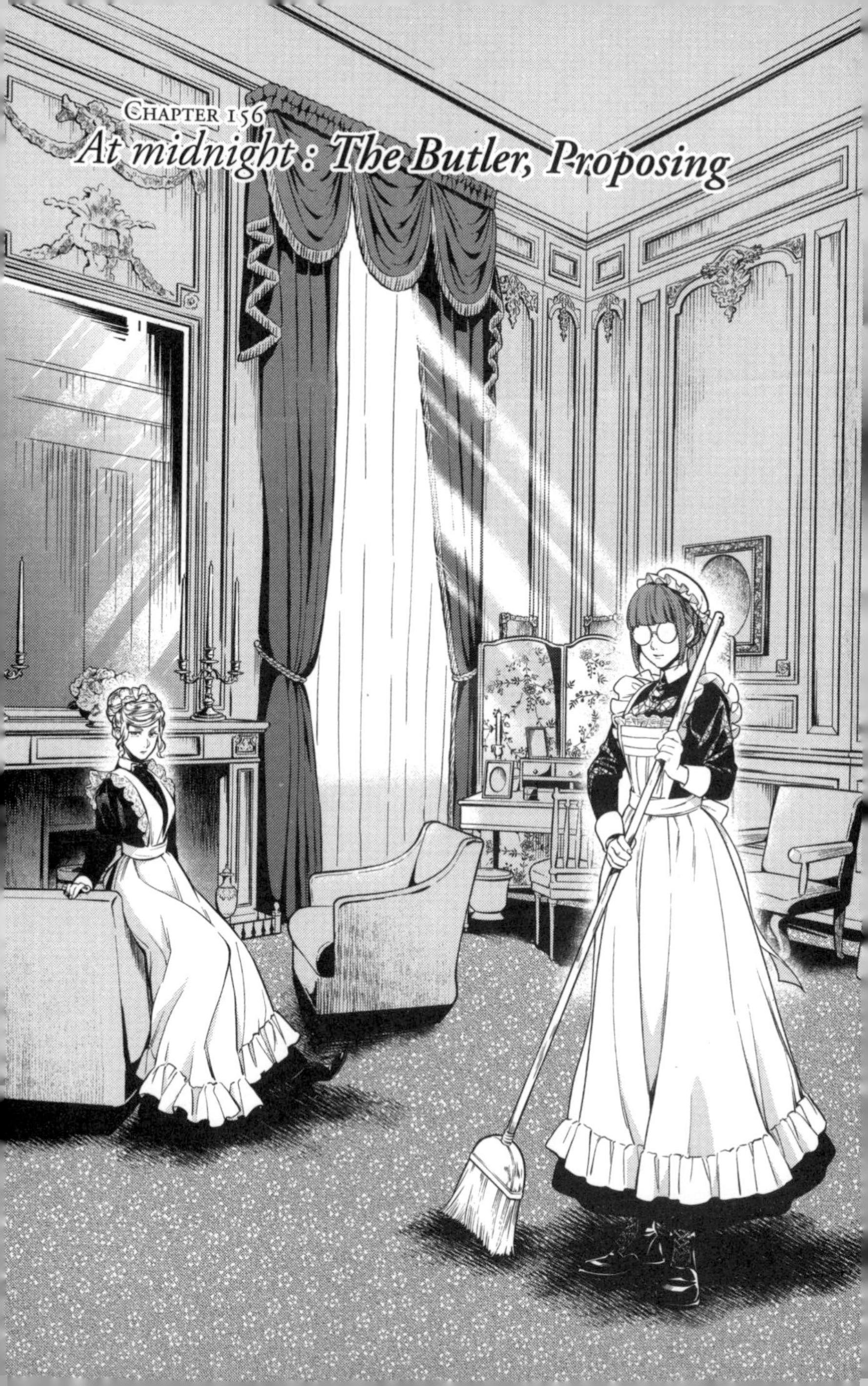
Chapter 156
At midnight : The Butler, Proposing

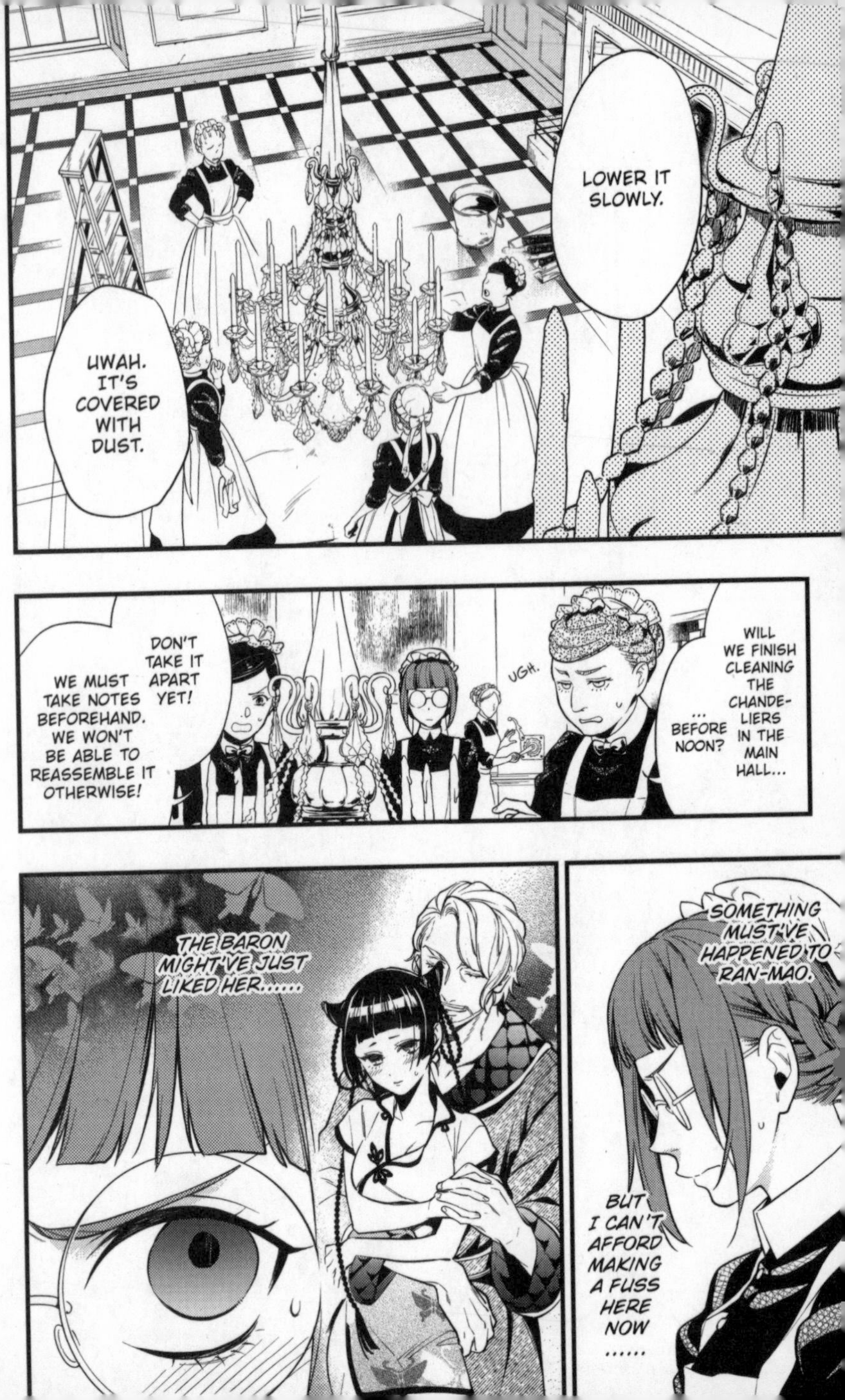
LOWER IT SLOWLY.
UWAH. IT'S COVERED WITH DUST.
WILL WE FINISH CLEANING THE CHANDELIERS IN THE MAIN HALL...
... BEFORE NOON?
UGH.
DON'T TAKE IT APART YET!
WE MUST TAKE NOTES BEFOREHAND. WE WON'T BE ABLE TO REASSEMBLE IT OTHERWISE!
SOMETHING MUST'VE HAPPENED TO RAN-MAO.
BUT I CAN'T AFFORD MAKING A FUSS HERE NOW ......
THE BARON MIGHT'VE JUST LIKED HER......

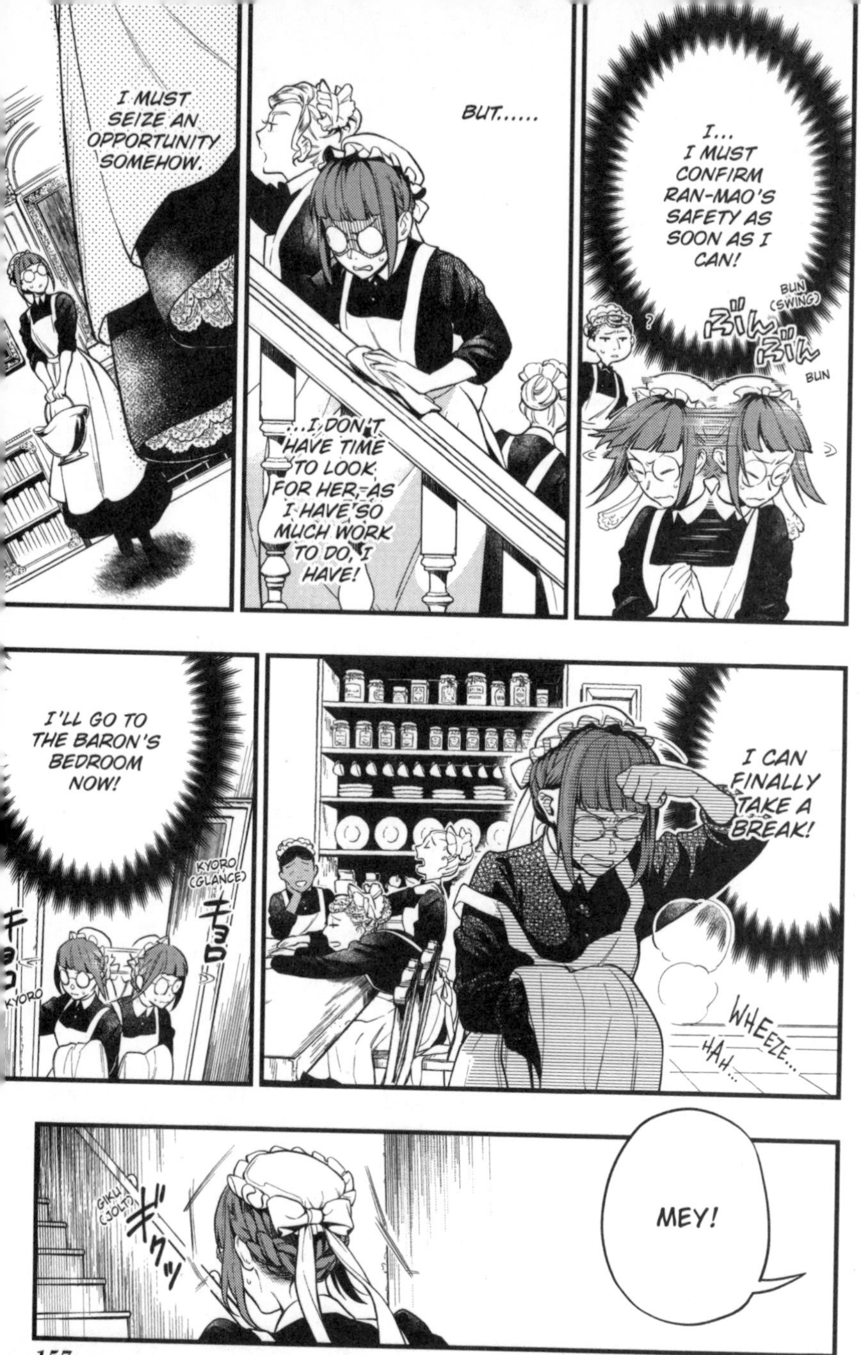
I... I MUST CONFIRM RAN-MAO'S SAFETY AS SOON AS I CAN!
BUN (SWING)
ぶん ぶん
BUN
?
BUT......
...I DON'T HAVE TIME TO LOOK FOR HER, AS I HAVE SO MUCH WORK TO DO, I HAVE!
I MUST SEIZE AN OPPORTUNITY SOMEHOW.
I CAN FINALLY TAKE A BREAK!
WHEEZE...
HAH...
I'LL GO TO THE BARON'S BEDROOM NOW!
KYORO (GLANCE)
キョロ
キョロ
KYORO
MEY!
GIKU (JOLT)
ギクッ

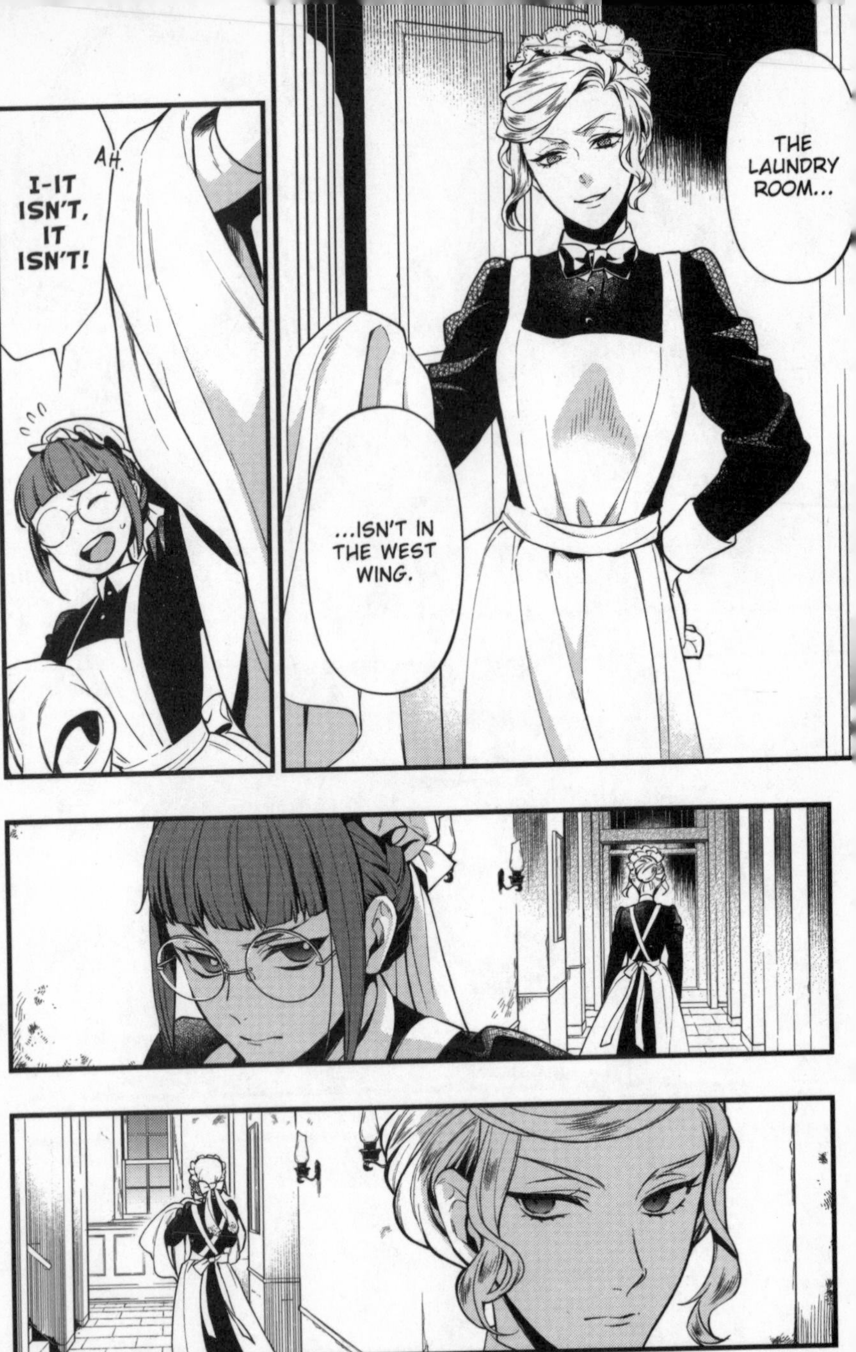
THE LAUNDRY ROOM...
...ISN'T IN THE WEST WING.
AH.
I-IT ISN'T, IT ISN'T!

I HAVE NO CHOICE—!

GATA
(CLATTER)

GASHA
(KASHAK)

KYU
(SHP)

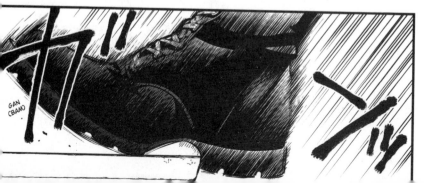

GAN
(BAM)

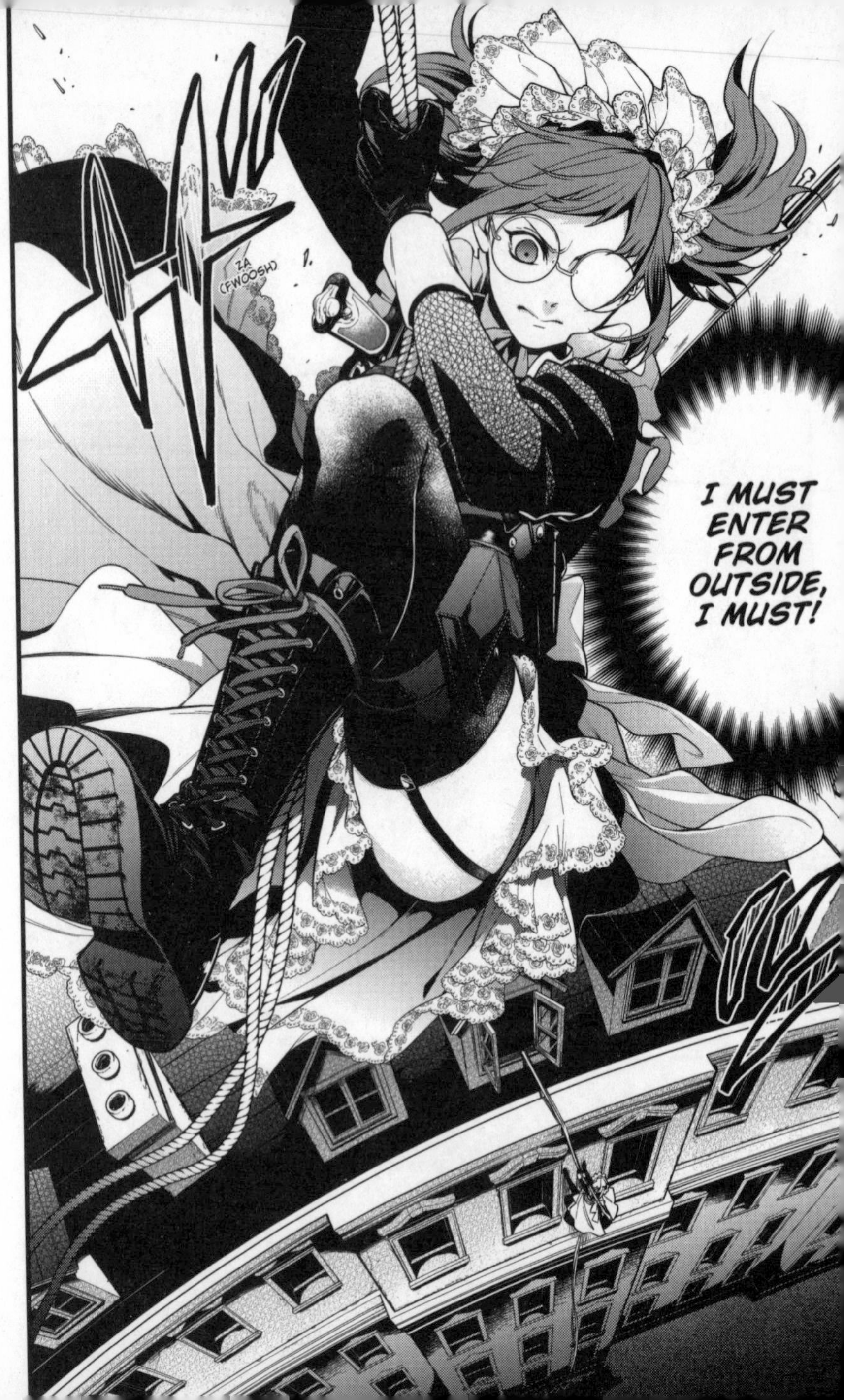
ZA (FWOOSH)
I MUST ENTER FROM OUTSIDE, I MUST!

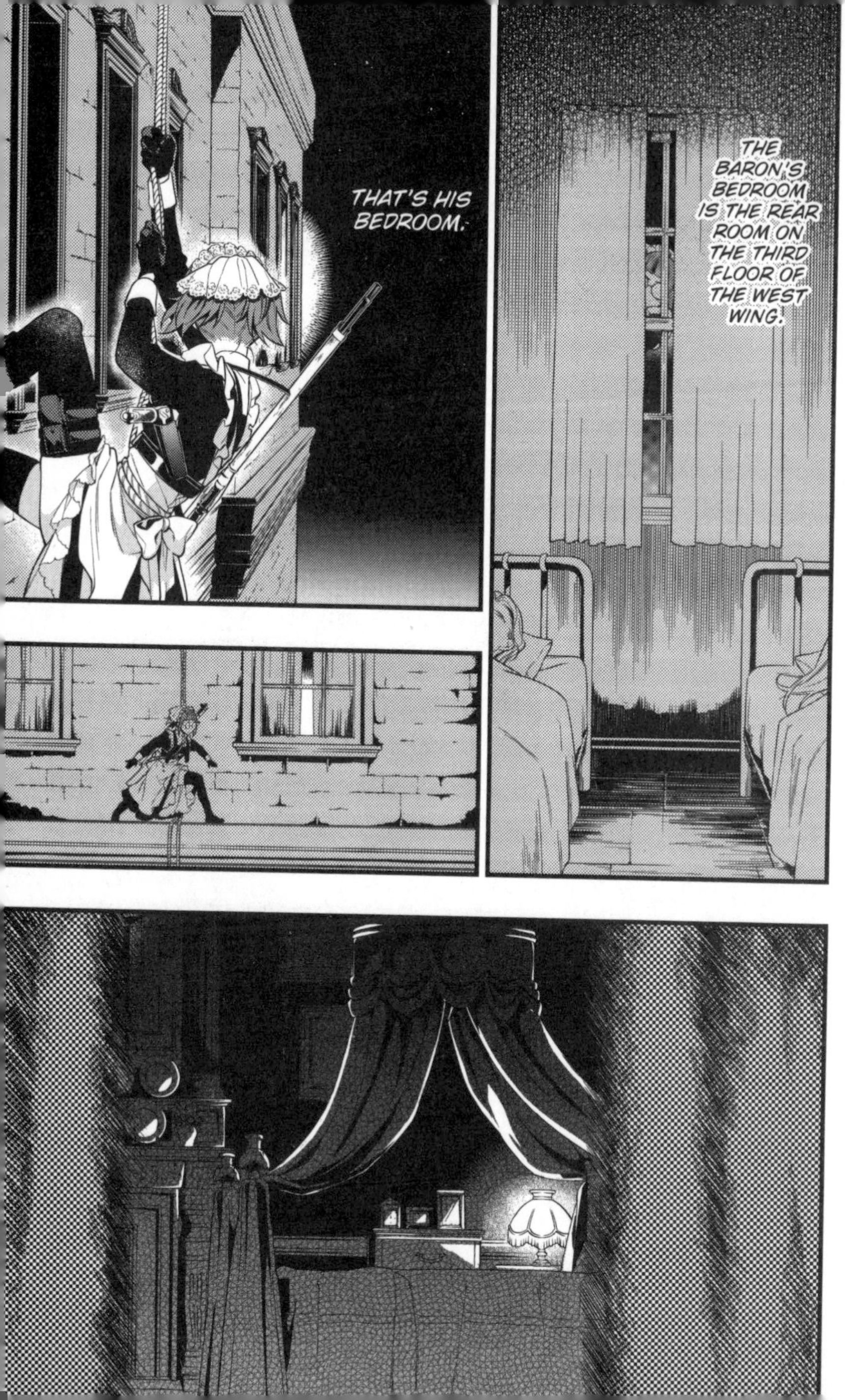
THE BARON'S BEDROOM IS THE REAR ROOM ON THE THIRD FLOOR OF THE WEST WING.
THAT'S HIS BEDROOM.

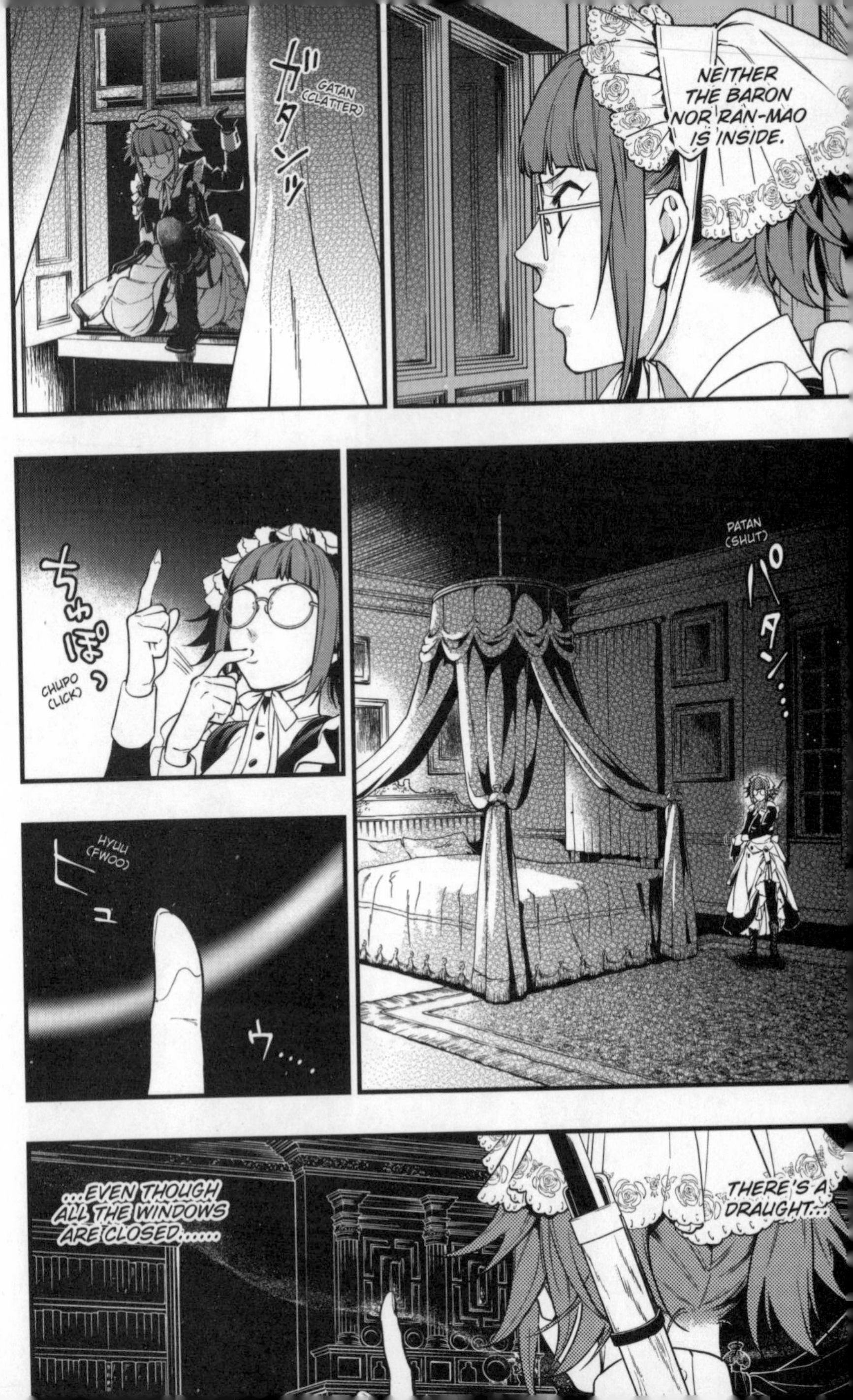
NEITHER THE BARON NOR RAN-MAO IS INSIDE.
ガタンッ
GATAN (CLATTER)
パタン…
PATAN (SHUT)
ちゅぽっ
CHUPO (LICK)
ヒュ
ウ….
HYUU (FWOO)
THERE'S A DRAUGHT...
...EVEN THOUGH ALL THE WINDOWS ARE CLOSED......

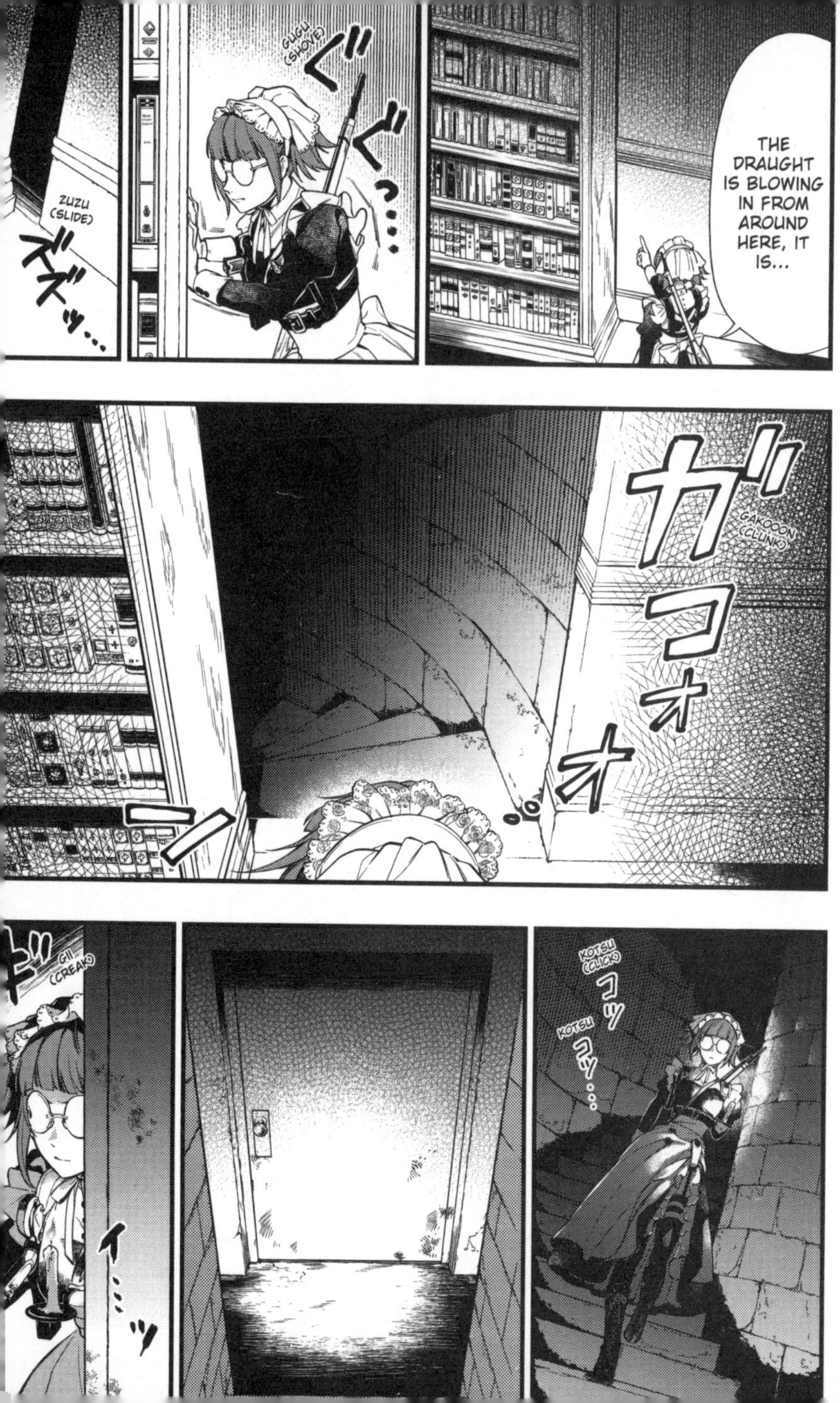
THE DRAUGHT IS BLOWING IN FROM AROUND HERE, IT IS...
GUGU (SHOVE)
ぐぐっ...
ZUZU (SLIDE)
ズズッ...
ガコォオン
GAKOOON (CLUNK)
KOTSU (CLICK)
コッ
KOTSU
コッ...
GII (CREAK)
ギィ...ッ

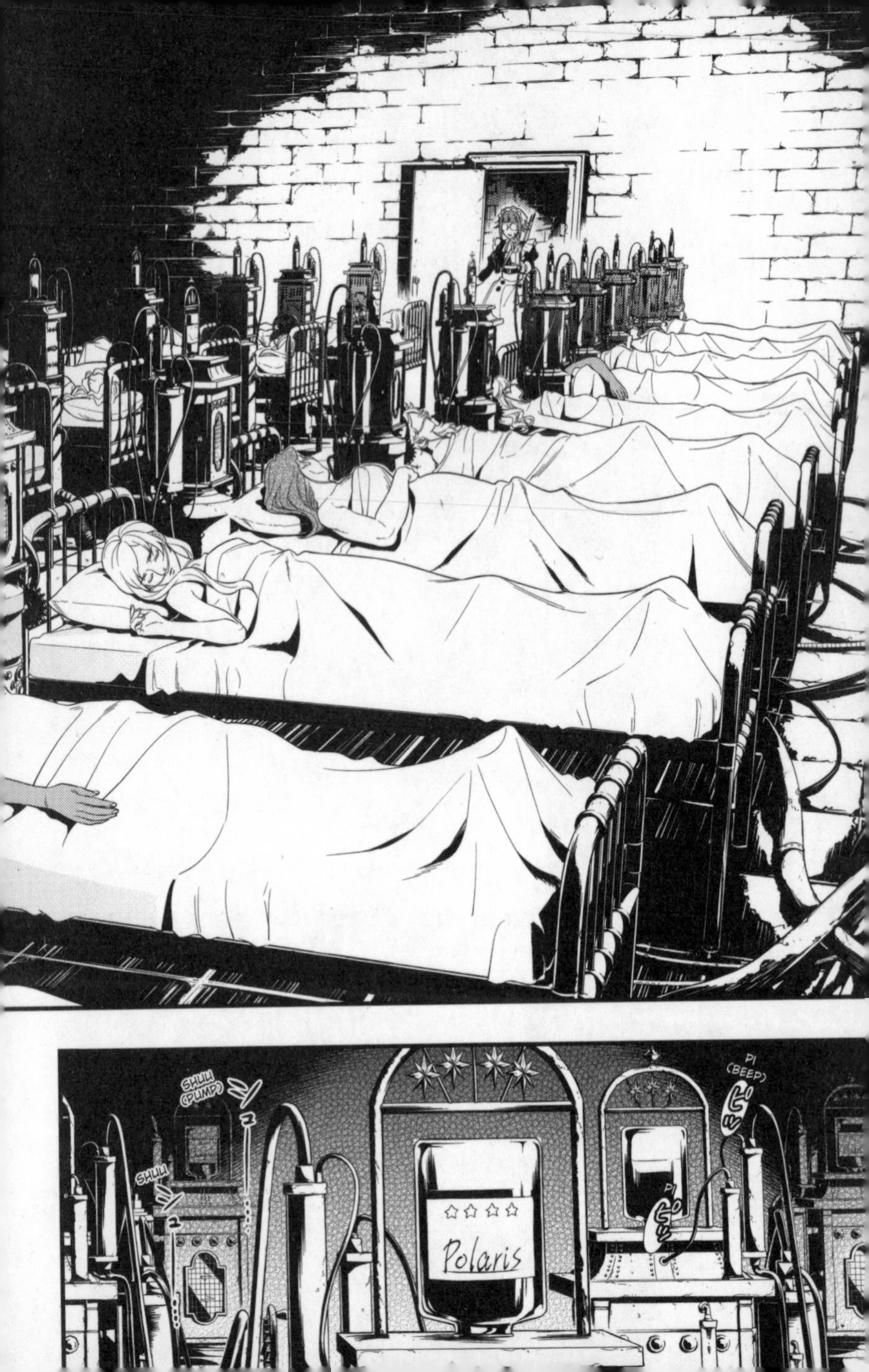
PI (BEEP)
PI
Polaris
SHUU (PUMP)
SHUU

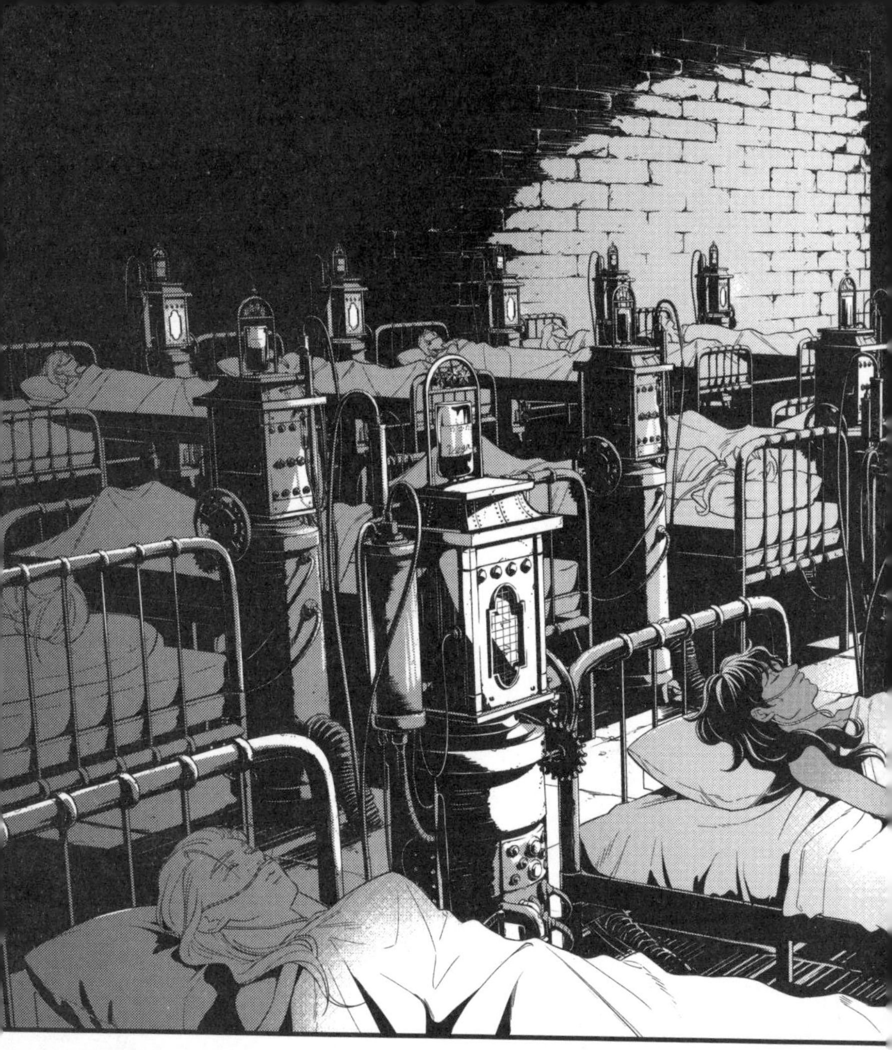

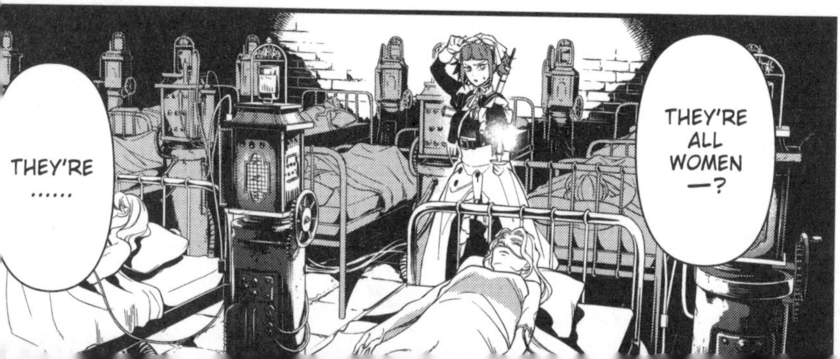
THEY'RE ALL WOMEN —?
THEY'RE ......

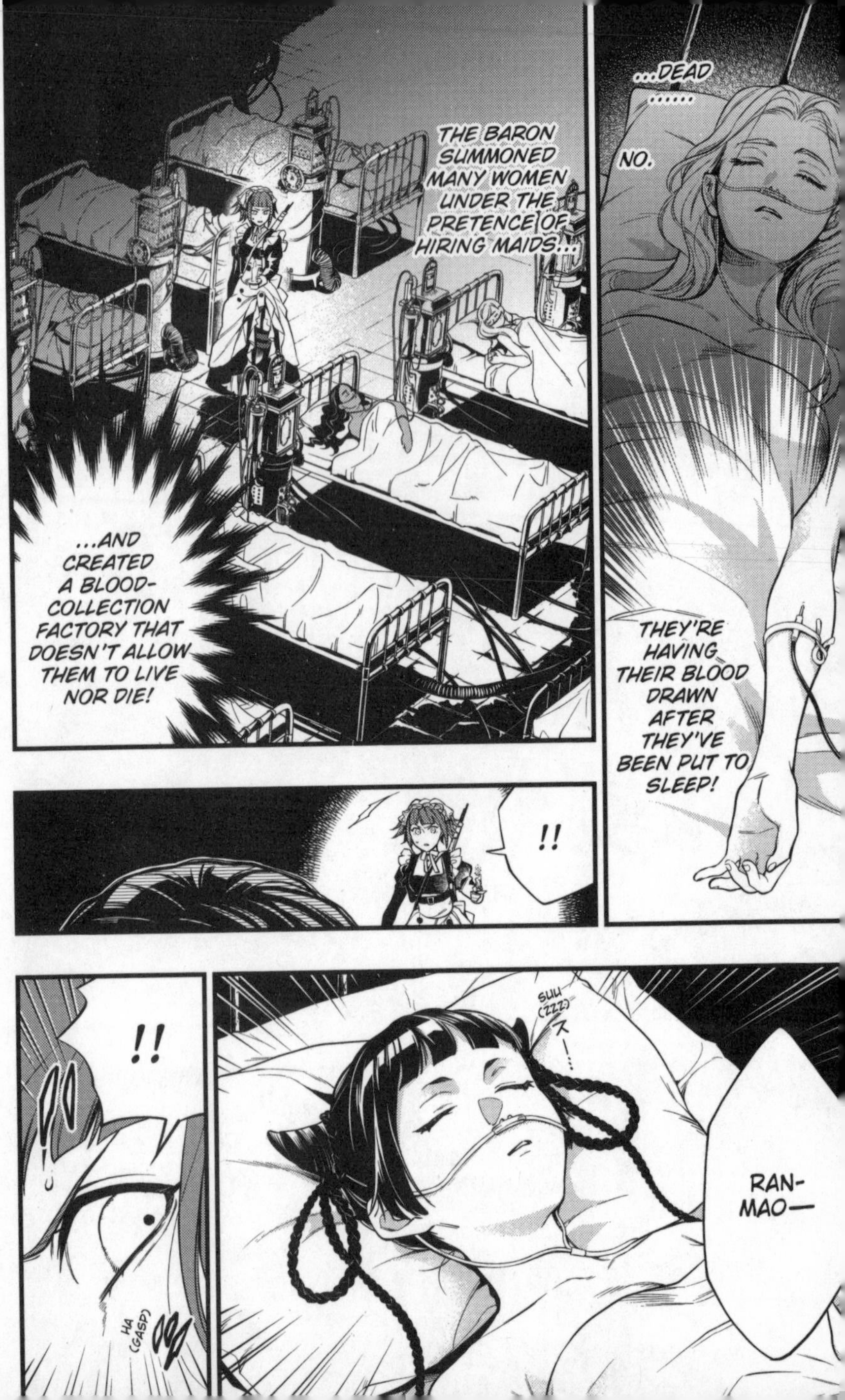
...DEAD ......
NO.
THEY'RE HAVING THEIR BLOOD DRAWN AFTER THEY'VE BEEN PUT TO SLEEP!
THE BARON SUMMONED MANY WOMEN UNDER THE PRETENCE OF HIRING MAIDS...
...AND CREATED A BLOOD-COLLECTION FACTORY THAT DOESN'T ALLOW THEM TO LIVE NOR DIE!
!!
SUU (ZZZ)
ス…
RAN-MAO—
!!
HA (GASP)

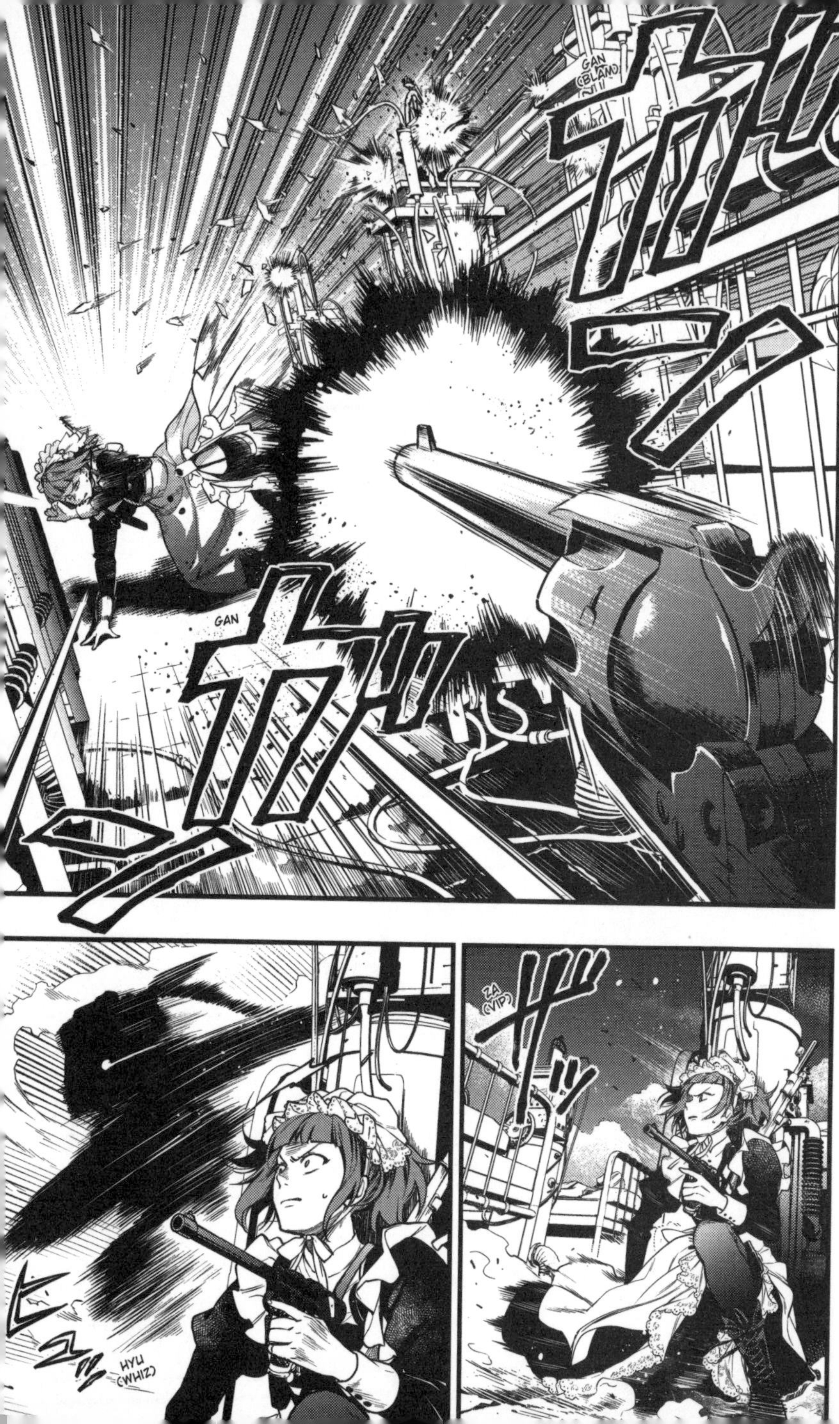
GAN
(BLAM)
ガッ
GAN
ガッ
ZA
(VIP)
ザッ
HYU
(WHIZ)

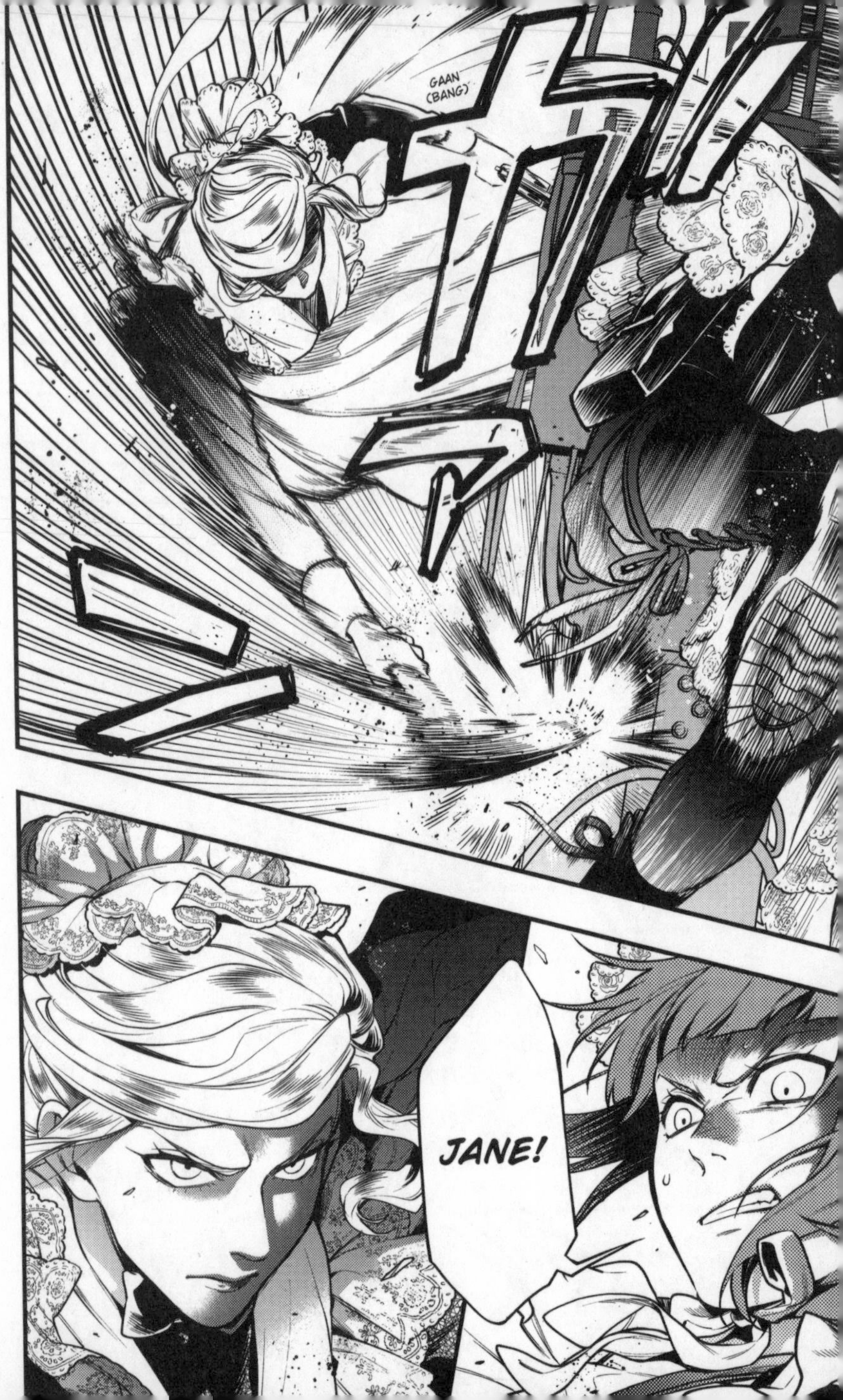
GAAN
(BANG)
JANE!

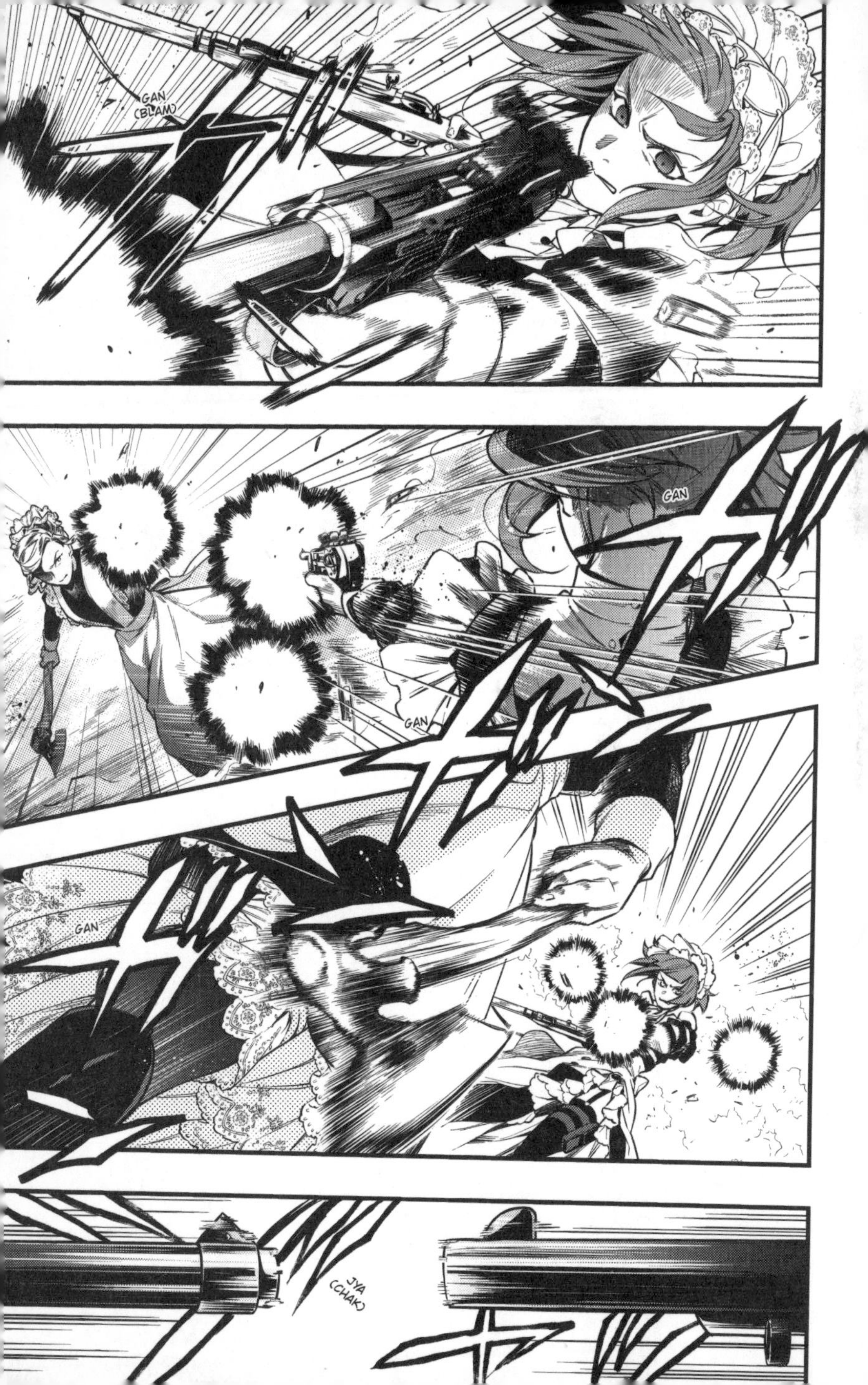
GAN
(BLAM)
GAN
GAN
GAN
JYA
(CHAK)

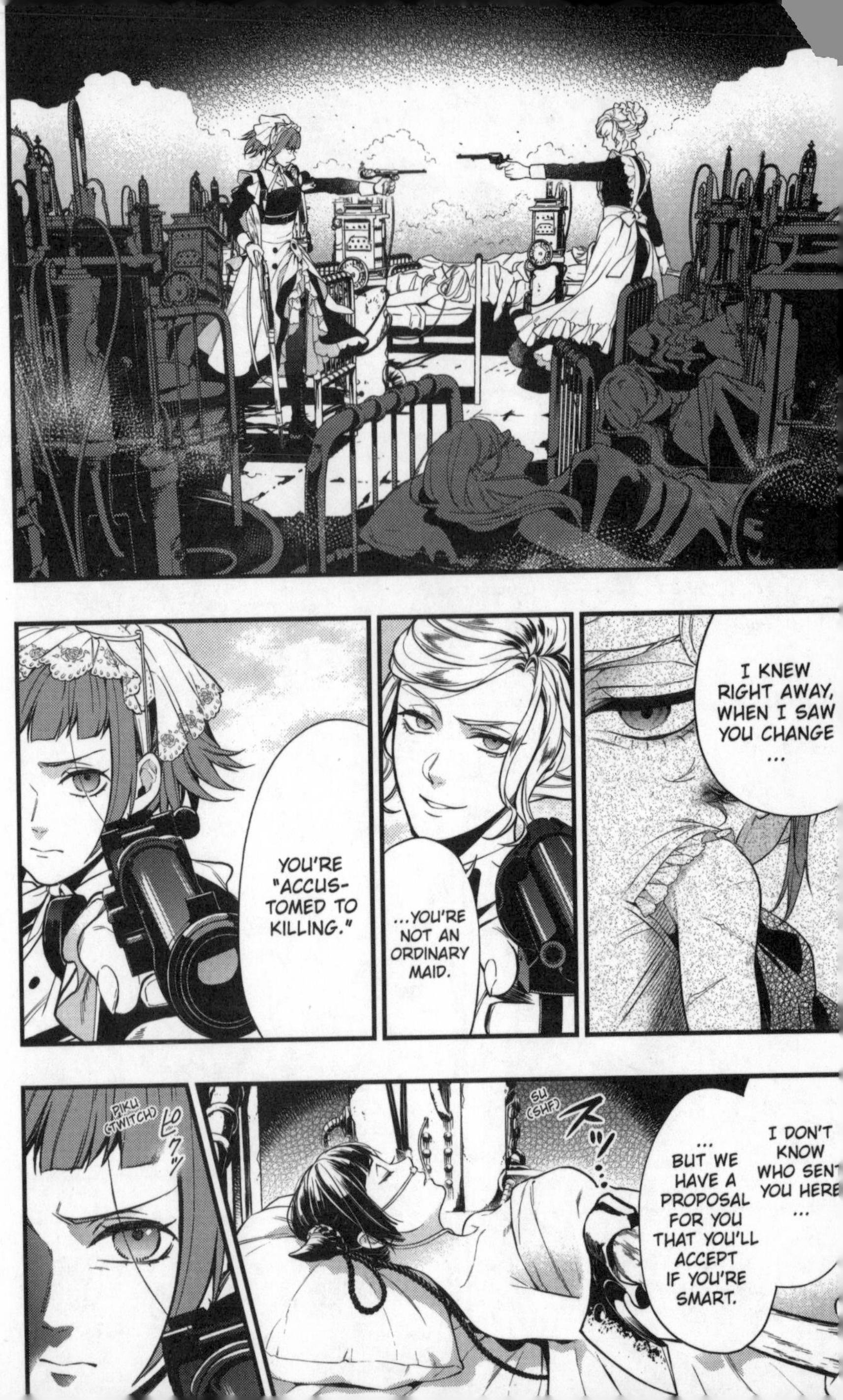
I KNEW RIGHT AWAY, WHEN I SAW YOU CHANGE ...
...YOU'RE NOT AN ORDINARY MAID.
YOU'RE "ACCUS-TOMED TO KILLING."
I DON'T KNOW WHO SENT YOU HERE ...
... BUT WE HAVE A PROPOSAL FOR YOU THAT YOU'LL ACCEPT IF YOU'RE SMART.
SU (SHF)
スッ
PIKU (TWITCH)
ピクッ

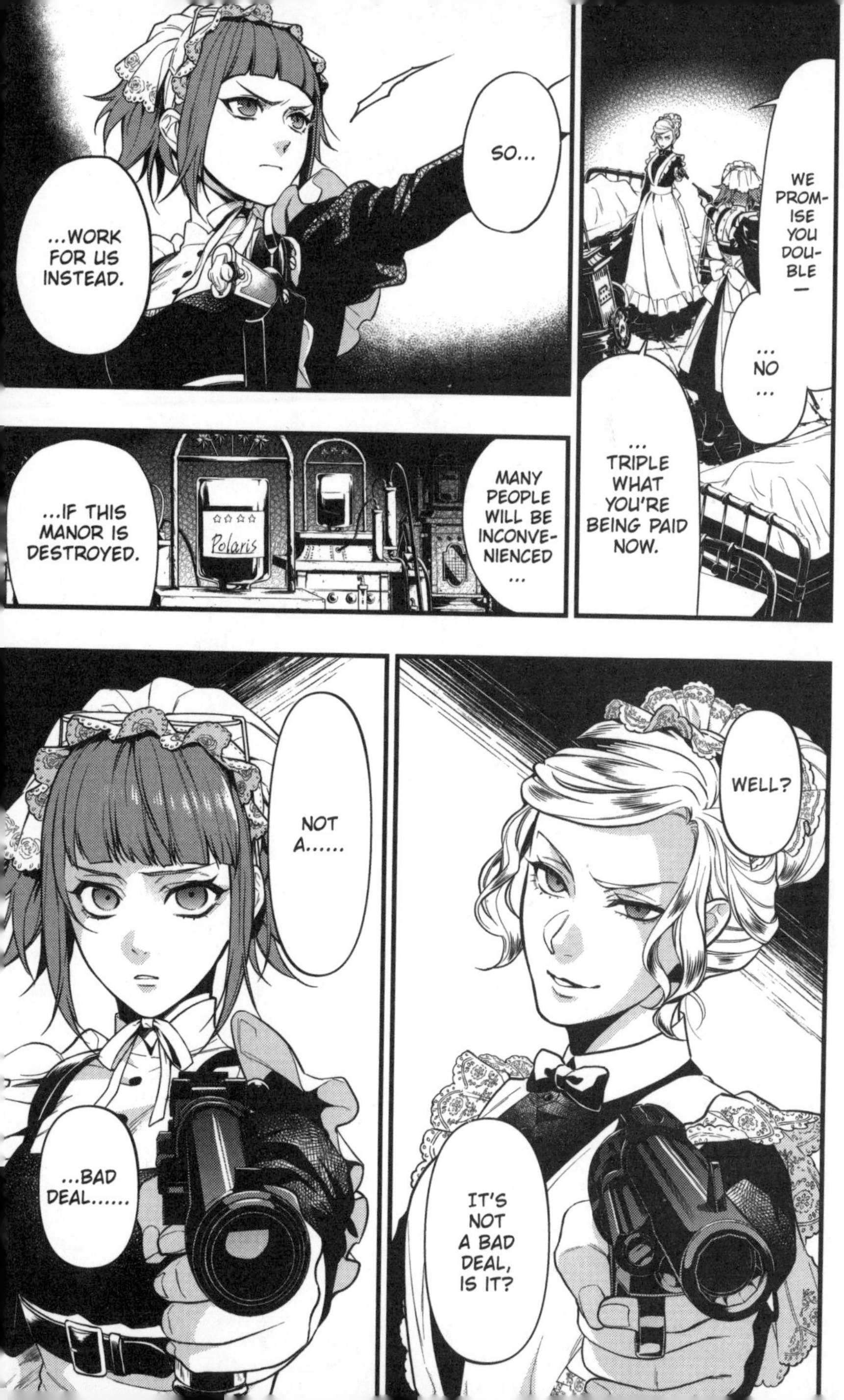
WE PROMISE YOU DOUBLE—
...NO...
...TRIPLE WHAT YOU'RE BEING PAID NOW.
SO...
...WORK FOR US INSTEAD.
MANY PEOPLE WILL BE INCONVENIENCED...
...IF THIS MANOR IS DESTROYED.
Polaris
WELL?
IT'S NOT A BAD DEAL, IS IT?
NOT A......
...BAD DEAL......

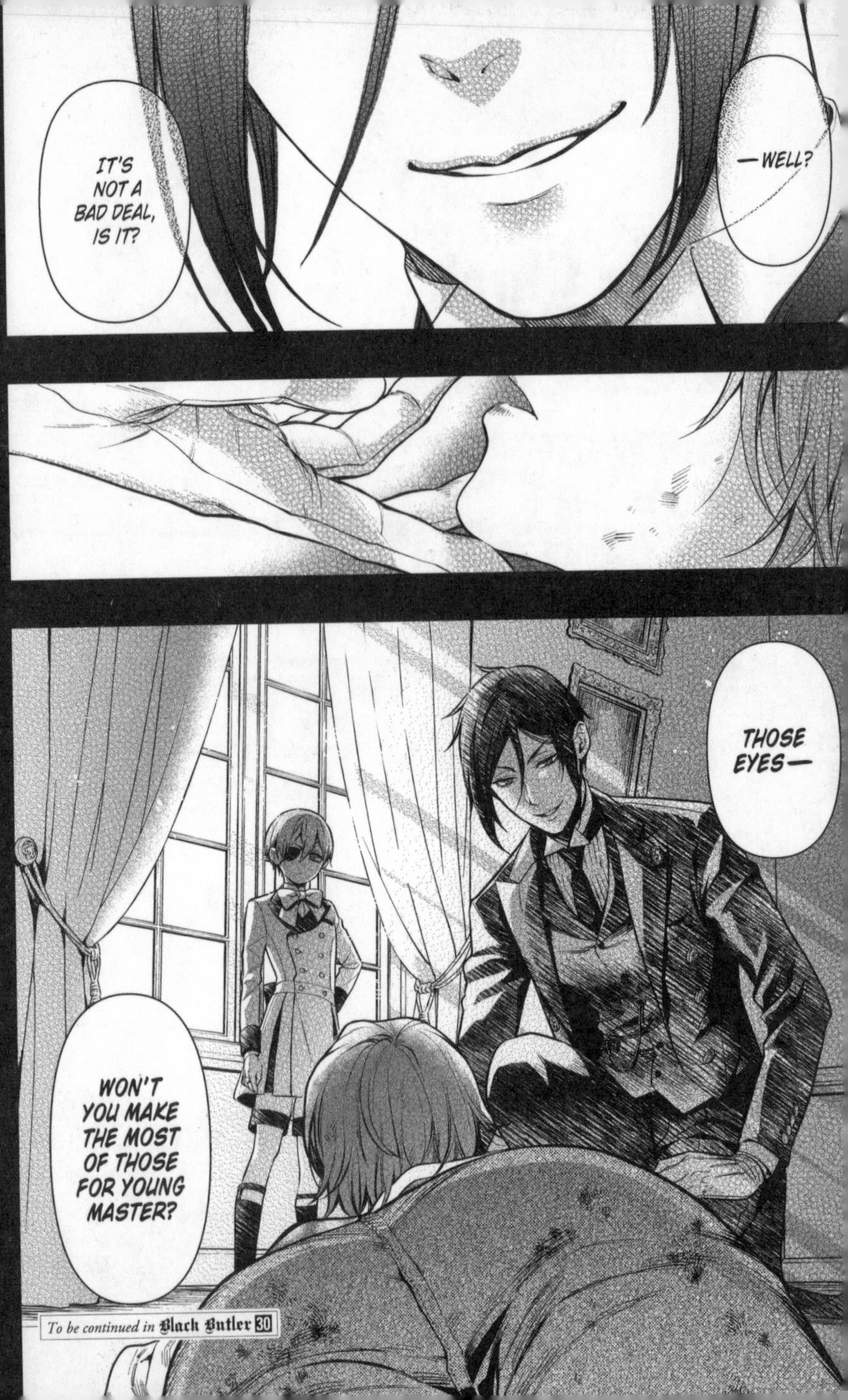
—WELL?
IT'S NOT A BAD DEAL, IS IT?
THOSE EYES—
WON'T YOU MAKE THE MOST OF THOSE FOR YOUNG MASTER?

To be continued in Black Butler 30

⇜ Black Butler ⇝

黒執事

Downstairs

Wakana Haduki
7
Tsuki Sorano
Chiaki Nagaoka
Sanihiko
Seira
Jun Hioki
*
Takeshi Kuma
*
Yana Toboso

Adviser

Rico Murakami

Special thanks to You!

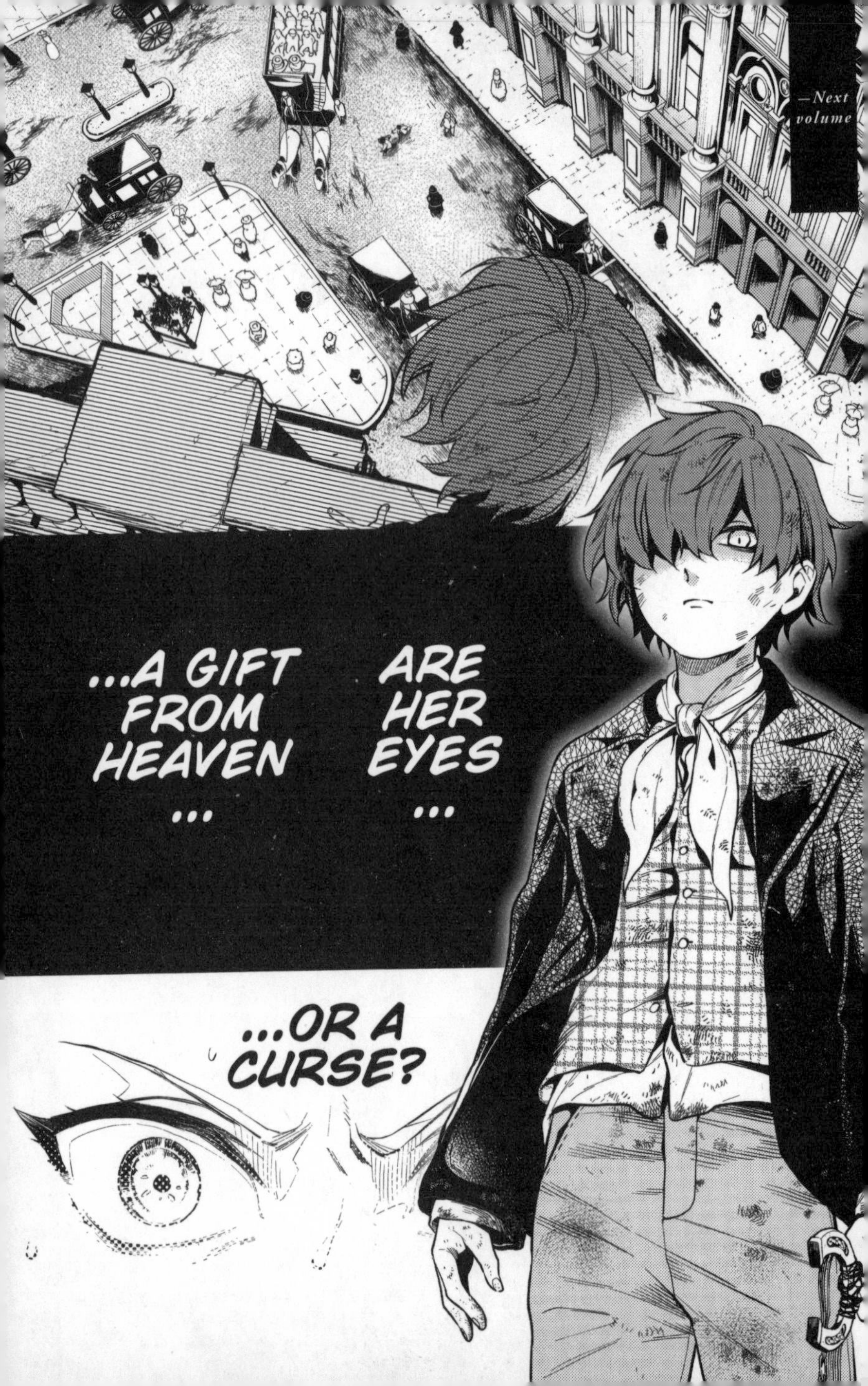
—Next volume
ARE HER EYES...
...A GIFT FROM HEAVEN...
...OR A CURSE?

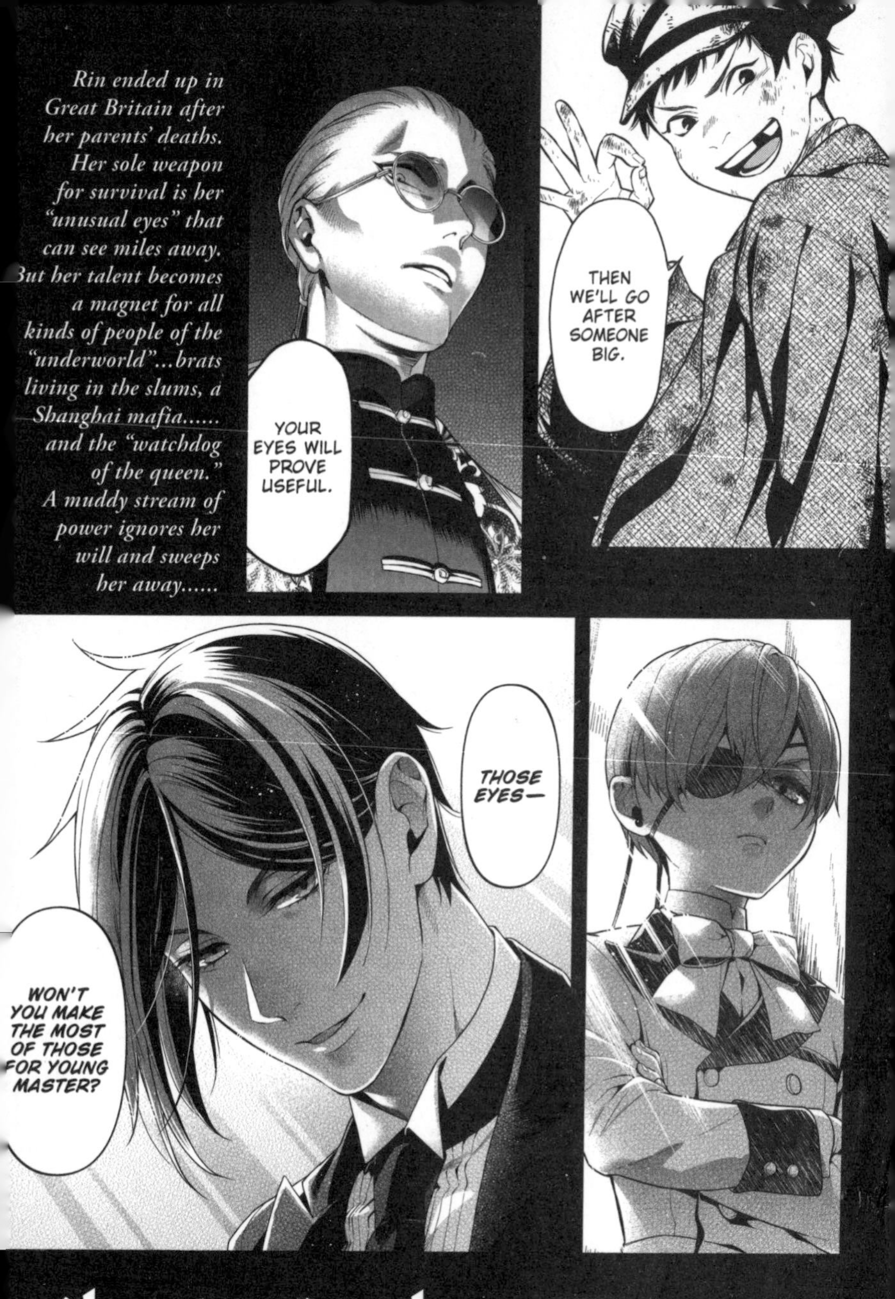
THEN WE'LL GO AFTER SOMEONE BIG.
YOUR EYES WILL PROVE USEFUL.
Rin ended up in Great Britain after her parents' deaths. Her sole weapon for survival is her "unusual eyes" that can see miles away. But her talent becomes a magnet for all kinds of people of the "underworld"...brats living in the slums, a Shanghai mafia...... and the "watchdog of the queen." A muddy stream of power ignores her will and sweeps her away......
THOSE EYES—
WON'T YOU MAKE THE MOST OF THOSE FOR YOUNG MASTER?

Black Butler 30

On sale 2020!

Translation Notes

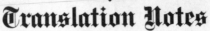

PAGE 87

Tea clipper

Tea clippers were fast sailing ships that were in use during the mid-19th century. They carried tea from China to London. Faster delivery enabled owners of the cargo to pick up the best price for the first teas.

PAGE 177

GFantasy

The magazine *Black Butler* releases monthy chapters in is called *GFantasy*. Due to the serialized nature of the work, the chapters are collected for full volumes, and often art or scripts are touched up for its release in print. The monthly chapters of *Black Butler* are available to read in English as digitally released simul chapters.

Yana Toboso

AUTHOR'S NOTE

When I receive a new issue of *GFantasy*,
I sometimes think "I could've drawn this
better......" or "This part is bad......"

But when I read the chapters again while
working on a collected volume, I often
think "I drew this well!" and "This is
great!" Thus, I feel human eyes are not
to be trusted.

And so, this is Volume 29.

BLACK BUTLER ㉙

YANA TOBOSO

Translation: Tomo Kimura
Lettering: Bianca Pistillo, Lys Blakeslee

KUROSHITSUJI Vol. 29 © 2019 Yana Toboso / SQUARE ENIX CO., LTD. First published in Japan in 2019 by SQUARE ENIX CO., LTD. English translation rights arranged with SQUARE ENIX CO., LTD. and Yen Press, LLC through Tuttle-Mori Agency, Inc.

English translation © 2020 by SQUARE ENIX CO., LTD.

Yen Press
150 West 30th Street, 19th Floor
New York, NY 10001

Visit us!
† yenpress.com
† facebook.com/yenpress
† twitter.com/yenpress
† yenpress.tumblr.com
† instagram.com/yenpress

First Yen Press Edition: August 2020
The chapters in this volume were originally published as ebooks by Yen Press.

Yen Press is an imprint of Yen Press, LLC.
The Yen Press name and logo are trademarks of Yen Press, LLC.

Library of Congress Control Number: 2010525567

ISBNs: 978-1-9753-1489-7 (paperback)
         978-1-9753-1488-0 (ebook)

10 9 8 7 6 5 4 3 2 1

WOR

Printed in the United States of America